*The Showman of Vanity Fair: The Life*
*of William Makepeace Thackeray*

*The Ordeal of George Meredith*

# The Ordeal
## of
# GEORGE
# MEREDITH

*A BIOGRAPHY*

*by* LIONEL STEVENSON

*New York 1953*

CHARLES SCRIBNER'S SONS

## ACKNOWLEDGMENTS

I wish to thank the Trustees of the George Meredith estate for their gracious permission to quote from Meredith's letters and other writings.

For the privilege of consulting and quoting from letters and other documentary material in their possession, I am grateful to the authorities of the Yale University Library (Altschul Collection), the New York Public Library (Berg Collection), and the Harvard University Library (Widener Memorial Collection).

Messrs Bradbury, Agnew & Co. (through Mr Allan G. Agnew, Managing Director) and Messrs Charles Scribner's Sons kindly granted me access to material in their archives.

The registers of St Thomas's Church (now Portsmouth Cathedral) were consulted through the courtesy of the Provost, the Very Rev E. N. P. Goff.

For permission to quote from books on which they hold copyrights, I acknowledge with thanks the courtesy of the following firms:

THE BRITISH BOOK CENTRE, INC. (*Portraits*, by Desmond MacCarthy).

DOUBLEDAY & CO., INC. (*The Romantic Nineties*, by Richard Le Gallienne).

HARPER & BROS. (*The Life and Letters of Sir Edmund Gosse*, by the Hon Evan Charteris, and *The House of Harper*, by J. Henry Harper).

HOUGHTON MIFFLIN CO. (*Shapes that Pass*, by Julian Hawthorne, and *Grey of Fallodon*, by G. M. Trevelyan).

HUTCHINSON & CO., LTD. (*Salt and His Circle*, by Stephen Winsten).

ALFRED A. KNOPF, INC. (*My Diaries*, by Wilfrid Scawen Blunt).

LITTLE, BROWN & CO. (*Memories and Reflections*, by the Earl of Oxford and Asquith).

THE MACMILLAN CO. (*The Record of an Adventurous Life*, by H. M. Hyndman).

JOHN MURRAY, LTD. (*Works and Days*, by Michael Field).

THE OXFORD UNIVERSITY PRESS (*A Long Retrospect*, by F. Anstey).

CHARLES SCRIBNER'S SONS (*The Letters of George Meredith*, *The Greenwood Hat*, by J. M. Barrie, *Memories of George Meredith*, by Lady Butcher, *The Letters of Henry James*, and *The Life of Francis Thompson*, by Everard Meynell; also the various novels by Meredith).

ST MARTIN'S PRESS INC. (*Autobiographic Memoirs*, by Frederic Harrison, and *Recollections*, by John, Viscount Morley).

Similarly I acknowledge the courtesy of the management of the *Queen's Quarterly* in allowing me to quote from "Meetings with Some Men of Letters," by Morley Roberts.

Parts of Chapter III have already been used in different form in an Introduction which I wrote for the Modern Library College Edition of *The Ordeal of Richard Feverel*. The material is used here with the permission of RANDOM HOUSE, INC.

L. S.

# Table of Contents

*J. Thomson*

George Meredith

# CHAPTER

## I

# *The Lonely Child*

DURING a prolonged war the business of a naval outfitter in an important port used to be not only profitable but downright romantic. From whatever ships were in harbor, officers flocked ashore to order new underlinen and uniforms and to arrange for the repair of battle damage in their old ones. Released from the rigors of shipboard discipline and meeting friends in the informal surroundings of shirt-sleeves and tapelines, they expanded into boisterous anecdotes of adventure. The staff of the shop, probably the first civilians seen since the previous shore leave, were included in the genial conversation. The shop took on some of the functions of an officers' club.

At the time of England's war against Napoleonic France, the chief naval station was Portsmouth, and in Portsmouth the chief outfitter's establishment was Melchizedek Meredith's, at 73, High Street. To inmates of cramped officers' quarters on frigates and brigs, it became a symbol of the amenities of life ashore—leisurely conversation and clean linen. "Oh! with what joy did I first put my foot on the shingle beach at Sallyport," says Peter Simple, hero of Captain Marryat's naval novel, after his escape from captivity in France. "We did not go to the admiral's, but merely reported ourselves at the admiral's office; for we had no clothes fit to appear in. But we called at Meredith's the tailor, and he promised that, by the next morning, we should be fitted complete. . . . By eleven o'clock the next morning, we were fit to appear before the admiral." Such dependable promptitude would become a byword throughout the fleet.

The Meredith concern, however, held its supremacy even more through the personal popularity of its proprietor. Mr Meredith was so urbane in manner, so witty and well informed in discourse, that even an admiral, while being fitted for a new pair of silk smallclothes, would find himself chatting to the outfitter in easy intimacy. And the sordid matter of payment was ignored as far as possible. The gallant officers were not apt to haggle, and Mr Meredith could never bring himself to press vulgarly for prompt settlement. As long as there was an occasional instalment on account, he remained solvent enough to live with all the elegance a provincial town could supply.

The name Meredith is of Welsh origin; and a loyal Welshman, like his kindred in Ireland and the Scottish Highlands, is likely to feel convinced of his descent from ancient chieftains and kings. Even when this conviction is unaccompanied by worldly prosperity, its possessor considers himself socially commensurate with any aristocrat of the upstart Saxon and Norman breeds. After two or three bottles of port Melchizedek Meredith would boast eloquently of his princely forebears, kinsmen of the Tudors who gave a royal dynasty to England. And he had not only these shadowy noble ancestors, reinforced by his solid commercial success, but other gifts of fortune also. He was tall and handsome, distinguished in bearing and irresistible to ladies. At many a county dinner the Portsmouth tradesman with his lively anecdotes and his affable manners cut a more notable figure than the worthy squires who tolerated his presence.

Behind his back, no doubt, they referred to him often enough as "that damned tailor." The dignity and prosperity of the naval establishment did not wholly obscure the dim days of peace when Meredith's had been merely a tailor's shop. Originally its proprietor must have learned the mastery of scissors and stitch as apprentice to some workaday clothier. Whatever the reason may be, the tailor's vocation was traditionally regarded in England with a peculiar mixture of humor and contempt. No other calling has been the butt of so many jests and sneers. In part perhaps the reason was the tailor's undignified posture, cross-legged on a table, with the grotesque "goose" at his elbow. Another reason may have been the informality of his relationship with his customers, to whom he ministered in the unbuttoned privacy of the fitting-room. At any rate, the ambiguous proverb about "nine tailors to make a man" and the legend of the "three tailors of Tooley Street" were typical of the disdain that attached to the craft. All this prejudice Mel Meredith had lived down by sheer force of social acumen.

Between his immediate forebears and the legendary Welsh princes of seven centuries before, the history of the family remains obscure.

In the middle of the eighteenth century they were established in the neighborhood of Portsmouth. One John Meredith was living at Portsea in 1763 when his son was baptized at the local parish church, St Mary Kingston, with the sturdy Old Testament name of Melchizedek. In his early twenties Melchizedek set up as a tailor in Portsmouth and married a woman ten years older than himself. Her name was Anne, and she may have been the daughter of an attorney named Mitchell. Tall and stately, she was gifted with much practical ability as well as strong will power, which had a chance to display itself in defense of her marriage to an untried youth of so humble a calling. Both her marriage portion and her sensible counsel must have aided him vastly in the development of his business.

The mellow old brick house at 73, High Street was spacious and well situated for its purpose, for the street led directly up from the Sallyport, which was the landing-place from ships in the harbor. The tailoring business occupied the ground floor, with the workshop in the rear, running back to White Hart Road. From the bow window of the parlor, above the shop front, the family could look out across Battery Row and the Platform to Spithead and the Isle of Wight. To the left lay the Grand Parade, an open space that was the scene of glittering naval and military spectacles.

Seven children were born to the Merediths in this pleasant house and were christened at St Thomas's Church, a little way up the street. The first son, Charles Melchizedek, died in childhood in 1794. Five daughters came into the world between 1786 and 1794, and finally another son, Augustus Urmston, was born in 1797.

With his business flourishing, Mel Meredith began to take his place among the solid burghers of the town. As early as 1796 he could describe himself as "gentleman" in the register of the Phoenix Lodge of Freemasons. He was a churchwarden of St Thomas's in 1801 and 1804, and joined with his fellow-warden in presenting two silver alms plates. Soon he was gaining the good graces of the county squires by riding to hounds.

As the five girls grew up with a full share of the beauty of their parents, they had no dearth of eligible suitors. The two eldest were both married in 1809—Anne Elizabeth to Thomas Burbey, of Grant and Burbey, bankers and wholesale grocers, of 46, High Street, and Caroline Melchizedek to William Price Read, a silversmith. Two years later the next two sisters made even better matches: Harriet Eustace married John Hellyer, an insurance broker whose family had a brewery at Newington, Surrey, and Louisa Mitchell married John Read, and they soon went to live in the Azores Islands. The young son, Augustus, meanwhile, was being educated for the medical profession.

These auspicious beginnings were soon shadowed by tragedy. Mrs Burbey, the eldest sister, died in 1812, and Caroline only five months later. After the lapse of another year, on July 10, 1814, Melchizedek Meredith died at the age of fifty-one.

His seventeen-year-old son may have been abroad at the time, on a visit to his sister Louisa. Augustus's grief for the loss of his father was merged into another sort of gloom when he came home to Portsmouth and learned from his mother that the accounts of the shop were in sad confusion and that he would have to adopt the trade forthwith and accept the responsibilities of management.

Augustus Urmston Meredith had inherited something of his father's handsome physique and aristocratic mien. Brought up during the years of prosperity, he absorbed the illusions of royal ancestry without the saving modicum of common sense that old Mel had retained from his boyhood days as the apprentice tailor. Before long it was gleefully reported that when the slim, dark young man was on a holiday in Bath his expensive raiment and courtly air gave rise to a rumor (which he did nothing to quell) that he was a foreign count traveling incognito. The nickname "Count Meredith" stuck to him in Portsmouth as long as he lived there.

Thus fancying himself as an elegant gentleman, Augustus could not display his father's geniality in dealing with the public. Instead his manner was inclined to be aloof and his tastes were bookish and intellectual. He was a member of the Portsmouth Literary and Philosophical Society, and a notable chess-player. With his self-dramatizing imagination, his fluency, and his love of reading, he might have become a writer—if only a dilettante one—had he been free to shape his own career. But the inflexible will of his mother decreed that he must carry on the business that her husband had built up.

"A perfect gentleman and not the least like a tailor," was the tribute that one of Augustus's later acquaintances paid to him; but customers prefer to patronize someone who does appear to be a representative of the craft he professes, and so they began to drift away to less pretentious competitors. Besides, he had assumed the control of the business at a difficult time. The ending of the wars meant a sharp reduction in the naval outfitting trade and in the general prosperity of Portsmouth. Many of the bills that Mel had allowed to grow year after year had to be written off at last as bad debts, in spite of Mrs Meredith's best efforts to collect.

The size of the family had shrunk sufficiently to allow curtailment of the old lavish way of living; and in October, 1819, the last of the daughters, Catherine Matilda, was married to Lieutenant Samuel Burdon Ellis, of the Royal Marines, a member of a family that had supplied officers to the armed services through several generations. For the next three years Mrs Meredith and her son lived alone, and then Augustus got engaged to Jane Eliza Macnamara, a girl whom he had undoubtedly known all his life, as her father had been proprietor of the Vine, just around the corner, in Broad Street. It was one of the good inns of the town, and when Michael Macnamara had died eight years earlier he left Jane and her sister and brother well provided for, her dowry being a thousand pounds, invested in four-per-cent annuities.

As a safeguard against the bridegroom's impulses toward extravagance, the marriage settlement stipulated that he could never touch either the capital sum or the interest, and that the trustees could not sell the annuities. After her death, the trust fund was to descend to any child or children who might survive. With this matter ratified, the wedding took place on May 1, 1823.

Jane Meredith's brother, Thomas Pellew Macnamara, a purser in the Royal Navy, and their spinster sister, Anna Maria, both lived in Portsmouth; and although they were respectable citizens the connection with an innkeeper's family cannot have been entirely gratifying to Augustus Meredith's sisters, who had all succeeded in marrying into a higher social station. Nor did the bride's income go far enough to restore the former affluence of the household. By this time some of the rooms were being let as lodgings: in 1827 Rear Admiral Sir Thomas Hardy, Bt., the officer who had held the dying Nelson in his arms, wrote to his brother: "I can give you a bed. I am at Meradith's, the tailor, 73 High Street, opposite the Parade Coffee House."

The only child of Augustus and Jane Meredith was born on February 12, 1828, and was christened George in St Thomas's Church on April 9. On November 8 of the same year a firm guiding hand was removed from the household by the death of his grandmother, the indomitable Mrs Mel.

A high-strung, pretty child, George was brought up in the family tradition of superiority, so that the little boys of the street regarded him with a mingling of envy and scorn. The next-door neighbor, a bookseller named Price, had a son about two years older, who left some amusing recollections, the earliest dating back to a time when George was not more than three years old. Invited to play with him in the large front parlor, Jem Price found a pretty little boy in a white frock with the sleeves tied up with blue ribbons. The visitor was shy in the presence of this dainty child and his mother, and was deeply impressed by the assortment of picture books and elaborate toys that George paraded before his admiring gaze. In particular there was a handsome white horse and toy cart which played tunes when George pulled it about the room. After a while Jem went home without much feeling of friendship for a child who was endowed with such unfamiliarly gorgeous playthings.

He describes also a grand party in honor of George's fourth or fifth birthday. "The Misses and Masters Price" received a formal invitation to the "Tea and Ball." The four of them were the first to arrive and sat in lonely discomfort on a sofa until other guests came, more adults than children, to the eventual number of about fifty. Mrs Meredith attended punctiliously to introductions, rout seats were distributed about the room, tea and coffee and cakes were passed around by servants. Now "out of the frock-petticoat period," George "was made much of by everyone." After tea the company was shifted into the adjoining room for the ball, at which Mrs Meredith's brother acted as M.C. After being pushed through one set of a square dance by a grown-up partner, Jem Price retired from the unequal struggle, sat against the wall for the rest of the evening, and was regaled at intervals with almonds, raisins, and quarters of oranges, along with weak negus, until he was too sleepy to hold his head up. Upon the announcement of supper there was a rush back to the front room for cake and tarts. When Mrs Meredith finally said, "It's time those children went home," the young Prices were more than willing to go.

With this sort of social display to be sustained, it was not easy for the Meredith household to make ends meet. When George was two years old an act of Parliament reduced the interest on bank annuities to 3½ per cent, and Mrs Meredith's income was thus cut to £35 a year. Three years later, in July, 1833, she died, and the legal machinery of the marriage indenture went into effect. The income could no longer be used for general household expenses, but must be applied by the trustees solely "toward the maintenance and education" of the boy. The Macnamara family and their solicitor kept a watchful eye to make sure that the provisions were enforced.

The widower and his five-year-old son were obviously incapable of taking care of themselves. Mrs Ellis may still have been living in Portsmouth, while her husband was on foreign service; but if so, she was busy with the care of her own three boys, the youngest of whom was the same age as George Meredith and may have been his playmate.

In later life, Meredith gave the impression that he was fonder of Mrs Ellis than of her sisters. The only other relation on the Meredith side remaining in Portsmouth was Mary Burbey, daughter of Augustus's eldest sister. Her father, who was mayor of the town that year, still lived on the opposite side of the street, and the children of his second marriage sometimes came to play with George. Young Miss Burbey could do no more than run in occasionally to see how things were going with her hapless uncle and cousin. The housekeeping was left in the hands of a servant girl, and the drawing-room and a large bedroom were rented to Sir Edward Synge, an eccentric Irish baronet.

This retrenchment did not mean that Meredith put an end to all the hospitable habits that he had been brought up in. He still gave dinner parties; and being an abstemious man himself, he would withdraw from the dining-room soon after the bottles began to circulate, and leave his guests to help themselves to the wine as long as they pleased.

George was too young to feel any acute grief at the time of his mother's death. Rather, he told a friend many years later, he "merely wondered." His father, who was devotedly fond of him, made every effort to keep him happy. Lacking congenial playmates, the child spent much time in his father's company and listened rapturously to eloquent accounts of the family's past splendors. From these stories the boy acquired a belief that he was of predominantly Celtic descent on both sides. His mother's family name was, of course, an indication of Irish ancestry; but in point of fact both the Merediths and the Macnamaras had been rooted in Hampshire long enough for intermarriage with the local stock, and Jane's mother had had the thoroughly Anglo-Saxon name of Dale.

Thanks to the £35 a year that he had inherited, George was able to attend St Paul's School, Southsea, a fact which widened the chasm between him and the other sons of High Street tradesmen, for they went to Frost's Academy in St Thomas's Street. "The boys of St Paul's looked down upon us, Frost's boys," Jem Price records; "but George Meredith and I when we met always exchanged salutations: 'How de do, Price,' in his usual drawling, patronizing way. He was certainly a good-looking youth, with bright blue or grey eyes, and a nice, light, curly head of hair, and always well dressed, much better than any of us boys, all sons of tradespeople." The jolly lads of Frost's amused themselves with marbles, hoops, whip and peg tops, and such games as rounders and prisoner's base, and by concocting fireworks out of the discarded powder when the soldiers drew their cartridges at the

Guard House; but "to these sort of things George Meredith never stooped, and, in consequence, he got the name of 'Gentleman Georgy' among us boys."

To a great degree this aloofness resulted from fear. Near the end of his life he told an interviewer that "I was a very timid and sensitive boy. I was frightened of everything; I could not endure to be left alone." He had been terrified when an Irish nursemaid told him that the wind whistling through the keyhole was the spirits of the starved. He dreaded the dark, which his lively imagination peopled with ghosts. And during the impressionable years between six and ten he must have grown vaguely aware that all was not well in the house in the High Street. His father's suave manner could not always disguise the growing financial anxiety. As time went on, Augustus Meredith seems to have found the ministrations of his housekeeper, a girl named Matilda Buckett, increasingly important, and it is not impossible that she assumed the functions of wife in other respects as well as domestic management. Whether or not the little boy was aware of any undue intimacies between the two adults in the house, his sensitive nature must have cringed to witness this woman's domination in the place of the mother who was described to him as having been "handsome, refined, and witty." An increasing sense of insecurity undermined the fascination that his father had once exerted. In spite of the good clothes, the superior school, and the legends of Celtic nobility, the memories of his childhood were bitterly distasteful to him in later years.

He saw little of his aunts and their families during this era. Louisa occasionally made a descent upon Portsmouth, garbed in the most elaborate Parisian modes and full of anecdotes about noble and royal foreigners. After being left a widow, she had married again in 1829, her second husband being probably a relation of her first, as he had the same name; but he was of higher social station. William Harding Read had been for nearly twenty years the British Consul-General in the Azores, where he became a personal friend of the ruling house of Portugal and Brazil, and was created a Knight of the Order of the Tower and Sword. Louisa's daughter married Antonio da Costa Cabral, a Portuguese aristocrat, in 1834. No wonder Senhora Luiza Read, whenever she honored her English relatives with a visit, spoke with a Continental accent and showed an elegant ignorance of everything connected with trade. Little George Meredith was profoundly impressed with her shrugs and gestures, her voluble vivacity, and her contempt for English boorishness. He resolved that he would always treat ladies with the courtesy that she lauded in her Continental friends.

In September, 1837, Aunt Catherine's husband, Captain Ellis, was anchored for a few days at Spithead, en route to India. His journal indicates that he dined with the commandant of the Royal Marines, visited Sir Philip Dunham, the commander-in-chief of the station, and spent a good deal of time with the affluent Burbeys, now living at Southsea, where they provided "music and dancing." Alongside these amusements, there is a trace of anticlimax in the entries: "8th September . . . Returned at a late hour, and slept at Mr Meredith's in the High Street . . . 12th September . . . Returned and dined with Mr Meredith in Portsmouth."

The business had gone from bad to worse in Augustus Meredith's incompetent hands. In November, 1838, a firm of clothiers in Cheapside brought an action for a fiat of bankruptcy against him. He apparently had not enough cash to pay his fare to London for the hearing; the court order included a proviso that the petitioner was to "pay the said Augustus Urmston Meredith his expenses of attending . . . and to be reimbursed . . . out of the estate and effects of the said Augustus Urmston Meredith." In *The Times* of November 17, the list of bankrupts blazoned the name of "Augustus Urmston Meredith, Portsmouth, draper."

At this time of crisis, eleven-year-old George manfully kept up his pose of sophistication. The last time Jem Price saw him in the High Street, a knot of Frost's Academy boys were clustered in front of the Parade Coffee House, among them being Joe Neale, whose father, the proprietor of the coffee house, owned a racehorse. With his most affable and worldly air, George strolled over to them and remarked to Joe, "I was at Stokes Bay races last week and I saw your father's horse come in second, but I think he is a grand horse. By George, he's got some blood in him!"

The business passed into the hands of a rival tailor, Joseph Galt, from No. 63, and Augustus Meredith moved to London in the hope of starting a fresh career where the stigma of his failure would not be known. George seems to have continued as a day-boy at the school in Southsea, and in all probability went to live either with the Burbeys or with his mother's relations. Matilda Buckett, the young housekeeper, must have followed Meredith to London, for on July 3, 1839, six months after the bankruptcy sale, he married her in the precinct chapel of Bridewell. Although on the marriage certificate he defiantly described himself as "gentleman," he had been obliged to find humble employment as a journeyman in a tailor's shop. Two years later, in one of the numerous affidavits connected with his son's inheritance, he was designated as a tailor living in Tudor Street, which is in a modest region between Ludgate Hill and the river.

Miss Anna Maria Macnamara died intestate in April, 1840, leaving £1818.12.11, which was divided equally between her brother and her nephew George Meredith. When this was added to his legacy from his mother, the total inheritance held in trust for him until his majority became £1909, and his annual income £66.12.6. More than a year elapsed before the new funds were available to him. In a petition to the court, granted on August 6, 1841, Augustus Meredith testified that he was "desirous of giving the said George Meredith such an education as will fit him for the profession of solicitor," and that his son's previous income of £35 was inadequate for the purpose. As part of the arrangement, he surrendered "the curation or guardianship" of his son, and gave his consent to the appointment of Charles Henry Binstead, the Macnamara solicitor, as trustee. This meant that George became a "ward in Chancery." He had seen little or nothing of his father and stepmother during the past two years, and now, when he was thirteen, the authority of the parent was largely abrogated.

This does not imply callousness on the father's part. Augustus was devoted to the boy and proud of his abilities. He was rightly convinced that George was better off in Hampshire, with prosperous relatives, than he would be in shabby London lodgings under the supervision of a stepmother whom he did not respect. For George, however, an agonizing disillusionment was now complete. The handsome and indulgent father, once able to hold him spellbound with romantic tales, had allowed the family business to perish, had lost the family home, and had married a servant girl. Now he legally acknowledged his inability to support his son. The child who "could not endure to be left alone" was spiritually alone indeed. The consequence was a lifelong contempt for his father, which he expressed once, in later years, in the intemperate remark that Augustus was "a muddler and a fool."

Through these years of failure and anxiety, the ambitious daughters of Melchizedek Meredith seem to have made no move to help their brother and nephew. To be sure, none of them still lived in Portsmouth, but all three were in a position to offer some financial aid. The Hellyer brewery was piling up profits for Harriet and her husband. Louisa's husband died in 1839, and she made her home in Lisbon to be near her son-in-law, who had just become *de facto* dictator of Portugal as principal minister for Queen Maria II. Captain Ellis was winning honors as commander of the Marine Battalion in the war with China.

From somewhere among them a few pounds might have been forth-coming. But in their scheme of things, poor relations were a blight that could be endured only by being ignored.

On the strength of his increased income, George was sent to a boarding-school. In after life he concealed his early days under such an impenetrable cloak of silence that there is no positive evidence by which the school can be identified. On the strength of some passages of autobiographical flavor, in his novels, it has been generally assumed that the school was situated in the pretty Hampshire village of Peters-field. Viscountess Milner, however, who was the daughter of his most intimate friend, kept notes of a conversation in his old age, wherein he told her positively that he had lived for a while at a farm near Peters-field but that he went to boarding-school in Lowestoft. There is no explanation for this removal to a rather bleak fishing-town on the east coast. Perhaps some family connection linked him with that part of Suffolk, for in later life he went back to the vicinity several times.

His most vivid memory of the school was associated with the rigidity of its religious practices. Twenty years afterwards, he gave a painfully precise description of

*how all love of the Apostles was belaboured out of me by three Sunday services of prodigious length and drowsiness. Corinthians will forever be as-sociated in my mind with rows of wax candles and a holy drone overhead, combined with the sensation that those who did not choose the road to Heaven enjoyed by far the pleasantest way. I cannot hear of Genesis, or of the sins of amorous David, or of Hezekiah, without fidgetting in my chair, as if it had turned to the utterly unsympathetic Church-wood of yore. In de-spair, I used to begin a fresh chapter of the adventures of St George (a serial story, continued from Sunday to Sunday), and carry it on till the preacher's voice fell. Sometimes he deceived me (I hope, not voluntarily) and his voice bade St George go back into his box, and then ascended in renewed vigour once more, leaving me vacant of my comforting hero, who was not to be re-vived, after such treatment.*

Apart from boredom, the school did not cause him undue distress. The realm of his imagination was peopled not only with St George and other knights of romance but also with the cadis and sorcerers of *The Arabian Nights*, his favorite book. A real-life hero was provided for his worship in the person of the head-boy; many years later he described how he used to feel "towards our big boy champion against the bullies at school: that is, I admire, believe in him, feel that it is my fight, but can aid only very little—by gesticulation chiefly." His lifelong love of cricket must have been fostered on the school playing-field; and he began to develop sinewy strength that could command respect. In later years he flattered himself that he had possessed a sort of telepathic insight into the very minds of his schoolmates which enabled him to read their characters "consummately." And he enjoyed rambles along the seashore and among the lanes behind the town. His finding of a fine lump of amber on the beach always lingered pleasantly in his mind. It may have been during this period that he acquired his affection for long lonely walks and his acute observation of birds and rodents and the pattern of clouds in the sky. This training in the lore of nature stood him in good stead through his whole life; but so far as the formal education of the schoolroom was concerned, he had no high opinion of what was offered him. Throughout his English schooling, he said later, he "learned very little."

On August 18, 1842, he entered the Moravian School at Neuwied on the Rhine. Here his £66 a year could go further than in England; and the stamp of a Continental education, with the facility in languages that might be acquired, would be a better qualification for the boy than anything obtainable in a small and obscure English school. During the preceding decade English boys had been sent to Neuwied in large numbers, drawn by the advantages of sound instruction, low fees, and devout but gentle and tolerant Protestant principles.

Neuwied was a neat little town, eight miles down the Rhine from Coblenz, among the cliffs and forests that border the right bank of the river. A spur of the rugged Westerwald lies not far behind the town. The school had been established in 1756, at a time when the tiny principality of Neuwied was a famous place of sanctuary for adherents of all religious faiths, who were allowed to conduct their services without official interference. Among the sects taking advantage of this liberal edict were the Moravian Brethren, who were being driven out of many regions for their refusal to be absorbed into the Lutheran Church. For centuries they had been persecuted for their opposition to war and to oaths, and their insistence upon the separation of church and state. They were the first Protestant sect to make conversion of the heathen a primary duty but it was on a basis of Christlike example, rather than on sectarian dogma.

There were about a hundred and fifty boys in the school. All slept together in one huge stuffy dormitory; there was not room to walk between the beds, and the windows were never opened. Every boy made his own bed. In the course of a day the boys moved from one class to another, not according to age but to their ability in the various subjects.

Henry Morley, later to be well known as a journalist and professor of literature, was a pupil at Neuwied ten years before Meredith. An article that he wrote in 1854 is the best source of information about the school and reveals why it was a formative influence in Meredith's youth:

Why do I believe, as I do firmly, that I learned precious things in that German school which suffered me to forget my little Greek, and to dwindle down from a precocious bolter of Virgil to a bad decliner of rex, regis; which administered its Euclid in homeopathic doses; which taught me to write in mystic characters that had to be unlearnt at home; and in which I cannot re-member that I ever did a sum? Why do I believe that I learned more than ever in the same time before or after? . . .

By incidents occurring almost daily, our imaginations were appealed to, and our hearts were touched . . . The multitude of boys, living together as a sort of federal republic, was not only maintained in perfect discipline with-out an act of violence, but very few went away from among us whose minds had not been, to some degree, enriched, enlarged, and ennobled. During the two years that I spent there, not a blow was struck, except the few that sea-soned our own boyish quarrels. They were few enough.

We were not milksops. We braved peril in many of our sports; we were for true knights, not for recreants; cowardice was abhorred among us . . . A spirit of truthfulness, of gentleness, of cordiality between the teachers and the taught, pervaded our whole body; punishments of the most nominal kinds sufficed for the scholastic discipline; insubordination, there was none; secret contempt of authority, there was none. New-comers brought vices with them very often, or began their new school-life in the wrong tune; the good spirit soon infected them; they fell into the right harmony within a week or a month . . .

Every one of us was being humanized in the best way, and trained to be-come a thinker and a student for himself thereafter . . . Our fancy worked in all our play. We spent many a summer afternoon in a craggy dell, acting robber tales that we created for ourselves . . . It was no great check on the play of our imaginations that the pious Moravians forbade novels and plays as reading, and restricted us to edifying stories about Easter eggs and other holy things . . . We still found, however, many fanciful books, and there was no reason why we should not contribute to each other all we knew con-cerning Schinderhannes, Eulenspiegel, and such worthies. We were en-couraged to tell tales of wonder to each other . . .

*We always went out in the warm spring weather at Whitsuntide, for a long—perhaps, week-long—ramble from hill to hill and town to town: now mounted upon donkeys, now rumbling in country-carts, now floating down the river in flat-bottomed boats, but always proudest and best pleased when we were a-foot. How intense was our enjoyment of these walks! We slept where we halted for the night: in barns, in kitchens—once in an old ruin— commonly on straw—one night only, in a town hotel on feathers, which we hated . . .*

Morley describes in detail the Christmas festivities and birthday parties, explains how English boys were gently cured of boastful exaggeration about their homeland, and insists that the pupils gained a sane feeling toward sickness and death by being encouraged to visit a master while he lay dying, to pay their respects to his corpse, and to participate in his funeral.

Naturally enough, one effect of the school's spiritual earnestness upon Meredith was an adolescent bout of religious fervor. "When I was quite a boy," he told a friend in after years, "I had a spasm of religion which lasted about six weeks, during which I made myself a nuisance in asking everybody whether they were saved. But never since have I swallowed the Christian fable."

This spell of evangelical zeal must have prevailed about the end of his sojourn at Neuwied, for its tone infects his earliest surviving letter, written to a schoolfellow in January, 1844, not long before he left the school. In the smugly trite language of self-conscious sixteen, he speaks of the feeling of fellowship which "has agitated our respective bosoms . . . O may God grant that all may have the same feeling towards you to make your life happy. But true fellowship is not to be had without Christianity; not the name but the practice of it. I wish you the greatest of all things 'God's blessing,' which comprehends all I would or could otherwise say."

Though Meredith so quickly abandoned the literal acceptance of the Bible, which was the fundamental doctrine of his Moravian teachers, his two years at Neuwied shaped his whole future view of life, in far more profound respects than his lasting interest in German music, German political thought, and the medieval legends that clung about every crag and castle along the Rhine. Every one of the qualities that Henry Morley listed as inculcated at the Moravian school can be clearly recognized throughout Meredith's writings. He was permanently indued with impatience toward sham and servility, contempt for conceit, admiration for courage, and devotion to candid and rational forthrightness. Being grafted on to his proud, introverted nature, however, these tenets did not produce a benevolent saint after the Moravian pattern, but more often aroused his fierce exasperation with his fellow-men for failing to fulfill the ideal.

When he came home to England, his father was actively planning a future career for him and seeking the necessary funds. In an application to the Court of Chancery, on March 15, 1844, identifying himself as a tailor living at 16, King Street, Holborn, Augustus declared that he "has not had at any time since his said bankruptcy and has not now any income except what is derived from his business as a tailor." The petitioner stated that the time had come for binding his son as an apprentice in "some trade or business with a view to providing for his future support and advancement in life," and consequently he requested the release of £400 by the sale of bank annuities from the estate of George's Aunt Anna, to cover the fees for apprenticing him for five years to John Williams, a bookseller and publisher, of 44, Paternoster Row. Williams had "proposed and offered to take this . . . son out with him to the settlement of Hong Kong on the coast of China where he . . . intends to carry on his said business of a bookseller and publisher, together with the business of taking portraits, landscapes, and other representative objects by the Photogenic System and of precipitating metals by Galvanic electricity." It was stated that the trustees of the estate would agree to the arrangement, and an accompanying affidavit added that "the deponent's said son is desirous so to do if he can be supplied with the necessary funds for that purpose." The court ordered that the petition be referred to the Master in Chancery for inquiry and recommendation.

It may be noticed that the earlier proposal of educating George to be a solicitor had been silently abandoned, in favor of a humbler vocation. The source of the new idea can scarcely have been the boy himself, as he had been isolated from all business matters in the almost monastic serenity of Neuwied. Nor is it likely that he had been writing to his father with demands to be released from school and launched in the world on his own account; he seems to have been happy enough at the German school, and his ambitions never showed a worldly bent. It is more probable that Augustus, in a sudden spasm of paternal responsibility, decided that at sixteen his son was too old to waste more time on schooling. His lodgings in King Street were only a few yards from Paternoster Row and with his love of reading he is sure to have been a browser among the bookstalls; he could thus have become acquainted with Williams. Chancing to hear that the bookseller needed an apprentice, he would be fascinated by the two elements of novelty and adventure in the project—first, the art of photography, which had emerged only within the preceding four years, and second, the colony of Hong Kong, which was equally recent in origin, having been nothing more than an anchorage for British warships when ceded by China in the Treaty of Nanking which ended the Opium War in 1842.

Of all the unfulfilled schemes that crop up in biographies of authors, this one is perhaps the most tantalizing to speculate on. What would have become of George Meredith if he had indeed learned how to take daguerreotypes and had gone out to the barren and unhealthy island of rocky peaks at the mouth of the Canton River, where a handful of Britons were securing a base for their opium trade and incidentally for the Empire?

The project did not materialize, and no further reference to it has been found in the Chancery records. Probably the Master's report was unfavorable; or perhaps when George discovered all the implications of the plan he rebelled and forced its withdrawal. The £400, in any event, was not made available for his apprenticeship fees.

A gap now occurs in the existing knowledge about his doings. After his return from school in the spring of 1844, more than half a year elapsed before the next stage of his career was even suggested, and another year was required before the proposal went into effect. Inference alone can be offered as to what may have been going on during these eighteen months.

The long alienation from his father would have been intensified, rather than mitigated, by the proposal of shipping the boy off to Hong Kong. Augustus was still, apparently, only a journeyman tailor, living in cheap quarters. It is scarcely believable that George could have made his home with his father and stepmother in London, or taken any hand in a tailoring shop. One possibility is that while awaiting a ruling from the Court of Chancery he went to work for Williams as a mere errand boy, without the dignity of an apprentice's articles. The other and more likely alternative is that he took refuge for at least a part of the time in Hampshire with the Macnamaras, who had always been solicitous for his welfare.

The possibility accords well with a further assumption that must be offered here in regard to his experiences at the crucial age of seventeen. Admittedly, caution is essential in inferring details of an author's private life from episodes in his books. It will be abundantly demonstrated, however, that Meredith derived all the major characters and situations of his novels from real life; and when we find one particular example occurring more frequently than any other, and with an intensity of feeling that marks it apart from its context, we are justified in assuming that it could originate in the author's own experience.

In three of Meredith's novels, as well as in his best-known and most erotically emotional poem, a significant character is a farmer's daughter —very young, very naïve, golden-haired and rosy-cheeked—who inspires a passion of romantic love in a young man of higher social or intellectual status. In both "Love in the Valley" and *The Ordeal of Richard Feverel* the idyllic devotion and innocent sensuality of first love are portrayed with keenest sympathy. In two later novels, *Rhoda Fleming* and *Harry Richmond*, a more realistic attitude prevails; both stories emphasize the essential incompatibility between the lovers, and culminate in abandonment of the girl. The internal evidence of personal feeling which they all convey is verified by his most profoundly personal poem, *Modern Love*. In a sonnet which has no inherent connection with the story and which therefore can only be a morsel of autobiography, he states openly:

> *I have known rustic revels in my youth,*
> *The May-fly pleasures of a mind at ease.*
> *An early goddess was a country lass:*
> *A charmed Amphion-oak she tripped the grass.*

The combined evidence of two poems and three novels thus suggests what easily can have happened when George Meredith, endowed with the exuberant emotions and romantic imagination of a poet, and embittered by a sense of neglect and frustrated pride, came home to England after two years at a school conducted on principles of strict moral austerity. When he went back to the Hampshire countryside there must have been a violent release of sentiment. If, at this acutely impressionable moment, a pretty, unsophisticated girl showed herself to be captivated by the handsome, moody lad, there was bound to be a sudden discovery of the raptures and agonies of sexual attraction.

The vivid glimpses of farmyard, byre, and kitchen, the portraits of bluff fathers, solicitous mothers, and sententious laborers, as well as the rosy glow suffusing the central figure who is variously Lucy Desborough, Dahlia Fleming, Mabel Sweetwinter, and the unnamed heroine of "Love in the Valley," combine to make these literary works yield an inescapably convincing picture of seventeen-year-old George Meredith haunting a snug old red-brick farmhouse for stolen moments of bliss with the blue-eyed young daughter of the family.

The outcome of the affair is also sufficiently obvious, both in terms of psychological probability and in terms of the inferences to be drawn from the books. Only in *Richard Feverel* does the young man actually marry the girl, and even in that story he causes her a long interval of misery by promptly deserting her and returning to his own social world. Futhermore, in a characteristic manner, Meredith repeatedly presented a sort of ironical antithesis to the pair of lovers. In several novels, and for no logical requirement of plot, he introduced the character of a gifted, idealistic young man who had impulsively "married beneath him" and had suffered the sequel of ostracism and remorse, while the wife drifted into drunkenness and promiscuity. This situation may have included a vague trace of the disgust that he felt over his father's second marriage (though Matilda Buckett proved to be a loyal help-mate), but it is more like a sort of hypothetical vindication of the author himself. In each instance the whole affair takes place offstage and the lowborn wife is a shadowy figure only mentioned in shocked whispers. For this contrast with the full-hearted sympathy with which the farmhouse love-idylls are presented, the most tenable explanation is that one set of episodes deals with something that Meredith knew well and felt deeply, whereas the other deals with something that had not happened, but which he constructed intellectually to represent the probable outcome that would follow such an irrational union.

If the foregoing reconstruction of the blank page in Meredith's life has any validity, he must have been dragged in different directions by his craving for the girl, his common-sense recognition that he was too young and penniless to marry her, and the restless ambition that was already driving him to seek social and intellectual distinction. Whether it was his own decision that drew him away from her, or whether his father or other relations intervened, the next positive record shows George back in London and making a start at last on the career that had been selected for him. But one can be sure that he not only suffered infernal tortures in the separation but also imagined vividly the misery of the girl left behind, and that he tried lamely to vindicate himself with the argument that she would not have made a suitable wife for the distinguished, witty gentleman that he expected to become.

A report of the Master in Chancery, dated December 20, 1845, summarizes the developments with regard to Meredith's prospects. In February, 1845, the month of his seventeenth birthday, there had been a flurry of affidavits. The new plan was that George Meredith was to be articled to a young solicitor named Richard Stephen Charnock, thus resuming the earlier objective of a career in the law.

There are several ways in which Charnock may have come upon the scene. At this time his address was 44, Paternoster Row, the same as John Williams's, whence it is clear that his chambers were above the bookshop. He could have met Augustus Meredith and his son at the time when the proposed apprenticeship to Williams was being debated. Moreover, Charnock was devoted to Germany and took walking tours there. This would give him a common interest with the youth who had been at school in the Rhineland. It is conceivable that when the apprenticeship scheme was first conceived Williams commissioned Charnock to visit Neuwied during one of his tours and to obtain George's formal consent to the proposition.

George had grown up to be an attractive lad with thick curly chestnut hair, delicately chiseled features, and a large mobile mouth. He retained the drawling intonation that had antagonized his young contemporaries in Portsmouth, but it was effective in giving point to the sarcastic remarks and poetic images that adorned his conversation. While he could not be described as well educated, he had begun to read the authors who make history come to life. He said in old age that after he outgrew his addiction to *The Arabian Nights* his next formative books were those of Scott, Gibbon, and Niebuhr. All this would appeal strongly to a man of Charnock's stamp.

The Charnock family had been active in English scholastic, theological, and legal circles since the seventeenth century. Richard Stephen Charnock had been articled to his father and then had gone into partnership with an aged relative, John Charnock. These established connections ought to have given him a good start toward a successful career in law, but there is no evidence that he built up any sort of practice. His tastes were for travel and philological scholarship, and also for such amenities as tobacco and vintage wines. In the course of a long life he lapsed into deplorable habits of slovenliness, but also acquired some distinction in his chosen lines of knowledge. For thirty-four years (1865–99) he edited Bradshaw's *Illustrated Handbook to Spain and Portugal*. He published books on the Tyrol and Transylvania, and many quaintly learned treatises on the Essex dialect, the etymology of place names and personal names, and similar topics. He became a Doctor of Philosophy of Göttingen University, and a Fellow of the Society of Antiquaries. In his early days, at any rate, he was no stuffy pedant, but a genial boon companion and a lover of the open air.

Meredith later declared in a characteristically ruthless phrase that "he had neither business nor morals"; but to a boy of seventeen with an active mind and literary impulses this sardonic young attorney, only eight years his senior, was a fascinating specimen of the talented man of the world.

The Court of Chancery apparently had doubts as to Charnock's fitness to assume responsibility for a pupil. The list of affidavits does not specify their contents, but his first one was presumably a statement of his qualifications. The next day it was supported by one from Richard Charnock, under whom he had studied law. In the same week Augustus Meredith swore an affidavit which may be supposed to have added his consent. A slight improvement in his circumstances is suggested by the fact that he was now described as "assistant" to a tailor named Mackie, in Southampton Row, Bloomsbury. During the next few months six further affidavits were submitted by other persons, chiefly solicitors. Still later George Meredith himself was called before the court for questioning. On November 6, Charnock swore a second affidavit, but not until December did the Master give his approval to the arrangement.

The Court ordered that £630 was to be realized by the sale of annuities from George's portion of Miss Macnamara's estate. Of this sum, £500 was to be paid to Charnock to bind George for five years' study of law, according to a "proper Deed or Articles of Clerkship," which the Master in Chancery must approve. The remaining £130 was to be applied "in and towards the Duty and other expenses attending the said Deed or Articles of Clerkship." The income derived from what remained of George's legacy from his aunt was to be paid to Augustus for George's maintenance during his minority or until further orders of the Court.

Charnock undertook to supply his pupil with good and sufficient food and lodging, £20 per year, and instruction in the law. On February 3, 1846, one week before his eighteenth birthday, the register of the Law Society recorded that George Meredith of Southampton Row was articled to Richard Stephen Charnock of Paternoster Row for five years.

NOTE. It has always been assumed that George Meredith was born in the family home at 73, High Street. He himself believed that his birth took place at a farm, owned by relations of his mother, near Petersfield. It is entirely probable that his mother chose to undergo her confinement in the quiet countryside, attended by her own kinsfolk, rather than in the rooms above the shop, under the domination of her mother-in-law.

# CHAPTER

# II

# *The Young Poet*

When Meredith told an interviewer that in his boyhood he was frightened of everything, he went on, "But when I came to be eighteen I looked round the world (as far as a youth of eighteen can look) and determined not to be afraid again."

This access of self-confidence must have come from his association with the easygoing, freethinking Charnock and the group of kindred spirits who were his friends. To find himself accepted into such a sophisticated circle, in spite of his youth and inexperience, would give Meredith a sense of achievement that he had never felt before. Charnock's scientific predilections must have opened a whole new field of thought to a boy brought up in strict Protestant dogmas. In 1846 such books as *The Vestiges of Creation* were popularizing new theories of physical science and providing ammunition for the foes of orthodoxy. Meredith would have listened eagerly to the wide-ranging discussions around Charnock's dinner table, and before long he undoubtedly added his own share to the talk. Thus he was encouraged to "look round the world" and reshape his whole conception of life.

Not only his ideas but his manners took on at this time their permanent mold. The somewhat foreign air of courtesy that he had cultivated in imitation of his Aunt Louisa had been strengthened by his residence abroad; and two years of hearing and speaking German sufficed to obliterate all lingering traces of Hampshire accent and to replace it with a faintly artificial articulation that betrayed no clues as to local or social origin. To offset these traits of formality, he gained from the Charnock coterie a habit of strenuous banter. Nicknames and scandalous innuendoes were pelted back and forth. These young men had grown up during the thirties, when the most popular humorists were Tom Hood with his puns and Theodore Hook with his improvisations and practical jokes. And the thirties was also the age of a debased Byronism, when the young bloods of London took Don Juan as their model in cultivating a cynical disrespect for convention. This pose of superiority to the common illusions of mankind was another element in the amalgam from which Meredith's personality was being shaped.

If any pretense at the study of law was ever attempted, it was soon abandoned. The records of Chancery yield no indication that the Master ever approved the "proper Deed or Articles of Clerkship" which had been decreed. The whole transaction fulfilled its purpose when it pried loose from the administrators a sizable portion of the inheritance that had been locked up in Chancery for so long. Charnock removed from Paternoster Row to 10, Godliman Street, Doctors' Commons, but the closer proximity to the Law Courts did not necessarily induce any stronger enthusiasm for the law.

This easy abandonment of Meredith's legal studies left unsolved the question of how he was to earn a living when the £500 should run out and the shelter of Charnock's chambers should no longer be available to him. His father, indeed, was beginning to clamber back to some degree of prosperity. In February, 1845, he had been "assistant" to Mackie, in Southampton Row; by 1846 he was Mackie's partner; and the next year he set up in business for himself in a more fashionable region, at 26, St James's Street. But even if Augustus should eventually be restored to comfortable circumstances, his son was far too proud to accept any identification with the tailoring trade.

Several considerations dictated George's choice of a calling. It must be something as remote as possible from both the dull routine of law and the intolerable servitude of business. It must give scope to his free-ranging fancy and his lively wit. Above all, it must offer opportunity for a young man without either means or social connections to achieve a distinction that would establish him in the true aristocracy of the spirit, since he could not claim any rank in the aristocracy of birth. These requirements all pointed in one direction. He would be an author. And to a youth of soaring aspiration this meant that he would be a poet.

He must have begun writing soon after he threw in his lot with Charnock, for he later told a friend that "I wrote verse before I was nineteen." Encouragement was easily forthcoming among his new friends. In addition to Charnock, those particularly interested in authorship were Henry Howes, of the Adjutant-General's Department, Horse Guards; Hilaire C. de St Croix, of 4, Mincing Lane; and Peter Austin Daniel and Edward Gryffydh Peacock, junior clerks in the East India Company.

Meredith felt most drawn to young Peacock, because he was the son of Thomas Love Peacock. Never before had Meredith found himself in proximity to a distinguished author; and Thomas Love Peacock was just the sort of author to inspire Meredith's admiration. In his early days Peacock had been an intimate friend of Shelley, and at intervals through his life he had published works of fiction which could only by courtesy be called novels, being plotless satirical dialogues that rambled capriciously over politics, literature, and scholarship, and in which the characters were easily recognizable caricatures of eminent contemporaries. *Headlong Hall, Melincourt,* and *Crotchet Castle* had baffled the critics and attracted few readers; but for this very reason Meredith was prepared to believe in their superior value, while their rationalism and worldliness, their ironical contempt for all popular fads and fallacies, appealed strongly to his taste. Besides, Peacock was a fanatical admirer of Wales, and had married a Welsh wife; and Meredith was becoming convinced that the Welsh strain in his own ancestry was the chief reason for his lack of sympathy with the average Englishman.

As there was a coolness at this time between Edward Peacock and his father, arising from a dispute about the young man's marriage, Meredith did not get to know the father immediately. His friendship with the son flourished on their shared love of open-air exercise, for the younger Peacock was a noted oarsman and boxer. They went to prize fights together, and enjoyed long walks through the Chelsea market gardens to the Surrey hills, and even as far as Brighton. And soon, at young Peacock's rooms, Meredith was introduced to his widowed sister, Mary Ellen Nicolls. She was a handsome and gifted woman, who had inherited much of her father's exuberant wit. When the group of friends decided to conduct a manuscript magazine for the interchange of their literary exercises, Mrs Nicolls was the only woman included in the undertaking.

The first number of *The Monthly Observer* was compiled early in 1848, when Meredith had just reached the age of twenty. Each contribution was written on quarto sheets, and these were stitched together and circulated among the group, one of whom served as editor and added critical comments on the whole contents of the number. The whereabouts of the first ten issues are unknown, but five of those from January to July, 1849, were preserved by Charnock.

An editorial comment implies that the earlier numbers had been largely occupied with controversial essays evoked by the "turbulent political ferment" which had engulfed Europe in 1848; and the editor welcomed "a return to Literature for its own sake and for real, practical, social purposes." Number eleven contained a poem by Meredith, "Saint Thérèse," an elaborately descriptive piece, full of echoes of Tennyson's "Saint Agnes' Eve" and also strangely like "The Blessed Damozel," though Meredith could not possibly have seen that poem, which was not printed until a year later. In the March number Meredith supplied two poems: "Brotherhood," a ponderously didactic piece that harked back to the teachings of Neuwied with its insistence on the Lord's law of Brotherhood and on the miseries caused by religious factionalism; and an equally didactic sonnet, condemning the "false themes of speculation" that were being propagated by materialistic scientists. Meredith's conversion to skepticism was not yet apparent.

The editor, Austin Daniel, was somewhat patronizing in his comment on these poems:

There is great beauty of sentiment and in parts, great beauty of execution; . . . but Mr Meredith to our mind, has a great fault; his poems are too unfinished, he does not appear to have studied enough the verse in which his ideas are embodied . . . He will no doubt by practice acquire a firmer mode of writing, he has genius we think, and if he has that perseverance so indispensable to its development, there is no reason why, in time, his name should not rank high.

To the April number Meredith contributed a poem on the Battle of Chillianwallah, written immediately upon hearing the news of the disaster, which had occurred on January 13, in the Second Sikh War. This time, apart from pointing out a couple of solecisms, the critic was more enthusiastic:

Our Poet, for he deserves the name, has chosen a theme of deep interest to many an English home, and right ably has he worked it out . . . We must offer our hearty congratulations to Mr Meredith for his poem, it is one of his best.

It was announced in this number that Meredith had been elected to take the next turn as editor; and in the June number he stated his policies, promising that his comments would contain neither jokes at the expense of the contributors nor "servile and deceitful praise," but would encourage merit and "deal justice." His "Propositions for Articles" display the trend of his mind:

*The first a philosophical examination of the Union of Poetry with general life and advancing science— The second on the inviolate claim of the Hungarian people to absolute independence and the Choice of Republican Government; with a glance at the chances and results of the present war and the resources of the country— We think this last well suited to the Pen of Mr St Croix if he is so far interested in the subject as to study it and sufficiently diligent to develope it— The first could find no better expounder than Mrs Nicolls.*

For this number Meredith translated four German lyrics, one by Heine, one by Eichendorff, and two by Goethe. Alongside his versions he gave the originals, carefully transcribed in German script.

From Mary Nicolls's contributions to the various numbers it is possible to gain hints of her tastes and attitudes. She wrote a sympathetic review of *A Saint's Tragedy,* by Charles Kingsley, who at the moment was being widely condemned as a subversive radical because of his humanitarian activities. Her partiality for France was revealed when she wrote an essay in French on "*La Mort*" and when she announced herself to be "a citizen of the great French Republic." In the June number she was represented by a poem, "The Blackbird," which she stated to be "the true history of a blackbird known to me," but which—it has been suggested—may have contained a personal allegory, as it describes the grief of a bird which has lost its mate and which assuages its sorrow by offering solace to a lonely friend in a cage. Meredith praised the poem lavishly in his critical note, rising to a climax of sensibility:

*Yes! the Universe is but a succession of links and we are all united—in nobility—and gentleness and Love. All that is brutish is alien of kin—but gentle Love uniteth all. And this the Poet has sung most worthily and well . . .*

His enthusiasm was not inspired solely by the merit of the poem. Meredith had also fallen completely under the spell of its author's cleverness and charm.

The details of their love affair are obscured by conflicting evidence. After Meredith's death, his biographers found that the only source of information about the episode was Mary Nicolls's daughter, who was inevitably biased in her favor. According to this account, Meredith's proposals of marriage were rejected six times before his persistence prevailed. On the other hand, Meredith told his version, under strict vows of secrecy, to two or three later friends; and while his confidence has never been violated, elusive hints indicate that he claimed to have been drawn into the engagement through some compulsion or trickery. When evidence is tainted with so much bitterness on both sides, the just verdict can only be that the truth lies somewhere between the two opposing testimonies.

If Mrs Nicolls did reject Meredith's first proposals of marriage, she had good reasons for doing so. Her witty brilliance was a mask for a nature that knew disillusionment and grief. Born in July, 1821, she was nearly seven years older than Meredith. When she was six years old her mother became a permanent invalid in consequence of the death of a younger child, and was never again capable of looking after her family. Mary Ellen and her brother and sister were brought up by their grandmother until 1833, and were then handed over to housekeepers and governesses. Peacock, being an important official in the East India Company, came down from London to the family home only on weekends. He insisted that his elder daughter should study modern and classical languages; he took her with him on holiday travels in Wales; and he sometimes had her at his side in the theatre, which he attended as critic for various papers. From infancy she had been a pet of his friend Thomas Jefferson Hogg, who in his youth shared Shelley's expulsion from Oxford. As she grew up she was in the habit of dropping into the kindly old lawyer's office to lend or borrow books. By this sort of training the girl was molded to think for herself and to share in masculine conversations on an equal footing.

In January, 1844, she married Edward Nicolls, a lieutenant in the Royal Navy. Two months later she was with him on board his ship, the *Dwarf*, in an Irish roadstead when a yacht that was anchored nearby began to drag its moorings. While his wife watched from the deck of the *Dwarf*, he put off in a gig to render aid. The gig jibbed and upset; and the officer and one of his men, stunned by a swinging block, never came to the surface. In the autumn the young widow gave birth to a daughter.

To a woman thus hardened by trouble, Meredith's enthusiasms and poetic ambitions must have appeared far from mature. With no money, no prospects, no profession, and family antecedents that he was ashamed of, he could not be regarded as a suitable husband. But he was handsome, magnetic, and intense. And he would not take "no" for an answer.

His eagerness for marriage roused him to concern about his financial position. Having reached the age of twenty-one, he was now in possession of the thousand pounds that had been held in trust for him since his mother's death, and also of the small residue—about £150— of his legacy from Miss Macnamara. He later became involved in legal proceedings over the inheritance, and blamed the trustee for having "squandered the little estate by fraud or folly"; but the court records indicate that at the time when he reached his majority the fund had been scrupulously conserved, the only deduction being the sums for his legal apprenticeship. As he remained with Charnock for only three years, instead of five, and received little of the instruction that had been contracted for, it is even possible that some of the fee was refunded to him; but of this there is no proof.

As soon as he came into his estate he moved away from Charnock's chambers and took lodgings at 7, Upper Ebury Street, Pimlico. This final abandonment of any pretense of law studies coincided with an active start in the literary profession. His first maneuver was to seek the help and advice of a successful author. On March 8, 1849, he wrote an ingratiating letter to Richard Henry Horne:

> You are a Poet and a Critic, and from certain of your writings I understand your sympathies in either phase to be with the young Poet. As this is a fact seldom found even among literary men, I have taken the liberty to address myself thus abruptly to you.
>
> I wish to lay before you certain Poems I have composed that I may obtain your opinion (in which I can trust) as to their merit—or more especially— the power of the Poetic Faculty in me . . . If you really can and will assist me with your advice, I shall be exceedingly indebted and obliged to you.

There were obvious reasons why Horne attracted the young poet's attention. Handsome, athletic, and restless, Horne had versatile literary talents that nearly carried him to real greatness. In the Byronic tradition he talked extravagantly and behaved picturesquely. As a schoolboy he threw a snowball at Keats. Later he served in the Mexican Navy, lived with the Indians in the United States, survived shipwreck, mutiny, and fire at sea. He was one of the few people able to penetrate the wall of seclusion protecting Elizabeth Barrett, and she helped with the writing of his book *A New Spirit of the Age*, which dealt favorably with the younger contemporary authors. In addition to several tragedies in the pseudo-Shakespearian style, Horne had written a classical epic, *Orion,* which was only slightly too rhetorical to be a first-rate poem. As an agitator for the wider distribution of poetry, he attracted somewhat unfortunate attention to *Orion* by putting the first editions on sale at the price of one farthing a copy. The poem was a mystical, Hegelian allegory, depicting the impulse for progress that drives mankind to spurn passive comfort, and preaching an ideal of love as the "combination of the mind with the senses which best helps the noble progress and happiness of certain beings." True happiness comes from the sympathy gained through experience of active, passionate love. Meredith was entranced with the theory.

In spite of the youthful pomposity of Meredith's letter, Horne was sufficiently impressed to answer encouragingly. He read the poems and made acquaintance with the poet. Goethe's poems came into their talk at their first meeting, and Horne said that he did not own a copy. Meredith promptly sent him one, with a letter of thanks for "the instruction you have already given me in the Art. I believe that I am now steadily improving. I have but flickered heretofore."

Under this guidance he revised and shortened "Chillianwallah," and on June 4 he sent it to *Chambers's Edinburgh Journal,* with a letter which assured the editors, "If you are not overstocked with engagements for poetical contributions, I should be very glad to supply you regularly." The poem being accepted, he offered to send a translation of a life of Kossuth, the Hungarian leader: "I could abridge it for one number even, or give it literally. The accounts of the man now afloat are flimsy and unconnected." Undoubtedly he made similar advances to other editors. At an earlier date (perhaps even before his legal apprenticeship began) he had tried a venture into daily journalism by sending a leading article on Lord John Manners to *The Standard.* Stanley Lees Giffard, the editor, called him in for an interview and asked for further contributions; but as the first one was never paid for, Meredith gave up for the time any thought of becoming a journalist. Now, however, there was a new motive for thinking about earning money by his pen.

These activities did not diminish his devotion to *The Monthly Observer.* The whole file offers a pleasant picture of Meredith among his friends: Charnock, the most prolific and punctual contributor, writing travel sketches and philological essays under his punning pseudonym of "Aretchid Kooez" (A Wretched Quiz); St Croix, excited about the political upheavals on the Continent; Mrs Nicolls, exuding a vague, melancholy mysticism; Meredith, self-consciously earnest as the youngest member and the only one with serious literary ambitions; all of them worshippers of the thrilling new poets, Tennyson and Kingsley and Horne and P. J. Bailey.

The July number, however, reflected a crisis. It had shrunk to only four contributions, including another of Meredith's translations of German lyric poetry. In an editorial note he announced that "Mrs Nicolls, being suddenly called on a journey to France, has been obliged to solicit our consideration this month—we expect to be favoured with two articles next month according to regulations."

In some way this absence may have been connected with Meredith's courtship; either just before her departure or after her return she said "yes" to one of his proposals, and took him down to Lower Halliford to make him known to her father. It was during this visit that her five-year-old daughter Edith, running suddenly into the drawing-room, surprised the lovers in a passionate embrace. When Meredith had left the room Edith threw herself into her mother's arms with an angry wail: "Mamma, I don't like that man!"

A possessive parent, who fell out with both his son and his younger daughter over their marriages, Peacock cannot have been favorably impressed by Mary's penniless young suitor. But she was old enough to do as she pleased, and she had a strong will. He not only gave his consent but was present to sign the register when they were married at St George's, Hanover Square, on August 9. According to the register, Meredith's address was then Maddox Street, and the bride's was Devonshire Street, about half a mile away—both temporary lodgings. The groom was identified as the son of "Augustus Meredith, Esquire" (no profession stated); but Augustus Meredith was not present at the ceremony. The shop in St James's Street had been disposed of, and on April 15 he had sailed for the Cape of Good Hope.

Within a week of his arrival in Cape Town he issued an advertisement in both English and Dutch:

A. U. MEREDITH, *Tailor and Professed Trouser Cutter, from St. James's Street, London, Begs to announce to the Gentry and Public of Cape Town, and the surrounding neighbourhood, that he has just arrived from England per 'Countess of Zetland' with a well-selected stock, and has taken the business of Mr HUME as above; and from long experience in all the branches of his trade can ensure Style, Fit, and Comfort, combined with the economy of his predecessor.*

N.B.—*A.U.M. is not so bigoted in his own style but that he willingly yields to gentlemen's own peculiarities.*

The business flourished, Matilda soon joined him, and George Meredith was left with the comforting knowledge that his father and stepmother were in easy circumstances, and five thousand miles away.

As *The Monthly Observer* went out of existence with the marriage of its current editor, the bride did not have to write the two articles. The young couple spent some of the groom's available funds in a honeymoon on the Continent, particularly in the Rhineland that he already knew and loved. In a poem published seven years later he depicted their lyrical delight in the scenery at Andernach:

> *Home-friends we pledged; our bridal maids;*
>     *Sweet wishes gaily squander'd;*
> *We wander'd far in faerie glades,*
>     *Up golden heights we wander'd . . .*
>
> *No longer severing our embrace*
>     *Was Night a sword between us;*
> *But richest mystery robed in grace*
>     *To lock us close, and screen us . . .*
>
> *Against the glooming of the west*
>     *The grey hawk-ruins darken,*
> *And hand in hand, half breast to breast,*
>     *Two lovers gaze and hearken.*

During the honeymoon his literary projects were suspended. Not until November did he send to *Chambers's Journal* the first four sheets of the promised biography of Kossuth, with a lame explanation: "I trust it is not too late—but the fact is I was determined to ascertain if the character of Kossuth was as fine as . . . I had imagined . . . You are at liberty to erase all passages which suit not the purpose or politics of the Journal." The subject had certainly become less topical, for after a dictatorship of three months Kossuth had been defeated and had fled to Turkey, where he was interned.

Meredith was planning also, he said, to write a biographical sketch of Gottfried Hermann, a German classical scholar who had died a year before; "there is as yet no English account." The next day he wrote again urgently: "Let me know about the article on Hermann as early as you can as the sooner that is printed the better." He also submitted some sonnets on "Two Kings of England": "I think they would do very well if taken as a series and I have a great many already finished."

It must have been a blow to the eager young writer that neither the Kossuth article nor these other offerings ever came out.

At that time the Merediths were occupying Peacock's London quarters at 22, John Street, Adelphi. Not long afterwards they moved away to Surrey, and took lodgings with Mrs Macirone (or Maceroni), at "The Limes," Weybridge, across the Thames from Peacock's home at Lower Halliford. Mrs Macirone was the English widow of an Italian soldier-of-fortune, who had been an aide-de-camp to Joachim Murat during the brief period while that innkeeper's son and Napoleonic marshal was King of Naples. Colonel Macirone later went to South America and was appointed a brigadier general in the Colombian Army. After he settled in England he invented an improved method of paving highways and constructed a "steam road carriage" which when tried out on the Edgeware Road ran fast enough to pass stage-coaches.

Mrs Macirone was interested in literature and had two lovely dark-eyed daughters, Emilia and Giulia. The elder was an impulsive, generous girl with a magnificent singing voice and also with literary ambitions; in 1851 she published a little Christmas book called *Magic Words,* with a hero not unlike Meredith. On holidays in the country, it was her unconventional custom to gather the farm hands into the barn at night and hold them enchanted with her singing. About the time Meredith made her acquaintance she married a young barrister and journalist, Edmund Hornby, whose autobiography chronicles a tiny specimen of Mary Meredith's caustic phrases. When Hornby confessed that the only poets he liked were Pope, Dryden, and Goldsmith, and that he couldn't understand Tennyson and the other moderns, Mrs Meredith remarked sharply, "You have a Manchester mind."

A spacious house with a pretty garden, The Limes was a gathering place for artists, musicians, and writers. One of these was Tom Taylor, a witty Cambridge man, barrister, journalist, and dramatist. When Meredith met him he had recently been appointed assistant secretary to the Board of Health, but he was also writing leading articles and art criticism for newspapers, sitting at the editorial round table of *Punch,* and supplying numerous farces to the London stage. In contrast with Horne, Taylor appealed to an opposite side of Meredith's character. Taylor was a sophisticated Londoner, whose scholarly gifts did not debar him from mingling in fashionable society and who made a good living from authorship without appearing to work hard at it. Horne was a poet of the romantic model, oracular and unconventional, a devotee of Nature. Meredith felt that he would like somehow to resemble both men at once.

Busily producing poetry, he applied himself to a course of self-training in poetic forms. The rugged simplicity of the English and Scottish folk ballads appealed to him, and he went through Ritson's and Kinloch's ballad collections and copied out examples. He also welcomed Horne's continued help. His most ambitious pieces were on Greek mythological themes, following the example set by Horne himself as well as by Keats and Tennyson, and perhaps fostered by the classical predilections of Peacock. One of the longest of the poems was "Daphne," presenting the legend of Apollo and the laurel with something of the sensuous elaboration of Keats's *Endymion*, though in a lighter meter. When sending a copy of "Daphne" to Horne, Meredith added some lines dedicating it to this "deep-hearted friend and earnest man," and extolling his "noble lyre."

Horne responded with praise of the poems, but advised that before publishing a volume Meredith ought to vary the classical theme by writing some ballads and some poems on modern topics. Horne also gave practical help by recommending Meredith to the editors of *Household Words*, the weekly that was just then being launched by Dickens. During 1850 three poems by Meredith appeared in that paper, though according to the account book one of them was in collaboration with Horne and another with the sub-editor, W. H. Wills. One of these poems, "The Two Blackbirds," was a retelling of the same sentimental episode that Mary had first narrated in her poem in *The Monthly Observer*.

It may have been through Horne, too, that he got in touch with another new weekly journal, of a different stamp, *The Leader*, founded by Thornton Hunt and George Henry Lewes as an organ for the radical thinkers, such as Mazzini (freshly exiled from Italy), Harriet Martineau, and Charles Kingsley. Meredith's translation of a German song appeared in it in September, and he may have contributed book reviews or other unsigned items. It is likely that he worked for other papers also: in his old age he told a reporter from *The Manchester Guardian* that he had written two articles for that paper when he was twenty-two.

Among the literary inhabitants of Weybridge were John and Sarah Austin, who had come there to take refuge from the revolution in Paris. Mr Austin was an erudite authority on jurisprudence and his wife was noted as a translator of French and German books and as a friend and correspondent of eminent authors. The daughter of the Austins was Lady Duff Gordon, a well-known personality in London society at the time. Combining the intellectual ability of her parents with much personal charm and an outspoken, unconventional manner, she was the center of a devoted group of literary men, notably including Tom Taylor, A. W. Kinglake, and Thackeray.

Sir Alexander and Lady Duff Gordon and their eight-year-old daughter, Janet, spent the summer of 1850 with the Austins at Weybridge. Janet was well accustomed to literary conversation, for it was one of the easygoing habits of the household to let the child meet the guests on equal terms. Now a new author was added to her roster, and one who delighted her even more than the older and more sedate ones who formed her parents' circle. It was arranged that she should go sometimes to The Limes as a playmate for Mrs Meredith's six-year-old Edith. Soon she was on the best of terms with Edith's stepfather, and imperiously named him "My Poet." When he escorted her home after her visits, often carrying her perched on his shoulder, he kept her entranced with wonderful fairy tales that he made up as he went along.

One day he happened to be at the Duff Gordons' when another guest was Baron August von Haxthausen, a celebrated traveler and authority on Russia and the Caucasus. The baron launched out upon a narrative of his battle with the Queen of the Serpents,

*whose crown he wore in a little red silk bag that hung round his neck from a gold chain. With flashing eyes and vehement gestures he described how he fought with the Queen. "She called her subjects to her aid with loud, shrill hisses, and the earth became alive with snakes. I killed, and I killed, and I killed, and then ran for my life out of the burning hot gulley, followed by hundreds of gliding, writhing, venomous creatures. The owner of this crown is the ruler and head of all the serpents," said he, proudly tossing his head. By dint of much persuasion, M. de Haxthausen was induced to show his treasure, which was inside a small gold box in the red silk bag. It looked like a miniature crown fashioned out of dark amber, and a doctor who was present said, after careful examination, that it undoubtedly was a bony excrescence from a reptile, and probably from the head.*

While this tale was being told, Meredith never took his eyes off the traveler; and the next time he carried Janet home from The Limes to Nutfield Cottage he had a new and marvelous fairy tale to tell her, in which the Queen of the Serpents played a leading part.

In the Duff Gordons and Taylor, Meredith was associating with people of higher social rank than he had previously known. The well-bred ease of their conversation, passing allusively from theme to theme, and brightened with glancing shafts of wit, made him realize how obvious and rowdy had been the talk of the Charnock group, which had delighted him three or four years earlier.

By the end of the year he considered that he had more than enough poems in hand to make a book, without using any of the juvenile pieces from his *Monthly Observer* days. Following Horne's advice he had tried some modern topics, although three or four of the longest poems were the classical ones. There were some brief lyrics whose melodious patterning of words recalled Tennyson's early work. Tennysonian, too, was the descriptive and reflective technique in two symbolic poems, "The Olive Branch" and "The Sleeping City"; and in particular Tennyson's "Two Voices" was closely echoed in a didactic piece called "Sorrows and Joys." A grimmer note of social protest and sordid detail appeared in "London by Lamplight." Recollections of Meredith's school days at Neuwied and of his honeymoon provided material for a pleasant descriptive sequence, "Pictures of the Rhine."

A fresher and more genuine quality, however, showed in several poems that dealt with the beauty of the English countryside and the joy of the open air. Chief of these were "South-west Wind in the Woodland," "Love in the Valley," and a group of six "Pastorals." All these displayed individuality in technique. The pastorals experimented with a variety of unrhymed stanzas and syncopated meters; one of them was an adaptation of the classical hexameter. The "South-west Wind" poem was in quickly running tetrameter lines that were peculiarly effective in conveying the wind's boisterous rush. And the eight-line stanzas of "Love in the Valley" used a singing duple-triple beat that was almost unprecedented in English poetry.

This group of poems combined earlier recollections of Hampshire with keen delight in the Surrey neighborhood where he was now living. In later years he pointed out a pine-ringed hill between Weybridge and Byfleet as the spot where he composed the "Pastorals." Several of them, as well as "Love in the Valley," hymned the joys of rural love-making. Sentimental critics have repeatedly inferred that "Love in the Valley" was inspired by Meredith's wooing of Mary Ellen Nicolls; but the details of the poem, in the light of biographical fact, make the suggestion untenable. Meredith's bride was a widow with a five-year-old daughter, whereas the keynote of the poem was the youth and virginity of the girl—"my young love . . . that dear one in her maiden bud . . . would she were older and could read my worth . . ."

> *Will not the virgin listen to their voices,*
>  *Take the honeyed meaning, wear the bridal veil?*

And in view of the unhappy incapacity of Mrs Thomas Love Peacock, it would have been the acme of bad taste if Meredith had been alluding to his wife thus:

> *When her mother tends her before the laughing mirror,*
> *Tying up her laces, looping up her hair,*
> *Often she thinks—were this wild thing wedded,*
> *I should have more love, and much less care.*

In significant respects the poem is linked with "Daphne," in which Meredith treated the same theme allegorically; and of this poem he stated in his epistle to Horne:

> *. . . You will know how in these after days*
> *First love still follows the fair, fleeting shape! . . .*
> *In your hands I place*
> *Daphne, the darling of my own first love.*

All the evidence points to memories of a boyish episode as the source of the ecstatic note in these poems. The short love lyrics in the volume, on the other hand, clearly originating in his courtship of Mrs Nicolls, are somewhat frigid in their conventional romanticism.

Many of the poems showed that their author was at work upon his interpretation of existence. The first in the book, "The Olive Branch," inspired by the plans for the Great Exhibition, was a paean of the current optimism regarding peace, prosperity, and scientific progress; but this bid for topical notice was offset in "London by Lamplight," which angrily denounced the ugliness and commercialized vice of the city, much in the vein of Hood's "Bridge of Sighs," and demanded succor for the abused prostitutes. In its contrasts between innocent childhood and depraved maturity, and between rural health and urban squalor, the poem echoed the old truisms of Rousseau.

The poems on Nature announced a fresher concept of man's relations with the forces of his environment. The basic tenet was that the processes of Nature are not only inevitable but beneficent, being the essential condition for survival and growth. As he stated it in "The Wild Rose and the Snowdrop":

> *Each, fulfilling nature's law, fulfils*
> *Itself and its own aspirations pure;*
> *Living and dying; letting faith ensure*

> *New life when deathless Spring shall touch the hills.*
> *Each perfect in its place; and each content*
> *With that perfection which its being meant.*

The theme was repeated strongly in "The Flower of the Ruins," the essence of it being stated in the line, "Thou art thy future, not thy past." Another poem, "Sorrows and Joys," was a more literal assertion of the doctrine of sublimating all regrets for the past and thus being able to share the unshadowed joy of Nature.

Again and again he emphasized that natural processes are joyful— not only "the primal joy of dawn," but the violence and strain of tempest, as in "South-west Wind in the Woodland,"

> *Each tree a harp, whose foliaged strings*
> *Are waiting for the master's touch*
> *To sweep them into storms of joy;*

and throughout the poem he depicted the gale-lashed trees as emitting sounds of "harsh delight" and "mighty melodies, sublime":

> *The voice of nature is abroad*
> *This night . . .*
> *And who that hears her now and yields*
> *His being to her yearning tones . . .*
> > *will gather in the flight*
> *More knowledge of her secret, more*
> *Delight in her beneficence,*
> *Than hours of musing, or the lore*
> *That lives with men could ever give! . . .*
> *For every elemental power*
> *Is kindred to our hearts, and once*
> *Acknowledged, wedded, once embraced,*
> *Once taken to the unfettered sense,*
> *Once clasped into the naked life,*
> *The union is eternal.*

In spite of the Wordsworthian ring in these lines, Meredith's view of man's kinship with Nature was not identical with Wordsworth's serene sense of communion. To him the human being is not a superior creature turning to Nature as to a kindly nurse, but is a participant in universal processes and can find happiness only by accepting this identity. Thus, in the symbolism of "Daphne," the abnormally chaste nymph's flight from Apollo was hampered by the trees and brambles that reached out to trip her: "All nature is against her!" And the "Pastorals" conveyed the same lesson of submission:

> A *thing of nature am I now,*
> *Abroad, without a sense or feeling*
> *Born not of her bosom;*
> *Content with all her truths and fates.*

Such insistence upon unquestioning obedience to natural processes sounds like stoicism; but in these poems and throughout Meredith's later work it was made the basis for the intensest delight.

Peacock was a friend of the junior partner in the publishing firm of John W. Parker & Son, West Strand. On December 12, 1850, Meredith sent Parker a list of the poems he intended to include in his book, with the manuscripts of several as samples. His accompanying letter struck a nice balance between confidence and modesty:

*If you think the specimens I forward you inferior to the requirements of the age, 'not saleable' and so forth, I shall very likely be content to abide by your decision for a time.*

When Parker suggested doubts as to the commercial value of the proposed volume, Meredith explained that he would be willing to have it issued at his own expense:

*By publishing I scarcely expect anything but loss; I know that a name must be successful before a book can. But to any achievement some first step must be made, both to the public and ourselves. In this first volume I hope to get a certain position among those who appreciate good poetry . . . If when left to themselves [the poems] have not vitality enough to survive, then I am content they should die.*

On this understanding the book was accepted, though on a smaller scale than Meredith had envisaged. A poem on "Cassandra," which he told Parker that he prized as his best work, was not finished in time. Nor was there any sign of "two or more numbers (but shorter ones)" that were to continue the theme of "London by Lamplight." A "Ballad," too, which in December he said he was writing for *Household Words,* did not appear in the volume.

When the book went to press, in May, 1851, Meredith prefaced it with a dedication "to Thomas Love Peacock, Esq., with the profound admiration and affectionate respect of his son-in-law." He invoked also the aegis of his other chief literary friend by quoting ten lines from Horne's *Orion* on the title page.

A glimpse of the publisher's effort to publicize the young poet can be caught in the fact that Henry Morley, a recent recruit to the editorial staff of *Household Words,* was invited to dinner at Parker's house to meet Meredith and Professor John Stuart Blackie of Aberdeen (later a humorous celebrity of Edinburgh University). Morley thought well of the Meredith poems, but apparently did not discover that the young author was a fellow-alumnus of Neuwied.

As part of the campaign of publicity, copies of the book were distributed liberally among literary personages. One of the first to respond with kindly praise was Edmund Ollier, son of a publisher who had brought out works of Shelley and Keats. Young Ollier was a minor poet and a disciple of Horne. Meredith thanked him warmly:

*It is the appreciation you give that makes Fame worth working for; nor would I barter such communications for any amount of favourable journal criticism, however much it might forward the popularity and sale of my book. I prepared myself, when I published, to meet with injustice and slight, knowing that the little collection, or rather selection in my volume was but the vanguard of a better work to come; and knowing, also, that the severest criticism could scarcely be more unsparing than myself on the faults that are freely to be found; knowing lastly, that a first volume of poetry is with the press a marked book; but some beginning must be made. The poems are all the work of extreme youth, and, with some exceptions, of labour. They will not live, I think, but they will serve their purpose in making known my name to those who look with encouragement upon such earnest students of nature who are determined to persevere, until they obtain the wisdom and inspiration and self-possession of the poet.*

In spite of all this gratitude and modesty, he went on to defend "The South-west Wind in the Woodland" vigorously against Ollier's complaint about its absence of rhyme.

Another copy of the book was presented to Alexander John Scott, Professor of English Literature in University College, London, with an accompanying letter that shows Meredith to have been on friendly terms with him and his family. An unorthodox Scottish divine, Scott possessed a sincerity and eloquence that won him the esteem of Thomas Carlyle, Edward Irving, and Frederick Denison Maurice. Meredith seems to have attended his lectures at the college, for his letter speaks of "having had the privilege of some of your instruction."

The book of poems went also to Charles Kingsley, whose novel *Yeast*, after two years of hesitation because of its dangerously Radical sympathies, had recently been published by the Parker firm. In a letter to Kingsley, Meredith declared:

*I am driven with a spur to tell you the delight & admiration with which I read your last book Yeast and the positive 'Education' I have derived from it. It was the very book I was in want of and likely to do me more good than any that I know.*

Kingsley responded with a promise to review the poems as soon as he returned from a trip to Germany.

The tribute that gratified Meredith most deeply was in a letter from Alfred Tennyson, saying that there was one poem in the book that he could have wished he had written. This was "Love in the Valley," and he had gone about the house chanting its cadences. He expressed the hope that the young poet would visit him.

The strong Tennysonian echoes in many of the poems reveal how deeply Meredith had been influenced by the man who had become Poet Laureate a year before. He answered the letter in a glow of pleasure:

*When I tell you that it would have been my chief ambition in publishing the little volume of poems you have received, to obtain your praise, you may imagine what pride and pleasure your letter gave me; though, indeed, I do not deserve so much as your generous appreciation would bestow, and of this I am very conscious. I had but counted twenty-three years when the book was published, which may account for, and excuse perhaps, many of the immaturities. When you say you would like to know me, I can scarcely trust myself to express with how much delight I would wait upon you—a privilege I have long desired.*

When the encounter took place, it supplied Meredith with a favorite anecdote of his later life. He contrived to have himself invited to a country house where the Laureate was also staying. Having arrived late in the evening, Meredith had not yet met his fellow-guest when he got up early the next morning and sallied out on his usual sunrise walk. Among the dew-drenched meadows he came upon the towering form of Tennyson, and drew near with eager anticipation. After eyeing him vacantly for some time in silence, Tennyson announced in his deep voice (which Meredith loved to mimic), "Apollodorus says that I am not a poet." Meredith racked his brains and identified Apollodorus as George Gilfillan, a Scottish clergyman and critic who had published an essay on Tennyson's work. The younger poet burst out with incoherent protests that Gilfillan was a miserable scribbler whose opinions nobody took seriously, and so forth. Tennyson listened with a gloomy scowl, and when the flood of expostulation ceased he rumbled, "Nevertheless, he should not have said that I am not a great poet." And the Laureate stalked on across the field, with Meredith speechless at his heels. Other little episodes heightened his impression of Tennyson's conceit; and (as he used to conclude his reminiscence) "I never wanted to see him again."

As a consequence of all the vigorous promotion, Meredith's book was fairly widely reviewed. In *The Leader* George Henry Lewes, knowing the poet personally, voiced qualified approval:

A nice perception of nature, aided by a delicacy of expression, gives to these poems a certain charm not to be resisted; and although they betray no depth of insight nor of feeling; although they are neither thoughtful nor impassioned, yet they rise from out the mass of verses by a certain elegance and felicity of expression which distinguish them.

The reviewer in *The Spectator* mentioned Meredith's tendency to imitate Keats, Tennyson, and the Brownings, and said that "this volume possesses considerable poetical feeling and poetical faculty, but displays more of promise than performance." He was warned about his "sensuous warmth of image and expression, which, though not passing propriety, might as well be tempered."

Disapproval on moral grounds was expressed more openly by *The Guardian*, a Church of England weekly. The reviewer admitted that "the author has considerable poetical capacity, and, if he is true to himself, may write things worthy to live." Then came the admonition:

He must, however, mend his morals and his taste. Coarse sensuality is no proof of power, and passionateness and vigour may be attained without impurity. Ovid is bad enough, but "Daphne" and "The Rape of Aurora" in this volume are worse, from their studied and amplified voluptuousness, than anything in the Metamorphoses. Mr Meredith is mistaken if he thinks this either classical or manly.

*The Athenaeum* gave him a two-column review, and achieved some masterpieces of noncommittal praise. The critic classified Meredith as "the minor minstrel, whose themes are generally as fugitive as his flight is brief"; but added that "he may even claim to be something more. His small volume contains some essays with epic ambition . . . They are not without poetic fervour . . . In the lyric poems, some of which might almost be called beautiful, we meet at times with stanzas that are quite prosaic in feeling and in diction." The critic concluded that "where the 'prentice hand' is so manifest as in this volume, we accept the signs of care and intention which it exhibits as indications of an artistic tendency in the 'singer,' and to a certain extent as pledges that one day he may become a poet."

The review in *The Critic* was written by William Michael Rossetti, the twenty-two-year-old youngest member of the Pre-Raphaelite family. He described Meredith as "a kind of limited Keats. He is scarcely a perceptive, but rather a seeing or sensuous poet." Praise was accorded to "Love in the Valley" for having "a clear voice of nature, as spontaneous and intelligible as the wooing of a bird." The main quality of the poems was stated to be "warmth of emotion, and, to a certain extent, of imagination."

Kingsley's promised review appeared in *Fraser's Magazine* in December. As the magazine belonged to the Parkers, who were Meredith's publishers and also his own, and as Meredith had written to him so flatteringly about *Yeast*, Kingsley was predisposed in his favor. "There is very high promise," he said, "in the unambitious little volume . . . Health and sweetness are two qualities which run through all these poems. They are often over-loaded—often somewhat clumsy and ill-expressed—often wanting polish and finish; but they are all genuine, all melodiously conceived." He quoted from "Love in the Valley" and praised its "instinctive melody," and he called "Daphne" a "charming poem." In view of other critics' complaints about the moral tone of the poems, it must have been a satisfaction for the author to be praised for "health and sweetness" by a clergyman of the Church of England; and Kingsley went out of his way to voice approval of particular poems that strait-laced reviewers had censured.

In spite of compliments from critics and poets, the book did not sell, and Meredith was out of pocket fifty or sixty pounds over the transaction. If the money was his own, and not supplied by his father-in-law, its loss must have sadly depleted the residue of his inheritance. Although he had defiantly predicted this outcome, the disappointment added a further element of bitterness and strain to his already difficult position.

# Passion Spins the Plot

WITHOUT a settled home or adequate income, the Merediths lacked any firm foundation for domestic happiness. Mary and her father had taken for granted that after the young man had had his fling at poetry he would be ready to undertake some sort of permanent employment. Peacock was ready to use his influence to get him an appointment in the East India House, as he had done for his own son a few years before. Inevitably Mary's seven years of seniority gave her the feeling that her young husband would sooner or later accept her guidance in matters of worldly prudence.

But he proved unexpectedly obstinate. His ambition for literary fame made him refuse flatly to consider an ignominious—even if lucrative—career at an office desk. They were glad enough, however, to avail themselves of any other sort of help from Peacock in the struggle to gain a living. One abortive scheme was the compilation of a cookery book, in which Mrs Meredith's father had a share. He was a famous epicure, and not only his favorite receipts but some of his classical erudition found a place in the text. The manuscript, which covers only joints, game, and poultry, never arriving at the other important matters of soups, fish, sweets, and sauces, is entitled *The Science of Cookery*. The handwriting is mainly Peacock's, but his daughter added passages throughout, and one page is in Meredith's hand, extending the sections on "Sir-Loin of Beef" and "Ribs of Beef."

The book was presumably intended for submission to the Parkers for publication; and a by-product of it was an article on "Gastronomy and Civilization" which appeared in *Fraser's Magazine* for December, 1851. Although it was signed with Mary Meredith's initials, her father's collaboration may be suspected from the stately style, the dogmatic opinions, and the classical allusions. Mrs Meredith, however, as the nominal author, undoubtedly received the payment; and this lengthy article in a leading magazine meant that her literary earnings for 1851 compared favorably with her husband's. One of his lyrics appeared in *The Illustrated Book of English Songs*, and his other identifiable publications during the year were one poem in *Fraser's*, one in *The Leader*, and twelve in *Household Words*, which usually paid him a guinea or half a guinea for each.

They were not, indeed, worth more, being glib and conventional pieces that were sometimes not far above doggerel. As they were unsigned, Meredith later came to hope that they had sunk into oblivion; and when they were identified more than half a century afterwards by means of the editor's account book, he insisted that some of them had been the work of his wife, and that he could no longer remember which were his, which hers.

Ample evidence of his authorship, however, survives in a notebook which is now in the Berg Collection of the New York Public Library. He entered about fifty poems in it, some extending to several hundred lines, others being unfinished jottings of a single stanza or less. It included several of those that appeared anonymously in *Household Words*, and the others were possibly contributed to obscurer periodicals where they have never been traced. The general level of the verse is mediocre. Some lyrics are charming enough, in a stereotyped style; but the more ambitious poems are deplorable. There are trite patriotic exhortations on the Crimean War, long narratives on classical and Oriental themes, half a dozen Arthurian pieces redolent of Tennyson, and even an "Ode on the Funeral of Arthur, Duke of Wellington." One amazing narrative poem on the California Gold Rush describes the lynching of a young woman. Apart from Tennyson, the closest affinity of the poems is with the pretentious and hectic compositions being produced in the same years by Alexander Smith, Gerald Massey, and Sidney Dobell, soon to be laughed into oblivion under the title of "the Spasmodic School." When compared with the vastly fresher and more thoughtful work in his already published volume, these verses of Meredith's offer a pathetic insight into the predicament of the young author, doggedly grinding out the sort of product that he thought editors would be willing to pay a few shillings for. All promise of creative power seemed hopelessly obliterated in this hack work.

The joint earnings of the two Merediths were not enough to support them. In search of cheap lodgings, and perhaps in actual flight from creditors, they moved away from The Limes. When Meredith wrote to Tennyson they were with Mrs Edward Peacock at Southend-on-Sea. On returning to Weybridge they lived for a time in a cottage near the parish schools. Between 1850 and 1852 more than one baby was born to Mary Meredith and did not survive. Her confinements and the grief over losing the infants must have intensified the discomforts of cramped quarters and inadequate funds.

Meredith's digestion gave him constant trouble—an indication of his nervous temperament rather than of the privations of poverty, for his wife continued to display her artistry as a cook. Jefferson Hogg, who visited them each summer, observed his beloved Mary's unhappiness with anxiety, and in his letters to her he tried tactfully to offer sympathy and to counsel patience. His first nickname for Meredith, "the Son of Song," gave place to "George the Fifth" (presumably in reference to his regal arrogance), and then to "the Dyspeptic." During 1852 the only known publications by Meredith were one poem in *Fraser's*, four poems and a prose article in *Household Words*. The article showed where greater profits lay, for it brought him four pounds.

Clearly, if he was to be a professional writer he must turn his pen to the less agreeable medium of prose. But at any rate his prose works would be endowed with the highest possible degree of imagination and poetic style. His earliest favorite reading had been *The Arabian Nights*, and the tales that he had invented for Janet Duff Gordon had been embroidered with the same Oriental coloring. Now he set seriously to work upon a fantasy in this vein. Perhaps under such a guise he might be able to entertain the fiction-reading public without descending too far from the heights of artistic creation.

He remarked long afterwards that it was "written at Weybridge, with duns at the door." Such material anxieties were a miserable handicap in the struggle to master a new technique and to create an atmosphere of exotic beauty. The story progressed with agonizing slowness, and meanwhile no money was coming in. Early in 1853 his wife was pregnant again, and they were at the end of their resources. With little willingness on either side, they went to live with Thomas Love Peacock, whose invalid wife had died more than a year before.

His house was large enough to accommodate them, being really two old cottages which he had thrown into one when he first settled at Lower Halliford thirty years earlier. The Thames ran alongside his garden and he still enjoyed going out in his boat. After many years of literary unproductivity he had begun to write again. Though a genial and kindly man, at sixty-eight he was rigidly settled in his habits, and the effort of adjusting himself to new inmates in his household was intolerable.

"His detestation of anything disagreeable," says his granddaughter in her recollections, "made him simply avoid whatever fretted him, laughing off all sorts of ordinary calls upon his leisure time. His love of ease and kindness of heart made it impossible that he could be actively unkind to anyone, but he would not be worried, and just got away from anything that annoyed him . . . He could not bear anyone to be unhappy or uncomfortable about him." The Merediths, with their financial anxieties and their sarcastic squabbles, were bound to distress him.

Meredith, to be sure, could discuss literature with him. On Shelley they were of one mind: "Peacock was never enthusiastic about him," Meredith recalled later; "he said to me, 'Shelley has neither head nor tail.' . . . Keats is a greater poet than Shelley; in this Peacock agreed." But Meredith had no success when he preached the beauty of Tennyson's "Oenone" and "The Lotus Eaters" to Peacock and Hogg.

On other matters, too, their views clashed. Peacock was a Tory, while Meredith sympathized with revolutionaries. Peacock disliked Germany, whereas Meredith was an admirer of German life and literature. Peacock hated tobacco, and Meredith smoked perpetually. Worst of all, Meredith was nervously intense, with habits of pacing the floor, fingering ornaments, or humming tunes; and Peacock loathed fidgeting. Little Edith Nicolls, watching her grandfather's encounters with her stepfather, became clearly aware that Peacock "could not stand him."

On June 13, 1853, Mary Meredith gave birth to a son, who was christened "Arthur Gryffydh," the second name being that of Peacock's Welsh wife. The addition of an infant to the household was a final exasperation to the old man. Though he enjoyed playing with children, they easily became a nuisance. "He entered with great amusement into any of our games in the garden," says Edith Nicolls; "in the house we were apt to grow too noisy, and he hated noise." As the only way to protect himself from the wailing and the cosseting of his new grandson, he rented a separate house for the Merediths, Vine Cottage, across the wide village green from his home.

The cottage was too small for the reception of any guests; even the faithful Jefferson Hogg had to forgo his visits. He wrote to express the hope that their new home might be "lucky" and his concern over Meredith's health and prospects: "I would that the Patient were well placed in E.I.H. [East India House] or elsewhere: how can we help him?" And again, when congratulating Mary on their wedding anniversary: "How is George the Fifth; is he less dyspeptic? Not to digest your delicate meats is to insult your art."

With the responsibility of a son, Meredith pushed doggedly on toward the conclusion of his Arabian fantasy, *The Shaving of Shagpat.* Two or three short poems are his only identified publications during 1853. In the summer of 1854, deep in a lawsuit over his inheritance, he was desperate to earn cash. Apparently he was writing from time to time for *Fraser's Magazine,* but of these contributions only one is as yet identifiable—a review of Bell's *Songs of the Dramatists.* He was undoubtedly grinding out hack journalistic work that appeared without his name. Perhaps he was experimenting with other types of literature and failing to sell them. In the summer of 1855 he submitted to Parker a volume of his recent poems. As the Crimean War was at its height, he emphasized the patriotic and popular note by naming the collection *English Songs.* His letter to Parker bluntly insisted that he must be paid for the book, "having spent on it, latterly, valuable time." Receiving no encouragement from the publisher, he afterwards destroyed the manuscript in disgust.

All the indications suggest that poverty, discouragement, and bitterness were cutting him off from his friends and almost stifling his creative power. The Duff Gordons lost touch with him when he moved away from Weybridge. Richard Henry Horne emigrated to Australia. The congenial friendships and ambitious dreams of his year as a Young Poet had evaporated.

It is clear enough that his wife showed little appreciation of the work he was trying to do. These frustrated years, when he was twenty-five and twenty-six, must have been particularly in his mind in later life when he said, "When I was young, had there been given me a little sunshine of encouragement, what an impetus to better work would have been mine. I had thoughts, ideas, ravishment; but all fell on a frosty soil, and a little sunshine would have been so helpful to me."

On the other hand, the blame for their increasing discord cannot be laid wholly upon the wife. Wrapped up in his literary ambitions, Meredith failed to consider her natural need for admiration and amusement. Her own bent for authorship made her feel sure that she should not be doomed to keeping house in a cheerless cottage and arguing with bill-collectors. William Holman Hunt, the Pre-Raphaelite painter, who knew her about this time, described her as "a dashing type of horsewoman who attracted much notice from the 'bloods' of the day." A woman so conspicuously seductive could not be expected to accept isolation and poverty without protest, especially when her husband seemed to be making no effective effort to overcome them. His charm and good looks only increased the sting of their indigence. Holman Hunt speaks of him as "both brilliant in wit and also singularly handsome in person. Of nut-brown hair and blue eyes, the perfect type of a well-bred Englishman." In his wife's eyes he was a self-centered dreamer who put his own chimerical artistic career before her legitimate right to happiness.

He had become thoroughly popular with his stepdaughter, who testified in after years that "he and I were great friends in those early days even. We played cricket together; he was a splendid playfellow." Nevertheless, the little girl was well aware of the tension between him and her mother. Both the husband and the wife were high-strung and impatient; both were gifted with a sarcastic tongue, and they knew each other's sensitive spots well enough to plant their barbs where they hurt most. As Edith Nicolls said, long afterwards, "they sharpened their wits on each other."

No wonder that the unsuccessful author grew morose and cynical, and took refuge more and more in long solitary walks which enhanced his loving familiarity with every mile of the Surrey countryside. Nature offered a healing relief for nerves rubbed raw by household friction.

*The Shaving of Shagpat: An Arabian Entertainment* was finally accepted for publication by a prominent London firm, Chapman & Hall, which had brought out novels by Dickens, Thackeray, and other celebrities. When the book was ready for the press, in December, 1855, Meredith wrote a prefatory note for it, to explain that he was "imitating the style and manner of the Oriental story-tellers. But such an attempt, whether successful or not, may read like a translation." He therefore avowed that "it springs from no Eastern source, and is in every respect an original work."

This preface betrays the author's consciousness that readers might be baffled by the book. From one point of view, it was a sheer fairy tale. While writing it he read it aloud to his little stepdaughter to discover whether it would be effective as a children's story. From another angle it was obviously an exercise in literary preciosity, a self-conscious mosaic of beautiful metaphors and melodious cadences, the prose reverie of a poet. But there were tantalizing clues that it might be more than either a fantasy for children or a frigid *objet d'art*. Several scenes of horror were too gruesome to be suitable for children's imaginations; many comic passages bore a flavor of satire; and the series of episodes were unduly elaborate to be devoid of ulterior purpose. Perhaps the whole thing was to be interpreted as an allegory.

Near the beginning, two or three short tales—particularly that of Bhanavar and the Serpents—were inserted with little relevance to the main narrative. Thereafter the story continued to be episodic but possessed increasing cohesion and suspense. Any symbolic element in the interpolated tales was simple and general, but the principal story was a complex allegorical satire. Echoes of A *Tale of a Tub* and *Sartor Resartus* can be recognized in the narrative of the pretentious clothier whose authority over a whole city was enforced through his possession of the densest hair and beard, and of the ambitious young barber who, aided by the spells of his enchantress sweetheart, finally cut off Shagpat's hirsute adornments and thus destroyed the single hair that was the source of his power.

Shagpat represents the whole structure of pretension and artificiality that dominates the modern social system, and Shibli Bagarag is the naïve young reformer who uses the tools of common sense to strip off the imposition. In his long preparation for the climax the barber hero is tested and toughened by a series of perils and temptations that represent the chief forces of worldliness and self-indulgence. All this is redolent of Carlyle, with his contempt for material advantages and his Calvinistic glorification of Duty. In the theme of "Mastering the Event" there are echoes of Browning's doctrine of valiantly facing the great test that confronts everyone at some time with a demand for positive action. But many touches convey special theories of Meredith's own, which were to remain basic in his thinking throughout his life.

One that is important for both its social implications and its psychological revelations is the role played by women. Shibli Bagarag is not remarkable for fortitude or clear judgment. The author mentions "his simplicity and his honesty, and his vanity and his airiness, and the betraying tongue of the barber." Again and again his conceit or his gullibility or his openness brings him to the verge of defeat. The evil forces opposed to him usually appear as beautiful and seductive women, avid for admiration—Rabesqurat and Princess Goorelka—who represent not only sexual lust but also ambition for power and greed for wealth. But the embodiment of wisdom and altruism is also a woman, Noorna bin Noorka, who with infinite patience endures her lover's boasts and blunders, and guides him to his ultimate victory. In feminine natures, then, Meredith sees not only the most primitive instincts, which hold man back in his struggle toward truth and self-mastery, but also the highest inspiration that draws him upward.

The second significant emphasis is upon egoism. Shibli Bagarag is always an easy prey to flattery; he goes wrong whenever he succumbs to self-indulgence or self-glorification. Only when he has mastered this inner handicap can he wield the sword that subdues the impostor. Humiliations and hard knocks ("thwackings") are an essential part of his training. As in many mystical allegories, his final ordeal is a symbolic experiencing of death and resurrection—"the dark night of the soul." Though Meredith was more prone than most men to vanity and pride, he was positive that these traits were the source of all the troubles of the human race.

Equally Meredithian is a recurrent emphasis upon the magic potency of laughter. At several crises this is the only thing that can defeat the evil enchantments. The souls of men held captive in the guise of birds by Goorelka are released when Noorna keeps them laughing for a whole hour with "a story of men, that rocked them on their perches with chestquakes of irresistible laughter." Later, when Shibli Bagarag finds himself paralyzed upon the throne that his conceit has tempted him to accept, he sees in a mirror that his crown is of asses' ears and monkeys' skulls, whereupon he is convulsed with laughter and is at once free to move. Having learned to laugh at himself, he escapes the bondage of vanity.

Like most allegories, *The Shaving of Shagpat* moves upon several levels of signification. On one it portrays the conflict of instinct and reason, the story of the human race in its painful struggle to overcome the heritage of animalism and develop the full power of mind. On another level it is the conflict of blind prejudice and critical intelligence, the story of the independent thinker who seeks to tell the truth as he sees it. In this light, Shibli Bagarag can be regarded as a projection of Meredith himself, the penniless youth of humble origin rashly setting out to expose the absurdities of entrenched dogma. If an autobiographic element is thus to be read into the story, a further notable detail is that Shagpat, the embodiment of pompous self-conceit, is a clothier. The description of him is irresistibly reminiscent of Mel Meredith:

Lo, one lolling in his shop-front, and people standing outside the shop, marking him with admiration and reverence, and pointing him out to each other with approving gestures.

The Freudian reader will probably infer that the plot thus reveals Meredith's hatred of the family trade and contempt for his would-be-gentleman father, just as the sexual theme in the book reveals his ambivalent feelings toward his wife.

The first reviews, while not unfavorable, showed that the critics were uncertain as to the author's purpose. *The Examiner* called the book "a charming one, full of lively fancy and bright invention," and termed the author "extremely clever." *The Athenaeum* gave it two columns, but devoted most of the space to extracts and a general discussion of pseudo-Oriental tales, and ventured only the comment that this work "exhibits power of imagination, ability in expression, and skill in construction." *The Spectator* described it as "a mistaken undertaking by an able man. It is intended for an Eastern tale of adventure, but it wants rapidity and purpose in its action, and what is of more consequence, the story wants power to carry the reader along." *The Critic* asserted that "an Englishman cannot think Eastern thoughts" but praised Meredith's humor and story-telling skill:

If he would write an *English* story in the *English* manner, laying his scenes among places familiar to him, and making his personages of those whom he has met in the actual world about him, he would, we believe, be entirely successful . . . [The book] has failed only because he has attempted that in which nobody has ever yet succeeded. Even burlesque comedy cannot be endured through so many pages.

A daily newspaper, *The Sun,* was lavish with compliments:

In Mr Meredith . . . we at once recognize a writer of real genius, of a genius large, true, and original . . . Henceforth he takes high rank among our chosen favourites by reason of his most remarkable power as a humourist, and by reason also of his prolific and splendid imagination . . . It may be regarded by those who list, as a satiric allegory, having reference to a certain hairy freak peculiar to our own generation. It will be perused by others, however, as by ourselves, without regard to any hidden significance in the incidents recounted, but solely with an eye to the luxurious enjoyment of the author's abounding drollery, and of the deft and wondrous play of his quaint, adroit, delicate, erratic, puck-like imagination.

George Henry Lewes, in *The Saturday Review,* calling it "an original and charming book," particularly praised the style:

Although written in prose . . . the work is a poem throughout. Not that he gives us that detestable hybrid vulgarly called "poetical prose." . . . The prose is prose—not broken-up verse; the language is simple, picturesque, pregnant—not ornate inanities addressed to the ear . . . The style, although Oriental in its figurativeness, is European in its concision . . . George Meredith, hitherto known to us as a writer of graceful, but not very remarkable verse, now becomes the name of a man of genius—of one who can create.

In view of Meredith's connection with *The Leader*, the review copy was assigned to the editor's favorite critic, Marian Evans, who had recently joined her personal career with that of Lewes, but had not yet come before the public as George Eliot, a writer of fiction. Her review hailed the book as "a work of genius, and of poetical genius." She extolled the "exquisite delicacy" of the love scenes, the "exuberance of imagery, picturesque wildness of incident, significant humour, aphoristic wisdom." She alone gave full credit to the allegorical purpose:

There is plenty of deep meaning in the tale for those who cannot be satisfied without deep meanings, but there is no didactic thrusting forward of moral lessons, and our imagination is never chilled by a sense of allegorical intention predominating over poetic creation.

The sincerity of Miss Evans's admiration is proved by a letter to her friend Sara Hennell, in which she said, "If you want some idle reading get *The Shaving of Shagpat*, which I think you will say deserves all the praise I gave it." And in the April number of *The Westminster Review* she repeated her encomiums, though with one qualification: "We confess to having felt rather a languishing interest towards the end of the work; the details of the action became too complicated and our imagination was rather wearied in following them."

A final favorable notice was in *The New Quarterly Review*, which predicted that the book was "destined to be classical":

Whether designed to be an allegory (a supposition not entertained by us) or a story written in imitation of Eastern fiction, we have in every line proof of a gorgeous imagination, literary skill of a high order, and considerable dramatic power.

The author ought to have been pleased with this chorus of praise, and interested to notice that each reviewer credited him with a different intention. To one the book was "a tale of Eastern adventure," to another it was "burlesque comedy." One admired his "abounding drollery," another his "simple, pregnant language." Of the three who even mentioned allegorical interpretation, two rejected the idea, and one of these confined the possible allegory to a satire on the current fashion of long whiskers.

Meredith may have taken a mischievous pleasure in the confusion he had stirred up among the pundits; and certainly his feeling of intellectual superiority had impelled him to make his meaning as elusive as possible, so that only a few select minds could share the secret. On the other hand, he had not intended merely a literary hoax. He had worked long and hard on the book, enriching it not only with verbal beauty but with esoteric wisdom, and had pinned high hopes on its success. If the professional critics failed to perceive the serious symbolism, could he hope that there were any elect spirits who might discover it?

In order to supply a clue without descending to a vulgarly obvious statement, he took the opportunity of a second edition, ten years later, to point out the symbolic purpose by the old device of pretending to deny it:

It has been suggested to me by one who has no fear of Allegories on the banks of the Nile, that the hairy Shagpat must stand to mean umbrageous Humbug conquering the sons of men; and that Noorna bin Noorka represents the Seasons, which help us, if there is health in us, to dispel the affliction of his shadow; while my heroic Shibli Bagarag is actually to be taken for Circumstance, which works under their changeful guidance towards our ultimate release from bondage, but with a disappointing apparent waywardness. The excuse for such behaviour as this youth exhibits is so good that I would willingly let him wear the grand mask thereby offered to him. But, though his backslidings cry loudly for some sheltering plea, or garb of dignity, and though a story-teller should be flattered to have it supposed that anything very distinct was intended by him, the Allegory must be rejected altogether. The subtle Arab who conceived Shagpat meant either very much more, or he meant less; and my belief is that, designing in his wisdom simply to amuse, he attempted to give a larger embrace to time than is possible to the profound dispenser of Allegories, which are mortal; which, to be of any value, must be perfectly clear, and when perfectly clear, are as little attractive as Mrs Malaprop's reptile.

After a while Meredith discarded this preface and became franker in admitting the allegorical purpose. In a letter of 1892 he said:

*I suppose [Shagpat] does wear a sort of allegory. But it is not as a dress-suit; rather as a dressing-gown, very loosely. And they say he signifies Humbug, and its attractiveness; while Noorna is the spiritual truth. Poor Sh. Bagarag being the ball between the two. I think I once knew more about them and the meaning, but have forgotten, and am glad to forget, seeing how abused I have been for having written the book.*

Again in 1906, to a Scottish admirer who had published a treatise on the symbolic meaning of the story, Meredith wrote:

*An Allegory is hateful to the English, and I gave it clothing to conceal its frame. But neither that nor the signification availed. Very few even of my friends have cared to read the book, and of these I can count but two who have said a word in favour of it.*

His bitter tone shows that the non-success of the book still rankled after more than half a century.

Apart from two poems in *Household Words*, Meredith is not known to have published anything in 1856. The public did not take to *Shagpat*, which eventually went into the cheap stalls as a remainder; but Meredith started upon another experiment in pastiche prose fiction, this time an imitation of the medieval legends of the Rhineland.

The nomadic way of life continued. For a while the Merediths lived at Felixstowe, on the east coast; but by the summer of 1856 they were spending most of their time at Seaford, a fishing village on the English Channel, not far from Newhaven. It was an ill-conditioned sort of place, with a straggling row of villas facing a muddy beach; but it had its own attractions for Meredith. The South Downs, which towered up behind the village, gave him the breezy walks that he loved. Cheap lodgings with good food were provided by the local carpenter's wife, Mrs Richard Ockenden. And a new, congenial friend was also a frequent lodger at the Ockenden house. This was Maurice FitzGerald, a handsome, worldly young man who owned property in the neighborhood. His father, John Purcell FitzGerald, of Boulge Hall, in Suffolk, was fanatically religious; and his Uncle Edward, whose eccentricity ran toward skepticism and dilettante scholarship, was at this time teaching himself Arabic and beginning to translate some old Persian quatrains.

Maurice FitzGerald had made a name for himself at Trinity College, Cambridge, as a classical scholar; but like his uncle he was indisposed to work hard on a career. His greatest pleasures in life were whist and food. It was his expert advice that put the final touch of perfection upon Mrs Ockenden's superlative cooking.

Another new friend at this time was Eyre Crowe, a painter who had recently traveled with Thackeray as his secretary during his tour of the United States. In a letter inviting Crowe to spend a week at Seaford, Meredith gave a seductive résumé of the summertime pleasures of the place: "Here is fishing, bathing, rowing, sailing, lounging, running, pic-nicing, and a cook who builds a basis of strength to make us equal to all these superhuman efforts." He added that "Mrs Meredith says you must come under pain of her displeasure."

Although the couple kept up a charming display of mutual admiration and sparkling repartee while visitors were with them, they welcomed any excuse to escape from each other's company. In this same summer Meredith took his little son to stay with Edward Chapman, his publisher, at Folkestone; but there is no indication that his wife accompanied them. He delighted the Chapman children by talking to them in a burlesque of the style of *Shagpat*. "Take care, birdy boy," he called to Arthur, playing on the sand, "and don't wet thy golden feet."

The attractions of Seaford did not survive into the winter season. Writing to Chapman in December, Meredith explained:

*I remain here, as I can work better than elsewhere, though, engaged as I am, the DULNESS is something frightful, and hangs on my shoulders like Sinbad's old man of the Sea . . . Mrs Meredith is staying at Blackheath . . . I am anxious she should spend Xmas in town. Dulness will put out the wax lights, increase the weight of the pudding, toughen the turkey, make lead of the beef, turn the entire feast into a nightmare, down here, to one not head and heel at work.*

In the same letter he demanded a prompt remittance of £25 to complete an advance payment of £70 which had been promised. Though wishing that he could spend Christmas with the Chapman family, he told the publisher conscientiously:

*It is doubtful if I shall quit hard work for a day, till the book is finished. I will come Manuscript in hand . . . The name of this novel is to be "The Fair Frankincense." Tell me what you think of it?—There are to be two Prophets in the book, and altogether a new kind of villain; being Humbug active—a great gun likely to make a noise, if I prime him properly.*

Chapman's faith in the young writer had survived the unsatisfactory sales of *Shagpat*. The publisher repeatedly told his family that it was "the finest Eastern story outside *The Arabian Nights*"; and the whole household became so fond of the author that whenever he was in London an extra knife and fork were always laid at their table in case he should drop in to dine. The young Chapmans never forgot a notable dinner party at which Meredith was a guest along with Thackeray, Charles Lever, and John Forster, who were highly amused by Meredith's remark that "Chapman has a larder in Piccadilly, where he hangs up poor authors, to use as he wants them."

In spite of the intimacy and the seventy-pound advance payment, Chapman's firm did not accept the new book. There is little reason to doubt that *The Fair Frankincense* was the story published in August, 1857, under the title of *Farina: a Legend of Cologne*; and it was brought out by a rival company, Smith, Elder & Co., which had recently come to the fore as publisher of the Brontës, Ruskin, and Thackeray.

In this fairly brief tale Meredith was attempting a difficult type of art—the grotesque, or comic-gruesome. A minor vogue for it had developed in the eighteen-twenties, as a symptom of the decadence of romanticism. R. H. Barham's *Ingoldsby Legends* were masterpieces of the genre, and Meredith's father-in-law had done something similar in his two burlesques on medieval themes, *Maid Marian* and *The Misfortunes of Elphin*. Some of Browning's poems, such as "The Pied Piper of Hamelin" and "The Flight of the Duchess," were in the same vein, and Thackeray also tried his hand at "A Legend of the Rhine."

In Meredith's story the central situation was a conventional specimen of the sentimental historical romance, with beautiful heroine, valiant lover, hearty father, savage villain, and assorted minor characters providing comic relief. But Meredith portrayed these stock personages with traces of caricature that suggested burlesque, and into the midst of it he inserted supernatural events—the conflict of St Gregory with Satan and the intervention of the Lorelei to save the heroine. Furthermore, the conclusion—the invention of Eau de Cologne—was so palpably an anticlimax that it seemed a piece of intentional bathos.

Nevertheless it serves to bring out the autobiographic substratum that links this book with *Shagpat*. Like Shibli Bagarag, Farina is a base-born young tradesman who defies entrenched privilege and wins honor by performing great public service. Meredith's secret ambitions are revealed in both books. Moreover, even in this short and simple tale there are traces of symbolism, shadowing forth some of Meredith's dominant ideas. Margarita, the heroine, is one of the straightforward, intelligent girls who reject all feminine wiles and pretenses and suspicions. Her courage and honesty, matched with her lover's, contrast on the one hand with the brutality of her bourgeois admirers and the feudal nobles alike, and on the other hand with the austere monk, embodiment of asceticism, who falls victim to spiritual pride and has to accept the service of the practical Farina to purge Cologne of the ill effects of his error.

Meredith was not wholly adept in the elusive magic that can evoke laughter simultaneously with superstitious shudders. His familiarity with the Rhineland made the landscape descriptions effective, and the grand storm scene in the Drachenfels stimulated his poetic eloquence. Warm affection for German life and German tradition pleasantly suffused the tale. But the comedy often depended on mere exaggeration, and the total impression was weakened by uncertainty in the author's attitude. Just as the reader of *Shagpat* was piqued by doubts as to whether the story was an allegory, so the reader of *Farina* kept wondering whether it was meant to be a sympathetic reproduction of the naïveté of folk tales or a malicious parody of their incoherence.

On the whole the reviewers treated the book kindly. *The Examiner*, *The Spectator*, and *The Critic* all considered it an improvement over *Shagpat*. The reviewer in *The Spectator* disliked the "forced quaintness and facetiousness" but admitted that "the larger portion of the story consists of scenes with action, persons, and purpose, that possess interest in themselves." *The Leader* dwelt chiefly upon the style:

Farina is a wild, quaint, surprising story, written with excessive elaboration. Mr Meredith seems to take up one sentence after another, not laying it down until it has been wrought, chased, polished, and tinted into a separate bit of art and fancy . . . He is a heraldic artist in the use of colours in bright contrasts.

*The Athenaeum* complimented it ambiguously as "a full-blooded specimen of the nonsense of Genius," calling it "wild, impudent, and fierce . . . full of a riotous, abundant fancy . . . a real, lively, audacious piece of extravaganza." Similarly *The Morning Post* said that "the story is told in a spirited and captivating style, and is full of the wild dreamy romance of the German school." *The Saturday Review*, on the other hand, was severe: "The subject does not seem to us worth handling, and the comic part is more grotesque than piquant . . . The whole seems to us flat and dull. It is true that the dulness is that of a clever man."

George Eliot's remarks on it in *The Westminster Review* began with warm praise of *The Shaving of Shagpat* for its creation of "the bright world of imagination."

*It was with something like disappointment, therefore, that we found ourselves brought down to the vulgar limits of time and place, and our appetite for the marvellous entirely spoilt by scenes which challenge prosaic considerations of historical truth and the fitness of things . . . As a whole we think Farina lacks completeness, and the ghostly element is not well worked in. The combat between St Gregory and the Devil is made ludicrous by its circumstantiality . . . Nor can we admire many passages in which the author has sacrificed euphony, and almost sense, to novelty and force of expression . . . Farina is both an original and an entertaining book, and will be read with pleasure by all who prefer a lively, spirited story to those dull analyses of dull experiences in which the present school of fiction abounds.*

This invidious comment related to the fact that she was reviewing *Barchester Towers* and *Madame Bovary* in the same article. An exactly opposite opinion was voiced in *The Eclectic Review*, a nonconformist periodical, which advised the writer to deal with "the problems of our time and the wants of men around us":

*The story has its defects, among which we reckon language sometimes coarse, and especially expressions in connexion with religious subjects, which, however common, we deeply and earnestly deprecate. But the Legend is cleverly conceived, and very well told . . . We look for the time when the talents of popular writers of fiction shall be directed to more elevated and appropriate subjects.*

In general, the reviews might have encouraged the author to continue in the manner of his first two prose works. But his vein of poetic fantasy had reached its end. Smith, Elder & Co. showed no sign of interest in publishing another book from his pen, and the realities of his personal crisis became too insistent to allow any further escape into realms of magic.

He and his wife were spending more and more of their time apart. Their complex and tormenting relationship, compounded of physical passion and intellectual rivalry, of nervous sensitivity and fluent declamation, had settled into a pattern of violent quarrels. The embers of their love for each other lent heat to the hatred that flared up in their disputes. When Meredith was hard at work in Seaford, his wife sought amusement in London; when Mary came back to the dim little Sussex town, George found that business called him to the city. Before the end of 1857, he had taken lodgings for himself at 7, Hobury Street, Chelsea.

Among their artist friends was a particularly agreeable young painter named Henry Wallis, whose favorite subjects for pictures were episodes in the lives of authors, painted in the vivid new Pre-Raphaelite manner. His admiration for both George Meredith's talent and Mary Meredith's beauty was shown by a painting called "Fireside Reverie" which he exhibited in the Royal Academy in 1855. Its epigraph was four lines of verse written by Meredith, and the model for the woman sitting beside a glowing hearth was Meredith's wife. His most popular painting, "The Death of Chatterton" (exhibited at the Academy in 1856), was painted in the chambers of the Merediths' friend Austin Daniel, and the model for the dead poet is said to have been Meredith himself. When Meredith realized that his wife's unhappiness was taking on a more poignant intensity, and when marital intercourse between them was brought to an end, he began to suspect that she was in love with Wallis.

The painter was two years younger than her husband, and for a thirty-five-year-old woman it was intoxicating to discover that she could still fascinate a much younger man. His flattering attentions, his easygoing Bohemian kindliness, were in conspicuous contrast with the inconsiderateness and irritability of her husband. In the summer of 1857 she was visiting the beauty spots of North Wales, and there can be no doubt that Wallis was her companion. When she became pregnant it seems to have been assumed by everyone concerned that Wallis was the father of the unborn child.

In January, 1858, Wallis painted a rather unsatisfactory portrait of Thomas Love Peacock. The spring exhibition of the Academy contained three of his pictures. Meanwhile, Mary withdrew to a cottage at Clifton, near Bristol, where she was looked after by her foster sister, a girl whom Peacock had adopted in childhood; and there a son was born to her on April 18. As she had a legal husband, the registration of the birth gave the father's name as "George Meredith, author." Meredith, however, must have felt certain that the child was not his, for he would not let his wife come back to him or let her see their son Arthur. In the autumn she left England in company with Wallis, and they sought sanctuary in the paradise of artists, Capri. Her husband began to realize that he was left to cope with a desperate burden of debts.

Their elopement marked the end of a year of torment for Meredith. First the gradual conviction that his wife loved someone else, then the grim farce of keeping up a public appearance of amity between them, next the shame and bitterness of the decision over the baby's paternity, and finally the open disgrace of her flight—all these combined to inflict upon him an incalculable shock. In addition to jealousy arising from his unextinguished love for her, he was wounded in all his most vulnerable spots. His personal pride was affronted by the fact that she preferred another man. His social prestige, imperceptibly erected by the elimination of all connections with his own family and childhood home, was imperiled by the scandal that she brought upon his name. The loneliness that had overshadowed his early years now returned upon him with redoubled strength. He solaced himself with every specious argument he could muster: the difference in their ages (which he later exaggerated to nine years); the mental collapse of her mother, with the inference that Mary, too, must have lost her reason; the evidence of heartlessness in the fact that she could abandon her five-year-old son. But underneath all this rationalization was a gnawing conviction that somehow he was equally to blame for the catastrophe, that he had been guilty of some indefinable failure.

His one instinct was to withdraw from all former associations, to hide the disaster under a shroud of silence, and to abstain from every emotional commitment. It was the practical application of his philosophic theory of banishing regrets and living in the present. There was one exception, however, to his renouncing of human ties. The little boy whom Mary had left behind must now be his own exclusive care. His unacknowledged remorse for some vague neglect of family duty might thus be assuaged. By devoting his entire love and attention to Arthur, he could atone for the mother's treason and prove his own rectitude. No doubt he had always been proud of having a pretty little son, but now he engulfed the boy in a flood of fiercely protective affection.

He retained the rooms in Hobury Street for himself and the boy, but he could never feel at home in the city and grasped every opportunity to escape from it. For one seaside holiday, he took Arthur to Lynmouth, in Devonshire, where a fellow-visitor, F. B. Barwell, obtained a lasting recollection of him: "He and one or two other men often spent an evening together at my rooms, and his conversation was very amusing and often witty. Meredith had his boy with him at Lynmouth but no nurse, for he considered that a good lad who could wash and dress the child was better than a woman. He was himself devoted to the little fellow, whom I often saw with his boy-nurse." Meredith believed that he had good reason to be distrustful of the female sex.

The best panacea for personal agony is hard work, and Meredith flung himself fiercely into the writing of a novel. In a long letter to Eyre Crowe, in April, 1858, he tried to keep up a flow of forced gaiety, but his depression broke through here and there: "If I speak much, old fellow, I shall get to speaking of myself, & this is not a cheerful theme. . . . I am ill, overworked, vexed. I'll do better by degrees." The friendship of his publisher, Frederick Chapman, was one of his strongest supports at this gloomy time. It was at Chapman's that George Henry Lewes had "a pleasant chat" with him early in the spring of 1859; a few days later Lewes and Meredith went for a stroll together on Wimbleton Common. By that time the new novel was reaching its end.

On inadequate evidence, it has usually been assumed that Meredith had started the novel at Seaford as early as 1856; but there is no reason to doubt his own statement that it was written at Hobury Street and took one year. It was so thoroughly interpenetrated with his own problem and his own grievance that it could not have been conceived before the break with his wife. *The Ordeal of Richard Feverel* was published by Chapman & Hall in three volumes at the end of June, 1859.

This year was an *annus mirabilis* of English literature. It marked a crucial turning-point. The senior authors were at the height of their power: Carlyle had just issued the first volumes of *Frederick the Great*, and Ruskin was about to issue the final volume of *Modern Painters*; Tennyson brought out the first major part of *Idylls of the King* that summer, and John Stuart Mill published his essay *On Liberty*; the pre-eminent serial novels of the year were *A Tale of Two Cities*, by Dickens, and *The Virginians*, by Thackeray. But several epochal books were also put forth in those months by previously obscure writers. Charles Darwin touched the match to the greatest intellectual explosion of the century with *The Origin of Species*. Edward FitzGerald unintentionally made himself the laureate of the young skeptics with his translation of Omar Khayyám. And George Eliot came before the public with her first full-fledged novel, *Adam Bede*.

Her novel and Meredith's share the credit of endowing English fiction with artistic and intellectual self-respect. During the preceding thirty years it had expanded vastly in popular appeal and in variety of material; but the chief novelists were still letting their creative fecundity produce stories without discipline or structure. After 1850 a new generation of writers began to supply more intelligent analysis and artistic self-consciousness: Trollope undertook a restrained, objective portrayal of ordinary human nature and Collins demonstrated the effectiveness of suspense and a rigorously planned plot. When George Eliot turned to fiction she had already been steeped for a dozen years in philosophical controversy. To her the novel offered an opportunity for expounding basic ethical problems and for probing the complexities of character.

Like her, Meredith was interested in motive and environment, in the elusive interplay of one personality upon another. But more than any of the other novelists he was fascinated also by prose style. He was eager to display his virtuosity in diction and rhythm. The book was an ambitious venture, as many young men's first novels are; but it was ambitious in peculiarly diversified directions. He undertook to write a witty, urbane social satire which should be at the same time a profound tragedy of young love and naïve idealism. He assumed his ability to impose artistic coherence upon stylistic extremes ranging from oblique epigram to extravagant poetry. To achieve this blending of incongruities, he practiced several devices: he put many of the sarcastic remarks into the mouth of the young cynic, Adrian Harley, and he created Sir Austin's book of aphorisms as a medium for inserting philosophical generalizations which he could simultaneously exploit and disavow. He departed entirely from the ironic, sophisticated style in his scenes of emotional climax, especially the famous love scene in the woodland and its later counterpart, the storm scene in the Rhineland. In contrast with his elaborate descriptive phrases and outpourings of metaphor, the conversations were uncommonly realistic. Unlike the formal and rhetorical speeches uttered by the characters in other novels of the time, Meredith's dialogue had much of the brevity, simplicity and fragmentary allusiveness of actual talk.

Diverse influences can be recognized in his manner. A fondness for Jean-Paul Richter and other German writers of emotional prose had made him an admirer of Thomas Carlyle's grotesquely imaginative and allusive style. From his father-in-law, Peacock, he derived the devices of discursive dialogue and tongue-in-cheek satire. The "fashionable novel," established by the early books of Disraeli and Bulwer-Lytton, provided a precedent of paradox and epigram in the portrayal of sophisticated society. Meredith, however, mingled these elements with poetic symbolism and subtle implication peculiarly his own.

In unfolding the story he had a habit of alluding to certain events and characters without explanation, and then later incidentally revealing their real significance. It seems to be an attempt at well-bred casualness, an under-emphasis to avoid the formal expositions practiced by other novelists. At first the reader is disconcerted by this absence of explanation; he feels that he must have overlooked something. Gradually a degree of naturalness invests the technique. In real life we are seldom provided with a summary of every situation as we encounter it; instead, as in Meredith's method, we pick up hints and apparently irrelevant details and later recognize their import.

Throughout the book he subordinated the external events to the psychological pressures that produced them. The early chapters depicted the hero's boyhood not for chronological or sentimental reasons, but because his whole future character and behavior were shaped by these adolescent conflicts. And with disregard for all conventions of romantic fiction, the marriage of the young lovers occurred at the middle of the story, instead of forming the final climax.

Richard's character, too, was a departure from the standard noble hero. He was impatient, selfish, arrogant. Even his humanitarian project for rehabilitating prostitutes was shown as essentially a manifestation of his self-importance. And his conceit rendered him an easy victim when Mrs Mount seduced him. It is *The Shaving of Shagpat* over again. Like Shibli Bagarag, Richard must suffer a series of hard knocks before learning to conquer his ego; and like Noorna, Lucy embodies supernatural forgiveness and intuition in her loyalty to him.

Into this emotional situation Meredith inserted an intellectual complication—Sir Austin Feverel's experiment in training his son according to a rigid theory. It has been suggested to me by Professor R. C. Bald that Meredith may have derived it from Sir George Thomas Staunton's memoir of the life of his father. As Staunton had been M.P. for South Hampshire or for Portsmouth during most of Meredith's boyhood, Meredith would have had an interest in reading his memoirs, and there he could have learned how Staunton's father, an opinionated baronet, brought up his son by an abstract educational "system." Herbert Spencer's book on education, issued in 1858, may also have contributed something. Whatever the source, this element brought the story into touch with a current controversy over ideas.

In both plot and characters, the novel distinctly resembled Shakespeare's first tragic play. Both Richard and Romeo are impulsive, headstrong, moody; both Lucy and Juliet are youthfully frank and unexpectedly obstinate; Mrs Berry is almost a twin sister to the nurse, both in her conversation and in her role in the plot; and the satirical onlooker, Adrian, has much in common with Mercutio. As in *Romeo and Juliet,* there is love at first sight between two young people separated by family opposition, resulting in secret marriage, enforced separation, and cumulative misunderstanding that leads to death on the threshold of reunion.

The author was not entirely successful in justifying the separation of Richard and Lucy after their marriage. Though he offered many reasons for it, the reader not only questions the probability but also loses too much of his sympathy for Richard. The duel, too, is a survival of old melodramatic techniques that seems out of place in a novel claiming to deal realistically with mid-Victorian life.

Weak spots in the structure, however, are offset by the psychological plausibility. Sir Austin's antipathy toward the marriage was not merely the traditional prejudice of the "heavy father." The failure of his own marriage rendered him suspicious of romance and intolerant of women; he constructed his educational theory with its rejection of all sexual passion partly out of an acute sense of parental responsibility but much more as a solace for his former disaster in love. And yet—paradoxically but logically—the defection of his wife had been caused by these same qualities of his, the arrogance and coldness that he regards as dignity and wisdom.

It is the more remarkable that the novel implies this vindication of the wife's infidelity, because the author treats her and her lover with manifest bias, showing repugnance toward even mentioning them. Lady Feverel is never described; in her rare appearances she remains a shadowy figure, as though the author were grimly denying her the gift of life. And he appears to relish the heartbreak and poverty that she has earned by the escapade. Her lover, who lurks in the background as far as the story is concerned, is sketched in two or three passages of venomous contempt.

This attitude might be explained as merely reflecting Sir Austin's disgust toward the guilty pair, or as being dictated by Victorian evasiveness in mentioning sex. But the bias obtrudes too uncomfortably in the midst of the cool impartiality that Meredith maintains toward the other characters. He could not suppress his own vindictive feeling for the two people who had played the same role in his own life.

As a study of relations between father and son, the novel was doubly Meredith's own confession. The lack of understanding between a devoted but pompous father and a proud, sensitive son had overtones of the old Portsmouth days. Like Richard, Meredith had admired his father and yet rebelled against him and lived apart from him. But he now resembled Sir Austin, as a deserted husband faced with the problem of how to bring up an only son whom he was determined to shelter from the evils of the world. The character of the baronet was not intended to be a self-portrait, for his combination of family pride, intellectual conceit, and lack of sympathetic imagination made him eventually the villain of the tragedy that engulfed his son. He retained, however, a few resemblances to his creator: he was an author, though strictly an amateur one; and there is an allusion both to possible plebeian origin and to a Welsh strain in the ancestry. Rather than being a self-portrait, Sir Austin might be regarded as a self-admonition—an objectifying of the potential danger to his son's welfare that lurked in Meredith's traits of self-sufficiency and intellectual intolerance. Similarly, the novelist's inherent loyalty to psychological truth obliged him not only to indicate why the errant wife preferred the worthless poet to the self-righteous baronet, but even to make the reader sympathize with her choice.

As already suggested, the passionate intensity of the Richard-Lucy love scenes may be based on personal feeling, an idealized memory of some boyish infatuation, to which Meredith's imagination reverted eagerly for its contrast with the hyper-civilized frustrations of his married life. Other characters in the novel were closely modeled upon real people. Adrian Harley, "the wise youth," was drawn from Maurice FitzGerald. Hippias Feverel, the dyspeptic wine-bibber and author of scholarly treatises, recalled Richard Charnock. The scenes, too, were drawn from the author's experience. Raynham Abbey has been identified as Woburn Park, close to Weybridge, and Richard's adventures in Germany were in the Rhineland.

At several points Meredith introduced ideas which were to recur throughout his later work. In opposition to the inflexible caste system, which could not admit the possibility of marriage between a baronet's son and a girl of the farming class, Meredith argued for his doctrine of the superiority of Nature over artificial customs. When Sir Austin interviewed his aristocratic friends in search of a suitable bride for his son, he found physical and moral degeneration; but instead of recognizing the fruits of inbreeding he blamed the absence of a system of training in continence such as he was inflicting on his son. The next chapter shows the lad succumbing easily and blissfully to the natural promptings of sex, while the whole panorama of the woodland harmonizes with the young lovers' rapture.

Meredith's exaltation of Nature was the reason for his contempt for sentiment:

*Here I think yonder old thrush on the lawn who has just kicked the last of her lank offspring out of the nest to go shift for itself, much the kinder of the two, though sentimental people do shrug their shoulders at those unsentimental acts of the creatures who never wander from Nature.*

This anti-sentimental acceptance of natural impulse led Meredith to his doctrine that confident fortitude is the chief virtue—that one qualm of doubt or dread entails subjection to miserable fatalism:

*Though every man of us may be a hero for one fatal minute, very few remain so after a day's march even: and who wonders that Madam Nature is indignant, and wears the features of the terrible Universal Fate to him? Fail before her, either in heart or in act, and lo, how the alluring loves in her visage wither and sicken to what it is modelled on! Be your Rubicon big or small, clear or foul, it is the same: you shall not return.*

This thought resembles Browning's favorite tenet of the crucial moment, and is equally reminiscent of Carlyle's glorification of the "everlasting yea."

More exclusively Meredith's own is his identification of the power of Nature with the art of comedy. Adrian expounds the paradox that "the wise do love the Comic Muse." Meredith points out that Sir Austin's fatal flaw was his lack of a sense of humor:

*A good wind of laughter had relieved him of much of the blight of self-deception, and oddness, and extravagance; had given a healthier view of our atmosphere of life; but he had it not.*

Nor is laughter to be confined to intellectual wit. Adrian asserts that "no Art arrives at the artlessness of Nature in matters of Comedy. You can't simulate the ape." A few pages later the virtue of natural laughter is more earnestly displayed when young Richard is saved from a crucial blunder by the triumph of his sense of humor over his outraged dignity:

*It was a genial strife of the Angel in him with constituents less divine; but the Angel was uppermost and led the van: extinguished loathing: humanized laughter: transfigured pride.*

The implication is that in this moment of comic vision Richard took an essential step from childhood into maturity.

Meredith had undertaken to write as a poet, as a philosopher, and as a man of the world. He enriched his descriptive passages with glowing imagery and his emotional scenes with rhythmic movement. He offered deep spiritual implications and subtle ideological analysis. He stood aloof from vulgar prejudices and sentimental triteness. All this put his book into the special category that may be called "the intellectual novel," which stemmed from *Tristram Shandy* and flowered in Peacock. About the time of *Richard Feverel*, Bulwer-Lytton was using the same technique in *The Caxtons* and *My Novel*.

Such novels stand almost as far apart from the serious "novel with a purpose" as from the average story of action. The primary intention is not the imitation of reality but the display of the author's ideas and opinions. He is not setting out to reform abuses or to convert his reader to any dogma. He is chatting about things that interest him and trusts to find readers who will enjoy the conversation. This type of novel is an extended personal essay in the guise of fiction.

In one of his digressions Meredith discussed the novelty of his method:

At present, I am aware, an audience impatient for blood and glory scorns the stress I am putting on incidents so minute, a picture so little imposing. An audience will come to whom it will be given to see the elementary machinery at work: who, as it were, from some slight hint of the straws, will feel the winds of March when they do not blow. To them will nothing be trivial, seeing that they will have in their eyes the invisible conflict going on around us, whose features a nod, a smile, a laugh of ours perpetually changes. And they will perceive, moreover, that in real life all hangs together: the train is laid in the lifting of an eyebrow, that bursts upon the field of thousands. They will see the links of things as they pass, and wonder not, as foolish people now do, that this great matter came out of that small one.

Thus confidently prophesying an era of psychological acumen, Meredith bequeathed *The Ordeal of Richard Feverel* to posterity.

# CHAPTER
## IV

# *Settling into Harness*

Just when a tentative new interest in life and basis of self-respect had been established for Meredith by the completion of his book, his wounds were torn open again by the news that his wife was back in England. Wallis must have returned too, as he exhibited a picture, "Back from Marston Moor," in the Academy that summer, giving his address as 62, Great Russell Street, Bloomsbury; but Mary and he had separated. After spending Easter with her daughter, Edith Nicolls, at Seaford, she took lodgings in Twickenham. Her consuming passion was to see her son Arthur again, and perhaps she even had some fantastic hope that this might lead to a reconciliation with her husband. But to all her appeals Meredith was adamant. The boy must never be allowed to see her, or hear from her, or be aware of her existence.

In the midst of this torment he took Arthur away from London and found quarters in Esher, only a few miles from Weybridge, where he had spent the first years of his marriage. Their rooms were upstairs in an old house on the main street, and from his bedroom at the back Meredith could look out across the garden to the park of Claremont, the mansion where the French royal family were living as refugees.

One day when his son had gone to play out of doors, Meredith heard a ring at the bell and went down to open the door. On the step stood a beautiful girl in riding-costume, holding her horse with one hand and a disheveled Arthur with the other.

"Your little boy fell in the road, just in front of my horse," she explained. "But he didn't cry at all, because he told me that 'Papa says little men ought not to cry.'"

Meredith kissed the child anxiously; then he suddenly fixed his eyes upon the young woman. "Are you not Lady Duff Gordon's daughter?" he asked. Before she had time to reply he clasped her in his arms, exclaiming, "Oh, my Janet! Don't you know me? I'm your Poet."

In the eight years since they had seen each other she had grown into a splendidly handsome and forthright young woman. Some years previously the Duff Gordons had taken Belvidere House in Esher, which came to be known as "The Gordon Arms" because of the crowd of guests continually coming and going. Janet cantered off to meet her father at the railway station; but she brought Sir Alexander back with her to invite Meredith to dinner and to reproach him for having vanished from the sight of all his friends. "I had no idea you were living in Esher," Meredith replied. "Now that we have discovered each other again, I will come and live near you." The next day Janet joined him in a search for a suitable cottage, and before long they found one that would soon be available.

By this time Meredith was absorbed in a new literary project. The London journalistic world was reeling from a feud between Dickens and the firm of Bradbury & Evans, who had published his weekly *Household Words*. For complicated reasons, partly connected with his separation from his wife, Dickens quarreled with the publishers, and set up a new paper, exactly like its predecessor, with the title *All the Year Round*. In retaliation, Bradbury & Evans were determined to create a rival weekly with all the best available talent. As it was three years since Meredith's last contribution to *Household Words*, he was not one of the group that Dickens had carried with him to his fresh venture. He was therefore enlisted by Frederick Mullet Evans, of the publishing firm, and by Samuel Lucas, who was to edit their new journal, *Once a Week*. They would accept as many good poems and prose articles as he could supply, and they would be interested in considering his next novel for serial publication.

Meredith took a cautious attitude, remarking in a letter to Tom Taylor that if the paper was to try to duplicate *Household Words* he would not be a suitable contributor, as he could not "properly do facts on the broad grin, and the tricky style Dickens encouraged." He felt sure that the paper could succeed only by following a totally different line.

In twenty years of publishing *Punch*, Bradbury & Evans had gained experience in the use of illustrations, and so they hired some of the ablest young artists in black-and-white to make drawings for their new weekly. The first issue included a poem by Meredith, "The Song of Courtesy," which was accompanied by a drawing by John Tenniel. Dickens and his staff were watching every move of what they called "the Whitefriars crowd" with a mixture of anxiety and contempt, and apparently they had some special joke about this contribution, for on July 8 Dickens wrote to his sub-editor, Wills, "I got your letter this morning, and Wilkie [Collins] and I have been much delighted by your account of Meredith's poem."

Meredith was chagrined to find that none of his friends were strongly impressed with the first number. Though aware of the danger of speaking unpleasant truths to an editor, he wrote a detailed criticism of it for Lucas, declaring that most of the contributions were too short and inconsequential. He was not penalized for his candor, and by the end of the year five more of his poems had been printed.

There was no hurry about starting the new novel, as *Once a Week* had set out with a serial by Charles Reade; but the prospect of it was enough to give Meredith a sense of security. When he and his son settled into Copsham Cottage it was the first time since his marriage that he had any feeling of being in a permanent home; and the little house suited him admirably. Well out of the town of Esher, on the road to Oxshott, it was alone except for one farmhouse nearby. A thick hedge surrounded the cottage, with a white gate opening upon the road, while all around were unfenced heaths and common land, covered with heather and gorse and dotted with mossy hillocks. The largest of these, known as "The Mound" or "Round Hill"—probably a prehistoric burial mound—was close beside Copsham Cottage, providing Meredith with a convenient height on which to enjoy the wind sweeping across the heath and the magnificent view of Claremont Park and the hills beyond. Not far away were dense woods of larch and pine, and deep in their center was a little lake, haunted by a white heron and so overshadowed with trees that it was known as "The Black Pool."

Along with the cottage Meredith acquired a housekeeper, Miss Grange, a member of the landlord's family. He soon realized that she was just the person he needed: "excellent temper, spotless principles, indefatigable worker, no sex." She had a young niece who became a playmate for Arthur and accompanied him to the local school. Although the Granges occupied some of the rooms, Meredith enjoyed the luxury of having a spare bedroom that enabled him to entertain friends under his own roof. The arrangements were so primitive, however, that he could not invite a married couple to stay overnight unless he was assured that the lady could put up with great inconvenience.

As soon as the Merediths were established, Maurice FitzGerald came on a visit. Soon he was joined by his college friend, Francis Cowley Burnand, who was desultorily reading law in London and nursing impulses to be a playwright. Burnand had never heard of Meredith, and so, while walking with him across the Common, FitzGerald coached him respecting his friend's books. When they came in sight of the cottage, Meredith could be seen at the gate, greeting the plump, red-faced figure of "dear old Pater Evans."

*As the latter disappeared within the gate [Burnand recounts], George strode towards us. George Meredith never merely walked, never lounged; he strode, he took giant strides. He had on a soft, shapeless wideawake, a sad-coloured flannel shirt, with low open collar turned over a brilliant scarlet neckerchief tied in loose sailor's knot; no waistcoat; knickerbockers, grey stockings, and the most serviceable laced boots, which evidently meant business in pedestrianism; crisp, curly, brownish hair, ignorant of parting; a fine brow, quick observant eyes, greyish—if I remember rightly; beard and moustache a trifle lighter than the hair. A splendid head; a memorable personality. Then his sense of humour, his cynicism, and his absolutely boyish enjoyment of mere fun, of any pure and simple absurdity. His laughter was something to hear; it was of short duration, but it was a roar; it set you off—nay, he himself, when much tickled, would laugh till he cried (it didn't take long to get to the crying), and then he would struggle with himself, hand to open mouth, to prevent another outburst.*

Young Burnand being an accomplished humorist, there was much of this uproarious laughter during his visit. He was also replete with songs from the London music halls, especially a catchy new tune from one of H. J. Byron's burlesques. "During our country walks, and in the quiet evenings," he reports, "Meredith would 'call' for this song . . . What used to delight George was the 'swing and go' of it, and the catch of the rhythm . . . The lilt of this to some old American jingle called '*Skid-a-ma-lik*' used to take Meredith's fancy." This fascination with a syncopated popular tune is consistent with the flair for strongly accented meters in many of Meredith's poems at the time, and with his habit of improvising rollicking nonsense rhymes about his friends.

In the midst of jokes and songs, one little incident was not a laughing matter; and it revealed the difficulties that beset Meredith in bringing up his son unaided, and the spoiling that resulted from a mixture of indulgence and irritability. At dinner one day, excited by the liveliness of the three men, the six-year-old boy piped up asking for a drink of wine. When this was denied, he kept on demanding it until his father suddenly lost his temper. "All right," he shouted, "if you will have it you *shall*," and he poured out a full tumbler of wine. While the guests looked on in embarrassed dismay, he insisted that Arthur must drink the whole of it. In a short time the child lapsed into a semi-coma, and his subsequent illness was serious for several days.

About this time Meredith acquired a new friend who was less convivial than FitzGerald and Burnand. This was Captain Frederick Augustus Maxse, who had won fame five years before through his naval exploits in the Crimean War. The young officer's emotional and idealistic temperament had been outraged by the incompetence shown in the direction of the war and by the needless suffering that resulted; and he had come back full of lofty visions of political reform and international co-operation. He was wealthy and well connected, his mother being the former Lady Caroline Fitzhardinge, daughter of the Earl of Berkeley. Meredith was drawn to him by genuine sympathy with some of his theories and by admiration for his valor in war, his aristocratic self-confidence, and his naïve enthusiasm. At the same time there was a rationalistic streak in Meredith that made him critical of his friend's Utopianism. As Maxse was busy writing pamphlets to expound his theories, he welcomed the advice of a professional author.

*The Ordeal of Richard Feverel* had been reviewed sparsely and unperceptively. *The Leader* called the story "wild, fantastic, and in some degree enervating," though "not without its moral and its purpose." The ending was condemned as too disastrous. "George Meredith can write well and conceive grandly, but he has yet to learn to correct, or at any rate to conceal his eccentricities." *The Critic* was equally severe: "Mr Meredith is a man who has evidently thought much and deeply; but there are many passages in his book that lead us to believe that his mind is none of the purest . . . His work is certainly meat for strong men rather than food for babes . . . It has great merits and great defects, and we believe that these are very evenly balanced."

*The Saturday Review* devoted itself to fault-finding, but ended with an illogical gleam of encouragement: "If this is all that Mr Meredith can do, it is a failure; but it gives us hope that it may prove the prelude to a work that will place him high in the list of living novelists." *The Athenaeum* was less optimistic:

*This "Ordeal" is about as painful a book as any reader ever felt himself inexorably compelled to read through, in spite of his own protests to the con-*

*trary . . . The book is very clever, with a fresh, vigorous vitality in the style;
but it is not true to real life or human nature, only true to an abstract and
entirely arbitrary idea . . . It affects the reader like a painful reality to see
such cruelty and blindness, and blundering, such child's play with the most
sacred mysteries of life, even though he is quite aware of the fiction that
lies at the root of this "seeming show." . . . The only comfort the reader
can find on closing the book is . . . that it is not true.*

*The Spectator* was more generous, saying that Meredith's "Shandy-
ism" was less plagiaristic than Bulwer-Lytton's, and terming the story
"a moving and suggestive one, in which there is more of vigorous
thought, imagination, wit, humour, and pathos, than would suffice to
make the fortune of a score of average novels." *The Illustrated London
News* also saw a resemblance to *The Caxtons,* by Lytton.

The inadequate reviews were a blow to the author's hopes, and a
graver disaster followed. In an era when few private customers could
afford to buy a three-volume novel costing thirty shillings, the profits
came from the sale of copies to the circulating libraries. The largest
organization of this sort, Mudie's, would buy hundreds of a popular
new book, and thus in turn would promote its fame and widen its
market.

Mudie had begun by ordering three hundred copies of *Richard
Feverel,* telling Chapman & Hall that the book seemed destined for
success; but shortly afterwards it vanished from the list. When Chapman demanded an explanation Mudie answered that there had been
"urgent remonstrances of several respectable families who objected to
it as dangerous and wicked and damnable." There were reports, too,
that some clergymen had banned it from their parish book clubs. "O,
canting age," Meredith fumed, "I predict the deluge." And again he
grumbled, "There are grossly prurient, and morbidly timid people,
who might haply be hurt, and with these the world is well stocked."
The stigma of indecency was the most fatal affliction that could befall
a new writer's first novel. Meredith lamented that "I would rather have
Mudie and the British Matron with me than the whole army of the
press."

He was willing to concede that he now saw "dulness and weakness"
in the book here and there; but he affirmed that "the main design and
moral purpose I hold to. I have certainly made it too subtle, for none
have perceived it." This remark was in a letter to Lucas, and he went
on to point out that Sir Austin Feverel's "system" had succeeded for a
while, through Richard's "luck in finding so charming a girl." But the

"moral" of the story was that "no System of the sort succeeds with human nature, unless the originator has conceived it purely independent of personal passion." Sir Austin invented his System less out of love for Richard than out of "wrath at his wife," and therefore it "carries its own Nemesis." Meredith had thought that he made his thesis plain enough, "but I do not insist on it and lecture my dear public. . . . It requires twice reading to see this, and my fault has been that I have made the book so dull that it does not attract a second reading. At least, not among newspaper critics."

The harmful consequences of Mudie's action disturbed Lucas also, as he had recently agreed to serialize Meredith's next novel in his eminently respectable weekly. Luckily he could do something to offset the bad publicity, for he was the chief reviewer of fiction for *The Times*. On October 3 Meredith wrote to thank him for his "kind intention to stand forth and defend my character."

Though its four months' tardiness might have roused suspicion, Lucas's two-column review in *The Times* of October 14 was mainly favorable. Terming *Richard Feverel* "an extraordinary novel," it said:

*Mr Meredith is an original writer, and his book is a powerful book, penetrative in its depth of insight, and rich in its variety of experience. But it is also very oracular and obscure in parts, and, as we conceive, extremely weak in the development of its main purpose. On the other hand, it is so crystalline and brilliant in its principal passages, there is such purity mingled with its laxness, such sound and firm truth in the midst of its fantastic subtleties, that we hesitate whether to approve or condemn.*

The critic pointed out justly that Meredith belonged to a limited class of novelists, "the *humourist* class, which draws its presentment of mankind to a large degree from its inner consciousness . . . His characters are more entirely symbols and shadows of his thought than ordinary every-day denizens of the world about him."

Using the very phrase that Meredith had supplied him with, Lucas said that the purport of the book was "to explode the system" of Sir Austin, who "gratified his wrath at his wife" at the expense of his son. The reviewer's verdict is that "the System is arraigned, but it is never tried fairly, its merits or demerits are unsolved to the last." He concluded, however, with further praises of the book, and with a challenge to "the over-fastidious":

*It certainly touches a delicate theme, and includes some equivocal situations, but of impurity, in the sense of any corrupting tendency, we see not a trace, and we will not endorse the imputation. It is a novel, in short, which may be read by men and women with perfect impunity if they have no corrupt imagination of their own to pervert the pure purpose of the author.*

As a further counterpoise to Mudie's blow, the book made Meredith known to one of his literary idols, Thomas Carlyle. The story, as Meredith loved to recount it in later life, was that Mrs Carlyle, when she began to read *Richard Feverel*, was so irritated that she threw the volume on the floor. Soon, however, she found herself impelled to pick it up again, and before long she was reading passages aloud to her husband. Eventually the Sage of Chelsea growled, "That young man is nae fule. Ask him here."

Having been a neighbor when he lived in Hobury Street, Meredith had seen Carlyle from time to time out walking, but had never plucked up courage to speak to him. When Mrs Carlyle asked his publishers for information about him, he hastened to call at Cheyne Row. Carlyle talked lengthily about deep philosophical matters, being gratified to discover the devotion to Goethe that had been increasing in Meredith ever since his schooldays in Germany.

Toward the end of the interview, Carlyle paid Meredith what was apparently intended as a compliment: "Man, ye suld write heestory! Ye hae a heestorian in ye."

"Novel-writing is my way of writing history," Meredith answered, and Carlyle chewed over the epigram as though it suggested a new idea to him. He asked the young author to come again and come often, and their interviews left a permanent impress upon Meredith's beliefs. Forty years later he stated that Carlyle "commended the study of Goethe to me constantly."

His new medium of publication, *Once a Week*, was not the sole cause for Meredith's being stimulated at this time to a fresh outburst of creative activity in poetry. It was evoked by his daily communion with Nature in the Surrey woods and hills, by the admiration of his circle of friends, and by an unwonted sense of freedom and achievement. Both in his personal relationships and in his professional career the long years of hopeless struggle had come to an end, and his genius displayed a flowering in poems that had little in common with the trite hackwork that he had manufactured in the early days of *Household Words*.

The poems were given gratifying prominence in *Once a Week*. During the autumn three of them had pictures by Hablôt K. Browne ("Phiz"), who had formerly been Dickens's own illustrator. While

Meredith retained much of his melodious lyricism he was now striving for a closer contact with the realities of life. His fourth contribution (September 3), "The Last Words of Juggling Jerry," was a study of low life that combined humorous realism with pathos and philosophic depth. Copsham Common was a favorite haunt of gypsies, tinkers, and tramps, and Meredith made a habit of getting into conversation with them and picking up their ideas. Phiz's drawing for "Juggling Jerry" was a faithful portrayal of Meredith's "Mound."

The poems were signed with his name, but a group of four brief humorous stories that he contributed to the Christmas number came out anonymously. In submitting them, Meredith pointed out to Lucas that they were not like the conventional seasonable tales that Dickens had popularized: "There is no ghost-walking, and picture of the season, as we are accustomed to see . . . I think the stories are rather amusing; but I have not worked them up, purposely not." He set the price at ten pounds, and added an urgent request for payment "in a day or two." This financial stress must have been responsible also for the fact that he had purloined the plots of the stories from a friend. As soon as Frank Burnand read the Christmas issue he recognized "A Story-telling Party" as consisting of anecdotes of his own, which he had told Meredith during his stay at Copsham Cottage.

George never informed me of his design [Burnand states], and made use of them without a "with your leave or by your leave." . . . Seeing a point to be scored for myself, I wrote to George, asking him as a set-off against the "honorarium" he had received for my stories ("only infinitely better told") to recommend a story of mine to the editor. George replied, expressing his regret, excusing himself by saying that he never thought I was going to make capital out of them (here he was right), and that he would have great pleasure in submitting my story to the Once a Week editor.

The story was duly published four months later and was Burnand's first contribution to any magazine. The connection with Bradbury & Evans culminated with his editorship of *Punch*, which earned him a knighthood.

At the moment short stories were hasty potboilers for Meredith, as he was under pressure to make a start with his new novel. Reade's *Good Fight* (later to be revised as *The Cloister and the Hearth*) had abruptly vanished from *Once a Week* in October, owing to a dispute with the editor, and the paper limped along for three months without a regular serial. In response to Lucas's urging, Meredith wrote on

December 6 that the serial could not begin before February, and a few days later he again pleaded, "I would save you perplexity, if I thought it wise to begin next month. But I have the fear that I should only cause you greater in the end."

Aware of the importance of the opportunity, he was eager to cooperate with the editor at every turn. Even the title of the novel was a matter for prolonged conference. He consulted George Henry Lewes about the first one that was suggested, and Lewes didn't like it. "Besides," Meredith explained to his editor, "it binds me too much to a positive course, and tempts to extravagance in the unfolding of situations." For a while he thought of using simply the name of his hero, *Evan Harrington*; but as his own family background was supplying the principal theme, he wanted to throw strong stress upon the conflict of social caste. Near the end of December he submitted a list of possible titles. *The Substantial and the Essential* he considered "bad, but better than *Shams and Realities*." He rather liked the double significance of *All but a Gentleman*, and he also proposed *The Gentleman-Tailor's Family* or simply *The Tailor's Family*, as this last would avoid the snobbish overtone of "gentleman" and would commit him to no "special developments." A few days later he was willing to settle for *Gentle and Genteel*, though protesting faintly that *Gentility and a Gentleman* might be better. Eventually they compromised upon the hero's name with a subtitle attached: *Evan Harrington; or, He Would Be a Gentleman*.

In a burst of energy Meredith had completed three chapters, enough for the first instalment, by the middle of December; and he suggested that they should be set up in type at once, as he knew he would be "cutting at it, correcting, polishing—unless I see it as a fact in print." Two more chapters were turned in before Christmas. Lucas promptly complained that the action was not getting under way fast enough to catch the flighty attention of weekly readers. Meredith had already impressed upon him that the story was to be a "study" in which "the incidents shape and are dependent on character." Now he begged him not to "hurry for emotion. It will come." He argued that, as he was not writing a mystery story of the Wilkie Collins type, "interest, not to be false and evanescent, must kindle slowly, and ought to centre more in character—out of which incidents should grow."

A week later he returned to the argument: "Remember, I have called this a Comedy. To invent probabilities in modern daily life is difficult, you can't work up the excitement of melodrama and 'Women in White.' " He admitted that "in a 'serial' point of view, there may be something to say; but I fancy I am right in slowly building up for the scenes to follow." He asked for a continuation of open criticism but added pathetically, "if you see good points, mention them. Praise nourishes."

In spite of his self-justification, Lucas's objections had thrown him into difficulties with the next two chapters, and on December 27 he confessed that he was still struggling with them. His trouble was partly in fitting the story to serial division, and he kept appealing for clearer instructions as to where each instalment was to end. He explained that he was rewriting two chapters to improve the endings. He was confident that his "idea and meaning was clear and safe," but he "did not sufficiently *lead on*." Lucas was growing so impatient over the delay that Meredith, promising copy shortly, besought him on New Year's Day to "try and spur me on without giving me the sense that I am absolutely due; for then I feel hunted, and may take strange leaps."

Not sure whether the editor would consider the rewritten sixth chapter to contain enough movement, he explained that "small incidents . . . best exhibit character," and argued that a serial ought to offer not only "excitement enough to lead on" but also "amusement of a quiet kind." The comparison with Collins must have rankled, for Meredith remarked that "the tension in 'W. in W.' is not exactly pleasant, though cleverly produced. One wearies of it." He sent chapters eight and nine on January 13, but withheld the troublesome seventh until a week later, which was less than three weeks before the first instalment was due to appear.

In a subsequent letter Meredith offered to make cuts, promised that in the next chapter there would be a cricket match that ought to be "rather liked," and gave assurance that after two more chapters the hero's arrival at Beckley Court would result in "the intrigues of the Countess, the loves of Evan and Rose, etc., and then I think we shall do." Editorial anxiety might well be aroused by this cool prediction, two weeks before the serial began its run, that ten instalments would be consumed before the plot really came to life.

Before the first instalment appeared, Meredith asked Lucas about his rights for disposing of an American edition, as "I'm horribly poor, and £30 or £40 is a windfall." James T. Fields, a Boston publisher, who was in England on one of his scouting expeditions, had praised *Richard Feverel* so highly that Meredith felt sure he would pay "a *sum*" for the new book. Instead, however, Evans undertook to negotiate with Harper & Brothers, and the author was equally hopeful over this prospect. He asked Evans to tell the New York firm that "the story will suit Yankee sentiment and Yankee principles. Exalt me tolerably . . . Perhaps. should it be needful, you may say that we are going to be guilty of no *impropriety* in this tale, and will never again offend young maids."

*Evan Harrington* began its run in *Once a Week* on February 11, 1860. The illustrations were provided by Charles Keene, a gifted young artist. The editor continued to beg for cuts and from time to time dropped a hint about the merits of other novelists—not only Collins but also Smollett. In admitting that "this cursed desire I have haunting me to show the reason for things is a perpetual obstruction to movement," Meredith added, "I *do* want the dash of Smollett and I know it." But the next week, regaining self-confidence, he boasted of having rejected "many temptations to incident," and pointed out that "in Smollett conduct is never accounted for." Besides, it was to be remembered that "full half the incident of Smollett trenches on amusing matter not permitted me by my public."

Through the spring and summer he struggled on with the novel, never more than a few weeks in advance of publication date. When near the end, he asked anxiously whether Lucas was "in a state of disgust with the story," and confessed that he himself could see faults in it—"the points I missed, and the lengthiness I should have cut short" —but he claimed that the novel was "true to its title, and that I avoided making the fellow a snob in spite of his and my own temptations." It was a shock to him to learn that some readers were sending in complaints that the story was dull. At the end of September, submitting the final instalment, he remarked dejectedly, "It is finished as an actor finishes under hisses. Sincerely I am sorry for you mainly and will do you more justice another time."

The serial publication ended on October 13, and the author was paid a satisfactory sum approaching £400. In spite of the grumbling of a few readers, Meredith had every reason to believe that his connection with a magazine of wide general circulation had established his reputation with a public that previously knew little or nothing about him.

During the year he also contributed two poems to *Once a Week*, both illustrated by John Everett Millais, the co-founder of the Pre-Raphaelite movement. In connection with one of the poems it is surprising to find that in spite of the separation from his wife he was still receiving friendly help from Peacock. In a book published in 1898, T. H. Sweet Escott told a circumstantial anecdote which must be accepted as authentic, as Escott—who knew Meredith personally— affirmed in his preface that "every doubtful case of personal and historical statement" had been verified by the person dealt with. The story is that when Thackeray was editing *The Cornhill Magazine,* Peacock showed him Meredith's poem "The Meeting," a brief ironic vignette, in the manner later used by Hardy, of an unmarried mother and a young man yearning for his mistress. Thackeray was impressed with the verses. "They have the ring of truth about them," he commented to Peacock. "Were it not my fate to make enemies of so many of my contributors by not always being able to meet their views, I should ask you to let your friend fill many pages of *The Cornhill.*"

The moment *Evan Harrington* was off his hands, Meredith committed himself to a new sort of occupation, which left him less time for his writing. In August, 1860, when John Forster resigned as reader for Chapman & Hall, they appointed Meredith as his successor. The position required him to go through stacks of the manuscripts submitted to them; these were sent to him at Copsham Cottage, six or eight at a time, and he visited the office in London once a week to turn in his reports.

He applied himself to the job conscientiously, and his opinions were trenchantly expressed. His first recommendation entered in the record book was on *The Two Damsels: A Spanish Tale,* by C. M. O'Hara. His comment was "Childish: return without comment," and Miss O'Hara's tale never achieved the glory of print. *Market Harborough,* a fox-hunting story by one of the best-selling authors of the day, G. J. Whyte-Melville, he described as being "of the order of *Soapy Spunge's Sporting Tour.* Not so funny: appeals to same class." This was construed as an acceptance, and the book was issued by the firm.

Whether the proffered material was by sentimental amateurs or by formula-ridden professionals, he considered most of it to be rubbish and was strengthened in his determination that his own fiction would never cater to popular fashions. The endless reading of manuscripts was dull, tiresome work, consuming much of the time that he would rather devote to his own writing; but it earned the steady income that kept a roof over his head and his son's.

During his first year at Copsham he was more than a little in love with Janet Duff Gordon. After all, he was only thirty-two and she was a mature seventeen. As a friend of her childhood he was accepted on terms of uninhibited intimacy; and her mother's contempt for conventions and for feminine affectations had encouraged the girl to acquire a frankness and self-reliance that paid no heed to current social laws about chaperons and modest blushes. She and Meredith took long walks together over the Common and through the woods, the tree-screened Black Pool being one of their favorite haunts. "My Poet would recite poetry or talk about his novels," she records. "I made him write down some of the verses he improvised as we sat among the heather." These lyrics, which Janet kept safe for sixty years, included many gay nonsense rhymes; but several of them were love songs of unmistakably genuine emotion.

On days when Meredith had to be in London, Janet took charge of little Arthur and coached him in German. Once, while staying with her godmother in town, she scandalized the strait-laced old lady:

When one day Meredith came to take me on the top of an omnibus to the Tower of London, which I had never seen, she wanted to send her daughter's French maid to act as chaperon. Fortunately Camille was busy making a ball dress, and could not be spared. My godmother was, however, somewhat consoled when she found that little Arthur was going with us.

In his admiration for the girl Meredith determined that she should be his protégée in a literary career, and he used his new influence in the publishing business on her behalf:

To my great delight and pride my Poet proposed that I should translate Herr von Sybel's Geschichte und Literatur der Kreuzzüge for Chapman & Hall, on condition that it should be published as edited by my mother, her name being so well known. [It] was finished in about ten months.

Janet had a circle of other and more distinguished men who also admired her, and Meredith was inclined to be jealous. One of the closest friends of the Duff Gordons was Alexander W. Kinglake, a famed conversationalist, who had won renown with his book of Near-Eastern travels, Eothen, and with his reports on the Crimean War. In September, when Kinglake was staying at the Duff Gordon house and suffering from eyestrain, Janet volunteered to become his amanuensis. Meredith obviously did not like the proposal. He and Kinglake, Janet says,

often met at dinner at the "Gordon Arms," but I do not think they cared much for each other. Both were shy in different ways, and both were at their best when alone with one or two friends . . . When strangers were there, or people who were not congenial to him, [Kinglake] was absolutely silent. My Poet, in the early days when I saw so much of him, was a delightful companion when he knew he was liked; before strangers his shyness took the *form of asserting himself rather loudly, and trying to be epigrammatic and witty; he gave one the impression that he was not quite sure on what footing he stood.*

Naturally Meredith was perfectly well aware that his attentions to Janet could be only romantic make-believe. Even if he had not been the husband of the banished Mary, who hovered perpetually in the background of his consciousness like an opiated ache, there would still have been no possible chance of a marriage between the brilliant, beautiful daughter of a baronet and the overworked author who—after ten years in the profession—could barely afford a lonely cottage to house himself and his little boy. And since a genuine love affair between them could not conceivably materialize, he indulged himself with the novelist's prime gratification: he projected the whole situation into the book he was writing and there provided it with the fulfillment that it could never have in actuality.

*Evan Harrington* was an even more autobiographical story than *Richard Feverel* had been; and like that novel it inextricably combined the author's present and his past. In many respects the hero was a portrayal of Augustus Urmston Meredith, the handsome lad with a soul above tailoring. Augustus's father appeared actually under his own name, "the great Mel"; his mother was there, with her indomitable common sense; the three ambitious sisters and their husbands were true to life in all essentials; even the neighboring shopkeepers in the High Street were reproduced, often without change of name. Portsmouth was "Lymport" and Petersfield was "Flowerfield." The death of the flamboyant old tailor and the unwilling accession of his son followed the real events of forty years before.

But when Evan rebelled against his mother's plans and set off to seek his fortune, the focus suddenly changed to Meredith's own immediate surroundings. Evan was now a projection of George Meredith himself, the man of humble origin received on sufferance in a brilliant aristocratic household and constantly suspecting some supercilious sneer from his fellow-guests. The portraiture remained faithful: Sir Alex and Lady Duff Gordon became Sir Franks and Lady Jocelyn; Janet was their daughter Rose; a spinster friend of the family, Louisa Courtenay, who often stayed with them at Esher, appeared as Miss Current.

The Duff Gordons were fully aware that they were being used as models; and, since the depiction was favorable, they were not displeased. "*Evan Harrington* was *my* novel," says Janet,

*because Rose Jocelyn was myself . . . With the magnificent impertinence
of sixteen I would interrupt Meredith, exclaiming, "No, I should never have
said it like that;" or, "I should not have done so." A young Irish retriever,
Peter, which I was breaking in and afterwards gave to little Arthur, was im-
mortalized in the pages of the novel at my special request.*

In developing the love story of Rose and Evan, and particularly in
narrating the poignant interview on a beautiful spring night, when
Evan nobly renounced the girl, Meredith was externalizing his own
secret wishes and regrets. Although under a comic mask, there are
revealing touches in a dialogue that he wrote for Janet during a visit
with Maurice FitzGerald to their old haunts in Seaford. He depicts
himself, as "Poet," struggling with a love scene for *Evan Harrington*
while Fitz constantly interrupts with remarks about a sybarite meal
that he is planning. The Poet's phrases about Rose Jocelyn are inter-
mingled with others referring unmistakably to Janet. Whether or not
the Duff Gordons recognized the degree of personal emotion in the love
episodes, it is certainly improbable that Meredith let them have any
inkling of the degree of autobiography prevailing in the chapters about
Evan's antecedents.

In January, 1861, the novel was issued by Bradbury & Evans in
three volumes. "I wish I could have done more for Ev: Harrington, for
both our sakes," Meredith wrote to Evans, "but I should have had
to cut him to pieces, put strange herbs to him, and boil him up again
—a toilsome and a doubtful process: so I let him go much as *Once a
Week* exhibited him. We must take our luck, and do better next time."
All his agonies over the instalment divisions and the need of action,
all his cuts and rewritings, may have caused some inequalities in the
story; but on the whole he had withstood the pressure to cater to
popularity. As he remarked to Lucas, "the charge of dulness comes of
an author giving himself a problem to work out, and doing it as
conscientiously as he could."

As compared with *Richard Feverel*, the narration was much less
capricious and the style less mannered. After the preliminary chapters
the novel had a unity of place and time like that of a well-made play:
the principal action all took place during a few days at Beckley Court,
and one episode was even called "the fourth act of our Comedy." In
other respects, however, it was a reversion to more primitive narrative
techniques. The wanderings of Evan after he left Lymport were told
in the simple picaresque manner of *Joseph Andrews*. There were too
many minor characters, not well integrated into the story, and atten-

tion shifted too often from one to another. Some of these were caricatured in the style of Dickens's earlier work, and for several of them specific models can be found in Dickens: The Cogglesby brothers resembled the Cheerybles, and Jack Raikes, the fantastic talker, was a composite of Jingle and Dick Swiveller. The machinery of the plot, too, was sometimes implausible, with the Cogglesbys performing as *deus ex machina*. But the high comedy scenes and the Countess de Saldar compensated for any defects.

Once again the theme of the story is a young man's testing. Meredith's theory was that the energy of youth possesses boundless potentiality for either good or ill, and that the hard blows of experience can purge the worthless elements and strengthen the genuine ones. Evan runs a grave risk of being a foolish social climber, as his sister tries to force him to be; but love and his mother's common sense succeed in winning him to candor and the wise acceptance of natural facts.

Both this novel and its predecessor dealt with the possibility of a crack in the rigidly stratified class system. *Feverel* showed the aristocracy starting to slip downward; *Harrington* shifted the emphasis and showed the bourgeoisie surging upward. One novel told the story of a baronet's son marrying a girl of the people; the other told of a tailor's son winning the hand of a baronet's daughter. Meredith was careful to indicate that the date of the action was a generation earlier than his own day; trains and steamships were not in use, and he commented sarcastically that "it was a time before our joyful era of universal equality."

There is one explicit mention of the guiding spirit that informed the whole story. "You may think," he told the reader, "the Comic Muse is straining human nature rather toughly"; and he proceeded to explain the psychological reasons for the Countess de Saldar's behavior at that point. Indeed, the Countess was responsible for some uncertainty in the author's touch. A chief function of the Comic Muse being to unmask affectation and pretension, the Countess ought to have been the prime victim; but Meredith admired her indomitable aplomb too much to give more than rare and furtive glimpses of her faults. As a lady of unscrupulous charm and boundless resource she was almost worthy to rank with Becky Sharp and Beatrix Esmond.

Meredith's satiric shafts were not aimed solely at the particular persons of his story. He took opportunities to scoff at English snobbery, English complacency, English inconsistency. These criticisms of national traits align him with a tradition of ironic protest extending from Arnold to Shaw. And he could not resist one sneer at the prudes who had condemned *Richard Feverel*:

*This is a comedy, and I must not preach lessons of life here: but I am obliged to remark that the husband must be proof, the sister-in-law perfect, where arrangements exist that keep them under one roof . . . What is the use of telling this to a pure generation? My constant error is in supposing that I write for the wicked people who begat us.*

The critics paid little attention to the book. *The Spectator* termed Meredith "a writer of uncommon ability," and said that his "vein of humour in literary composition is clearing and fining down as he grows older." A brief note in *The Examiner* remarked that the story "is cleverly told in vigorous and pointed English, and abounds in shrewd sketches of character." A more thorough discussion was in *The Saturday Review*, which called it "a surprisingly good novel . . . a story new in conception, new in the study of character, fresh, odd, a little extravagant, but noble and original." But the favorable tone of the review was painfully qualified in its last sentence: "It is not a great work, but it is a remarkable one, and deserves a front place in the literature that is ranked as avowedly not destined to endure." The longest and most laudatory review was in a moribund weekly, *The Literary Gazette*, and was written by John Morley, a youth of twenty-two who had just arrived in London to seek a literary career. "We scarcely remember perusing a more fascinating work," he declared. "In our opinion *Evan Harrington* is the only novel of the day that is entitled to a place on the same shelf with such works as *The Woman in White*." The other journals did not deign to mention the book at all.

CHAPTER

V

# Wider Horizons

AFTER finishing *Evan Harrington*, Meredith added further sources of income to his salary from Chapman & Hall. One of these was an engagement as editorial writer for *The Ipswich Journal*. On the death of its owner, in 1855, this prosperous provincial paper had been inherited by his widow and young son, and in 1858 the widow married a barrister of the Inner Temple, Thomas Eyre Foakes, who had known Meredith since the old days in Charnock's office. Foakes's mother lived at Walton-on-Thames, not far from Halliford, and so the two young men remained in touch with each other during Meredith's married life. Now Mr and Mrs Foakes had a house on Weybridge Heath, near enough to Esher for visits, and Arthur Meredith became a playmate of Mrs Foakes's little boy, who was about the same age. The only lasting impression that George Meredith made upon this six-year-old observer was of his yellow dogskin gloves and his reddish whiskers.

When Foakes wanted to hire someone to write leading articles and a weekly commentary on the news, he offered the appointment to Meredith at £200 a year. His normal weekly stint was to be two columns of news notes and one leading article. He sometimes added a second, for which he was paid separately. No visits to Ipswich were required, and even a detailed familiarity with local conditions in Suffolk was not essential. Some of the work could be done at home, and on Thursdays he had to spend the day at Foakes's London office, putting his week's copy into final shape.

Although Meredith's views on many social and political issues were far from orthodox, he considered himself to be a Conservative, and therefore had no objection to the fact that his editorials had to reflect the politics of the paper, which was uncompromisingly Tory. He had a natural tendency to dogmatize and to assume authority on subjects with which he was not thoroughly acquainted, and this trait enabled him to compose fluent "leaders." Habits of generalization and pontifical assertion, inherent in editorial writing, insidiously grew upon him and were bound sooner or later to invade his novels.

Another new engagement was more remunerative. A rich and eccentric old lady, Mrs Benjamin Wood, who lived in Eltham, a Kentish suburb of London, offered him a snug salary, reported to have been £300 a year, if he would become one of her "gentleman readers." His duties were simply to come to Eltham Lodge for an hour once or twice a week and read aloud to her, with perhaps some discussion of literary topics to follow.

The widow of a Member of Parliament, Mrs Wood was a competent classical scholar who had privately printed several volumes of her poetry, essays, and translations. At this time she was about sixty-five years old and had acquired an amazing array of fads. Dressed in the modes of forty years before, she had lived in complete seclusion since the death of her husband, emerging only for a drive every day in her ponderous chariot. She had only once been in a train. The curtains in her handsome Georgian house were kept drawn to exclude the sunlight, and her servants were trained to walk noiselessly on tiptoe. No visitor was allowed to step on the polished floors; and to keep the carpets clean the gentleman reader was required to take off his boots in the front hall and put on a pair of slippers that were kept in the cloakroom.

Had she been no more than this bundle of crotchets Meredith would have found her intolerably boresome. But she was also an able and independent thinker. On religious questions she was an outspoken rationalist, and her literary taste was rigidly classical: apart from the Greek poets her chosen authors were Racine, Swift, and Addison. Her archaic diction and mannerisms encouraged Meredith to treat her with an elaborate courtesy that they both enjoyed, and her vigorous wit came into play in their arguments over literary points.

Toward the end of the year Meredith's make-believe romance with Janet Duff Gordon came to an end with the announcement of her engagement. In December she was to marry Henry James Ross, twenty years her senior, who had won her heart by his prowess in riding to hounds. He was an amateur archaeologist and head of a banking firm in Egypt, which meant that after the wedding she would leave England and go to live in Alexandria. Meredith gave utterance to his sorrow in a melancholy lyric. "My Poet," says Janet, "was very fond of music, and his favourite song was Schubert's 'Addio.' I complained about the commonplace German words, so he wrote for me the following verses, which have brought tears to many eyes":

> . . . *I dare not basely languish*
> *Nor press your lips to mine;*
> *But with one cry of anguish*
> *My darling I resign.*
>
> *Our dreams we two must smother:*
> *The bitter truth is here:*
> *This hand is for another,*
> *Which I have held so dear.*
>
> *To pray that, at the altar,*
> *You may be bless'd above—*
> *Ah, help me, if I falter,*
> *And keep me true to love!* . . .

After this *cri du cœur*, he displayed his devotion by helping her to select and order the large collection of books that she had asked Ross to give her, instead of jewels, as a wedding present. In due course she left her native land, to spend much of her long life abroad; and half a century later she wrote of her Poet that "he lives in my memory as the lithe, active companion who so often strode by the side of my cob over Copsham Common, brandishing his stick and talking so brilliantly."

At the beginning of 1861 Meredith's circumstances were better than ever before. He was drawing three salaries, and *Evan Harrington* as a serial and in book form—including the American edition—had brought him a good sum. There is a confident note in his letter to Lucas offering two alternative projects for the 1860 Christmas number of *Once a Week*. One was to show King Arthur listening to stories of the modern world; the other was to consist of tales told by a group of people stranded at a lonely inn by an accident to their coach. Still harping on the rivalry with Dickens's paper, he said, " 'The Old Stage Coach' will be more homely and easier; but we must be careful not to seem to be copying the enemy . . . I'm for the higher effort." And a little later, having submitted other short stories, he notified the editor that he expected to be paid at higher than the normal scale:

*If you do, I'll give you some very good stories, but I must have money . . .
As to those that I write for the occasion, they have not my stamp upon them,
and I would prefer not to append my name. In the matter of verse, also, I
shall rarely be able to give my time for the money I get for it.*

His ultimatum was not at all effective. The suggested Christmas
features never materialized; and of the two stories that he mentioned
in the other letter, only one, which he then called "The Highwayman,"
was printed in the paper. It appeared anonymously in the issue of
February 23, 1861, under the title "The Parish Clerk's Story," and he
was paid five guineas, the same rate per page as he received for "A
Story-telling Party" a year earlier. During the next twelve months he
contributed five poems, paid for at the same rate as his previous ones.

"The Parish Clerk's Story" was a complete departure from his usual
style. The events were narrated in the simple phrases of an elderly
villager, and were seen through his naïve eyes. It was a melodramatic
tale of a village girl's wooing by the squire's son, who, when disowned
by his father, became a highwayman. There was also the supposed
seduction of the heroine's cousin by another young gentleman. After
various misunderstandings it all came to a happy ending. The im-
probabilities of the trite plot were made all the more obvious by the
unvarnished and summary style in which it was presented; but the
story was not much worse than some of those that such masters as
Dickens and Trollope were publishing in the magazines in the same
decade. At that era the art of the short story was but little understood
in England.

In spite of the improvement in Meredith's finances, he was not
feeling satisfied. He thought for a while of giving up Copsham Cottage
and going to live in two rooms in London, so that he could save money
for Arthur's education. He was trying to push on with a new work of
fiction—indeed he had made a start with three different ones—but his
health was giving him anxiety. As in the days of his first troubles with
his wife, exasperation and nervous strain led to acute indigestion. In
November, 1860, doubtful whether he would be well enough to attend
Janet's wedding, he wrote to her, "I have been knocked down again
by the old illness. It's horribly dispiriting." And again, "On the earth
I lie, and imagination will picture the idea that I am going under it."
Similar gloomy allusions recurred through the winter and spring.

In the hope of stimulating his sluggish digestive system, he became
more and more fanatically addicted to long country walks. Captain
Maxse took a cottage at Molesey, close to Esher, and they undertook

"expeditions together on foot" into distant lanes and villages of Surrey, Sussex, and Hampshire. Maxse introduced Meredith to the sons of King Louis-Philippe, living in exile at Claremont Park. He found the two younger princes more charming than the eldest. "I never felt attracted," he used to say afterwards, "by the vague and slow intellect of the Comte de Paris. When he talked to me about making certain reforms when he should be re-established in his hereditary place upon the throne, I mentally hoped that he might never be seated there." Not long after their conversation, the young Count went off to serve in the Union Army in the American Civil War, and Meredith remarked, "He was courteous and kind to me here, and so I wish him well—and well out of it."

By coincidence, just at the time he met the Bourbon princes he became acquainted also with a scion of the rival dynasty, the Bonapartes. This was William Charles Bonaparte Wyse, whose father, Sir Thomas Wyse, an Irish landowner and diplomat, had married Letitia, the daughter of Napoleon's brother Prince Lucien. The Princess and her husband had separated seven years later; and Sir Thomas, who eventually became British ambassador in Athens, paid little attention to his two sons, who remained in France with their mother. While living in Avignon, Bonaparte Wyse became enthusiastic about the revival of Provençal language and poetry under the inspiration of Frédéric Mistral. He studied the dialect, composed poems in it, and was admitted to the Society of Félibres, who claimed to be the successors to the medieval troubadours. Wyse spent some of his time also in his native Ireland, where he became a captain in the County Waterford Militia and in 1855 high sheriff of the county. When Meredith met him he was thirty-five years old and was living at Guildford, twelve miles from Esher. Meredith was at once attracted by his Gallic charm and his literary enthusiasm. "He has nice tastes," he reported to Janet Ross, "and is an odd mixture of Irishman and Corsican."

They read their poems to each other and laughed together over "jokes improper to quote," as Meredith mentioned in one of the impromptu rhymes that diversified his letters to Wyse. Having expressed a liking for long walks, Wyse was bombarded with invitations in doggerel verse and Shakespearian prose to join Meredith and Maxse in their two-day and three-day outings. On occasions when he failed to keep a rendezvous he was reproached with melancholy eloquence or with mimicry of his Irish brogue. In one letter Meredith described a walk to Mickleham on which he had taken Keats's *Endymion* with him in order to read it at the Burford Bridge Inn, where the last lines of it were written: "The nightingale saluted me entering and departing. The walk has made of me a new man. I am now bathed again in the Pierian Fount. I cannot prose." And with a half-serious note in his jesting, he begged Wyse to join him for a day in the "nightingale vale" of Mickleham: "We will have poetizing, no laughter, no base cynical scorn, but all honest uplifting of the body and soul of us to the calm-flowing central Fire of things."

Of the three books that Meredith was trying to write, he had made most progress with *Emilia Belloni*. Dealing with "a feminine musical genius," it was based on the character of Emilia Macirone, his friend of ten years before. In the interval she had lived for some time in Constantinople, where her husband had been sent as commissioner to administer the Anglo-French loan to Turkey during the Crimean War, and she had published a book of her experiences. Meredith had never lost his interest in her, and when writing to Janet Ross about his new book he reminded her that "I gave you once, sitting on the mound over Copsham, an outline of the real story it is taken from. Of course one does not follow out real stories; and this has simply suggested Emilia to me." He read some of the chapters aloud to Lady Duff Gordon, and she praised them.

To follow *Emilia Belloni* he was planning another novel, of which he told Janet, "I think it will be my best book as yet." His tentative name for it was *A Woman's Battle*; and it may possibly have been the same one that he was calling *The Dyke Farm* a few weeks later when he submitted the beginning of it to Lucas in the hope that it would be accepted for publication in *Once a Week*. If so, however, he was curtailing it, for *The Dyke Farm* seems to have been intended to run anonymously through only two or three issues of the paper, whereas *A Woman's Battle* had been described as "my next novel." He was working at the same time on a third piece of fiction, *Van Diemen Smith*, which he considered "weaker in breadth of design" than *A Woman's Battle*, but "interesting as a story." In the back of his mind he was also hatching the project of a new volume of poems.

Under this stress of composition, in addition to his regular employments, his health showed no improvement during the spring, in spite of the invigorating week-end walks. He complained to Wyse: "I must go somewhere soon; for my work is beastly . . . I am getting temporarily tired of my *Emilia*." He confessed that he had written only two chapters since reading Wyse the first part of the story. "The dawdling dispirits me."

Wyse was leaving soon to visit his relations on the Continent, and was pressing Meredith to join him there. Meanwhile, Meredith persuaded Lady Duff Gordon to learn Provençal so that she could share his ecstasy over Mistral's poems, which Wyse had given him. Always prone to enthusiasm over a new friend's work, he was urging Chapman & Hall to accept a book on Rabelais that Wyse intended to write.

He was not so favorably impressed with a project that was proposed to him by Dante Gabriel Rossetti. Still known chiefly as the leader of the Pre-Raphaelite painters and not as an author, Rossetti was in ecstasies about the biblical poetic drama *Joseph and his Brethren*, by Charles Jeremiah Wells, which had attracted no attention when first published, thirty-seven years before. He wrote to Meredith flatteringly about *Evan Harrington* and went on to propose that Chapman & Hall should bring out a new edition of Wells's play. "But a poem on a scriptural theme," Meredith demurred, "you know how little chance it has with the British public, be it never so good . . . *Sale*, as well as merit, is what we shall have to look to."

Rossetti's own work roused a warmer response in him. In a letter of May, 1861, he mentions meeting the painter in Fleet Street and going with him to his studio, where Rossetti gave him a copy of his *Early Italian Poets*, which was just off the press. "Some are perfectly exquisite," he reported to Wyse; "as for the translation, it is so good that he will rank as poet as well as an artist from the hour of its publication."

Late in May Meredith consulted his doctor, who told him that "the 'knot of the nerves' is irritated and has been long so. I must not smoke. I must not work." The first essential was a complete rest for six weeks, and then a holiday in the mountains. Meredith accordingly wrote to Wyse and proposed that they should meet in Switzerland or the Tyrol.

His affection for his son was a continual source of both joy and anxiety. Facing unhappily the prospect of eventually sending Arthur away to school, he tried to be with him as much as possible and to shape his character in the right molds. "At present he is not brilliant," he told Janet Ross, "but he is decidedly hopeful. I don't want to force him yet. I wish to keep him sound and to instill good healthy habits of mind and body. In writing, spelling and reading, in memory for what he acquires, few children surpass him. And he really thinks—without being at all instigated to think." On Arthur's eighth birthday they spent the whole day together in the woods. The thought of leaving him behind cast a gloom over the plans for a holiday abroad, and so eventually it was decided that the boy must come too; and while in Switzerland

Meredith would investigate a school at Hófwyl which had been recommended.

The stimulus of the prospective trip made him feel better quickly. Relieved of work on his novels, he applied himself happily to poetry. He finished the polishing of "Cassandra," a poem that had originally been intended for his first volume, ten years before. He "remoulded and made presentable" a queer piece entitled "Phantasy," a grotesque erotic nightmare that was linked in some obscure way with the theme of *The Ordeal of Richard Feverel*. And he composed one of his series of contemporary character studies, "The Patriot Engineer."

Departure was delayed until he could find someone to substitute for him on *The Ipswich Journal* and until Arthur was supplied with suitable knickerbockers. Luggage was confined to a knapsack. "I shall not bring a hat or a tail coat," Meredith warned his friend. At the beginning of July the father and son crossed from Dover to Ostend. The earlier part of the trip—by train to Coblenz and by steamer to Mainz—was familiar to Meredith from his German school days and his honeymoon tour; but when they went on to Zurich he was in new territory.

His first view of the Alps affected him deeply, as he reported to Maxse. "They have the whiteness, the silence, the beauty and mystery of thoughts seldom unveiled within us, but which conquer Earth when once they are. In fact they have made my creed tremble.—Only for a time." He soon realized that even these heaven-touching peaks were part of the unity of Nature, and not "a rebuke to us below." Thus he regained his tenet that "the error of all religions" has been "to raise a spiritual system in antagonism to Nature." The stainless summits were a symbol that "in you and in me there may be lofty virgin points, pure from what we call fleshliness."

Obeying his doctor's orders "to get much tonic glacier air, to pass many mountain passes, to keep to the high land," he and Wyse and the boy proceeded from Zurich to Munich, and on to Innsbruck, where they shouldered their knapsacks and walked to Landeck, taking three days on the road. Meredith began to be disillusioned in his companion:

Wyse does not walk in rain, or when it's to be apprehended; nor when there's a chance of nightfall; nor does he like it in the heat; and he's not the best hand in the world at getting up in the morning; and he's rather excitable. But still thoroughly kind and good.

At Landeck, Meredith was fascinated by the turbulent Rosanna River and wrote a poem about it, in the same surrealistic vein as

"Phantasy," the poem he had been working on before leaving England. He dedicated the poem to Captain Maxse, who seemed to him to resemble the river, "perhaps because it is both hearty and gallant, subtle, and sea-green." Arthur was left behind at Landeck to devote himself to butterfly-collecting, while the two men spent the next three days in walking on to Meran, in the South Tyrol. Meredith was astonished at the tropical heat: "The flies sting, and the sun is relentless. We drank at the wells every ten minutes, sat over the brooks naked legged, dipped our heads desperately."

His health soon improved, and he boasted of being able to walk thirty miles a day under the scorching sun without ill effects. "Nevertheless the nerves are not yet right." The immediate result was eagerness to resume writing: "I am very anxious to finish my 'Emilia'; and have gentle prickings about other matters in my mind." He pestered Evans with inquiries as to whether Lucas wanted him to go on with *The Dyke Farm*, and he announced that "I have an autobiographical story in view for O. a W. when Chapman's 3 vols. are out of hand."

Through miscalculation of his supply of money, Meredith by this time was totally out of funds. He had written to Evans from Zurich and to Chapman from Landeck, requesting advances of cash, but their replies did not reach him, and in Meran he found himself "dependent on a civil landlord for wherewithal to make merry abroad." At last a second urgent appeal produced twenty pounds from Evans, and he was able to move on.

As he reported later to Janet Ross, "The Alps gave me shudderings of delight; but I didn't see enough of them, and I can't bear being coop'd long in those mountain-guarded valleys; so I shot through them in two weeks." The fact probably was that he was glad of an excuse to get rid of his companion. Wyse bored him by asking sympathy for his financial problems: "The old boy is very desponding about his circumstances, and he won't buckle up to brave them." Besides, Wyse was deeply involved in an affair of the heart, and the lady had made her appearance on the scene: "Mrs W. is really in love with the Irish-Corsican. They spoon terribly. Perhaps I am getting old, for I don't envy them, though I feel a kind of emptiness—an uncared-for feeling. A good friendship would satisfy me." And Wyse was tactless enough to talk about Meredith's solitariness: "Wyse is lost in astonishment at me because I don't look out for a 'woman.' 'You're a pote, and I can't think how a pote can get on without one. I'd go mad.'"

Early in August the travelers crossed the Adige into Italy, which was seething with threats of revolt against Austrian rule. In Verona,

Meredith watched the white-coated Austrian troops with keen interest and admired their efficiency. Upon arrival in Venice Wyse went off to visit his mother at Como. This, Meredith confided to Maxse, "was a blessing, for somehow or other dear old Wyse isn't at all the right sort of companion . . . The fact is the dear old boy (meaning excellently) is irritable exceedingly: tiffs twenty times a day, and now and then a sulk. Then ensues reconciliation . . . You may imagine this sort of schoolboy business is not to my taste. When one does meet a woman, it's better to have her in petticoats."

Meredith reported that Venice was "a dream and a seduction to the soul of me." He learned to love Giorgione, Titian, and Paul Veronese; in spite of Ruskin's praise, he ranked Tintoretto lower. He planned to write an ode on the Campanile. He felt a thrill when his gondolier claimed that in his boyhood he had seen "Lord Birren." He discovered the exact spot on the Lido where Shelley had stood with Byron, as described in "Julian and Maddalo," and had seen the sunset through the bell tower on the island. "I have seldom felt melancholy so strongly as when standing there," he told Maxse. "You know how I despise melancholy, but the feeling came. I love both those poets; and with my heart given to them I felt as if I stood in a dead and useless time. So are we played with sometimes!"

He did not ignore the charms of the Venetian women: "They have a gracious walk and all the manner one dreams of as befitting them." And he exchanged amorous glances with a pretty girl who leaned seductively out of her window to admire him as he passed in his gondola. The exciting atmosphere of the place was heightened by the tension between the inhabitants and the Austrian garrison.

His enjoyment of the glamorous city was handicapped only by his duties toward his son: "I had to watch the dear boy like tutor, governess, courier, in one." Arthur didn't like art galleries and loved bathing in the warm Adriatic. Therefore his father saw fewer pictures than he wanted to, and every morning they both went to the Lido and spent an hour floating and splashing under enormous straw hats.

From Venice they moved on for a short stay in Milan, where the heat was even more fiery; then they went to the Villa Ciani, on Lake Como, to meet Wyse's mother, the Princess Letitia. Here Meredith threw himself gleefully into the drawing-room comedy of a counterfeit court. As Mme la Princesse insisted upon proper use of her royal title, and responded avidly to flattery, he had full opportunity of exercising the Continental courtesies that he had practiced in his youth under the tutelage of his Aunt Louisa. "She has no difficulty in swallowing a compliment," he told Janet Ross. "Quantity is all she asks for. A good gross compliment, fluently delivered, I find to be best adapted to a Frenchwoman's taste. If you hesitate, the flavour evaporates for them. Be glib, and you may say what you please."

With the Princess's handsome daughter Adeline he struck up a lively flirtation. The young lady sang to him and encouraged his attentions until her fiancé, General Stephan Türr, came in, whereupon she suddenly grew discreet. The general's young aide-de-camp, a dashing Hungarian, then began plying the matronly Princess with compliments and Meredith joined the contest. Praises of her shoulders and her bust, assertions that she was not eclipsed by her lovely daughter, grew more and more extravagant, and the Princess accepted it all complacently, and rewarded each of the competitors with a photograph of herself. General Türr produced some royal Tokay that had been given him by Victor Emmanuel, the newly proclaimed King of Italy, "and we were merry over it . . . Before dinner we all bathed in Como, ladies and gentlemen ensemble. Really pleasant and pastoral." Narrating these amusements in strict confidence to Janet, Meredith said, "I was vastly entertained. Look for it all in a future chapter."

Crossing the Mont Cenis, Arthur was so excited that he stayed awake all night in his father's arms in the *diligence*. A night's sleep at Macon restored them both somewhat, but the boy was now eager to be back in England, and was not interested in Paris, though his father found the city "delightful." Meredith reported regretfully that "under the circumstances, with a remonstrating little man, there was nothing for it but to return hastily. Thank heaven! I got him home, safe—a little worn: but he soon got over that."

The two months abroad had done much more for Meredith than merely improve his health. His German school days and his honeymoon trip had indeed shown him some aspects of Continental life; but now for the first time he had traveled widely and mingled with foreigners of all ranks, including the sophisticated international aristocracy. His interest in public affairs became more serious, his observation of social nuances more incisive; and his wit gained a fresh assurance based upon a wider perspective.

During this same summer Mary Meredith became seriously ill. Since her return to England, two years before, she had moved restlessly from one lodging to another, sometimes contriving to snatch short and secret interviews with Arthur when his father was away from home. She treasured such small belongings of the boy's as she had been able to retain, and carried a lock of his hair over her heart. She wrote

bitterly to her old friend Hogg that life was *"une froide plaisanterie."*
In moods of depression she talked much about death and declared that
the only inscription she wanted on her tombstone was Tennyson's
harsh lines:

> *Come not, when I am dead,*
> *  To drop thy foolish tears upon my grave,*
> *To trample round my fallen head,*
> *  And vex the unhappy dust thou wouldst not save . . .*

Often in tears, she would pace the floor of her lonely lodgings till she
wore out the vehemence of her grief.

Her final residence was at Grotto Cottage, Oatlands Park, Weybridge—the very town in which her early years with Meredith had
been spent. Disquieting symptoms of kidney disease were developing;
but when she stayed with her father early in August he considered that
she showed no sign of serious illness. Three days after going home, however, she wrote to him that her condition was grave, and when he
hurried to her he was shocked at the change in her appearance. Thereafter he was with her every day, while she grew steadily worse. Her
malady was diagnosed as "renal dropsy," a form of Bright's disease.

After Meredith came back from the Continent she sent him a final
appeal to come and see her; but again he refused. Emilia Hornby, who
had remained on friendly terms with both Merediths, then decided to
take matters into her own hands. With characteristic impulsiveness
she drove to Copsham Cottage late one evening to demand that Arthur
should come and visit his mother. Meredith would not let him go at
that moment, but he must have soon relented, for in a letter to Janet
Ross at the end of September he said, "Arthur is now at Weybridge
seeing his mother daily."

Meredith's circle of friendship had been widened by several congenial additions. He was already intimate with the family of George
Virtue, a publisher of art books, who lived at Weybridge; and Virtue's
daughter got married at this time to James Cotter Morison, a young
man whose social charm and diversified tastes made him widely
popular. He had inherited wealth from his father, the vendor of a
renowned vegetable pill; a boyhood in France had given him a cosmopolitan outlook; at Oxford he became a Senior Commoner of Lincoln
College; and he was an ardent admirer of books and authors. When
Meredith met him he was one of the group of able and independent-
minded men contributing to *The Saturday Review*. He was also deep

in the writing of an ambitious biography of St Bernard of Clairvaux, and before long he submitted the manuscript to Meredith for criticism. Morison was deeply under the influence of Carlyle; and in view of the accusations of obscurity and over-elaboration leveled against Meredith's own writing, it is ironical that he objected to Morison's turgid Carlylese. He read some passages from the manuscript aloud, exaggerating the rhetorical effects so mercilessly that at last the discomfited author jumped to his feet and declared he would abandon the whole undertaking. Meredith assured him, however, that only the manner was at fault, and so Morison went to work and rewrote the book in a more straightforward style.

About the same time that he met Morison, Meredith acquired another new friend. For the summer months of 1861 a house at Esher had been rented by a London barrister named William Hardman, who dabbled in journalism and photography. Meredith was immediately drawn to both Hardman and his pretty, musical wife. Hardman was a bluff, jolly man of Lancashire origin, plump and bearded, often accused of resembling Henry VIII. His voluminous journal, which was sent monthly to a friend in Australia, records his first impression that Meredith was "very clever, original, and amusing." Arthur is described as "one of the finest lads I ever saw . . . The boy is well worthy of his father's pride and affection."

Meredith took to Hardman for his sincere amiability, his liking for long walks, and his fund of Rabelaisian humor. They soon came to regard themselves as a secret Pantagruelian society to which a few choice spirits among their friends were eventually admitted. As to Mrs Hardman, Meredith decided that he could grant her "private's rank in Janet's Amazonian regiment, with chances of promotion," because she was "one of the rare women who don't find it necessary to flutter their sex under your nose eternally, in order to make you like them." Although he detested having his picture taken, and never was satisfied with the result, he allowed Hardman to photograph him.

Meredith's friendship with Rossetti was also ripening. He reported to Captain Maxse that Rossetti had lent him the manuscript of a book of original poetry, containing "some very fine things. He would please you more than I do, or can, for he deals with essential poetry, and is not wild, and bluff, and coarse; but rich, refined, royal-robed." Rossetti had been fascinated with Meredith's poem on Cassandra and volunteered to draw an illustration for it. Hence grew his lifelong unfulfilled project of a large canvas to be based on the pen-and-ink drawing that he made.

Through Rossetti, Meredith encountered Algernon Charles Swinburne, aged twenty-four, who had just settled in London to pursue his poetical career. In October, mentioning his recent poems in a letter to Monckton Milnes, Swinburne said, "my friend, George Meredith, has asked me to send some to *Once a Week,* which valuable publication he props up occasionally with fragments of his own." At the same time Meredith was notifying Lucas that he intended to bring "little Swinburne" to meet him, as "I think you will find him valuable."

Among Swinburne's current passions was the collecting of Border ballads, with a view to publishing a volume of them; and Meredith turned over to him the manuscripts of seven or eight that he had transcribed in his poetic apprenticeship. He listened to Swinburne's reading of his outrageous burlesque of a French novel about English society, *La Fille du Policeman,* and was enchanted with its farce and naughtiness; but of the young poet's serious talents he was doubtful:

*He is not subtle; and I don't see any internal centre from which springs anything that he does. He will make a great name, but whether he is to distinguish himself solidly as an Artist, I would not willingly prognosticate.*

In October Meredith spent a week in a quiet corner of Suffolk, "the Giles of Counties," as he called it; and on his emergence he received the news that his wife was dead. He mentioned it in a letter to Wyse in four words, and to Hardman he was not much more explicit:

*When I entered the world again I found that one had quitted it who bore my name: and this filled my mind with melancholy recollections which I rarely give way to. My dear boy, fortunately, will not feel the blow, as he might have under different circumstances.*

In spite of his taciturnity Meredith was deeply moved by the event. The pitiful story of his married life, which he had rigidly suppressed for three years, paraded through his mind and besieged him with terrible questions as to his degree of responsibility for the disaster. He was driven to embody the whole story and its moral crux in grim poetry, a more powerful and sustained work than any of his previous poems.

Throughout the autumn his two novels remained at a standstill while he devoted himself to verse, intending to publish a volume in the winter. His two peculiar poems, "By the Rosanna" and "Phantasy," appeared in *Once a Week,* though Lucas expressed doubts about them and wanted cuts. After "By the Rosanna" was printed, the editor told Meredith that readers were complaining they could not understand it.

Meredith replied unrepentantly that "I do my best always, and let it take its chance. I never publish anything that hasn't a meaning distinct to *me*, and not indistinct to fellows here and there. You will find by and by, that when taken altogether I am clear."

The Hardmans spent a week-end with him late in October, and Hardman's journal gives a good picture of his way of life:

*The heartiest of welcomes awaited us at the really humble cottage . . . Meredith is a man who abhors ceremony and "the conventionalities." After our first greetings were over we turned out for an hour and a half before lunch . . . The scent of the pine-woods, the autumn tints on the elms and beeches, the brilliant sunshine exalted us to a climax of ecstasy. We were children again. Luncheon on our return consisted chiefly of home-made products— bread, honey, jams, marmalade, etc., most delicious. Then came a general lighting of pipes and cigars, and off we started for another walk through lanes and wood to Cobham, a good six-mile business. We got back at five o'clock and dined at six. What appetites we had! Meredith's two other guests left at eight to walk home to Walton-on-Thames, and then we put a log of wood on the fire and sat down for a cosy talk . . . Up at seven, and away went Meredith and myself for a brisk walk of three or four miles, after taking a tea-cup of hot soup and a slice of bread. After breakfast, Meredith retired to work at his book of poems while we went to call on some friends in the neighbourhood. On our return he read to me the result of his morning's work—portion of a very pretty idyll called "Grandfather Bridgeman."*

For some reason he imagined just then that his poetry was more profitable than prose. "I am obliged to make money as I can," he told Maxse, "to meet these new claims on me, and so all my pieces must be published before they're collected." Informing Janet Ross that he meant to go to work on a long poem as soon as his volume of short pieces was out of the way, he felt a need of justifying himself: "If I have the power to do it, why should I not? I am engaged on extra pot-boiling work, which enables me to do this; and besides, I can sell my poems."

His confidence in his poetic power was strengthened by a letter from a stranger, the Rev Augustus Jessopp, headmaster of the historic Edward VI Grammar School at Norwich. Jessopp's immediate purpose was to remonstrate against a frivolous note in "By the Rosanna"; but most of the long letter was a eulogy of Meredith's other work. He said that he and some of his friends (Cambridge men, like himself) ranked Meredith next to Tennyson in poetic power; that the "enchantress" scene in *Richard Feverel* had made him ill for twenty-four hours; and that Meredith was one of the three men he had wished to see before he died—the others being the great scientists Humboldt and Bunsen.

Meredith was gratified by the unwonted praise, though he regretted that Jessopp found anything to admire in his first book of verse, which he was now making every effort to suppress—perhaps because of the dedication to his father-in-law as much as for the immaturity of the poems. He had destroyed the three hundred copies that remained unsold.

With some trace of self-pity, his reply to Jessop gave a statement of his literary creed:

*There is very little poetry to be done when one is severely and incessantly harassed . . . I have been virtually propelled into a practical turn, by the lack of encouragement for any other save practical work. I have no doubt that it has done me good . . . One result of my hard education since the publication of my boy's book in '51 has been that I rarely write save from the suggestion of something actually observed. I mean, that I rarely write verse. Thus my Jugglers, Beggars, etc., I have met on the road, and have idealized but slightly. I desire to strike the poetic spark out of absolute human clay. And in doing so I have the fancy that I do solid work—better than a carol in mid air . . . The worst is, that, having taken to prose delineations of character and life, one's affections are divided. I have now a prose damsel crying out to me to have her history completed; and the creatures of a novel are bubbling up; and in truth, being a servant of the public, I must wait till my master commands before I take seriously to singing.*

A yacht trip in November was only partially successful in improving his health and spirits. Every week he had to force himself to face the deadly sequence of mediocre manuscripts to be read for Chapman & Hall. On the rare occasions when one showed even a gleam of promise he was ready to offer encouragement. A collection of poems by Edwin Arnold, who had recently come home from India at the age of twenty-nine to find work as a journalist, elicited the opinion, "I should say this man will do something . . . He should wait till he has composed a poem likely to catch the public ear." *Alec Grange*, a novel by a twenty-year-old Scot, William Black, was found "promising," and Meredith advised, "Write very encouragingly. Don't lose sight of him." When the encouraging letter elicited a second manuscript, *James Merle*, Meredith wrote in person to the eager aspirant, telling him that the book "would not do," but giving suggestions for its improvement. Black revised the story and sent it back, but Meredith again had to decide against it, and it was brought out later by another publisher.

In contrast with these forecasts of success for writers who later fulfilled the predictions, he was positive in his rejection of one of the most egregious best-sellers of the century. Mrs Henry Wood's *East Lynne* came out as a serial in *Ainsworth's Magazine* during 1860–61; and William Harrison Ainsworth, being one of the best-known authors on Chapman & Hall's list, assumed that the firm would welcome his suggestion that it be submitted to them. Meredith, however, recorded his judgment in the strongest terms: "Opinion emphatically against it." Ainsworth was so horrified at the rejection that he called on the publishers again and insisted that they were making a mistake, the result being that Meredith was asked to read the story a second time. When he refused to alter his verdict, the head of the firm approved the rejection, "because he considered the tone of the book was not good for the general public." Mrs Wood found another publisher, who made a fortune out of it.

Meredith's dislike for the book was so inveterate that when it was favorably reviewed in *The Times* he wrote an angry protest to the critic, who was his friend Lucas:

*I have read [your notice] with almost less pleasure than the novel. It is (the novel) in the worst style of the present taste. What a miserable colourless villain, Levison; the husband a respectable stick; the heroine a blotched fool; all the incidents forced—that is, not growing out of the characters; and the turning-point laughable in its improbability. Why do you foster this foul taste? There's action in the tale, and that's all . . .*

Mentally comparing Mrs Wood's triumph with the public neglect of his own novels, he could not help feeling a sort of personal grievance against her.

As a change from the vexations of judging manuscripts, Meredith turned once a week with some relief to his other task of writing for *The Ipswich Journal.* The American Civil War was at its height, and at the end of 1861 the relations between England and the Federal government were perilously strained over the *Alabama* incident. Like many other Englishmen, Meredith was disposed to sympathize with the Southern cause; and as a strong English patriot he clamored for a defiant stand in the crisis. His two closest friends, though they represented opposite extremes of political thinking, were both of his mind:

Maxse, the Radical, was ready to postpone his impending marriage and go into active naval service at once against the Americans; and Hardman, the rabid Tory, loathed Yankees as fiercely as he loathed Radicals. It was no wonder that Meredith's articles were intemperate in their bias:

*Alas! with a President who cannot write grammar, and generals who lie to the public and snarl among themselves, and who all but turn tail to the foe, what can the North do but be abject and ask for a master?*

And when John Bright made a speech in Birmingham vindicating the American blockade, Meredith sneered in print, "We dub him Yankee and bid him goodbye."

As a sequel to the exchange of letters with Augustus Jessopp, the schoolmaster paid a visit to Meredith in December, and the two got along famously. Jessopp was a tall, handsome man with a lively sense of humor, and Meredith was delighted to find how liberal were his views on religious questions. Bitter controversy over the orthodox interpretation of the Bible was raging as a result of the recently published volume *Essays and Reviews,* which summed up the theories of "higher criticism." Jessopp was firmly with the modernist wing of his church, and Meredith thrashed out his own heterodox ideas in discussion with him. Jessopp, for his part, was so favorably impressed by the poet and his son that he offered to take on the full charge of Arthur's education at his own expense—an offer which Meredith's pride would not let him consider.

The intimacy with Hardman was also ripening. During December Hardman spent every week-end at Copsham Cottage, where he soon made the acquaintance of Cotter Morison. "Good heavens!" Hardman reported, "how he and I and Meredith did talk." Under Meredith's goading, Hardman had to improve his ability as a walker. After covering the five miles from Copsham to Weybridge in seventy minutes, and back at the same rate, he bragged, "smart walking for a man of my kidney, but I frequently do fifteen or eighteen miles at a stretch now."

On Meredith's weekly visits to London he usually saw something of Rossetti at his studio in Chatham Place. A note from Rossetti to Alexander Gilchrist, the art critic, in November, read, "Two or three are coming here on Friday evening at eight or so—George Meredith I hope for one . . . Nothing but oysters and of course the seediest of clothes." A few weeks later Hardman was taken by Meredith to Rossetti's house; he found the painter "a very jolly fellow, and we had a most amusing visit. I am going on Friday to his place again, to a social reunion of artists and literary men, short pipes and beer being, I am given to understand, the order of the day." At this party Swinburne was present, in outrageously assertive form; and Hardman, in spite of the lack of prudery in his own conversation, was disgusted with the young poet's eulogies of the Marquis de Sade.

Meredith's influence confirmed Hardman in a growing distaste for the law and an ambition to become a writer. Just as Meredith had used his connection with Chapman & Hall as a bait for persuading Janet Ross to translate a German history and Bonaparte Wysc to start a book on Rabelais, so he now decreed that Hardman was the very man to write a biography of William Cobbett, and he arranged an interview for his friend with the Chapmans, at which satisfactory terms were agreed upon. As it happened, neither this book nor Wyse's was ever completed.

Meredith had conferred on the portly Hardman the nickname of "Friar Tuck," while he himself naturally became "Robin." A variety of other nicknames and fantastic catchwords enlivened their inter-course. By January they were on such terms of mutual trust that Meredith confided some of the story of his marriage and its collapse. Not by any means, however, did they think alike on all points. Hardman describes their discussions:

*I come down in the midst of his many poetical rhapsodies with frequent morsels of hard commonsense. I interrupt him with a stolid request to define his terms. I point out discrepancies between his most recent sentence and some previous one. The consequence of this is that we get into long arguments, and it was only last Sunday, during one of our country rambles, that, in spite of the raw, inclement January day, we stopped a long time at a stile, seated on the top of which he lectured me, quite ineffectually, on his views of the future destinies of the human race.*

During the winter months Meredith was absorbed in the poem which grew out of his wife's death and all the memories it wakened. He called the component parts "sonnets," but some purists deny them the name, because each consists of sixteen lines. The general pattern, however, resembles that of the sonnet, and the whole group takes rank with the great sonnet sequences as a personal record of passion presented in a condensed and vivid series of emotional glimpses.

To some extent the actual experiences were changed, such as the circumstances of the wife's death—partly to disguise the autobiographical origin, partly to achieve dramatic intensity. The only major episode, however, which seems to depart from the real events is the cold-blooded affair of the husband with another woman, after he becomes aware of his wife's infidelity. There is the possibility that this, too, was a confession of what actually happened, though no corroborating evidence happens to survive. But Meredith probably invented the episode to give symmetry to the situation and also to make it typical of the artificial social complexities he intended to impugn.

As in his novels, but to a greater degree because of the extra compression of poetic technique, the story is told largely by indirection, the psychological reactions of the characters being depicted more fully than the external occurrences. A further difficulty for the reader arises from the absence of any names; after the second woman enters the story there is constant danger of confusion between the two "she's"— "Madam" (the wife) and "My Lady" (the friend). Even the references to the two male characters can be ambiguous, since the narrator sometimes uses the first personal pronoun, but elsewhere the third. Recurrent metaphors gave the whole poem unity.

For readers unacquainted with the real story underlying it, the action is not easy to decipher; and, once deciphered, it sounds like the plot of a conventional "problem" drama. This was merely the framework, however, on which Meredith displayed his interpretation of the ethical and psychological issues. The basic thesis was that neither the husband nor the wife was to blame. Both were helpless in the trap of their personalities. The man was egotistically wrapped up in his own concerns; the woman had never been allowed a chance to learn how to think for herself, and so was controlled by the primitive emotionalism that was the heritage of her sex. She could not realize that married love ceases to be solely a thing of the impulses and the senses, and becomes a mental union as well. But the husband was equally wrong in expecting her to continue to be his unquestioning adorer. Again and again he strove to see the situation rationally and to show tolerance toward the unhappy lovers; he reminded himself that he, too, had once indulged in an extra-marital escapade; but each time his reason was defeated by his feelings and he reverted to jealousy, hatred, and injured pride. With intentional cruelty he thwarted his wife every time she tried to reach an understanding with him.

As in *The Shaving of Shagpat,* a woman possessing intelligence and cool sense is contrasted with one who is both the exponent and the victim of uncontrolled impulse. The narrator draws spiritual sustenance from his Platonic affair with "My Lady," his charming friend, and yet he finds this no adequate substitute for sexual love. Meredith's doctrine was no ascetic one; as an apostle of obedience to the inflexible laws of Nature, he admitted the demands of the instincts; but he held that they must be joined with the restraints of the intellect.

Again the poem parallels *Shagpat* in that the central character finally learns self-control through his sufferings. In the last ten sections he achieves pity and forgiveness; but the tragic climax springs from the fact that his wife cannot comprehend his attitude, and kills herself in a blindly generous gesture of setting him free. Here at the end of the poem the wider application emerges: the misery of this couple arose from their impossible wish to retain the naïve sensuality of first love instead of growing into maturity and accepting inevitable change without regret.

> *Lovers beneath the singing sky of May*
> *They wandered once; clear as the dew on flowers:*
> *But they fed not on the advancing hours:*
> *Their hearts held cravings for the buried day.*
> *Then each applied to each that fatal knife,*
> *Deep questioning, which probes to endless dole.*
> *Ah, what a dusty answer gets the soul*
> *When hot for certainties in this our life!*

Unless there can be a fuller development of intelligence and mastery over the senses, Meredith believed, society is doomed to endless repetition of this needless tragedy.

While writing the poem he first gave it the ironical title of "The Love Match"; later it became "The Tragedy of Modern Love"; and finally it bore the brief and cynical name "Modern Love." He showed part of it to Rossetti, who pronounced it the best thing he had ever done; and Meredith began to have high hopes for the success of the book in which it was to appear. Remembering the accusations of moral laxity that had greeted his earlier books, he was aware that "Modern Love" might rouse an uproar. He seems to have asked Jessopp to obtain his wife's opinion, which was favorable. Meredith expostulated:

*Is she adapting her wisdom to the mind of the British matron, and of the snuffling moralist so powerful among us? . . . In the way of Art I never stop to consider what is admissible to the narrow minds of the drawing-room. But is it well to call up what is marked for oblivion? Isn't it a sort of challenge; and an unnecessary one?*

He circulated the poem also to Maxse, Hardman, and others, and he omitted at least one sonnet from the series, on Hardman's advice. As a warning to readers, respecting both the style and the moral problem, he prefaced the poem with a distich:

> This is not meat
> For little people or for fools.

The rest of the volume was made up mainly of his narrative poems and monologues on contemporary English scenes and types. Captain Maxse, whose literary taste was conventional, protested against the vulgarity of these familiar themes, but Meredith was determined to deal realistically with everyday life. The influence of Tennyson's rural poems was visible in "Grandfather Bridgeman," a sentimental story of Crimean War days which fell into abysses of triteness and prosiness, though Meredith said that it was "approved by friends who have heard it," and Hardman confessed that both he and his wife wept over it. Much in the same vein was "The Patriot Engineer." There was more humor and true pathos, with a touch of Browning's methods of characterization, in the monologues, "Juggling Jerry," "The Old Chartist," and "The Beggar's Soliloquy."

One of the last poems to be added to the collection stands apart from the others, though it has a close affinity with the "South-west Wind in the Woodland" of his first book. The new poem was called "Ode to the Spirit of Earth in Autumn," and again it is a rhapsodic description of the "glorious South-west" battling the woods in "a night of Pagan glee." It merges into a paean of the joy of Nature:

> For once, good souls, we'll not pretend
> To be aught better than her who bore us,
> And is our only visible friend.
> Hark to her laughter! who laughs like this,
> Can she be dead, or rooted in pain?
> She has been slain by the narrow brain,
> But for us who love her she lives again.
>     Can she die? O, take her kiss . . .
>
> Bacchante Mother! stern to those
> Who live not in thy heart of mirth;
> Death shall I shrink from, loving thee?
> Into the breast that gives the rose

*Shall I with shuddering fall?*
*Earth, the mother of all,*
*Moves on her steadfast way,*
*Gathering, flinging, sowing.*
*Mortals, we live in her day,*
*She in her children is growing.*

No previous English poet had ever hymned the creed of identification with Nature so rapturously or so frankly.

The poems were in type in January, but as late as March he was still discussing with his friends which pieces to include, and he had to report that "my book hangs a little. I am sick of the sight of it." And he undertook during this unsettled interval yet another engagement to work for pay. Maxse sometimes contributed to *The Morning Post*, and through him Meredith was introduced to the proprietor, Algernon Borthwick, who asked him to write for it. An addition to his income meant a further obstacle to creative work.

# CHAPTER

## VI

# *The House in Chelsea*

Now that he was a widower the question of his feelings toward women cropped up in his talk and his letters with fresh significance. A disillusioned attitude toward the sex was a natural outcome of the failure of his marriage. His supercilious remarks on the subject to Bonaparte Wyse having led the romantic Irish-Corsican to accuse him of misogyny, Meredith protested:

Women, my dear fellow, can occasionally be fine creatures, if they fall into good hands. Physically they neighbour the vegetable, and morally the animal creation; and they are, therefore, chemically good for men, and to be away from them is bad for that strange being who, because they serve his uses, calls them angels.

I respect many, I dislike none. I trust not to love one. For what if you do? Was there ever such a gambler's stake as that we fling for a woman in giving ourselves for her whom we know not, and haply shall not know when twenty years have run? I do blame Nature for masking the bargain to us. The darlings ought all to be ticketed. Nevertheless, I envy your state of mind with regard to them immensely.

This note of envy became clearer when Captain Maxse got engaged. The sight of his Quixotic friend boyishly and idealistically in love aroused disturbing emotions, and his almost paternal advice was interspersed with introspective remarks:

I am so miserably constituted now that I can't love a woman if I do not feel her soul, and that there is force therein to wrestle with the facts of life *(called the Angel of the Lord). But I envy those who are attracted by what is given to the eye;—yes, even those who have a special taste for woman flesh, and this or that particular little tit-bit—I envy them! It lasts not beyond an hour with me.*

And again, not long before the wedding:

*I wonder, now, whether any nice woman will ever look on me?—I certainly begin to feel new life. Also a power of work, which means money. There is evidently great folly kindling in me. All the effect of example!*

His women friends did their best to convert him. Mrs Hardman, in a letter to her friend in Australia, said she was endeavoring to prove to Meredith "that all women are not hypocrites and deluding actresses; we are not of those angels in the Honeymoon who turn into fiends before they have served an apprenticeship to matrimony." Under such pressures his cynicism on the subject was bound to totter.

His health was variable. The east winds of early spring always made him miserable, and in March he complained that he felt "as one who has run a gallant race ½ way to perdition." He was in good form, however, a month later, when Hardman gave "a very select dinner party" at his club, Rossetti being one of the two other guests. Hardman, as an expert in the matter of food and wines, boasted that "I flatter myself they never sat down to a better selected meal in their lives . . . We kept it up till 2:30, and Meredith (whom I with difficulty piloted through the Haymarket, he was so very rampant) came home and stayed all night with me." The Haymarket was the most notoriously disreputable area of London in those times.

The book of poems finally came out at the beginning of May, and on the eve of publication the author was able to say that it had "subscribed wonderfully well." He was looking forward eagerly to the first reviews, but they fell short of his expectations. *The Critic*, in a short notice, found the same qualities in Meredith's poems as in his novels—"much humour joined to very uncommon powers of observation and graphic painting." *The Parthenon*, since it was owned by his friend James Virtue and since the review was written by two other intimate friends, Cotter Morison and Stephen Hamilton, with aid from Hardman, naturally offered praise, proclaiming "the probable addition of a new original genius to the goodly company of England's poets." These trite compliments were acceptable, but the most influential journals had not yet spoken.

As May advanced, Meredith responded to the vitality of the spring-time. He rhapsodized to Hardman:

*The gorse is all ablaze, the meadows are glorious—green, humming all day. Nightingales throng. Heaven, blessed blue amorous Heaven, is hard at work upon our fair, wanton, darling old naughty Mother Earth.*

He had at last vigorously resumed the writing of *Emilia*, but he broke off for a week-end walking-tour with his friend. They left Copsham Cottage after dinner on a Friday evening, "enlivening the way with snatches of song, reminiscences of overtures, frequent bursts of laugh-ter, and absurd rhymes, as occasion suggested." After dark they reached the Running Horse Inn at Mickleham, arranged for their rooms, and strolled out to listen to the nightingales in the meadows beside the River Mole, while Meredith recited Keats's "Ode to a Nightingale." "We returned to our inn," says Hardman, "singing my music to Robin's madrigal addressed to myself, 'Since Tuck is faithless found,' amid renewed peals of laughter." Meredith had brought a bottle of capital brandy in his rucksack, and after "large potations" of brandy-and-soda, they went to bed about eleven; but as their rooms had a connecting passage they lay awake for an hour, shouting jokes to each other.

Having been wakened several times by rural sounds coming through his open window, Hardman was annoyed when his companion burst into his room at half past five, telling him to get up. He sent the intruder back to bed and they finally got up at seven. During the day's ramble they took lanes and footpaths whenever possible, and reveled in the landscapes and the "nutty smells" of the gorse. They went through Dorking, lost their way in consequence of Meredith's insist-ence upon seeking the birthplace of Malthus, and paused for ale and bread and cheese at the village inn at Shere.

After scrambles up and down steep hills, cruel to the portly Hard-man's lungs, they came to rest in a deep dell, where they lay and smoked their pipes while Meredith read extracts from a projected collection of aphorisms, "*The Pilgrim's Scrip*, by Sir Austin Feverel." Several more miles of tramping and view-gazing brought them to Guildford, a cold supper, and copies of the weekly papers, including *The Spectator* with a review of the poems.

The article was, in Hardman's phrase, "a regular stinger":

*Mr George Meredith is a clever man, without literary genius, taste, or judg-ment, and apparently aims at that sort of union of point, passion, and pictorial audacity which Byron attained in* Don Juan. *There is, however, no kind of harmonious concord between his ideas and his expressions . . . On the whole, the effect of the book on us is that of clever, meretricious, turbid pictures, by a man of some vigour, jaunty manners, quick observation, and some pictorial skill, who likes writing about human passions, but does not bring either imaginative power or true sentiment to the task . . . Meddling causelessly, and somewhat pruriently, with a deep and painful subject on which he has no convictions to express, he sometimes treats serious themes with a flippant levity that is exceedingly vulgar and unpleasant.*

The sonnet sequence, in the reviewer's opinion, was written "with occasional vigour, but without any vestige of original thought or purpose which could excuse so unpleasant a subject," and the poet "intersperses it, moreover, with sardonic grins that have all the effect of an intentional affectation of cynicism." After suggesting that a more accurate title would be "Modern Lust," the critic turned his attention to the other poems, in which he found "the same confusion between a 'fast' taste and what Mr Meredith mistakes for courageous realism, 'poetic Pre-Raphaelitism.' " The reviewer labeled most of the poems "a very thick solution of mental mud" and declared that much of the volume was "vulgar and tawdry."

Hardman comments that "Robin was naturally annoyed, for the review was most unreasonable, and was, in my opinion, written with a very decided personal bad feeling. Meredith did not agree with me in this, and eventually concluded that the review was written by a woman." The two friends did not let the onslaught becloud their pleasure. After supper they walked on through Godalming and put up for the night at a tiny inn near Milford, at which Meredith and Maxse had stayed during a similar tour a year before. Up again at seven, they were off after breakfast, "over heath and through hedges white with hawthorn bloom, most beauteous to behold." They climbed to the summit of Hindhead for the magnificent panorama over the Downs, and got to Haslemere in time for dinner at the White Horse Inn, "washed down by copious draughts of the best pale ale Meredith and I had ever tasted." There being no afternoon train from Haslemere, and Hardman having blistered his heels, they were reduced to the ignominy of hiring a chaise to take them to Godalming, where they caught the train for home.

Hardman's zestful description of this expedition displays Meredith in his most characteristic colors, walking indefatigably, talking and jesting and laughing without restraint, squatting on grass to smoke his pipe and invading rustic taverns for tankards of ale. Even if there was something almost pathological in this lust for physical exertion and primitive amusement and the lavish beauty of the English spring, it drew to him a band of friends who devoutly shared his enthusiasms.

Further reviews of *Modern Love* did little to counteract *The Spectator*. The one in *The Athenaeum* conveyed a similar distaste for the main poem, though in more temperate language: "The phases of the husband's torture are elaborately set forth, often with spasmodic indistinctness but now and then with real force and imagination." The style was described as "abrupt and obscure," the theme "morbid." Other poems in the book were found "more wholesome . . . free from the blemishes of caprice and obscurity"; but "Phantasy" and "By the Rosanna" came in for disapproval: "In poetry, even humour should not be prosaic and coarse, but Mr Meredith is both." The "Ode to the Spirit of Earth in Autumn" was praised for its "poetic feeling and truth of observation . . . But if these gifts are to produce a lasting result, Mr Meredith must add to them a healthier purpose, a purer taste, and a clearer style."

The poet's friend Maxse had undertaken to write the review for *The Morning Post;* but being away in Italy, he saw only an incomplete proof copy of the book, and his long article was in general terms. Meredith's loyal supporter, *The Westminster Review,* acclaimed his "freshness and vigour," but complained of "frequent roughness and occasional obscurity," and raised the inevitable moral protest: "It is unfortunate that the subjects of many of these poems are tales of guilt and sin, of women's temptation and fall."

After the *Spectator* diatribe, Meredith confessed that "I find, to my annoyance, that I am susceptible to remarks on my poems, and criticisms from whipsters or women absolutely make me wince and flush." He was disappointed at receiving no notice at all in *The Saturday Review,* to which so many of his friends contributed, but he found consolation in an encounter with Robert Browning, who said he was "astounded at the originality, delighted with the naturalness and beauty" of the poems.

A more doughty champion also appeared. Swinburne was so infuriated by the review in *The Spectator* that he sent the editor a long letter of protest, couched in his usual hyperbole. Terming Meredith "one of the leaders of English literature . . . a man who has won his spurs and fought his way to a foremost place among the men of his time," he went on:

*Praise or blame should be thoughtful, serious, careful, when applied to a work of such subtle strength, such depth of delicate power, such passionate and various beauty, as the leading poem of Mr Meredith's volume; in some points, as it seems to me (and in this opinion I know that I have weightier judgments than my own to back me), a poem above the aim and beyond the reach of any but its author. Mr Meredith is one of the three or four poets now alive whose work, perfect or imperfect, is always as noble in design as it is often faultless in result. The present critic falls foul of him for dealing with "a deep and painful subject on which he has no convictions to express." There are pulpits enough for all preachers in prose; the business of verse-writing is hardly to express convictions . . . As to subject, it is too much to expect that all schools of poetry are to be for ever subordinate to the one just now so much in request with us, whose scope of sight is bounded by the nursery walls; that all Muses are to bow down before her who babbles, with lips yet warm from their pristine pap, after the dangling delights of a child's coral, and jingles with flaccid fingers one knows not whether a jester's or a baby's bells.*

A week after the publication of this letter Swinburne and Rossetti spent a week-end with Meredith at Copsham. They arrived on June 14, following a visit from Edward Peacock and his son, who had stayed for several days to take part in celebrating Arthur's ninth birthday. The new visitors walked to Copsham from Esher, and when Meredith caught sight of them he saw that Swinburne was brandishing a pamphlet, with the gestures of a revivalist displaying a tract. As he drew nearer he could be heard declaiming sonorous poetry. It was a marvelous, unknown poem, he explained, which he had discovered in the twopenny box in front of Quaritch's bookshop. Though it was described as a translation from the Persian, its luscious melody and glowing phrases made it a masterpiece of English verse.

He was too much excited to go indoors, and so for hours the friends sat together on the Mound and read to each other the enchanting quatrains of Omar Khayyám. When the book had been printed, three years before, it had gained absolutely no attention; and as it was anonymous Meredith was unaware that its author was the uncle of his beloved Maurice FitzGerald. Intoxicated with the new music, the three poets stayed on the Mound till nightfall, paying no attention to the dinner bell; and after they finally went in for a meal they continued chanting the stanzas. Then Swinburne snatched paper, a quill pen, and a bottle of red ink, and within an hour wrote the first thirteen stanzas of "Laus Veneris," in the same pattern as the FitzGerald poem.

That evening on the Mound marked a turning-point in the fame of the *Rubáiyát*. Rossetti and Swinburne preached its marvels to all their friends, and within a few months it was becoming famous.

A different matter had been the proposed topic for discussion during the week-end at the cottage, and it eventually received attention. Although Rossetti had been a cheerful participant in Hardman's dinner party in April, he was actually going through a crisis of gloom. The beautiful tubercular wife, whom he had married only two years before, had committed suicide in February; and in remorseful grief Rossetti had buried the manuscripts of his poetry in her coffin. It was obviously bad for him to live alone, and so he was persuaded to rent a large house at 16, Cheyne Walk, Chelsea, in which the other members of his family could join him. "He also," says his brother, "particularly wanted to have Mr Swinburne in the same house with himself, thinking that, in his own depressed state of mind, he needed some inspiriting association such as he could scarcely obtain from mere family life, and that he could procure this better from Mr Swinburne than from any other available person."

On second thoughts it was realized that two shy sisters, an invalid mother, and an aged spinster aunt would scarcely be appropriate fellow-inmates with a pair of Bohemian poets who were cultivating "inspiriting association." Of Rossetti's family, therefore, only his brother, William Michael, actually joined the household, and the tenancy of the extra rooms was offered to Meredith.

Although he had become far too fond of the Surrey countryside to think of giving up Copsham Cottage, there were many times when the journey home at night was tiresome after a long day in town. If he stayed for a dinner party he had to beg some friend to let him have a bed for the night. He agreed therefore to rent a bedroom in Rossetti's "Queen's House" and to have the use of a sitting-room whenever he wanted to entertain guests. The inmates would have dinner and breakfast together. "We shall have nice evenings there," Meredith wrote to Maxse (still honeymooning in Italy), "and I hope you'll come."

He described it as "a strange, quaint, grand old place, with an immense garden, magnificent panelled staircases and rooms—a palace." His historical sense was gratified by the legend that it had been occupied by Sir Thomas More and afterwards by Catherine Parr and Catherine of Braganza; though in strict fact it had been built in the early eighteenth century, in the grounds of an old manor house that possessed some of these anterior associations. The modern distinction of the neighborhood was chiefly artistic and literary, as the Carlyles lived a few doors away, George Eliot and George Lewes just around the corner, and James McNeill Whistler in Lindsay Row, at the other end of Cheyne Walk.

Meredith was drawn to the Rossetti group because they despised social convention and because the Pre-Raphaelite doctrine insisted upon realistic frankness in art. But his nature had other facets, too, which resulted in friendships with men of diverse types, less temperamental than the Bohemian painters and poets.

One new friend was Lionel Robinson, who lived with his parents next door to the Hardmans in Bloomsbury. He was a perfect specimen of the urbane young dilettante that Meredith portrayed so often in his novels—imperturbable, witty, and self-indulgent. Meredith nicknamed him "Pococurante"—soon shortened to "Poco"—and derived endless amusement from his remarks.

Another young man was of a totally different sort. When Cotter Morison was a Senior Commoner at Oxford, his closest friend among the undergraduates was a talented, hard-working youth named John Morley, son of a North Country doctor. Now Morley had come to London to be a journalist, and with Morison's help had found employment on *The Saturday Review*. An introduction to Meredith followed in due course, and Morley's earnestness and ability impressed him deeply. Morley paid his tribute of gratitude more than half a century later, when he wrote his *Recollections*:

He, being ten years my senior, benevolently took to me, and extended a cordial, indulgent, and ever-faithful hand . . .

He came to the morning meal after a long hour's stride in the tonic air and fresh loveliness of cool woods and green slopes, with the brightness of sunrise upon his brow, responsive penetration in his glance, the turn of radiant irony in his lips and peaked beard, his fine poetic head bright with crisp brown hair, Phoebus Apollo descending upon us from Olympus. His voice was strong, full, resonant, harmonious, his laugh quick and loud . . .

His personality seemed to give new life, inner meaning, vivacity, surprise, to lessons from wholesome books and teachers, and to shower a sparkling cataract of freshness on them all . . . Loud and constant was his exhortation. No musical note from a lute, it was the call of the trumpet from live lips. Live with the world. No cloister. No languor. Play your part. Fill the day. Ponder well and loiter not. Let laughter brace you. Exist in everyday communion with Nature. Nature bids you take all, only be sure you learn how to do without. Even the trite commonplaces of conduct, set forth in all

*the tones of physical joy, as he strode over his own fir countryside, were
kindled in a new light as of planetary stars . . .*

*He lived at every hour of day and night with all the sounds and shades of
Nature open to his sensitive perception . . . To love this deep companionship of the large refreshing natural world brought unspeakable fulness of
being to him, as it was one of his most priceless lessons to men of dispositions
more prosaic than his own.*

*In the stillness of the country evening it was an experience both fascinat-
ing and edifying to hear his sonorous tones, as in a sort of plain-song he read
out to me chosen sections of the fine, profound, and subtle Modern Love, or
the genial and truthful Roadside Ballads, or some prose composition of the
finished day.*

The chilly reception of the book of poems drove Meredith back on
his prose writing with redoubled vigor. "What works I could throw
off," he complained to Maxse, "if I had the digestion of any of the
creatures that hope to be saved! I am fretted with so much in my head
that my hands can't accomplish." He heard enviously the gossip that
George Eliot was to receive £8000 for *Romola* ("Bon Dieu! will aught
like this ever happen to me?") After almost a year's interruption, what
he had previously written of *Emilia Belloni* did not satisfy him, and he
remodeled it completely, "making the background more original and
richer comedy." In July he read several chapters to the Hardmans when
they spent a couple of days with him.

New projects, however, competed for his attention. "I have a
comedy germinating in the brain, of the Classic order: 'The Sentimentalists.' I fancy it will turn out well." In fact, "I have an immense
quantity of work in store. Health is still weak and will never be much,
I fear, unless I can purchase two years' perfect rest and travel."

In August he reported that "a dreadful hitch in E. Belloni has been
distressing me of late. This day tides me over the difficulty." He was
just starting on a cruise in the Channel with the Morisons in the
Virtues' yacht, and he begged Hardman to write his week's articles for
*The Ipswich Journal* for him, so that he could accompany his friends
as far as the Channel Islands, instead of being put ashore at Wey-
mouth. "I have got a Pea-jacket and such a nautical hat, and such a
roll of the legs already."

For some months he had been unhappily aware of the fact that
sooner or later Arthur must be sent to boarding-school. Throughout
the summer he spent as much time with the boy as possible. Twice
they stayed in London for several days to visit the International Exhibi-

tion. The Jessopps continued to show an interest in the boy; Mrs Jessopp sent him a Bible for a birthday present, after the preliminary precaution of asking the father's approval. Meredith therefore wrote to Dr Jessopp in September to inquire about the steps necessary for Arthur's admission to Norwich Grammar School.

At this time he and Arthur were staying with a banker friend in Hertfordshire; and while they were there news arrived that the house-keeper's niece at Copsham had come down with smallpox, and that the cottage would be quarantined for two months. A hasty appeal to Jessopp brought a cordial response, assuring Meredith that he could bring his son to the school immediately, even though term had already begun; and they thoughtfully invited him to stay for several days, to soften the pang of parting. After a short visit to London to buy the boy some clothes (since most of his, and Meredith's own, were inaccessible at Copsham), they journeyed down to Norwich.

Meredith was so charmed with the kindly schoolmaster and his wife that he began to wonder whether he might somehow arrange to live near them. A household of sincere religious feeling combined with wit and wide-ranging intelligence was a new experience for him. In the evenings there was music and reading of Molière, with a pretty niece participating. Even the frequency of prayers was endurable in these surroundings, and Meredith reported gleefully to Hardman that he went "on his marrow bones 24 times per diem." The physical and moral health of the school filled him with satisfaction, and in his admiration for Mrs Jessopp he commented, "Does praying get us wives of this sort? If so . . ."

Jessopp took him to Cambridge for a couple of days while a meeting of the British Association was in progress, and Meredith was highly gratified at being supplied with the rooms and the gyp of an absent graduate of St John's, and at being invited to dine with Fellows. The hospitable Jessopps insisted upon his prolonging his stay in Norwich for more than a week. "They do not poetize me," he explained, "but honour me by treating me as simple flesh." Even though he had a temporary shock when Arthur fell from a seventeen-foot ladder during gymnastics in the school crypt, he went away in the assurance that he was trusting his precious son to the best possible hands. Just as he was leaving he was horrified to discover that in his ignorance of parental duties he had neglected to provide the bed linen, table silver, and other equipment that each boy was supposed to bring, and that Mrs Jessopp had silently contributed them herself. He sent apologies in rhyme— an amusing parody of "Lady Geraldine's Courtship"—and took the opportunity to inquire in confidence, "Do you find him such a darling 'tis no wonder that I dote?"

On his return to London he spent several days with Cotter Morison. Characteristically he was eager to show off his newly won familiarity with the Bible, and a group of his friends were convulsed to hear him citing "The Book of Micaiah," and quoting the text of a sermon as being, "And Jesus said, 'When ye think most of yourselves, then are ye least worthy.'" Though his hearers were far from being orthodox Christians, they recognized the blunders. "We all roared," says Hardman, "he himself as heartily as anybody."

By this time the house in Cheyne Walk was ready for occupancy. Of the four men who were to share it, only William Michael Rossetti had anything like an equable temperament. He was to be present for three specified days each week, and Meredith was normally to come only for Thursday nights. The younger Rossetti's description of his fellow-tenant hints at the lack of congeniality that was soon to develop:

Mr Meredith had a fine well-chiselled face, more noticeable, perhaps, for mould of feature, and for the air of observant intellect, than for the expression of indulgent fellow-feeling: an Italian would have called him "bello" rather than "simpatico." It is the face of a man not easily hoodwinked by the shows of the world. My brother was wont to say that Meredith bore a rather marked resemblance to the busts of the Emperor Hadrian; I think he improved upon them.

Meredith's association with the Bohemian household in Chelsea aroused misgivings in his former friend Holman Hunt, whose increasing religious fervor had led to a break with Rossetti and his lax companions. "When I was told Meredith was about to take up his residence with Rossetti in Cheyne Walk," he says, "I recognized that this combination would be an obstacle to the increase of my intimacy with the novelist at the time."

Meredith may have spent a few days at Queen's House toward the end of October, after which Copsham Cottage was again open to him. He celebrated his return to the heath by chopping down trees and sawing up the logs, as a new device for promoting circulation and improving digestion. He also derived benefit from a wet compress on his stomach. Before long he sliced through his boot and gashed his toe, but he still vaunted his "carpentering" as "great exercise." A few weeks later, however, he discovered a substitute that pleased him even more—an eighteen-pound iron weight on the end of a wooden bar.

which he swung, tossed in the air, and caught by the handle. He called it "the beetle," and thereafter his letters often lauded his "wondrous tricks" with this instrument. Another specific was to sally out at dawn and walk many miles without having eaten anything, the result often being that when he came back for breakfast he was too weary to digest his food, and therefore suffered new discomforts when he tried to fix his mind on writing.

No contribution of his had appeared in *Once a Week* for many months. A short story, "The Friend of an Engaged Couple," which survives in manuscript, has notations showing that Lucas accepted it, but for some reason it was not printed. Nevertheless Meredith continued to have a close association with both Lucas and Evans. In December he made a definite agreement to supply a serial for the paper as soon as he finished writing *Emilia Belloni*.

He had been waiting eagerly for the end of Arthur's first school term, and through most of the Christmas holidays the boy's wishes held priority over all else. In order that "Sons" might enjoy the merriment of a family Christmas dinner, an invitation to the Hardmans was accepted, though Meredith was full of forebodings: "I plunge with knowledge aforethought into a week's dyspepsia. I shall be ridden all night by a plum-pudding-headed hag: shall taste the horrors without the vacuity of Death!" For the next night, Hardman had asked father and son to the theatre; a farce at the Strand was rejected in favor of a pantomime, on Arthur's decision, and the two adults had to sit through a stupid performance at Drury Lane, with a riotous gallery mob, while the boy was ecstatic over it all.

For the middle of January Meredith had reluctantly agreed to go on a week's cruise in the Channel in a new yacht just bought by Cotter Morison. As might have been expected, there were violent gales, and much of the time was spent in harbors of Jersey and Guernsey. Meredith had the humiliation of being occasionally seasick, but during the intervals at anchor the party was very merry. The cook was excellent, and the time between meals was spent in smoking and playing whist. "Meredith showed a remarkable talent for revoking," says Hardman. "We only played for penny points, so there was no harm done, only great amusement was caused . . . It is impossible to reproduce the chaff, the laughter, the extempore verses of our poet. Robin was in wild spirits when he was not squeamish, and he composed numerous extempore verses on the voyage."

He returned to Copsham for another week with "Sons," ending in a heroic day's outing in London: "Expedition over Bank and Tower.

Thence to Pym's, Poultry: oysters consumed by dozings. Thence to Purcell's: great devastation of pastry. Thence to Shoreditch," the station for the Norwich train. "Never mind, Papa," was Arthur's calm farewell; "it's no use minding it. I shall soon be back to you." Only when all these distractions were at an end could Meredith resume the struggle with *Emilia*. "I hope to finish this dreadful work in six weeks," he wrote optimistically to Wyse; "then I shall be free to disport."

During the early months of 1863 his life followed its established routine. At the middle of every week "George Pegasus, Esq., goes into harness and understands what donkeys feel when they are driven." Thursday was always "Black Foakes Day," spent glumly in "Foakes-den," grinding out his copy for *The Ipswich Journal*. He slept at Cheyne Walk, and the next morning he put in his spell of duty at Chapman & Hall's, in Piccadilly. There were frequent dinners with the Hardmans, or the Chapmans, or Evans and Lucas of *Once a Week*. If there was unfamiliar company at one of these affairs, he had a tendency to talk glibly on subjects he did not know enough about. Hardman chronicles an example, when one of the guests was Mrs Atkinson, widow of a noted explorer and herself the author of a newly published book, *Recollections of Tartar Steppes*:

[Meredith] *was in high spirits, and talking fast and loud . . . G. M. asserted (I know not on what authority) that the view from the Hindhead was very like Africa. Mrs Atkinson pricked up her ears, and bending forward across the table asked in a clear but low voice: "And pray, sir, may I ask what part of Africa you have visited?" . . . No one could be more amused at his own discomfiture than he was himself, and he gave a very vivid description of his sensations when he saw Mrs Atkinson preparing the inevitable inquiry.*

His letters at this time had fallen into well-defined patterns, depending on the personality of the recipient. A different facet of his nature was shown to each correspondent. With Jessopp he was carrying on a running argument over asceticism, which he strenuously condemned for its animosity toward beauty. His manner in these letters was emphatic, flexible, metaphorical. To Maxse, whose health was giving him trouble, there were blunt, didactic disquisitions on the virtues of regular exercise and intelligent diet (with avoidance of beer, new wine, and too many vegetables). Hardman received innumerable notes of exuberant banter, adorned with comic rhymes. Meredith assumed, for example, an immense admiration for Hardman's mother, whom he dubbed "The Great Mother of the Pantagruelians," and this led him to the theory that she was actually Venus in disguise, and that therefore Hardman must be an adult Cupid, a legend which he embroidered to his heart's content.

The Morisons had gone off to the Mediterranean in their yacht and were importuning Meredith to join them there. But he was determined to push on with the interminable *Emilia*, so that he could make a start on the projected serial for *Once a Week*. Apparently he was in greet need of money; in a letter to Wyse he mentioned "voracious creditors," and other letters indicated that he was thinking about building a house. "I am overwhelmed with disgust at *Emilia*," he confessed in March. "Am hurrying her on like Ye Deuce. She will do. But, ahem!—she must pay. I have taken some trouble with her and really shall begin to think her character weak in this respect, if she don't hand in what I think due, speedily."

Arthur, home for the Easter holidays, came down with measles, and Meredith had to be up at all hours of the night to ply him with barley water. His quarantine was made the pretext for keeping him at home beyond the end of the vacation, and he was at last sent back to school reluctantly. "What strange dispensation is it," Meredith wrote to Jessopp, "which gives you my boy for the best portion of his young years?"

Having lasted for about half a year, the house-sharing arrangement in Chelsea now came to an end. Holman Hunt, writing forty years later, declared that Meredith told him "that he never slept at Queen's House"; but it is likely that, if such an impression was really ever conveyed, Meredith was merely humoring Hunt's antipathy to the Rossetti circle. Undoubtedly, however, the intimacy of living together, though for only one day a week, had soon got on Meredith's nerves. His fastidious ways and ironical attitudes were totally incompatible with the irregular habits and emotional extravagances of the other two poets. His addiction to ridicule, on such matters as the green eyes and carrot hair that Rossetti bestowed upon all the women in his paintings, was not likely to gratify the victims of his banter. William Michael Rossetti afterwards reviewed the situation in discreet language:

*Meredith and Rossetti entertained a solid mutual regard, and got on together amicably, yet without that thorough cordiality of give-and-take which oils the hinges of daily intercourse. It would have been difficult for two men of the literary order of mind to be more decisively unlike . . . Even in the mere*

*matter of household-routine, [Meredith] found that Rossetti's arrangements,*
*though ample for comfort of a more or less off-hand kind, were not conform-*
*able to his standard . . .*

   *Meredith had a far wider interest in life and society, the actual transac-*
*tions of men and women in their relations ordinary or exceptional, the inter-*
*action of characters and motives, than either my brother or myself had . . .*
*He understood, and liked to understand, many things to which I was mainly*
*indifferent—to some of them, as for instance everything connected with the*
*ordinary politics of the day, my brother was much more indifferent than*
*myself . . . The early termination of his sub-tenancy in Cheyne Walk was*
*due, not to any disagreement with anyone, but, on his own part, to finding*
*that practically he made very little use of the rooms, and, on Rossetti's part,*
*to a perception that, as his money-affairs continued to improve, his original*
*wish to abate the expense of his household had come to count for very little.*

   A similar impression is given by a comment which Meredith contributed anonymously to Joseph Knight's biography of Rossetti:

*I liked him much, though I was often irritated by his prejudices, and his*
*strong language against this or that person or subject. He was borné, too,*
*somewhat, in his interests, both on canvas and in verse, and would not care*
*for certain forms of literature and life which he admitted were worth caring*
*for. However, his talk was always full of interest and rare knowledge; and he*
*himself, his pictures, and his house, altogether, had I think an immense in-*
*fluence for good on us all.*

   There were many complicating factors. Swinburne's uncontrollable
behavior, especially when he was tipsy, was hard to endure; he was
apt to fly into ferocious tantrums or to take off all his clothes and
caper wildly through the house or slide down the banisters; and a year
or two later even Rossetti could no longer tolerate his vagaries. Then,
too, Rossetti's own lack of financial sense was disquieting to one who
was contributing to the upkeep of the house; the day the tenant handed
over his rent for the month, Rossetti was likely to go out on an orgy of
buying old china and to come home penniless. On the other hand,
Meredith was so short of funds that he was not always prompt in
making his payment.

   While it lasted, the association was productive of much merry-
making, as artist friends were in the habit of dropping in at Queen's
House at all hours. Meredith used to say afterwards that some of their
gatherings in the garden were so noisy that Mrs Carlyle sent a message

that her husband was being distracted by the uproar, even though a number of houses stood between. Whistler was often in and out; and in spite of the similarity in their sarcastic wit, he and Meredith got along remarkably well. "I never had a dissension with him," Meredith testified, "though merry bouts between us were frequent. When I went to live in the country, we rarely met. He came down to stay with me once. He was a lively companion, never going out of his way to take offence, but with the springs in him prompt for the challenge." Another intimate member of the group was Frederick Sandys, a Pre-Raphaelite painter and typical Bohemian, who seldom had a penny in his pocket, and borrowed money from everyone without any prospect of repayment, but who always wore a freshly starched white waistcoat and airily alluded to "five hundred" as his minimum fee. One of Sandys's reminiscences was of a day when he went to Hampton Court with Rossetti, Meredith, and Swinburne, and each of the three wrote a poem in the train between Waterloo Station and their destination.

Various legends became current with regard to the actual circumstances in which Meredith finally broke with his housemates. Ford Madox Brown's version was that the other two became so distressed over a cracked old pair of boots, which Meredith always left outside his door to be cleaned, that they bought a new pair of the same make and substituted them for the old ones, whereupon Meredith left in high dudgeon. This is too like a famous anecdote about Samuel Johnson's college days to be plausible. Whistler's story was that Meredith talked to a cabman on the corner about a disagreement that he was having with Rossetti, and Rossetti was enraged when he heard about it. At dinner that night he declared that anyone who could thus blurt out confidential matters to a cabbie was no gentleman; and to emphasize his disgust he slapped down a serving-spoon into the dish of meat in front of him, and squirted gravy into Whistler's face. In the midst of the confusion Meredith got up and stalked out of the house. This version has a close resemblance to the one that Wilfrid Meynell retailed, claiming Rossetti himself as his source. While they were sitting at table together, Meredith said something that roused Rossetti's annoyance. "If you say that again," growled the painter, "I will throw this cup of tea in your face." Meredith said it again, Rossetti threw the tea, and Meredith (as in all the other stories) marched out of the house and sent for his belongings later in the day.

A more widespread tale was that on the last morning of the joint tenancy Rossetti came down to a late breakfast and "devoured like an ogre five poached eggs that had slowly bled to death on five slabs of bacon," and Meredith left the house in disgust and did not return.

It is true that he protested against Rossetti's peculiar meals, but his objection was not on aesthetic grounds. Holding fanatical opinions about health and diet, he lectured many of his friends on the subject, and Rossetti was no exception. Five years later, in a letter to Hardman, Meredith said:

*Poor Dante Rossetti seems to be losing his eyesight, owing entirely to bad habits—a matter I foretold long ago: Eleven a.m. plates of small-shop ham, thick cut, grisly with brine: four smashed eggs on it: work till dusk: dead tired on sofa till 10 p.m. Then to Evans' to dine off raw meat and stout. So on for years. Can Nature endure these things? The poor fellow never sleeps at night.*

Here, obviously, is the factual basis of the legend. But in its more malicious form it was bandied about in print until Meredith felt impelled in the last year of his life to issue a public refutation:

*What I must have said to some friend was that Rossetti's habits were ruinous to his health, and I mentioned the plate of thick ham and fried eggs, taken at once on the descent from his bedroom. I ventured to speak to him of the walk of at least a mile before this trying meal. But he disliked physical exercise, and he was wilful, though he could join in a laugh at his ways . . . On no other subject have I spoken of this dear fellow but with the affection I felt—sometimes playfully with regard to his peculiar habits, I daresay; never in the gossip's manner.*

The other stories may be similarly exaggerated accounts of occurrences that contributed to the friction between the two. A more credible explanation of their parting is to be found in a scene described by both Whistler and Sandys. It occurred at a dinner that Rossetti had given in honor of some of his patrons. Meredith was in particularly brilliant form, and directed many shafts of wit at Rossetti and his pictures; and the artist was so mortified at being ridiculed in the presence of clients that he asked Meredith to terminate his tenancy. This dinner was probably the one given on April 30, 1863, at which Meredith and Swinburne were present, the guest of honor being a Newcastle lead merchant who had bought paintings of Rossetti's, and two or three other art patrons being included.

Two months later, however, Meredith was still paying his share of the rent, and had no idea that he was out of favor. In a note to William Rossetti, dated June 27, he said:

*Owing to an absurd confusion of dates in my mind, I had fancied the day of debit was this following week. I will bring you the money on Monday, and pray say to Gabriel everything in my excuse. I can conceive now that my recent absence from the house must look odd to him.*

The only conclusion to be drawn from the conflicting testimony is that a series of disputes and temporary coolnesses convinced both Meredith and Rossetti of their thorough incompatibility, and that the arrangement between them was quietly allowed to lapse. It was certainly at an end before August, when Rossetti mentioned in a letter to William Allingham, "I see hardly anyone. Swinburne is away. Meredith has evaporated for good, and my brother is seldom here."

Even if there ever was some sort of dramatic tiff faintly resembling any one of those cited above, Meredith's withdrawal from the house-sharing compact did not put an end to all friendship. As late as October, young George du Maurier, an adoring disciple of Whistler's, wrote with a touch of jealousy, in a letter to a friend: "Jimmy [Whistler] and the Rossetti lot, i.e., Swinburne, George Meredith, and Sandys, are as thick as thieves . . . Their noble contempt for everybody but themselves envelopes me, I know." The anecdotes of fights and door-slamming exits had conversational value, but the ascertainable facts shed a better light on the good sense and good manners of the household.

# CHAPTER

## VII

# *Second Marriage*

WHEN Arthur's summer holidays began in July, father and son went to Seaford to spend a week with a jovial party, including Maurice Fitz-Gerald and his brother Gerald, Frank Burnand, Samuel Laurence (a well-known portrait-painter), and a young friend of FitzGerald's, Henry Mayers Hyndman, an undergraduate at Trinity College, Cambridge, who was playing in the Sussex county cricket matches. Long afterwards Hyndman wrote his recollections of the "laughing, chaffing crew who, with the sons of the chief local landowner, were making merry at one of the few decent houses on the front, or at the New Inn."

*Meredith was almost as jolly as Burnand . . . He delivered himself without effort or artifice of all the really profound and poetic and humorous thoughts on men and things that welled continually within him . . . It was on one of these occasions, when we were all sitting together on the beach, tossing stones lightly into the sea, and Meredith was discoursing with even more than ordinary vivacity and charm, that Burnand suddenly came out with, "Damn you, George, why won't you write as you talk?"*

In Meredith's own report of the visit he said that he was there "as an animal. Our life is monstrous." He expatiated upon the huge meals and the games of loo that lasted until sunrise. Later in the summer he went to the Goodwood races with the same party and had a glimpse of high life: "We elbowed dukes, jostled lords, were in a flower-garden of countesses." He backed the wrong horses and lost five pounds; but it was all justified on the novelist's usual plea: "saw much life, which I wanted." The group stayed at the Dolphin Hotel in Chichester, and young Hyndman one day got into a playful wrestling bout with Meredith. "I was then strong and active," he says, "and thought I was pretty good at a rough-and-tumble, but he wore me down by sheer endurance. The only two men I ever met of similar physical characteristics are E. B. Mitchell, the famous old Oxford athlete, and Cunningham Grahame. Meredith was physically the equal of either of them, and he was always in training."

The Hardmans were touring Switzerland and France, and Meredith had been eager to go with them; but after prolonged indecision he had discovered that "I cannot get the reading and Foakes both done . . . Chapman must have some MSS immediately read. On the whole, I do see that it's the right thing for me to work straight on this year." Lucas was demanding the beginning of the new serial for the end of October, but Meredith doubted whether he could possibly obey, "and my last chapter of Emilia to retouch and the proofs." The book was being set up in type at last, and he intended to hand the proofs around among his friends for suggestions.

At the end of July he was relieved to learn that a serial by Tom Trollope had been accepted by *Once a Week*, which relieved him of the immediate pressure; but at the same moment he was asked to become reader for the firm of Saunders & Otley, which had been bought by C. Warren Adams, a friend of Lady Duff Gordon; and he decided to accept, even though it would have to be kept secret, since his acting in this capacity for two rival publishers would be questionable. "I never refuse work," he told Hardman defensively.

He suffered a shock to his nerves when Arthur, out alone on the Common, was offered a ride on a friend's horse, fell off, and was dragged for fifty yards. If his foot had not then pulled out of his boot, he would probably have been killed. Meredith was in a frenzy of anxiety for several days, before he was assured that no damage had been done. When the school term began, in the middle of August, "Sons" had recovered and was sent back to Norwich; but his father was so unmanned that he decided to take his postponed holiday on the Continent, leaving his new friend John Morley to write his columns for *The Ipswich Journal*.

After a pause at Rouen to interview an author on behalf of Chapman & Hall, he reached Paris in time to meet the Hardmans on their homeward way. Two days were devoted to sightseeing with them— the Louvre, the Panthéon, the Hôtel Cluny, Versailles, St Cloud, the Bois de Boulogne, and dinners at famed restaurants. Then Meredith went on to Grenoble to join his friend Lionel Robinson in some strenuous Alpine walking. Their first day's journey took them to the Grande Chartreuse. The next morning, supplied with nine bottles of liqueur, they set off to "toil over mountain passes" into Dauphiné. Walking at least ten hours a day, and sometimes thirteen, they crossed the Col de Genèvre into Italy, as far as Turin; then to Lago Maggiore, and back into Switzerland over Piedmontese mountains, to Geneva. "We went too fast," Meredith admitted. "We trudged like packmen. Still, I have much enjoyed the trip: am better, fresher." The friends separated at Dijon, and Meredith returned to Paris for "four days of delight," probably less orthodox than the two he had spent there with Mr and Mrs Hardman.

*Emilia Belloni* was now being circulated among his friends for their opinion. Captain Maxse, as conventional about women as he was revolutionary in politics, was horrified by an episode in which the heroine accepted Captain Gambier as her escort. "Every girl," he expostulated, "is conscious that she should never trust herself alone with a man." As the chief purpose of the book was to show the intuitive rightness of Emilia's unconventional actions, Meredith was exasperated. "So," he grumbled to Hardman, "the sentimental worshipper will always make them animals—with the finger of a fixed thought from their birth upward (and pressing more and more consciously) directed upon a certain spot. But we know, we libertines, coarse boys that we are." Though he rejected this protest of Maxse's, he acknowledged "the soundness of some of his criticism and the value of his advice."

Hardman's objections were on a different matter, "an absorbing tendency which possesses him for indecent *double entendre*. I am determined he shall not offend the public taste, if I can help it." Meredith agreed to leave out the obnoxious passages. Most of the revision, however, was not prompted by the advice of friends but by the author's own determination to achieve distinction of phrase. In later years Swinburne told various people that he had seen the first draft of *Emilia*, which was then written in "pure, sweet, Thackerayan English"; and that in his opinion it had been ruined by being "translated" into an artificial idiom. While there may be a touch of mischievous exaggeration in this reminiscence, as Swinburne was no longer on intimate terms with Meredith when he recounted it, there probably was a basis of fact.

All the delay and rewriting caused Meredith intense distress. In the course of three years the characters had come to life in his imagination and insisted upon behaving according to their own natures instead of conforming to the plot. "To him they are living beings," Hardman noted; "I know he has felt them as such for the past twelve months." His problem was complicated by the fact that his mind was already focused on a sequel, *Emilia in Italy*, for which the present novel must adequately prepare. Hence his letters throughout the winter were full of lamentation. "My fastidiousness," he told Mrs Jessopp, "has made me turn from my new work to cut to pieces four printed chapters of Emilia (who begins to dissatisfy me totally, as do all my offspring that have put on type)." At the beginning of November he was "dejected about this novel." A month later he said that it was impossible to tell "what difficulty I get myself into by altering my original conception of the scheme." To Mrs Jessopp, at the end of December, he wrote, "Of Emilia I cannot speak. She grieves me. I have never so cut about a created thing." And to Jessopp, on a foggy mid-January day:

*I am not all right. Emilia Belloni is not all right. She has worried me beyond measure, and couldn't expect to be all right. She will be, when she's in Italy. As to character, I think you will have no doubt of her flesh and blood. How you will like the soul of the damsel, I can't guess.*

A further complication lay in the financial arrangements. The story was set up in type before any agreement as to terms was reached with Chapman & Hall. In October he appealed to the practical Hardman for advice: "Do you think that, as novels go now, I may fix for something huge? or content me with a medium, and, snuffling a low content, say Such is the world? Or, if I can't get my price, take all the risk?" He eventually offered the alternative to Chapman, who welcomed this way of avoiding the large payment that the author asked for. "It's my undertaking," Meredith reported somewhat apprehensively, not long before the publication date, "the risk mine and the uncounted profits."

In spite of the current crisis in the American Civil War he was hopeful for an edition in the United States, and sent the proof sheets to Harper & Brothers, with an ingratiating letter:

*Mr James Virtue tells me that Evan Harrington made no mark among you. The present volume is of a different texture, and will not moreover offend as The Ordeal of Richard Feverel is said to have done. I think you refused to publish that; and though I have received testimony from certain of your countrymen that it was not distasteful to them, I must allow you to be the best judges of the saleable quality of a book . . . I have had offers previously*

*from Mr Fields, of Boston, but prefer, if possible, to have my books repub-*
*lished by the gentlemen who first made my name known in America.*

He went on to suggest that they might be interested in *The Shaving of*
*Shagpat:* "The taste, I am told, is growing to it gradually."

He had learned that before long Copsham Cottage was to come
on the market; if he could make enough money he might buy it and
remodel it so that he could entertain friends in some comfort. For
this reason, he told Mrs Hardman, he was confining himself to prose:
"When I write a verse I say, 'so many lines, so many leagues from your
cottage, my lad!' "

His letters to the Jessopps were full of loving concern over Arthur.
They reveal a pathetic conflict between his desire to regard his son as
a paragon and his realization that the boy was not exceptionally endowed:

*If you are only anxious as to his mental briskness, I am not alarmed; and I*
*know also that he "potters" and plays after his own fashion and is not a bois-*
*terous fellow. But I am always open to fear for his physical health. His circula-*
*tion is not rapid, his stomach is weak . . . I told you that his powers of ac-*
*quisition would not be marked. But you will find by and by that he has sucked*
*in much and made use of it in his own way. He will never be a gladiator: but*
*he may be a thinker: I expect him to be a man of sense.*

Such comments were interspersed with detailed suggestions about his
diet, the virtues of cod-liver oil, and the inspiriting possibilities of light
claret diluted with seltzer water.

The days of Meredith's own boyhood were suddenly revived in his
mind at this juncture. After fourteen years in South Africa, Augustus
Meredith was able to retire and come home. When his son's literary
fame penetrated to that distant region Augustus had felt natural
paternal pride, to the extent of lending copies of the first books to
some of his customers; but *Evan Harrington,* appearing serially in
*Once a Week,* pained him by its attitude toward the family. Augustus
and his wife settled quietly in Southsea, and thereafter George Meredith saw them occasionally, though rather on terms of duty than of
cordiality.

His varied anxieties engendered a mood of depression that found
unwontedly candid utterance when he was apologizing to Janet Ross
for the infrequency of his letters:

*I, who let grief eat into me and never speak of it (partly because I despise the sympathy of fools and will not trouble my friends), am thereby rendered rather weak of expression at times. The battle is tough when one fights it all alone, and it is only at times that I awake from living in a darker world. But I am getting better, both in health and spirit.*

Few of his friends were ever allowed to catch a glimpse of this hidden sadness. To them he always radiated vitality and merriment. Less than two weeks before writing the letter to Janet, he had dined at the Garrick Club with Maxse. Thackeray, who was to have joined them, was ill and could not come; but the evening produced a rich crop of anecdotes about Thackeray's Rabelaisian wit, and when Meredith arrived at Hardman's, where he was to sleep, at one in the morning, he was "full of fun and spirits" and ready to retail all that he had been hearing. Barely five weeks later he was "startled and grieved" by the news of Thackeray's death—"I, who think I should be capable of eyeing the pitch-black King if he knocked for me in the night!"

Friendly relations with Rossetti still survived in January, 1864, when Rossetti was painting Arthur's portrait, though this picture, like many others from the same brush, remained unfinished, and there was probably only one sitting, since even as far as it went the painting was largely taken from a photograph.

A permanent result of Meredith's association with Rossetti and Swinburne showed itself in the novel he had been writing. *Emilia Belloni* was saturated with enthusiasm for the cause of Italian freedom, and the projected sequel was to be even more ardent in the same devotion. It is true that the Rossetti family were not actively interested in the political upheavals of their fatherland; but they provided a rich study in the Anglo-Italian artistic temperament, which was the keynote of the novel. And on the political side Meredith was thoroughly infected with Swinburne's fanatical worship of Mazzini. He became acquainted with Mme Emilia Venturi and her sister, Mrs James Stansfeld, who were the chief English friends of the exiled patriot. One of Meredith's pro-Italian friends arranged to introduce him to Mazzini; but at the last moment some piece of bad news from Italy threw the refugees into such distress that the interview was postponed, and never took place. In the spring of 1864 there was an uproar over the Greco conspiracy to assassinate Napoleon III, in which Mazzini was accused of complicity; and capital was made out of his connection with Mrs Stansfeld, as her husband was a junior lord of the Admiralty. Meredith's excitement over the affair was recorded by Hardman, who despised Mazzini and admired Garibaldi and Cavour: "He and I have had several arguments, and I never saw him so angry as he was the other night. During the day or so before I had been poking him up with, 'Well, Meredith, what do you think of Mazzini now?' and such-like chaffy queries. He has often endeavoured to induce me to believe in Mazzini, but I have always resisted."

The political background of the novel was therefore thoroughly topical when it came out, early in April. The title was finally fixed as *Emilia in England*. The writing of it had occupied something like four years, with long interruptions and heartbreaking revisions, and the author was by no means confident about it. "The novel has good points," he told Jessopp, "and some of my worst ones. It has no plot albeit a current series of events: but being based on character and continuous development, it is not unlikely to miss a striking success." As a sequel was to follow, the story had no real conclusion. "Poor little woman!" he wrote to Maxse, "what will the British P. say to a Finis that holds aloft no nuptial torch? All she does, at the conclusion, is to leave England." And in the week of publication he said, "I foresee that I shall get knocks on the head from reviewers, and should like to be out of hearing for 3 months, but Courage!"

The central theme of the book was described by Meredith to Janet Ross as "a contrast between a girl of simplicity and passion and our English sentimental, socially-aspiring damsels." To strengthen the contrast he had taken liberties with the circumstances of his model, Emilia Macirone. The real-life Emilia was well educated and of good social status, whereas her counterpart in the novel was brought up in a London slum, the daughter of an intinerant musician, and owed her poise and intelligence wholly to innate gifts. For the fiery Italian patriotism of his heroine, Meredith probably borrowed from another Emilia of his acquaintance, Mme Venturi, who, as Emily Ashurst, had been Mazzini's secretary while he lived in London and had translated his writings into English. In the very week when *Emilia in England* was published, Meredith took enough time away from his other tasks to proofread the first volume of a collected edition of Mazzini's writings, which Mme Venturi was seeing through the press.

As a study of a socially ambitious family the novel dealt with a later stage of the process observed in *Evan Harrington*. That book had shown the simple antithesis of a small-town tradesman's family and the county landowers of the early nineteenth century. In mid-Victorian times the situation had grown more complex. Mr Pole was a wealthy

London businessman, owning a handsome suburban estate; his son was an officer in a good regiment and his daughters were models of refinement. But there was still a sense of insecurity. The girls were ashamed of their father's blunt manners and the boy lacked convictions and self-reliance. In Meredith's view they were victims of the new malady of the middle class—sentimentality. In revulsion from the crudities of their forebears they had cultivated artificial etiquette and "fine shades" as a substitute for emotions. The cult of Pre-Raphaelite aestheticism was satirized in the Pole girls with their persistent patronizing of the arts.

Emilia, of course, was utterly beyond their comprehension. The three Pole ladies cultivated her in the hope of winning social prestige through her marvelous voice, but they were shocked by her candor; Wilfrid Pole fell in love with her exuberant vitality but miserably failed to perceive her spiritual altitude. In depicting Emilia, Meredith achieved the rare success of making artistic genius believable. Emilia's childlike innocence and intuitive wisdom, her physical and emotional energy, her moods of exaltation and misery, add up to a memorable picture of the born artist.

The large cast of characters was portrayed with varying effectiveness. Mr Pericles, the Anglo-Greek impresario, was a successful blending of grotesque comedy and sincere feeling, and Tracy Runningbrook was a friendly vignette of Swinburne. It was necessary for the theme that the Misses Pole should not be sharply differentiated, since their true natures were concealed under standardized attitudes. Mrs Chump, however, a vulgar comic figure of the Dickens model, is out of keeping and the reader is apt to be embarrassed by her antics. The morbid Purcell Barrett does not ring true; and Merthyr Powys and his sister, whom Meredith intended his readers to admire, are too perfect. As usual, Meredith assigned Welsh lineage to his favorite characters: Merthyr and Georgiana were supposed to represent genuine sensibility and refinement in contrast to the poses of the Misses Pole, and to represent civilized emotional restraint in contrast to Emilia's primitive impulses. Above all, Merthyr's altruism was set off against Wilfrid's selfishness. But they are so perfectly controlled and so elegantly cultivated that they seldom become more than gentle voices uttering beautiful generalities.

More than once Meredith fell into his habit of presenting important scenes obliquely, through sketchy references by other characters; and he paused repeatedly to utter disquisitions in which he elaborated pet phrases and metaphors interminably, such as "Hippogriff," the horse symbolically ridden by sentimental lovers. Well aware that this tendency was inimical to the book's popularity, he took occasion to announce again his objective in writing novels:

*Right loath am I to continue my partnership with a fellow who will not see things on the surface, and is blind to the fact that the public detest him. I mean, this garrulous, super-subtle, so-called Philosopher, who first set me upon the building of THE THREE VOLUMES, it is true, but whose stipulation that he should occupy so large a portion of them has made them rock top-heavy, to the forfeit of their stability. He maintains that a story should not always flow, or, at least, not to a given measure . . . He points proudly to the fact that our people in this comedy move themselves,—are moved from their own impulsion,—and that no arbitrary hand has posted them to bring about any event and heap the catastrophe. In vain I tell him that he is meantime making tatters of the puppets' golden robe—illusion: that he is sucking the blood of their warm humanity out of them.*

And later he declared that total exclusion of the Philosopher "would render our performance unintelligible to that acute and honourable minority which consents to be thwacked with aphorisms and sentences and a fantastic delivery of the verity."

As in the preceding novels, there were unforgettable scenes that compensated for any vagaries: Emilia's battle of wills with Mr Pole in his office; her nightmarish flight through the London underworld; the love scene with Wilfrid by Wilming Weir; and the lovely culminating "Frost on the May Night." And in spite of some disproportion, Meredith never lost sight of his central theme—the "ordeal" of Emilia. A series of shocks and disillusionments transformed her youthful arrogance into wise maturity. Like Shibli Bagarag and Richard Feverel (and like Carlyle's Teufelsdröckh) she went through a spiritual death and was reborn with an absolute acceptance of "the eternal yea."

A few lukewarm reviews greeted the book, the best being by Richard Garnett in *The Reader*. He spoke of the "display of intellectual pyrotechnics" in Meredith's novels and called them "the best modern representatives of the genteel comedy of a hundred and fifty years since."

*It might easily be surmised that Mr Meredith experienced considerable difficulty in arraying his thoughts in their appropriate garment of speech, and that the frequent harshness of his exposition was the evidence of a victory won by a vigorous growth over an unkindly soil. Thus rich, original, strained,* and artificial, the general effect is very much that of a fine landscape seen through tinted glass—a pleasing variety, so long as there are plain windows in the house.

One critic considered the book important enough to justify an extensive survey of Meredith's novels in a serious quarterly. Justin McCarthy was a young Irishman on the staff of a London paper. He says in his *Reminiscences* that at that time "Meredith was not known to the general public at all. He had a small circle of enthusiastic admirers scattered here and there among English readers. Wherever you happened to go you were sure to meet a man or a woman to whom the reality of George Meredith's genius was an obvious and a positive fact . . . We of the very, very select group, most of us quite unknown to each other, who had read *Richard Feverel* and gone into delight over it, were perfectly certain that the novelist we fancied we alone had discovered, or at all events had been the first to discover, would come one day to the front and receive the world's full recognition."

McCarthy suggested an article about him to John Chapman, editor of *The Westminster Review.* Though Chapman, as a friend of George Eliot and Lewes, "knew Meredith intimately" and "had an immense admiration of him," he was reluctant to accede. The article, nevertheless, entitled "Novels with a Purpose," came out in the July issue. It was the first general analysis of Meredith's qualities:

*His works, as a whole, reveal undoubtedly the operations of a mind endowed with great and genuine power; of a quick, sensitive, feeling nature; of a rich and sometimes a prodigal fancy, of an intellect highly cultured, and matured by much observation . . . But the intellectual man predominates in them; and therefore they are no great works of fiction. The fusing heat of emotion which melts the substances of a novel into one harmonious and fluent whole is wanting . . . He is too much of a thinking man; he needs the spirit which abandons itself wholly to the work, becomes lost in it, and has for the time no arrière-pensée, indeed no individual existence apart from it. The critical faculty is too strong in him, and therefore, even when he begins to grow earnest, he forthwith sets about to analyze this very earnestness, and it naturally vanishes in the effort.*

During the months while *Emilia* ran the gantlet of criticism, Meredith was facing a crucial decision in his personal life. In the previous autumn he had made the acquaintance of an Anglo-French family named Vulliamy at Mickleham, a few miles from Esher. Of Huguenot origin, the family had lived in England for several generations, and

Justin Theodore Vulliamy's wife was English; but his active career had been in France, where he owned woolen mills, and his children were born in that country. The eldest daughter married a French army officer with an estate in Dauphiné, and the three sons took over the family industry in Normandy when their father retired. After their return to England Mrs Vulliamy died, and the widower settled down with his three unmarried daughters in a spacious old country house amid a pleasant atmosphere of musical and literary interests. If it were not certain that the first draft of *Emilia in England* was already completed at the time Meredith met the family, it could be suspected that they were portrayed clearly, though unkindly, in the Pole girls and their father.

Soon after their first meeting, Meredith lent them *The Ordeal of Richard Feverel*, though with misgivings that it might shock them; and he explained that he would be happy to walk over and call on them, without expecting to be offered a bed: "As to my walking back at night: I am an associate with owls and nightjars, tramps and tinkers, who teach me nature and talk human nature to me." The two elder sisters gained his admiration for their sincere religious belief and their practical work among the poor of their neighborhood, which had won them the enmity of the conventional local rector. The youngest, Marie, who was twenty-four, played the piano exquisitely; and though she talked little, Meredith began to realize that she was "intensely emotional."

His growing interest in these sweet, earnest young women made a breach in his misogyny. In January he surprised his friends by going to a ball at Esher, which bored him unutterably and left him with a bad cold and upset stomach, to the sardonic amusement of "Old Parsimony," as he nicknamed his housekeeper: "You changed thick breeches for thin, thick socks and boots for them capering patents, and out in that there frost, and then wonders you feels aches in your bones and calls it indigestion." Three days later he walked over to see the Vulliamys, taking Arthur with him; and in order that the boy should not get tired the father carried him on his back most of the way home and had to hire a fly for the last two miles, none of which was a good remedy for chills and fever.

Marie Vulliamy's gentle charm was in his mind when he wrote to Maxse, early in the spring:

*I progress excellently, but only to get into a higher circle of desires and hopes, despairs and dreams. And if a fair face touches me, what is there for me but to moan at my loss of philosophy? Can I go to her and say, "Love me"? She sucks my comfort from my life, and that's all. Or, not all! It's experience!—for this were we born. My philosophy distils again to just that bitter drop.*

His financial condition was not auspicious for marriage. He was in arrears with Arthur's school fees and had to petition Jessopp to wait until a month after the publication date of *Emilia,* in the hope that a first payment of profits might then be forthcoming:

*Nothing but my carelessness puts me behind in my money accounts. I make, apart from novels, enough for Arthur and myself. It comes and goes. If this novel does not pay well, I shall retrench rigidly, book my bills, deny friends, have no purse, and look above the head of the crossing-sweeper.*

Improved health and his sudden desire for funds impelled him to scatter his energy in half a dozen directions. "I regret to say," he admitted to Janet Ross in December, "that I can't give up writing poetry, which keeps your poet poor." Four months later he detailed his undertakings:

*Now that Emilia's off my mind, alas! poetry presses for speech! I fear I am, unless I make great effort, chained to this unremunerative business for a month or so. I am getting material for the battle-scenes in Emilia in Italy. But I have an English novel, of the real story-telling order, that must roll off soon and precede it. Minor tales, too, and also an Autobiography. Which is to be first, is the point, and while I hesitate comes a "Wayside piece," a sonnet, a song; ambition says, "Write that grand Poem." I smile idiotic and should act with all due imbecility but for baker's bills and Boy.*

What he called the "Autobiography" was a novel written in the first person, intended to fulfill his long-standing promise of a serial to *Once a Week.* In May he described it a little more definitely as " 'The Adventures of Richmond Roy, and his friend Contrivance Jack: Being the History of Two Rising Men,'—and to be a spanking bid for popularity on the part of this writer." In this month he was also at work on Odes to Garibaldi and Beethoven.

Meanwhile, in April Marie Vulliamy had been on a visit to friends in Norwich, and Meredith contrived to be staying with the Jessopps at the same time. He had brought plenty of work to keep him occupied while the boys were in school; but he found time to go "Cathedralizing" with the young lady. They traveled back to London in the train together, "alone in the carriage the entire length of the route," as he reported coyly to Jessopp; "and really it is hard, for a young lady demands all your resources to amuse her: and I wonder whether I did!" By this time he had no doubt that he was genuinely in love.

Life took on an unfamiliar rosy glow. "I am in the best of spirits," he told Hardman in May. "Health is good and so is power to work, and one can't pray for more." Through Maxse's nomination he was elected to the Garrick Club, the haunt of London's choicest wits and epicures. His young friend Harry Hyndman invited him to Cambridge for a fortnight as his guest in his rooms in Rose Street. "I believe he had a thoroughly good time," Hyndman says:

I had become accustomed to his incisive methods of expression, and the strange way in which he would of a sudden turn into ridicule about half of what he had said seriously just before. But my undergraduate friends did not know what to make of him . . . . He never seemed to be conversing on the same plane as themselves, clever fellows as some of them were, and I am confident that the lack of sympathy arose from the artificiality I have noted. For Meredith fully enjoyed and entered into the untamed fervour of youth just entering upon its physical and intellectual emancipation. Though no judge of oarsmanship or games, he took pleasure in looking on at rowing, cricket, racquets, and sports of all kinds, being himself always in training and very much stronger muscularly than he looked. In fact he was all wire and whipcord without a spare ounce of flesh upon him . . . And so Meredith saw Cambridge, looking in when possible at the lecture-rooms, lounging round the backs of the Colleges, watching the boats on the Cam, seeing much of interest in the Colleges and libraries, going down to Ely and running over to Newmarket.

It was perhaps a token of his new discretion that on this visit to a race meeting he did not bet. "I wanted to study the scene," he explained.

As Frederick Sandys's home was in Norwich, Meredith got better acquainted with him during visits to the Jessopps than in the hectic atmosphere of Cheyne Walk, and liked him for "a romantic turn that lets me feed on him" and "the quaintest stolid Briton way of looking at general things." Sandys came to stay at Copsham Cottage late in April and remained for many weeks, working on a painting of "Spring" and taking long walks with his host. Sandys in later years praised Meredith's brilliance as a talker but added that "it was at the expense of his friends. [He] often had three or four friends dining with him on Sunday and, if the humour seized him, would select one of the company and dissect him for the benefit of the others. It was like taking a butterfly, pinning it, still alive, to the wall, and examining every quivering detail. This lost him many friends." While Sandys was at the cottage they started negotiations with *The Cornhill Magazine* for a series of Meredith's "wayside pieces" with illustrations by Sandys. These could subsequently form a volume which, Meredith hoped, would prove popular.

In spite of reviewers' "slaps" at *Emilia in England,* he was able to report that "she moves, which is good. A favourable touch to her in the 'Saturday' or 'Times' would launch her into more than the middle of a 2nd edition." He was pushing on rapidly with the sequel, and felt that he ought to take a trip to Italy for local color. He expected to finish the novel in the autumn, and thought it might be accepted as a serial by *The Cornhill.* As Mrs Jessopp had complained of too much analytical comment in the previous book, he sent her assurances that *Emilia in Italy* would be "all story; no philosopher present; action, excitement, holding of your breath, chilling horror, classic sensation."

Although he had realized during the days of sightseeing with Marie Vulliamy in Norwich that he was thoroughly in love with her, he hesitated for two months before making a formal proposal, for he was aware that his poverty was only one of his handicaps. Justin Vulliamy was not only a successful businessman who despised improvidence; he was also a devout Christian of strict moral principles. The shadow overhanging Meredith's first marriage implied all sorts of impropriety. The suitor's chief problem was how to prove his respectability.

His first step was to appeal to his loyal friend Hardman, who was a man of means and a pillar of his community. Though Meredith had previously confided to "Friar Tuck" the main outlines of his unhappy marriage, he now told him the whole history of his life, which he had never divulged so fully to anyone. "I have much to pass through," he wrote to Maxse, "in raking up my history with the first woman that held me. But I would pass through fire for my darling." Hardman commented to his friend in Australia that it was "a curious and painful story," but he was left with an unimpaired conviction that Meredith would "make her a good husband." He summed up the matter by saying, "he *was married* before, he is going *to marry* now: you will understand the difference between the active and the passive." Hardman acted as Meredith's envoy to the young lady's father, and managed to overcome his objections.

"I have written of love," Meredith rhapsodized in a letter to Maxse, "and never felt it till now." To this romantic friend he could express his feelings in a vein that he would otherwise have scorned as sentimental. "When her hand rests in mine, the world seems to hold its breath, and the sun is moveless. I take hold of Eternity . . . There could not be a fairer, sweeter companion, or one who would more perfectly wed with me. She tries to make me understand her faults. I spell at them like a small boy with his fingers upon words of one syllable. Of course some faults exist. But she has a growing mind and a developing nature. Love is doing wonders with her."

He explained that she was very fond of Arthur, "not in a gushing way, but fond of him as a good little fellow whom she trusts to make her friend." She was eager to meet the intimates of her future husband and he besought them to write to her first, so that she would not feel shy when she saw them. Wyse, who was too far away to be introduced, received a word picture of her: "She is a very handsome person, fair, with a noble pose, and full figure, and a naturally high-bred style and manner such as one meets but rarely . . . When I do love, I love hotly and give the heart clean out of me. She does likewise . . . I trust I may have strength, as I have honest will, to make her happy."

To Jessopp he wrote in almost religious terms: "Me she fills with such deep and reverent emotion that I can hardly think it the action of a human creature merely. I seem to trace a fable thus far developed by blessed angels in the skies. She has been reserved for me, my friend. It was seen that I could love a woman, and one has been given to me to love."

He was full of good resolutions regarding practical affairs. "To speak materially, marriage will not increase the expenses of a man hitherto very careless . . . I know that I can work in an altogether different fashion, and that with a wife and such a wife by my side, I shall taste some of the holiness of this mortal world and be new-risen in it. Already the spur is acting, and health comes, energy comes. I feel that I can do things well, and not haphazard, as heretofore." As Marie had an income of £200 a year, and would have more after her father's death, she was independent of a husband and would not "be leaning on a literary reed." At the lowest estimate he ought to be able to earn eight hundred a year, "and I shall now hold the purse-strings warily."

He felt certain that his literary work would be benefited by his new frame of mind. "There is an end now to my working with puppets," he declared. "I enter active life with my people, and my resolve to merit money,—which should mean, to make it." He did not, however, trust solely to the possibility of increased profits from his books. He bearded the Chapmans to propose that he would increase his attendance at the office in Piccadilly to three afternoons a week, would write all the letters about manuscripts, and would even interview authors whenever it was imperative, though on the stipulation that his name must not be divulged to them. For all this he expected that his salary would be raised to £300, or £250 at the very least.

This was only one of his projects. He submitted an outline and some specimen chapters of *Richmond Roy* to Lucas, who was "charmed" with it, but could give no definite promise, as *Once a Week* was in a process of reorganization. Meanwhile Meredith accepted a definite request from Tinsley Brothers, a rival firm to Chapman & Hall, "to do a 1 volume story within a certain term." There was a scheme afoot for the establishment of a new magazine, and he expected to be appointed sub-editor, with "a fellow who is merely to be titular chief, acting as head." This, if it should materialize, would carry a sizable salary. "I have laid lines right and left," he told Jessopp; "in short, spread traps for money everywhere."

There was also the question of providing a suitable home for his bride. The project of buying and enlarging Copsham Cottage lingered in his mind; possibly with some financial help from the bride's father, this would be the best arrangement. If not, Mr Vulliamy might advance enough money for them to build a small house about the same distance from London, for Meredith was determined not to become a city-dweller. "I must have for my daily meal a good plateful of sky," he had remarked not long before; "and the sun must drop into it, or I'm not satisfied. I feed on him and the field he traverses." To begin with, they could rent a furnished house for six months or a year, while they looked for a permanent home that really satisfied them.

Throughout the summer Meredith worked tirelessly. His energetic new employer, Warren Adams of Saunders & Otley, had rushed over to Cherbourg, interviewed Captain Semmes of the Confederate raider *Alabama* on the very eve of its fight with the *Kearsarge*, and obtained the log and the captain's journal. Meredith offered to write the book; but when he found that Adams wanted to go to press in five days he "declined this fiery proximity to the printer's devil," and contented himself with supplying the first and last chapters, while Adams sat up day and night to produce the rest. Meredith's two chapters reflected the enthusiasm for the Southern cause which he had already expressed in his editorials, and he made a spirited narrative of the *Alabama's* last fight.

Good progress had been made with the second *Emilia* story. Early in June his report was that " 'Emilia' is running very fast in Italy, and we may hope to see the damsel of the fiery South (no longer tripped and dogged by Philosopher or analyst) by late Autumn." Six weeks later he was calling the book *Vittoria* and saying that it was "going on swimmingly. Sandys has heard the first 150 pages, and says it is extremely interesting, and likely to be by far the best thing I have done." Hardman, on a holiday tour abroad, made notes for him of the street names in Bellagio. By the end of August, the word was, "*Vittoria* does not proceed fast, but the matter is of a good sort." Marie copied each chapter when he finished it.

On the eve of the wedding Hardman described his friend's "rapturous condition": "His soul is filled with love dreams, which jostle rudely with the stern practical matters essential to the stern fact of matrimony. Kisses and Life Insurance, Angels and House Agents, Doves, Loves, and Leading Articles, etc., etc., do not assimilate." The wedding took place in Mickleham Church on September 20, with Dr Jessopp performing the ceremony, Lionel Robinson as best man, and most of the groom's old friends in the congregation.

The first two weeks of the honeymoon were spent at Pear Tree Cottage, across the river Itchen from Southampton, and then they moved to Ploverfield House, at Bursledon, a little further along the river. This was the home of the Maxses, who lent it to the newly married couple for a month, while they went traveling. Meredith was delighted with the panorama from the windows, and vowed that in seven years, if he had not become a "pallid ghost," he would be able to get a home for himself in the vicinity. The sea air gave him a glow of health; he took a bathe and a run before breakfast, and went on fishing expeditions on the river. To his delight he found that Marie had a lively sense of humor, and assured Hardman that she "is the wife of a Pantagruel; she is sublime in laughter. We sit on a humourous Olympus, and rule over the follies of mortals."

Honeymoon joys were not allowed to interfere too much with work, but once again he was being distracted among several projects. Because of the fixed date when a short novel was to be ready for Tinsley, he laid *Vittoria* aside and concentrated upon *Rhoda Fleming: a Plain Story*. He was determined that it should be the first example of the new straightforward manner that he believed himself to have acquired. Planning it as a one-volume novel (in a day when the standard length was three volumes), he thought he might be able to finish it by the end of the honeymoon; even if he could not compress it to such strict limits, he was confident that it would be "out in the winter."

As usual, strong creative concentration aroused the impulse of poetry. One night he woke up at three o'clock and wrote a poem on "Cleopatra" to go with a drawing that Sandys had made for *The Cornhill*, and he went on to compose part of an "Ode to the Napiers" and part of a "wayside piece" to be called "The Ex-Champion's Lament," his bride meanwhile supplying him with notepaper and assuring him that she did not mind being waked up. "I never had such a fit on me since the age of twenty-one," he declared.

His hope of contributing poems to *The Cornhill* was not fulfilled. When one of his "wayside" monologues, "Martin's Puzzle," was submitted, the editor, while "personally admiring it," had to reject it because its freethinking opinions might offend many readers. Nor did the "Cleopatra" poem see the light of print. Sandys's picture did eventually appear in the magazine, but the accompanying poem was by Swinburne. This disappointment may have influenced Meredith's unflattering opinion of the published poem, as recalled by Swinburne more than twenty years later: "Meredith, I remember, strongly (and no doubt justly) remonstrated with me for producing such a farrago of the most obvious commonplaces of my ordinary style. The verses were never intended for reproduction or preservation, but were simply scribbled off as fast as might be to oblige a friend whose work I admired." Apparently Sandys made a last-minute appeal to him when Meredith's poem proved unsatisfactory. Because of Meredith's strictures, Swinburne never included his poem in any collection.

In spite of setbacks, Meredith remained optimistic. When they left Ploverfield, at the end of October, he was talking of "A Plain Story" as running to 600 pages—i.e., two volumes—of which he had written 250. "*Vittoria* lags, but will be good, I see . . . A publisher with whom I have an appointment this week proposes to give me four figures (with no dot between) for a novel. Am I rising? The market speaks! . . . I shall be a MILLIONAIRE next year. My 'plain story' is first to right me and then the 3 volumer will play trumpets." Emile Forgues was translating *Emilia in England* for the *Revue des deux mondes*. All the auguries pointed to fame.

After their return from the honeymoon the couple stayed for a week with the Vulliamys at Mickleham and then moved into a house called The Cedars, in Esher, which they had rented for six months. In the preceding spring the Hardmans had bought a handsome property, Norbiton Hall, at Kingston-on-Thames, and the Merediths stayed with them several times during November and December to inspect a neighboring house, Kingston Lodge, which was available for lease.

Meredith's enlarged duties at Chapman & Hall kept him in London for several days each week, and he found the Garrick Club a useful shelter there. Shirley Brooks, the comic dramatist and *Punch* writer, who was a member of the Hardman coterie, reported after seeing Meredith one evening at the Club that "he looks exceedingly well and has somehow altered himself—seems less poetic and more social."

Some of his hopes of financial advancement had been dashed. The new magazine, which he had expected to edit, was now coming into existence as *The Fortnightly Review*; but instead of having Anthony Trollope as editor, as had first been proposed, it was under the guidance of the energetic George Henry Lewes, who did not need a subordinate to do the real work. Shortly afterwards *Once a Week* passed out of the editorial hands of Lucas and therefore the tentative approval of the "autobiographical" serial was canceled. In consequence of buying linen and plate and the other requisites of setting up a household, Meredith had fallen into further arrears with Arthur's school fees, and at the end of January he had to appeal again for Jessopp's forbearance, explaining that "in prospect of the needful" he had "put aside *Vittoria* (which contains points of grandeur and epical interest) to 'finish off' *Rhoda Fleming* in one volume, now swollen to two—and Oh, will it be three?—But this is my Dd. Dd. Dd. uncertain workmanship . . . However, I hope in six weeks to be clear of Miss Rhoda, into whose history I have put more work than she deserves. I write in the saddest spirits, rare with me. Stomach, my friend. I am not in the bracing air which befits me. But in future I will be punctual. By degrees I will reduce the portentous I.O.U.'s . . . *Vittoria* is one third towards completion." In another dispirited letter, to Maxse, a few days later, grumbling that the frost "nips and impoverishes me," he said of *Rhoda Fleming*, "I don't at all know what to think of the work."

This discouragement was a sad contrast to his confident resolutions of six months before. Even though his wife was doing everything she could to help him, "and would hush the elements, knowing me pen in hand," he was depressed by the difficulty of composition in the midst of changes of residence, with all the business details involved. It was finally decided that they would lease Kingston Lodge for three years; but the only feature of the house that gave Meredith any satisfaction was its being just across the road from the Hardmans. In a letter to Jessopp in February, complaining again of the "deadly" weather that "fits an iron cap on my brain," he gave a glum description of his future home: "No country around—brick, brick, brick; but a middling pretty little house, and Marie likes it, so I submit." He promised to send a cheque toward Arthur's expenses "within two or three weeks. If things don't go better (in this respect) he will have to go to Switzerland."

On April 24, after the removal to Kingston, he reported that *Rhoda Fleming* was finished, all but the last two chapters. As he had fore-seen, it had grown to the standard three-volume length, and so he was disappointed when Tinsley Brothers offered him only £400, which was presumably what they had intended to give him for the originally pro-posed one-volume story. Hesitating to sell it so cheap, he consulted Chapman, who told him to wait till November; but in his financial extremity a delay of seven months was unthinkable, and he had to let Tinsley bring it out.

Although he described the book to Jessopp as "six months' work, minus a week or two," its origin can be found three years earlier. It may possibly have incorporated some material from the stories that he had been writing at that time, *A Woman's Battle* and *The Dyke Farm*. Neither of these is identifiable in any other form, and both titles can be considered applicable to *Rhoda Fleming*, since the setting is a farm-stead and the plot centers on a girl's "battle" on behalf of her sister. Whether this hypothesis is valid or not, at any rate there is no doubt that the embryo of the book can be seen in "The Parish Clerk's Story," which he contributed to *Once a Week* in February, 1861. The rural setting, the main situation, and several of the characters emerged straight out of that source; but the short story's melodramatic im-plausibility was disguised by the psychological complexity that he developed in the ampler dimensions of the novel.

Written under pressure and amid growing depression of spirits, it was a simpler and a sadder story than his previous ones. To lure the public, he needed a vigorous plot, enacted by sufficiently stereo-typed characters. This requirement had been amply fulfilled in "The Parish Clerk's Story," with its conflict of peasantry against aristocracy, its theme of abduction and detection, its *dramatis personae* of con-ventional types from melodrama. The one recent writer to have soared up to the highest literary prestige and fortune was George Eliot, and so he invaded her domain by drawing the chief episodes and characters from farm life. His plot—the seduction of a pretty country girl by an unscrupulous gentleman, and her rescue by her heroic sister—was reminiscent of both *The Heart of Midlothian* and *Adam Bede*. It may have been influenced also by *The Scarlet Letter*, for Meredith was reading Hawthorne's novels about the time he wrote it.

The resemblance to George Eliot's novels extended beyond the rural setting and the emotional tone; there were specific parallels in characterization not only with *Adam Bede* but also with *Silas Marner* and *The Mill on the Floss*. Only when he introduced a London eccentric—the smug bank messenger—did Meredith revert to his former reliance on the Dickens technique of comic portraiture; and so Anthony Hackbut fails to merge into the texture of the novel. And among the major characters there was one, Robert Armstrong, who had conflicts and strengths and flaws that set him apart from the central male characters in any novel George Eliot had yet written. Moody, headstrong, and ill-tempered, he was living under an assumed name in hope of escaping from the disgrace caused by his bouts of hard drinking. He was not the first hero of an English novel to be a drunkard; but in contrast with Dickens's romantically charming Sydney Carton, Armstrong was a surly boor.

It was necessary to portray Armstrong as a man of tough fiber if he was to be an adequate foil to Rhoda Fleming; and even his obstinacy and occasional violence scarcely sufficed to prevent his seeming a weakling alongside of that obdurate girl. Rhoda has a good claim to the title of the least sympathetic heroine in fiction. She is gradually revealed as stubborn, unimaginative, and motivated by an almost pathological contempt for sexual love. The reader may admire her constancy and courage, but her hardness becomes repugnant. It was her relentless rectitude that finally caused the tragic doom of her sister.

As the reader's sympathy becomes alienated from Rhoda it is bound to attach itself to Dahlia, who has all the pathetic gentleness and kindliness that her sister lacks. There is a horrifying undertone of jealousy, revenge, and even masochism in the righteousness that makes Rhoda snatch Dahlia away from her betrayer and bully her into marriage with the repulsive Sedgett. Meredith was aware of the appealing quality in the girl who was nominally the wrongdoer in the story; he is reported to have said to a friend who was expressing admiration of Rhoda, "Don't you love Dahlia more? I do."

This partiality for the blond, innocent farm girl harks back to the theme of *Richard Feverel*. The story of Dahlia Fleming is basically similar to Lucy's. The lovely, trustful country girl falls in love with the ambitious and selfish young man of rank and wealth. They are separated when he goes abroad because he fears the wrath of his father. They are reunited too late, when he realizes his folly and returns to beg her forgiveness. Yet all the values are changed in the later book: instead of being an unworldly enthusiast, the man is a hard and calculating realist; instead of a secret marriage there is a betrayal; and instead of merely neglecting his devoted mistress, Edward initiates a hideous scheme to get rid of her by paying a ruffian to marry her. They are a hopelessly disparate couple, the girl so unintelligent that her only claim to admiration is her utter loyalty, the man so brilliant and experienced that from the beginning of the affair the reader suspects his sincerity. The outcome is mental collapse and attempted suicide for the girl, tortured beyond her strength by problems that she cannot fathom; while for the man there is the permanent curse of knowing that he alone has been responsible for the whole catastrophe. If this theme did indeed stem from some experience of the author's own youth, he had become disillusioned about it since his use of it in his first novel.

Whilst his bias in favor of Dahlia made him regard her as a sort of martyred saint, he was notably impartial in picturing her betrayer. Edward Blancove is a credible character and far from contemptible. His repentance at the end was not a conventional "conversion." As Meredith remarks, "There is a sort of hero, and a sort of villain, in this story: they are but instruments. Hero and villain are combined in the person of Edward." Though he is selfish and ambitious and can be called cruel, Edward has both intelligence and magnanimity which eventually lead to his self-abasement. Yet even his belated attempt at retribution has traces of the egotism that had caused all the trouble.

It has been suggested that Meredith modeled Blancove upon his brother-in-law, Edward Peacock, who similarly fell out with his father over his infatuation with a girl of lower status. If so, it may throw light on the presentation of Blancove's friend, the young widow Mrs Lovell. Here again Meredith departs far from the stereotype. She seems to fascinate him so strongly that he magnifies her capricious moments of generosity and condones her duplicity and her mercenary motives. As a portrait of a charming, shallow, worldly woman, hardened by early emotional disaster, she is fully convincing; and she is also startlingly like Edward Peacock's sister, Mrs Mary Ellen Nicolls.

Parts of the story, then, may have been as intimately interwoven with Meredith's past experience as his previous novels had been. And the implied "moral" of the book also linked it with its predecessors. The catastrophe resulted from several malign forces—egoism, social class prejudice, and the rigidity of self-righteous morality. All these had already functioned harmfully in the three earlier novels.

In construction, *Rhoda Fleming* was well handled, and avoided some of the weaknesses of the preceding books. The plot was close-knit and vigorous, sometimes verging on the melodramatic, but never wholly improbable. It was confined to a small group of important characters whose interplay produced the whole sequence of events.

Foreshadowing was used effectively, and the sense of inevitable consequences was powerful.

The author's idiosyncrasies of method and style were less obtrusive
than usual. Only two or three significant scenes were conveyed in-
directly instead of being narrated in their chronological context—
notably Armstrong's attack on Edward Blancove and the subsequent
waylaying and beating of Armstrong, and the scene at Dahlia's wedding
to Sedgett. Most of the style was straightforward, almost totally free
of oblique allusions. Auctorial comment, too, was held to a minimum,
not more than half a dozen passages offering brief excursions into Meredith's opinions on human follies, on national destinies, or on the art
of fiction.

In large measure the author's unwonted meekness of form and
style arose from his conscious effort to write a book that would earn
some money by conforming with the standards of the circulating-
library fiction that formed Tinsley's usual stock in trade. But there
is some likelihood that the novel would have been elaborated with his
customary involutions if it had not been safeguarded from revision by
the speed with which it had to be written and sent to press.

# The War in Italy

IN SPITE of all Meredith's concessions to popular taste, *Rhoda Fleming* did nothing to further his fame. Some reviewers hailed it as an improvement over his previous work because of its comparative clarity, but others still found trouble in following the thread of the story; and William Tinsley testifies glumly that the book "had a very poor sale."

Before its publication date, a new edition of *The Shaving of Shagpat* had come out, with a frontispiece by Sandys and a dedication to Hardman. A French translation of *Richard Feverel*, by Forgues, was printed in the *Revue des deux mondes*. There was a gleam of encouragement in these indications that his earlier work was not consigned to oblivion.

A more important event was the birth of a son on July 26. Hardman chronicled the remarkable fact that Meredith, who was "very superstitious," would not allow the infant to be weighed because of an old wives' belief that it was unlucky to do so. While not intending to have a formal christening—"a piece of the old secondary barbaric system of training men to be humane"—he asked his two closest friends, Maxse and Hardman, to regard the boy as their "lay godson," and he was consequently named "William Maxse."

Meredith was proud of the health and cheerfulness of his new son, and scoffed at visitors who suggested the baby ought to be bottle-fed; but he showed no signs of becoming a doting father to Willie as he had been to Arthur in the days when they were all in all to each other. In his comments on the infant there was often either a trace of amusement or a coolly scientific observation of his behavior. The day after the baby's birth, in a letter to Wyse, he remarked that, if the mother and child continued to go on well, he would be "free about a fortnight hence" to come and visit Wyse in the west of England, after which he would "walk on to Lynmouth and Ilfracombe. Perhaps subsequently run over to Brescia and the Subalpine cities, to see to my colouring in the novel, *Vittoria*." These plans did not materialize; but instead, when the baby was less than three weeks old, the father went off in Maxse's yacht to Cherbourg for several days to witness a joint review of the French and English fleets. It was Meredith's gesture of independence from domestic duties.

A new journalistic venture of the year was *The Pall Mall Gazette*, a daily newspaper of Conservative sympathies. Several of Meredith's friends were on the staff, and he soon became a contributor, and added the editor, Frederick Greenwood, to his intimate circle.

Plans were afoot for the publication of *Vittoria* as a serial in *The Fortnightly Review*. Lewes saw specimens of the manuscript during the autumn and gave encouragement. Toward the end of the year Meredith wrote to Maxse:

*I am very hot upon Vittoria. Lewes says it must be a success; and it has my best writing . . . I think one must almost love Italy to care for it and the heroine. There are scenes that will hold you; much adventure to entertain you; delicate bits and fiery handling. But there is no tender dissection, and the softer emotions are not kept at half gasp upon slowly-moving telescopic objects, with their hearts seen beating in their frames.*

Shortly afterwards, comparing his novels with Hawthorne's, he told Maxse that he tried to repress his own tendency to delineate morbid action:

*Much of my strength lies in painting morbid emotion and exceptional positions; but my conscience will not let me so waste my time. Hitherto consequently I have done nothing of mark. But I shall, and Vittoria will be the first indication (if not fruit) of it. My love is for epical subjects—not for cobwebs in a putrid corner; though I know the fascination of unravelling them.*

The arrangement with *The Fortnightly* was ratified early in December, when Meredith accepted £250 for the serial rights. "If my progress seems to you slow," he explained to Lewes, "remember that I am on foreign ground and have to walk warily. I read a good deal of the novel to Mdme Venturi the other day, who says that the Italian colouring is correct." The first instalment duly appeared in *The Fortnightly* on January 15, 1866.

As usual, Meredith had been confidently looking forward to success, and he was cast down when Chapman and others told him, after the first two or three instalments had appeared, that the story was not liked. He was therefore cheered by receiving an enthusiastic letter from Swinburne, and all the more so because there had been a coolness between them. Sandys was of the opinion that the disagreement arose because Swinburne was annoyed by Meredith's portrayal of him as Runningbrook in *Emilia in England*; but this is unlikely, as the portrait was not unfavorable. Meredith's frankness about the "Cleopatra" poem is a more probable cause. At any rate, Meredith now responded with almost pathetic cordiality:

*Why will you content yourself with only writing generously? Why will you not come and see me? My wife has constantly asked me how it is that you do not come. Must I make confession to her that I have offended you? It is difficult for me to arrange for spare evenings in town; I can't leave her here alone. If we meet, I must quit you only too early. I wonder whether Sandys would invite us to dine with him; when we might have one of our evenings together, and come to an understanding about future evenings at Kingston.*

Swinburne's *Poems and Ballads* were then going through the press, and Meredith warned him that he "had heard 'low mutterings' already from the Lion of British prudery; and I, who love your verse, would play savagely with a knife among the proofs for the sake of your fame; and because I want to see you take the first place, as you may if you will." In reply, Swinburne sent a copy of the new edition of Byron to which he had supplied a preface, and Meredith gratified him with a letter of high praise for the essay. The reconciliation was thus ratified.

Suburban life at Kingston Lodge grew no more acceptable with the passage of time. Both Meredith and Hardman were driven half to distraction by a loud and persistent peal of bells in the church tower near their homes. "I like nothing in Kingston," Meredith told Maxse; but he withstood the temptation to look for another house: "I have determined to save up and put by, and endure this place (if possible) for the three years' term. And when I move I will move to a fixed place. Rich men may be houseless rovers: it upsets poor ones. Besides, wives don't like foreign houses and won't let their hearts' fibres cling to any place not their own."

At the end of March, sending Jessopp twenty-five pounds and promising that the rest of the arrears would be forthcoming next month, he said he was "busy in a thousand ways," and added, "I think I shall give up the Ips. J., which doesn't (really) pay me. I am behind with you simply because Foakes owes me twice the amount, and pleads 'Expenses' here and there." In the same letter he broke the news that he would not be able to see much of Arthur during the Easter holidays. He had been accorded one of the contemporary marks of recognition— an invitation to stay at Fryston Hall, in Yorkshire, the estate of Lord Houghton, the former Richard Monckton Milnes.

Ever since the days when he had been one of the "Apostles" at Cambridge with Tennyson, Milnes had invited the cream of the literary and political world to his country mansion. Swinburne, who was one of his recent protégés, accompanied Meredith on the present visit; and the other guests were a variegated menagerie of celebrities: Samuel Baker, just back from discovering the source of the Nile; Henry J. Selwyn, M.P.; Connop Thirlwall, Bishop of St David's and noted historian; Rev Charles John Vaughan, former Headmaster of Harrow and an eloquent preacher; and Dr John Henry Bridges, a leading exponent of Comte's Positivist philosophy. It was not surprising that in this assemblage of theologians and philosophers Meredith felt out of his element and could not hold forth with his usual assurance. After his return home he reported that "Fryston is the dullest house with the dryest company in the dismallest country I have ever visited. Houghton, of course, was pleasant, but I think I could never travel two miles to go there again." A country house full of argumentative theorists was more entertaining in the novels of Peacock than in real life.

He might have enjoyed the visit more if he had been there a few days earlier, when his old friend Carlyle stopped for two days, accompanied by Tyndall and Huxley, on his way to Edinburgh to be installed as Lord Rector of the University. After returning to London Meredith spent the afternoon of April 20 with Mrs Carlyle, who had stayed at home in Cheyne Walk; it was a horrifying shock to him when he learned that she died suddenly the next day while driving in Hyde Park.

He did not carry out his impulse to resign from *The Ipswich Journal*, and he continued to write special articles for both *The Morning Post* and *The Pall Mall Gazette*. To identify these anonymous pieces is not practicable, but some inference may be drawn as to what type of work he did. When Maxse wanted him to put in an article on behalf of one of his political crusades, Meredith explained:

*Greenwood, and doubtless our B[orthwick] as well, don't regard me as a political writer, so I am always in danger of slipping into the waste paper basket, unless I write review or essay . . . And the truth is, I can only now and then afford time to write an experimental article on politics. When my last debts are paid, and I have finished my next novel, I shall have a free hand . . . I have not meant to say I will not write unless I see my pay—but that it's heart-breaking to feel that I have given up my time, with some amount of ardour for a theme, all to no purpose save to see my manuscript as the froth tossed up from the wheel of an editorial mill.*

Whatever else might change in his employments, he plodded on with the steady routine of reading manuscripts for Chapman & Hall. In the five years since taking the appointment he had curtly rejected books by "Ouida" and Mrs Lynn Linton, both of whom became celebrities soon afterwards in the hands of other publishers; and on the other hand he had approved a mediocre novel called *An Artist's Proof*, by Alfred Austin, who thirty years later became Poet Laureate. "Their reader had reported it was the best novel he had read for a long time," Austin says in his autobiography. "I confess I was surprised by what they said; for my opinion, even then, of the work, regarded as a novel, was much lower . . . I do not doubt that he was influenced by the thoughtfulness of the book, and the disquisitions, philosophical and other, it contained."

The kindly side of Meredith's treatment of authors can be seen in the case of a young woman named Jennett Humphreys. In 1864 a novel that she had submitted evoked two helpful letters from him, signed only by the firm and couched in the impersonal "we." He praised her "copious youthful feeling" but objected to the redundancy, the lack of naturalness in dialogue, and the exclamatory comments. When she wrote back to protest that the exclamatory style was naturally feminine, he replied patiently, citing George Eliot as evidence to the contrary, saying that interjections betrayed "raw thought" and "vagrant emotion," and prescribing "mental labour" to acquire "a well-trained mind."

As both letters had expressed encouragement, Miss Humphreys submitted another manuscript a year later. Intending to send her detailed advice about how to revise it, Meredith set it aside and forgot it. On discovering it some time later, he wrote her an apologetic letter, and offered to grant a personal interview, since a written criticism "will possibly not be so effective, and it may seem more severe." Written by "the Reader" in the third person, the letter ended with the remark that "it needs hardly to be said that obscurity is his most comfortable cloak, whenever he undertakes the thankless duty of looking at a MS."

Miss Humphreys duly presented herself at the glass-walled cubicle in a corner of the publishers' office. "He was studiously polite to me," she later testified; "and I have a memory of a man dressed with great care—leading even to lavender-coloured kid gloves—his hair of chestnut colour and lying in curls, or waves, round a handsome face. What he said was patiently said, my faults being pointed out, and his judgment over what I had done being several times repeated—'It will not go to the public.' I asked if I might know to whom I was indebted, and he said 'Excuse me'—which, of course, I was bound to do."

Subsequently Miss Humphreys gained some standing as a writer of children's stories and magazine articles, but it is a proof of Meredith's sound judgment that she never persuaded any publisher to accept one of her novels. She had no idea of her adviser's identity, and when she asked William Harrison Ainsworth about it five years later, on the strength of his being one of Chapman & Hall's most noted authors, he showed a total confusion between George Meredith and "Owen Meredith," the pseudonym of Robert Bulwer-Lytton: "I fancy the gentleman must have been Mr Owen Meredith. I do not know him, but I have heard that he was their reader. From his name he must be a Welshman." This vagueness on the part of one of the most active literary men in London is evidence of Meredith's success in keeping himself unrecognized.

The interview with Miss Humphreys was part of a hurried disposal of business prior to departure. War was about to flare up between Italy and Austria, and Meredith had accepted an appointment to serve as a special correspondent at the front for *The Morning Post*. On June 21, the day after the declaration of war, he reached Bologna, caught a passing glimpse of King Victor Emmanuel there, and pushed on to Ferrara, the headquarters of General Cialdini. From there he sent his first dispatch the next day, confidently forecasting success for the Italian army that was poised to cross the Po. The outcome, however, was indecisive, and Meredith withdrew to Milan, where on the 28th he interviewed General Durando, who had been wounded in the action.

One of the first people he encountered in Milan was his young Cambridge friend, H. M. Hyndman, who had got himself appointed as correspondent of *The Pall Mall Gazette*. They were only briefly together at the Hotel Cavour before Hyndman went off on a jaunt to Genoa and Meredith proceeded to Cremona. On July 2 he moved on to Bozzolo, the headquarters of the Eleventh Division, but his reports were already reflecting the uncertainty and confusion that soon led to the collapse of the whole campaign. Apart from narrating a few anecdotes of individual battle experiences which he picked up in interviews, he could only cite conflicting rumors, tediously guarded with "perhaps" and "it is thought." Though full of enthusiasm for the Italian cause and confident in the spirit of the troops, he grew doubtful as to the judgment of the leaders.

He wrote his third dispatch at Bozzolo at five in the morning and went on the same evening to Marcaria, a "little and dirty hole." After a visit to the front he arrived on July 7 at Torre Malimberti, the general headquarters, where the King was conferring with his advisers on the French offer of mediation. Meredith watched the generals scurrying about, but had no idea as to what was being decided, and the next day he drifted over to the headquarters of the First Army Corps, at Piadena.

Until this point his reports to his newspaper had been drily factual, but with war news remaining negative, his eighth letter was a vivid and exasperated narrative of an expedition from Torre Malimberti to Gonzaga. He started at three A.M., and before long his carriage became entangled with an endless procession of army supply waggons, so that he was half mad with impatience before he reached Casalmaggiore, and instead of crossing the Po there he branched off on a side road. After four hours he stopped at a little inn at La Colombina, and had to wait an hour for food. He had intended to cross the river at Viadana, but found the bridge demolished, and so he pushed on through intolerable heat and dust to Dosalo, where there was a ferry; and then he had to wait again while a herd of cattle took precedence on the crossing. He spent the night at Luzzara, got up at four the next morning, and went on through Reggiolo to Gonzaga.

A few days later he accompanied General Medici's division from Lusia to Motta, and then proceeded to Noale, near Treviso, where he continued hopefully collecting rumors and guesses. On July 20 he went to Padua, and in the middle of the night he was told that cannon fire could be heard in the direction of Venice. His next report gave a lively account of a three-hour ride toward the front, in pitch-darkness, heavy rain, thunder and lightning, struggling through a whole army corps on the march, blundering into ditches, and coating himself with mud. On reaching the village of Dolo, he and a staff officer climbed the church spire and peered into the blackness for two hours without the faintest idea as to what the cannonading was about.

As a matter of fact, the war—if it could be dignified by that name —was already fading out in negotiations, and Meredith's dispatches came to an end on July 24. He was unwilling to hurry home, however, and lingered in the hope that further assignments might be forthcoming. Part of August he spent in Austria, where a Viennese friend conducted him around the Höllenthal and up the Schneeberg. While in Vienna, he made the acquaintance of another wandering Englishman, Leslie Stephen. Formerly a tutor at Cambridge, Stephen had left the University a year before, impelled by his growing rationalism and by his hopes of becoming a journalist. A keen Alpinist, he had spent the summer climbing in Switzerland with his young American friend, Captain Oliver Wendell Holmes, and while there he had fallen in love with Minnie Thackeray, daughter of the late novelist. The foundations of a lifelong friendship with Meredith were laid during the days they spent together in Vienna.

At the beginning of September Meredith crossed the Semmering to Venice, which had just been reopened to foreigners, though still occupied by Austrian troops. After three days he went on through Padua and Vicenza to Milan. His love of Italy was growing so strong that he sought some way of settling there permanently and bringing his family to join him. In the hope that *The Times* might appoint him as resident correspondent, he enlisted the aid of his old friend Tom Taylor, who was on the staff of that paper. "In a settled position (I wish it were in Italy)," he wrote to Taylor, "and with command of news, or the sources of it, I believe I could show the requisite judgment." Taylor recommended him warmly to Mowbray Morris, the editor, describing him as a thorough gentleman, well acquainted with modern languages, and "quick and lively, so that he might be relied on to master rapidly any subject or study he had to turn his mind to."

Waiting for a decision on his application, Meredith went back to Venice to witness the festivities celebrating the province's freedom, in the hope that Borthwick might accept a report about it for *The Morning Post*. At the Hotel Vittoria he joined a lively group of fellow-correspondents, including Hyndman, Colonel C. B. Brackenbury, Henry Spicer, G. A. Henty (later famous for his boys' books), and— the most eminent journalist of the party—George Augustus Sala, a choleric and noisy *bon vivant*, who had traveled everywhere and was notorious in Fleet Street both for his productivity and for his excesses.

Hyndman realized that Meredith had not enjoyed his duties as a reporter:

*He wrote nothing worth reading in his new capacity, and this was the more astonishing, as walking through the calles of Venice and gondolaing through its canals on our visits to its places of interest, Meredith's observations on the works of art, the architecture, the history, and the people were extremely interesting; while his reflections and general talk on political matters, as we used to sit out before the Café Florian until the early hours of the morning, were certainly worth reproducing. But Meredith positively hated writing as a daily task, and could not bear to think of the whole thing as a mere matter of business. This disturbed his vision and cramped his pen.*

William Hardman took an opposite view in this matter. Terming Meredith's dispatches "admirable," he noted in his journal:

*He writes so much better when he has not time to finish, rewrite, and (as Anthony Trollope says) twist his work to curl-papers. The journey will do him good, for he wants facts and extended observation, being usually too much given to feeding entirely on his own imagination—a well that, however deep, is liable soon to run dry.*

The same subject happened to come up for discussion between Meredith and his associates in Italy. During one session around the table outside Florian's, says Hyndman,

*the conversation turned on Meredith's own writings, and we all agreed that he had the right to far higher and wider popularity than he had yet secured. Meredith declared that he always wrote with a standard of his own before him and that he did not care for popularity. This the rest of us would scarcely accept, and I blurted out, "I believe you will be popular enough one day, Meredith, and the funny thing is you will be appreciated even more for your defects than for your merits." Meredith laughed.*

The enforced propinquity of several weeks in Venice led to a nasty quarrel between the two most showy conversationalists in the group. Hyndman says:

*Meredith's keen and at that period rather sardonic and satirical intelligence grated on Sala's ebullience, and there was a continual friction below the surface from the first time they met . . . Meredith, though just in all his dealings and hospitable in his way, was by no means liberal, while Sala, though extremely liberal, was by no means always just. Anyway, there arose a tremendous storm on Sala's part, the accumulated outcome of weeks of irritation, and he insulted Meredith most grossly at the hotel table. Meredith kept a strong restraint on himself and simply went away. As I was on very good terms with them both it fell to me, though by far the youngest of the party, to endeavour to make peace, and I did contrive to bring about a temporary understanding.*

The principal event during Meredith's stay in Venice was the triumphal entry of the King of Italy. In the midst of a frenzied crowd watching a review in St Mark's Square he caught sight of a familiar face and shouted "Janet!" Mrs Ross greeted him with "infinite joy," as she tells in her memoirs. "As most of the party I was with were bent upon bric-à-brac hunting, we made several excursions together. One whole day we spent at Torcello, most beautiful of islands, and talked of the dear old Esher days, of the novels he had written and was going to write. I tried to persuade him to come with me to Egypt, but alas, he could not." The group of correspondents dispersed after the royal visit; and as there was no word of encouragement from *The Times*, Meredith reluctantly journeyed back to England.

*Vittoria*, having finished its serial run in *The Fortnightly Review* on December 1, was issued three weeks later by Chapman & Hall in three volumes. As a sequel to *Emilia in England* it inherited a few of the characters; but otherwise no two novels could be more unlike. Gone was the social satire, and the three Misses Pole evaporated with it. Their brother Wilfrid remained, still the well-meaning, puzzled Englishman, gradually winning a modicum of nobility under stress of the emotions swirling all around him, until his great scene when sheer exasperation drove him in mufti into battle, brandishing his umbrella.

Merthyr Powys continued to play the role of *deus ex machina*, and became even more than before an idealized projection of the author himself—the aloof, mature man who can love and sympathize and help without personal ambition. Understanding the heroine's nature, he was quietly devoted to her but set up no obstacle to her marriage with another.

The novel was supposed to derive its unifying force from the central character. Nomenclature is a minor annoyance. In the course of the earlier novel her first name, "Emilia," had been replaced by her second, "Sandra"; and now that she had become a professional singer she adopted an entirely new name, "Vittoria Campa." This, no doubt, was meant to signify her embodiment of the spirit of the Italian revolution; but the author was not entirely successful in drawing her simultaneously as a symbol and as a human being. In much of the book she is seen from a distance. Only in the second half does the reader ever get close to her feelings. Therefore her love for Carlo Ammiani is unexpected and inadequately accounted for. He worshipped her youthfully from the beginning but there was no indication of her response until she suddenly accepted him.

It was presumably part of Meredith's plan that Vittoria should marry a man of weak character, who would prove unworthy of her; but this could only have been rendered plausible by a detailed revelation of her attitude toward him, with emotion overcoming her judgment, as it had often done before. Meredith implies that she loved Ammiani because he seemed to be a symbol of the free Italy which was her only real devotion; but this is not developed far enough to be effective. The author glorified Vittoria to a point where he could not bring himself to display her feelings toward a lover. This was far different from the earlier novel, where her girlish infatuation with another attractive but weak character was analyzed with convincing intimacy.

Vittoria evoked a strong emotional response in almost everyone who encountered her, while she remained scarcely conscious of other people and their feelings. In addition to Carlo, most of the men were more or less in love with her: Pericles, the millionaire, wanted a monopoly on her artistic fame; Captain Weisspriess, the Austrian officer, expected her to be another easy conquest; old Agostino, the satirical poet, felt a fatherly affection for her; Wilfrid Pole (now Pierson—another unnecessary change of name) was so deeply under her spell that he lost his Austrian fiancée; and Merthyr Powys always hovered in the background. Several women, too, were fanatically fond of her. On the other hand, many people believed they had cause to regard her with hate and jealousy: the Italian conspirators, Corte and Rizzo, thought a woman had no right to dabble in public affairs; Irma de Kaski was a professional rival; Countess Violetta d'Isorella despised her for both political and personal reasons; the Leckenstein sisters wished revenge for their brother's death, for which they blamed Vittoria in part.

Thus she was used effectively as the emotional focus of the whole group; but there were many times when the group itself became submerged in the turmoil of the revolution. Meredith had undertaken the hard task of writing a historical novel without adequate perspective of time. The events took place only seventeen years before the book was written. Mazzini, the chief historical personage, was still alive and so he could not be depicted in detail; he remained a shadowy figure known as "the Chief." Meredith made use for the first time of all the melodramatic trappings of historical romance—escapes and pursuits, secret interviews, spies, cryptic messages, mistaken identities, kidnapping. His continual display of Italian and Tyrolese landscapes, local customs, and idioms was ostentatious in its thoroughness. And the plot was obviously manipulated to give an all-over picture of the whole course of the revolt. The characters were dragged about for no other reason than to have them on the spot where great events occurred. Otherwise, the plot was merely a series of contrived and unconvincing delays in the marriage of Vittoria and Carlo.

The real theme of the book was the psychology of revolution. It recreated the strange atmosphere of suspicion, hatred, pride, and vengeance, and especially the way in which the conspirators distrusted and misunderstood each other. Barto Rizzo was a masterly study of the professional plotter. In spite of Meredith's zeal for the cause of freedom, he reproduced with cruel clarity the futility and discord that prevailed in Italy as in all the other abortive revolutions that convulsed Europe in 1848. He showed the complete lack of harmony between the aristocratic liberals and the rebellious masses—the noblemen who wanted to defeat Austria so that they might govern Italy for themselves, and the populace who wanted freedom from all overlords, foreign or local. The elusiveness in the glimpses of Mazzini served to suggest, whether intentionally or not, the leader's aloofness from the emotions and agonies of the masses he claimed to represent.

This impression of aloofness extends to the author also. Meredith never seemed to be sharing the emotions of his characters: he watched them impartially from outside. His point of view was too universal for the reader to develop much sense of identification or even of participation. One's attention is shifted about among so many characters that they seldom seem more than the pieces being moved on a chessboard. At first there appeared to be an intention to build up strong sympathy with the Italian insurgents; but in later chapters the Austrian characters were gradually endowed with legitimate motives. While this was strictly proper in terms of abstract justice and of human psychology, it was disturbing to readers of fiction who instinctively want to identify themselves with one side or the other. The dispassionate attitude was appropriate in Meredith's social comedies; but the only comedy in *Vittoria* was the basic irony of events.

As well as showing the jealousies among the insurgents, Meredith brought out an anomalous feature of a revolution going on between parties which had lived in close proximity—the social and personal affiliations which cut across the partisan lines: Italian women were conducting secret love intrigues with Austrian officers, and other Italian ladies, wives of Austrian noblemen, were giving parties at which representatives of both sides met under one roof. Meredith was not the man to flout historical realism in favor of romantic sentiment.

His inability or unwillingness to manage scenes of action was conspicuous in this novel which contained so many episodes of melodramatic violence, such as the attempted assassination of Vittoria. When he passed over these in a sentence or two, he gave an impression of impassivity, as though he were virtuously repressing every impulse to make the scene exciting. Furthermore he used coincidence shamelessly at many points in connection with the spying and counterspying, and he took little trouble to render it plausible.

The novel had elements of power that did much to offset its defects. It succeeded in its purpose of displaying the fervor and self-sacrifice of the Risorgimento as a tonic contrast with the artificial genteel values that he had ridiculed in *Emilia in England*. Some of his most glorious descriptions of mountain scenery occurred in the book. And, as usual, he rose to a few unforgettable incidents, such as Vittoria's performance at La Scala, the duel in the Pass, and the vengeance of the Guidascarpi.

The reviewers were no more generous to *Vittoria* than they had been before. *The Pall Mall Gazette* led off with a friendly notice, but *The Saturday Review* declared that there was "a wide disproportion between the expenditure of ability and the result obtained . . . He has shown as much power of thought and style as would fit out a dozen writers of sensation novels. . . . Yet we fear that Mr Meredith's novel has the unmistakable fault of being hard to read. It is often so clever as to be on the verge of genius, but somehow we don't get on with it." The critic proceeded to a long recital of Meredith's faults of style and structure.

Geraldine Jewsbury, in *The Athenaeum,* followed a similar line: "The reader is lost in the maze of events . . . How are human beings with limited faculties to understand all the distracting threads of this unmerciful novel?" And *The Spectator's* indictment was ruthless. The author was "hitherto known as a novelist of some ability and a rather low ethical tone." He was afflicted with "literary egotism" and his style "often gasps with effort." The novel was "worth reading once, but written in such a falsetto key, that, apart from the crowd of un-interesting and dim figures on the canvas, no one would wish to read it again."

These hard knocks came not long after Meredith had returned from three carefree months in Italy to face the gloom of an English winter and the economic problems of his household. Only an occasional flicker of high spirits showed itself. He was deep in a friendly argument with Maxse, partly on the best way to train Maxse's little boy in sound religious views, partly on the Captain's rigidly ascetic contempt for wine. Meredith's favorite trick of inventing fantastic anecdotes about his friends is illustrated by one of the letters. Postdating it by four years, as "Christmas, 1870," he gave a detailed report of the lengths to which Maxse's vagaries would then have carried him—the adoption of priestly robes, the founding of a new religion, the enforcement of total abstinence by dowsing the mayor of Southampton with a fire hose in the midst of a banquet to the American plenipotentiaries who were over to admit England as a new state in the Union. The whole thing was written with such admirable gravity and corroborative detail that some of Meredith's biographers have accepted the tissue of grotesque nonsense as veritable facts about the ultra-dignified Captain's activities.

Such flashes of gaiety, however, were infrequent, for Meredith was struggling with a difficult decision. The increasing expenses of his family and the disappointment of his hopes for enhanced income rendered it imperative that Arthur should be sent to a cheaper school. Nearly six years before, Meredith had been impressed by accounts of a school at Hófwyl, near Berne, which was conducted on the progressive system of Pestalozzi. Perhaps this method, with its emphasis upon practical application of knowledge, would provide the best training for the boy, who at thirteen had not shown any marked aptitude or active ambition. Arthur was withdrawn from the Norwich Grammar School and sent off to Switzerland.

Sympathy and pity must be felt for this lad whose whole childhood had been exposed to abnormal emotional conditions. Even though he had been less than five years old when his parents separated, he must have retained some recollections of his mother's beauty and charm. During the next three years, while he was dimly aware that some unmentionable barrier separated him from her, he was passionately cherished by his father and allowed to associate freely with Meredith's circle of adult friends. A few hasty, furtive interviews with his mother, in London or in the avenue of Ham House, Petersham, increased the sense of mystery and grievance; and his final visits to her, when she was on her deathbed, cannot have failed to leave an impression of tragedy. The knowledge that the subject must not be discussed with his father formed a dark blot precluding full confidence between them.

At school in Norwich he was as happy as the kind and tactful Jessopps could make him, but remained aloof and taciturn. He cannot have been unconscious of the high hopes that his father had formed as to his intellectual and his physical development, or of the undertone of disappointment in the patient advice and encouragement filling the letters from home. Then, when he was eleven, came Meredith's second marriage, with the inevitable dislodgment of Arthur from the first place in his father's regard. Though Meredith had spoken optimistically of providing a new mother for his boy, Marie was not likely to idolize him as Meredith had done; and her more objective attitude was soon adopted by her husband. The birth of their son completed Arthur's expulsion from importance in the household.

There is an uncanny parallel between the early lives of father and son. George Meredith, like Arthur, lost his mother about the age of five, was petted and adored by his father, lived in isolation from other children, and was outraged when he was eleven by his father's remarriage. In both instances the father forfeited the son's respect by being unable to afford a projected education, and in both generations the boy was packed off at the beginning of his teens to a cheap foreign school.

Equally ironic is the parallel between the actual circumstances affecting Arthur and the fictitious ones that his father drew in more than one novel. The relationship between Sir Austin Feverel and Richard was prophetic of that between George Meredith and Arthur: the over-solicitous father, full of theories as to the boy's mind and body; the son's puzzled contempt when he discovered his father to be interested in a woman; the boy's defiant coldness for reasons that the father cannot fathom. A second instalment of the study, as it were, occurred in *Emilia in England*, in the frustrated character of Purcell Barrett:

As a child . . . he had grown up with ideas of filial duty perplexed, and with a fitful love for either [parent] that was not attachment: a baffled natural love, that in teaching us to brood on the hardness of our lot, lays the foundation for a perniciously mystical self-love. He had waxed precociously philosophic when still a junior. His mother died away from her husband's roof. The old man then sought to obliterate her utterly.

The pathetic end of Barrett, victim of his own sentimentality and indecision, read forebodingly like another prophecy of Arthur Meredith's future.

The ill success of *Vittoria*, as well as the pressure of newspaper work, deterred Meredith from going on with fiction. While in Italy he had written to Tom Taylor that "if you don't like *Vittoria* I promise you quite another sort of next novel"; but by March, 1867, the reviewers had discouraged him so much that he wrote bitterly to Swinburne, "*Vittoria* passes to the limbo where the rest of my works repose . . . I see the illustrious Hutton of the *Spectator* laughs insanely at my futile effort to produce an impression on his public. I suppose I shall have to give up and take to journalism, as I am now partly doing . . . I am being carried off from the Singing. I stand on an inexorable current."

Swinburne had expressed willingness to write a favorable notice of the book; and John Morley, who had become editor of *The Fortnightly*, agreed to consider something of the sort. But as the novel had first appeared as a serial in that periodical, he did not think that an ordinary review would be appropriate. Meredith therefore hinted that a general article on his books might be contributed by Swinburne "or some such good name . . . The writer could dwell on the work pleasing him best."

Meredith did not hesitate to admit to Swinburne that some of the condemnation of *Vittoria* was justified:

*The vast machinery pressed on me. My object was not to write the Epic of the Revolt—for that the time is yet too new: but to represent the revolt itself, with the passions animating both sides, the revival of the fervid Italian blood, and the character of the people . . . I am afraid it must be true that the style is stiff; but a less condensed would not have compassed the great amount of matter.*

Extolling Swinburne's "Ode on the Insurrection in Candia" as "the most nobly sustained lyric in our language," he added lugubriously, "for me there will never be time given even to try the rising to such a song." And he added a warm invitation to Swinburne to come and stay at Kingston Lodge.

The year 1867 was a drab one for Meredith. Still harassed by debts, and with no novel in hand, he plodded wearily at journalistic work. In addition to his assignments for three newspapers, he wrote for *The Fortnightly Review* a number of book reviews, a "Sonnet to ——"

which was an affectionate tribute to Morley, and a long experiment in galliambic meter called "Phaethon." "To my mind [the galliambics] are near the mark," he commented later to Jessopp, "but as the public is not near it, I might as well have missed."

One of his book reviews brought him a taste of editorial inter- ference. The book was *Chronicles and Characters*, a collection of poems by the Hon Robert Bulwer-Lytton, who wrote under the name of "Owen Meredith." His sentimental poetry enjoyed the sort of inflated reputation that George Meredith despised; and there was possibly a further touch of prejudice arising from the fact that the poet's choice of a pen name had caused confusion during the past decade, George Meredith repeatedly finding himself mistaken for the more popular writer. He composed a long and unfavorable review, mentioning that an earlier book of the same author's had been accused of plagiarism.

There were complications. Lytton's publishers were Chapman & Hall, who were Meredith's employers and were now also the proprietors of *The Fortnightly*; John Morley was a friend of Lytton's; and John Forster, who had much influence in the editorial counsels, was Lytton's chief literary sponsor. Morley sent proofs of the review to Lytton and Forster, who both protested so angrily that publication was delayed until the offensive passages had been toned down.

Morley entertained the chief supporters of *The Fortnightly* at dinner that spring at the Garrick Club; in addition to Meredith, the guests included Browning, Trollope, Lewes, Forster, Frederick Green- wood (then editing both *The Cornhill Magazine* and *The Pall Mall Gazette*), Alexander Macmillan (the publisher), FitzJames Stephen (the jurist), and Edward Beesly (the Positivist philosopher). A more distinguished intellectual group would be hard to find.

An assistant on *The Fortnightly*, W. Burnett Tracy, has described the conversations in the editorial office: "Trollope was the loud but sound-hearted John Bull of the trinity; he would sit probably on the table with a big cigar. Lewes, the smallest and most frail in appear- ance, would sit with his thin legs crossed, his big white bulldog at his feet, and murmur with captivating fluency a running commentary; Meredith would stand and gently swing a cane pendulum fashion, always with the philosophic air which had no taint of assumption, but fitted him as neatly and becomingly as did his clothes, and he was a born artist even in these details. Thus he would take his turn in the talk, and his expressions would frequently sound uncommonly like blank verse, uttered with an occasional hesitation that was the faintest suggestion of a meditative drawl."

During the summer his wife's sister and her husband and baby came to stay at Kingston Lodge, and while there the baby fell ill and died. The shock to the Merediths was so great that they went to stay with Mr Vulliamy for two months, and their dislike of the Kingston house was so much increased that they decided to give it up without waiting for the termination of the lease. They bought a small house on the edge of Box Hill, not far from Mickleham, and the lease of Kingston Lodge was turned over to Frederick Jones, a London solicitor.

John Morley left in November for a visit to the United States, and Meredith was appointed to act as editor of *The Fortnightly* in his absence. He took advantage of the opportunity to print in it a poem of farewell to his friend, "one of my dearest, whom I trust":

> *We send our worthiest; can no less,*
> *If we would now be read aright—*
> *To that great people who may bless*
> *Or curse mankind: they have the might.*

The editorial duties lasted for only three months, as Morley's travels were cut short by illness. During his brief tenure, however, Meredith learned something about an editor's troubles. When Chapman & Hall had taken over the periodical from the group of literary men who founded it, they discovered that it had lost money under amateur management, and rigid financial control was applied. The editor had a fixed budget which had to be apportioned among the contributors. Meredith accepted two poems from Swinburne, and when the poet received his payment he wrote to the editor with a complaint about the inadequate sum, adding that a poem which Morley had printed the preceding month had not been paid for at all. In reply Meredith explained the financial arrangements and assured Swinburne that for his own "Phaethon," a poem of 150 lines, he had received only five pounds. "I propose to come and lunch with you some afternoon," he added. "Will you have me? I will stay from two or three till six, and if we are alone, we will give and take, though I shall take ten times the worth of what I give."

According to Sandys, the encounter actually occurred at dinner at the Garrick Club, which indicates that Meredith or Sandys, and not Swinburne, was the host. After dinner Swinburne again raised the question of his fee for the poems, and Meredith reminded him that it was what he usually received for his own.

"Yes, for yours," said Swinburne, "but for mine?" Meredith tried to point out the justice of it: what was enough for him was enough for Swinburne. Swinburne got up, came over to him, and slapped his face. That was the end of their friendship.

There was certainly less cordiality between them after this episode, but relations did not wholly cease. Two years later, in a letter to Bonaparte Wyse, Meredith mentioned he was intending to send Swinburne a copy of one of Wyse's Provençal poems. In January, 1873, however, he remarked in a letter to Greenwood, "I never see him, and have to imagine that he has taken offence."

# CHAPTER

## IX

# *Box Hill*

AFTER spending the Christmas weeks with the Vulliamys in Mickleham, the Merediths moved into their new home early in January, 1868. Flint Cottage, as its name implied, was a grey little house, built of the local flint, with brick facings. Though the road from Mickleham to Dorking passed nearby, the house was secluded in a ravine and was almost hidden by high box hedges. The hillside ran up sharply behind and was crowned with a dark wood of larch and firs. The opposite side of the ravine was formed by the steep green rise of Box Hill, already a favorite spot in Meredith's long walks, because it commanded a glorious view over the Surrey Downs.

The rooms were small, and to Meredith's regret there was not much spare accommodation for friends; but they could be put up at the historic Burford Bridge Hotel, only a few hundred yards away. In the cottage Meredith's bedroom was in the northeast corner of the upper floor, so that from his window he could see the sun rise over Box Hill, on the rare occasions when he did not climb up to meet it. He reported ecstatically to Hardman:

*I am every morning on the top of Box Hill—as its flower, its bird, its prophet. I drop down the moon on one side, I draw up the sun on t'other. I breathe fine air. I shout ha ha to the gates of the world. Then I descend and know myself a donkey for doing it.*

He needed this renewed energy to sustain him under his load of work. In addition to his *Fortnightly* editorship, he explained, "incessant composition and pot boilers" kept his hands tied. "But I am training my toes (first and second of right foot) to indite epistles and *Ips. Journal* while I pursue my course complacently above."

The one drawback of his new home was its remoteness from his friends: "I can't sleep away from home, as it appears to upset Marie, and we have not yet a dog, and do on the left side lean on the wilds, where there are rabbits, and may be weasels." A watchdog was soon supplied by Captain Maxse—a brown retriever named Ben—and a few congenial new friends were discovered in the neighborhood. In the next house, separated only by the high hedge, lived Charles Mackay, a well-known editor who had written dozens of rousing songs, such as "A Good Time Coming" and "Cheer, Boys, Cheer." The elderly journalist had a young daughter by his second wife, and when the two writers walked up Box Hill together, discussing literature or politics, thirteen-year-old Minnie usually accompanied them. The girl was fond of playing the piano, sometimes improvising her own pieces, and Meredith gratified her father by saying that she had "the divine fire." He little guessed, however, that Minnie Mackay's blond curls, round face, and slightly crossed blue eyes masked a personality of intense ambition which later pushed her to literary notoriety under the pen-name of "Marie Corelli."

Within half a mile lived Dr Gordon, whose house was a gathering-place of good talkers. In June a fourteen-year-old grandchild of the Gordons, Alice Brandreth, came to stay with them. She chronicled the consequences in a book half a century later:

My cousin, Jim Gordon, an Eton boy of sixteen, suggested to me that we should get up early in the morning, unknown to our parents, and walk up Box Hill to see the sun rise . . . We started long before it was light, and as we groped our way along the Leatherhead road, Jim Gordon said to me, "I know a madman who lives on Box Hill. He's quite mad, but very amusing, he likes walks and sunrises. Let's go and shout him up." So we trudged up the little drive to Flint Cottage, and began to throw small stones at the window of his bedroom.

It was quickly thrown up, and a loud and cheerful voice asked "What we meant by trying to break his window." We explained that we wanted him to climb up Box Hill with us and see the sun rise. In a miraculously short time Mr Meredith joined us, slightly clad, his nightshirt thrust into brown trousers, and his bare feet into leather slippers, no hat on his head, twisting his stick, and summoning his brown retriever dog. He started to walk very fast up the steep grass incline of Box Hill . . .

"Come on, London-pated girl," he shouted, and up I struggled to sink exhausted on the top, and then we sat and watched the sun rise and glorify the valley and the hills. I insisted on reading aloud to Mr Meredith one of the hymns from Keble's Christian Year, while he gravely listened to the birds singing around us . . .

He poured forth the most wonderful prose hymn to Nature, Life, and what he called obligation, by which I understood he meant Duty. His enthusiasm, his personality, so one with Nature, the summer, and the morning, startled and bewildered me, and for the first time in my spoilt only-child life I was awake and interested in something outside myself . . .

During the days that followed we made several more excursions and picnics with Mr Meredith . . . [He] used to advise us to go to our Mother Nature and learn of her, and not to look upon trees, mountains, fields, and lakes as merely the background of our own little ephemeral lives. He told us that he had trained himself when he walked "to observe, not to feel."

In those days his laughter, rhymes, and jokes were constant, but he was ever a master of exquisite chaff, and his words never really hurt. They only stimulated us to try and find a retort.

In spite of sociable interludes, he was depressed by the tediousness of journalism and the feeling that his career as a creative artist was at a standstill. In October, realizing that he had not answered a letter from Jessopp for more than a year, he explained remorsefully:

I had to buckle to newspaper work to pay debts, and this has gone on ever since, with now and then a dash at verse. But I've not had heart to write to friends, my way being to go up in a corner when I don't flourish, and trouble none that I can't help. I still hope for that leisure which will let me do the work I can do.

When this letter was written, Captain Maxse was standing for Parliament as a candidate of the Radical party, and Meredith was staying with him in Southampton in order to help with the campaign. He was not an enthusiastic canvasser. He told Jessopp that it was "a dismal business, but I take to it as to whatever comes." He was far too impatient with human stupidity to find any satisfaction in the manipulating and temporizing expected of a politician. Indeed, his own political views were far from clear. His journalism had all been done for Conservative papers; and his closest friend, Hardman, regarded him unequivocally as a fellow-Tory. Both of them, of course, enjoyed private gibes at the royal family and other cherished institutions; but both of them, as zealous patriots and believers in energetic action, were disgusted with the "peace at any price" policies of the Liberal government, which seemed to them to be destroying British honor and prestige in such issues as the Prusso-Danish war and the *Alabama* claims. Meredith's personal revolt from his shopkeeping heritage, reinforced by the deep and early influences of Carlyle and Peacock, both sworn enemies of commercialism, made him even more antagonistic to the materialistic standards of the "Manchester School." Some of his most scornful editorials in *The Ipswich Journal* were directed against the "money-grubbing" philosophy of Cobden and Bright:

*What has not been the power of Manchester in the Legislature of late? Say, what has tarnished the chivalry of England before Europe? What has made the thirst for gold a fever throughout the country? What has caused the accumulation of wealth to be followed up with almost the fervour of a religious inspiration? Have not the instigation and the rule of Manchester been heavy on us for years?—and yet its representatives are disappointed!*

On the other hand, Meredith's newer friends on *The Fortnightly Review* were intellectual Liberals who were hoping to inject fresh vitality into the party's ideas, and Meredith was strongly drawn to their doctrines of tolerance and humanitarianism. His interest in the Italian war of liberation had roused his fervor for advanced democratic theories. These varied influences combined to make him contemptuous of the existing political organizations but did not help him to formulate a very coherent doctrine of his own.

Captain Maxse, governed more by emotion than by logic, was himself a political anomaly. A scion of the aristocracy and an officer in the armed forces, he was as ardent a patriot as Meredith or Hardman. He, too, contributed from time to time to *The Morning Post*, and would probably have claimed to be a Tory rather than a Whig. Yet he was a red-hot exponent of all sorts of utopian schemes of reform. In the political scene of 1868, with no Socialist or Labour party yet in existence, he could only identify himself as a "Radical"—a vague classification for men of diverse doctrines who agreed only in disagreeing with the prevailing scheme of things. His supporters in the Southampton election were therefore the ideologues and the malcontents.

Meredith's letters to him had always been full of arguments against his extreme views. Sometimes it was the Christian religion that Maxse was assailing, sometimes the monarchy, sometimes the eating of meat and the drinking of wine. Meredith in reply counseled moderation and acceptance of gradual processes.

"The fanatical worship of truth will always be fruitless," he told him, three years earlier, apropos of a crusade against Christianity; "it is nothing better than the embracing of a phantom . . . Live on and be placable under some trifling irritation, till men are near a majority (or nearer to one) in contempt of imposture . . . Let Philosophy sap the structure and work its way . . . Objectless (that is, indistinct, blind) protests are like all unseasonable things, useless, and are shelved as mother nature shovels away the dust which does not serve her. . . . When the Ministers of Religion press on for an open rupture by attempts at persecution, it will be time enough to take rank under colours: until when I hold myself in reserve. I don't want the day to be advanced. I think you are altogether too impetuous: 500 years too fast for the human race."

In the same Fabian spirit he discussed politics: "I take no interest in reform. I see no desire for it below. If there were, I would give it; I have no fear of Radicals. Democracy must come, and the sooner it overflows rulers who are cowardly, the better for all. We say—Democracy, as if it were some deadly evil; whereas it is almost synonymous with Change. Democracy never rests. The worst of it is that it can be violent in its motion."

And when Maxse was ferociously condemning liquor, because he felt better after giving up wine, Meredith expostulated: "You are right just now. Nevertheless you must needs lay down positive principles as if your existing state were the key of things. You will become a fanatical Retired Admiral advocating Maine liquor laws for every natural appetite on earth, and dogmatically refusing to hear an opinion. I foresee it,—unless you can be humble while there's yet time, and admit that I am right, who preach moderation, and you are wrong, who raise the banner of abstinence with all its tissue in tatters."

These doctrines of reason, moderation, and tolerance sometimes led him toward pessimism about the state of the country. He asserted that the government, the newspapers, and the public were swayed only by "apprehension and panic" in their foreign relations and "by little else in their doings at home. The aristocracy has long since sold itself to the middle class; that has done its best to corrupt the class under it. I see no hope but in a big convulsion to bring a worthy people forth. The monied class sees the same, and dreads it—will do anything to avoid it." In the same mood, three days later, ridiculing the fulsome flattery lavished on Queen Victoria's new book, he exclaimed to Hardman, "May thine and mine live in the Age of the final Eradication of

Humbug. But then wilt thou and I be flying particles on the breath of the South-West."

This disillusioned realism could supply no incentive for vigorous electioneering, and particularly on behalf of an unpopular cause. Meredith went to Southampton from a sense of loyalty to his friend and with a novelist's interest in observing another social situation. Maxse was soundly beaten, and Meredith felt that his two months away from home were "a dead loss of time." He and his friend solaced themselves with the conviction that the winners had engaged in wholesale bribery.

The prolonged absence from work had set him sadly back in his earnings. In December he grumbled that he "must work with three heads" to meet the Christmas bills, which he termed "the obscene artillery of the stinking pit." Wife and son, fondly though he loved them, were not only a financial responsibility but also a source of interruptions for a busy writer in a small house. His boasts about Willie's health and spirits usually included some allusion to the little boy's loud tuneless singing and noisy playthings.

News of Arthur from Switzerland was encouraging, though the boy's letters hinted that he did not like the place and had made no friends among the pupils. Always reticent, he withdrew further from human contacts and devoted himself to languages. His headmaster reported that the boy had become reasonably proficient in French and German, was mastering Italian, and had taught himself enough Spanish to be reading Cervantes. Meredith reconciled himself to having a plodding, bookish son without brilliance or physical energy. In a letter full of affectionate advice, he suggested that if Arthur felt ready to advance beyond the Swiss school he might be sent to Dresden, rather than to Spain, as Spanish would be of little practical value. "I think it quite as well that you should not return to England until you do so finally to begin your apprenticeship to some business—I don't mean trade, unless you like it,—nor do I suppose that you much desire to come home at present." He proposed various plans by which they might meet somewhere on the Continent during the summer vacation and have a little tour together. But he made it plain that he was still financially straitened: "Our commercial failures of two years back still press on us. Artists and authors suffer particularly. But the strain will be over with me very soon. My novels have been kept back by having had to write for the newspapers—the only things that paid. So take this as a moral: don't think of literature as a profession. I believe you to have too much good sense."

In his capacity of reader for Chapman & Hall he made at this time what proved to be one of his most momentous judgments. In December the manuscript of a novel entitled *The Poor Man and the Lady* was turned in by Thomas Hardy, then a young assistant in a London architectural office. He had first offered it to Macmillan & Company; and Alexander Macmillan, "apparently in some doubt about it," gave Hardy an introduction to Chapman & Hall, with the suggestion that he submit the book to them. After the usual weeks had elapsed, the firm wrote to ask him if he could "meet the gentleman who has read your MS, as he would like to speak to you about it."

On an afternoon in January, 1869, Hardy was shown into the little back room at the publishers' office, "such a dusty, untidy place," as he later recalled it. The reader was waiting for him. "I felt," says Hardy, "that he was an unusual sort of man to discover in a back office in London, though I knew nothing about his personality, Mr Frederick Chapman, who presented me to him, not having told me his name."

At the time of Meredith's death, Hardy recalled that "Meredith was very kind and most enthusiastic. He gave me no end of good advice, most of which, I am bound to say, he did not follow himself." The novel was satirical in tone and radical in its social criticism. Meredith pointed out that a novel—especially a first novel—could appeal to the public only if it had a "plot." From his comments Hardy derived the idea that this meant "sensational" action in the manner of Reade and Collins. He therefore discarded *The Poor Man and the Lady* and went to work on *Desperate Remedies*, "a story quite foreign to my own instincts, and which therefore, oddly enough, owed its existence to Meredith."

Hardy made no note of the conversation, "the only words of his I remember being, 'Don't nail your colours to the mast just yet.' But I well recall his appearance—a handsome man with hair and beard not at all grey, and wearing a frock coat buttoned at the waist and loose above." And in his memorial poem he voiced the impression that Meredith's stimulating personality produced:

> *He spoke as one afoot will wind*
> *A morning horn ere men awake;*
> *His note was trenchant, turning kind.*

In the summer, when Meredith went abroad with his friend Lionel Robinson, they picked Arthur up at Berne and took him to the Obersimmenthal and the Rieder Alp, where his father was delighted to find that "he is bold on ice and endures fatigue well; projects his head and chin." But though Arthur had a clear and honest eye, and was reported to have become popular in school, he made his father anxious by his abnormal silence and impassivity. He preferred to go off on walks by himself, and when he was with his father and Robinson he could not be drawn into conversation except on the unboyish subject of philology, which could always rouse a gleam of response. Thwarted in the satisfaction that he expected to feel in his son's company, Meredith had to derive his whole pleasure from the beauty of the Alps—sitting on a terrace at Berne to watch the Jungfrau all aglow in the sunset light, listening to the roar of glacier waterfalls as he climbed in the Obersimmenthal, lying on dwarf juniper and harebells and gentian on the summit of the Riederhorn. "A month of this every year would always keep me right," he wrote home to his wife; "I felt the change as soon as I set foot on the springy turf. . . . The clear, thin air revived me exquisitely."

At the end of the holiday Arthur was escorted to Stuttgart, where he was to attend the Gymnasium, living in the house of a professor. His letters soon indicated that he was making good headway in Latin and Greek, but despising his fellow-students.

During the later part of 1869, more than three years after the completion of *Vittoria*, Meredith was at last able to return to the writing of fiction. The novel on which he now went to work was an outgrowth of the "autobiographic" tale, *The Adventures of Richmond Roy*, which he had outlined five years earlier as a possible serial for *Once a Week*. The long immersion in his subconscious mind produced immense change and enrichment. The original sketch, being a bid for acceptance in a popular magazine of wide circulation, projected a picaresque story of adventure and mystery, reminiscent of *Martin Chuzzlewit* or *Nicholas Nickleby*. Young Richmond Roy, seeking his fortune in London, falls in with a cocksure character, Contrivance Jack, of the Dickensian model. While Roy is secretary to a blind gentleman, Jack takes various makeshift employments; then Roy's aunt articles him to a solicitor, and Jack gets innocently involved in a murder and falls in love with the daughter of a racetrack tout; next Roy meets a beautiful girl at a country house, and as she is in mysterious danger he undertakes to escort her secretly to London, afoot and in disguise.

This is as far as the outline extended. Its atmosphere of romantic adventure did survive into the novel that was actually written, and two or three incidental episodes in the original outline grew into major elements. At one point, Richmond Roy went to a London mansion which he thought was his father's residence, only to find that his father was merely employed there as a singing-master. Among Jack's temporary employers was "one who believes himself Dauphin of France." During the five years' interlude these fragments linked themselves in Meredith's mind with the familiar theme of the pretensions to noble ancestry cherished by his father and grandfather. This in turn interwove itself with the character of Bonaparte Wyse, the charming and improvident grandnephew of a French emperor, and for immediate models he probably used two brothers, John and Charles Allen, sons of a naval officer, who about 1842 assumed the name of "Stuart" and announced that they were legitimate grandsons of Bonnie Prince Charlie. Handsome and courtly, they both married Englishwomen of means, and while spending some years in Bohemia they were accorded the privileges of royalty. When Meredith was writing his novel the "Stuart" brothers were living in London, in great poverty, but still using royal insignia and appearing in society decorated with the stars and crosses of orders of chivalry.

These various sources contributed to the creation of a character so vital that he dominated the book and changed its whole nature. The conception burst on Meredith with the vividness of an actual experience. "When Harry Richmond's father first came to call on me," he told a French visitor, long afterwards, "when I heard the pompous speech of this son of a duke of the blood royal and of a seventeen-year-old actress, I remember I absolutely roared with laughter." The name "Richmond Roy" was now transferred to the pseudo-royal father; and the title of the book, still alluding to the young man who narrates it, became *The Adventures of Harry Richmond*.

In dealing with a problem of hereditary royalty, the novel was bound to touch upon matters of fundamental political principles. Meredith, in his usual way, did not state these directly when Richmond Roy brought his suit against the government, but by such apparent digressions as philosophical debates with a wise German professor. The Southampton election being strongly in the author's mind, he arbitrarily made his young hero stand as a candidate for Parliament, near the end of the book, in order to introduce some sidelights on the English democratic process in action.

Meredith was going through a serious revaluation of his own beliefs, making for the first time a synthesis of his opinions on science, religion, and the structure of society. Ten years of weekly commentary on current events for *The Ipswich Journal* had made him better acquainted with national and international affairs than English novelists usually were; but while he was immersed in this task he had little opportunity of seeing the occurrences in their permanent perspective. Giving up his employment on the Ipswich paper about this time, he could ruminate with more leisure and form a more coherent and more radical outlook.

His young friend Alice Brandreth was startled by his iconoclasm:

*I do not think Mr Meredith liked the company of very rich people, and I remember well as a child how puzzled I was when I heard him say that in many cases the vision of rich people was limited to their personal possessions, and that their mental horizon was bounded by their own park gates . . . He was by nature very proud, and haughtily resented anything like patronage. He had a certain carriage of the head that we grew to recognize whenever he suspected any one of attempting to patronize him. They did not do it a second time.*

*With his Surrey neighbours who were his personal friends, however rich they were, he was very genial, and chaffed them constantly about their French cooks, orchid houses, and well-filled stables, and would ask them when they returned to their country residences from their town mansions, "Well, have you been going to many gabble-gobble dinner parties?"*

He became particularly exasperated with "the Parsonry" about this time and engaged in sharp arguments with clergymen of his neighborhood. He was therefore deeply impressed by Charles Bradlaugh, when he accompanied Maxse to a meeting addressed by that militant spokesman of free thought. Bradlaugh was in the midst of his fight for the Evidence Amendment Act, to enable atheists to testify in lawsuits without taking a religious oath; and he had recently defended his newspaper against a government prosecution for blasphemy and sedition. Meredith tried hard to impress Greenwood with the fact that Bradlaugh was an important phenomenon, "neither to be laughed nor sneered down, nor trampled."

In letters to Maxse, Meredith revaluated the leading writers of the day—Carlyle, Ruskin, Tennyson. He deplored the latest portions of *Idylls of the King* for disregard of contemporary ideas, and arraigned the public for having "corrupted this fine (natural) singer. In his degraded state I really believe he is useful, for he reflects as much as our Society chooses to show of itself . . . Tennyson has many spiritual indications, but no philosophy, and philosophy is the palace of thought." His other early mentor, Carlyle, also disappointed him in his current writings, by being "irritable" and "impetuous" in his comments on practical affairs. But Meredith continued to regard Carlyle as the greatest seminal influence of the era, so long as he stayed clear of legislative recommendations: "I hold that he is the nearest to being an inspired writer of any man in our times; he does proclaim inviolable law; he speaks from the deep springs of life . . . Philosophy, while rendering his dues to a man like Carlyle and acknowledging itself inferior in activity, despises his hideous blustering impatience in the presence of progressive fact."

His recurrent emphasis on "Philosophy" in literature was combined with an active attention to poetic technique. He spoke of studying the French alexandrine, and added, "When I have leisure I hope to write some papers on poetry and versification." His own poetry, naturally, was affected by his change of interest. He stopped writing the "roadside idylls" which had been his distinctive mode for the preceding ten years, and turned to presenting his poetic vision of reality through symbols and gnomic apothegms, rather than by literal portrayal of human types. This was not a new departure; it had been foreshadowed in his first book of poems by "South-west Wind in the Woodland" and ten years later by "Ode to the Spirit of Earth in Autumn." But his sunrise rites on Box Hill, his rambles through the woods of Norbury Park, renewed his conviction that trees and hills and the southwest wind were the poet's best clues to the essential meanings of life. He gave utterance to it in a long poem, "In the Woods," published in *The Fortnightly* in August, 1870.

Through the early months of 1870 he worked hard on *The Adventures of Harry Richmond*. In January he remarked that "I fear I am evolving his personality too closely for the public, but a man must work by the light of his conscience if he's to do anything worth reading." Later he told Jessopp that he was "busily finishing a novel for the *Cornhill Magazine*, one of three or four that are carved out and waiting . . . The English public will not let me probe deeply into humanity. You must not paint either man or woman; a surface view of the species flat as a wafer is acceptable. I have not plucked at any of the highest or deepest chords. Hence possibly those who have heard some of the chapters say it must be the best novel I have written." By the beginning of July he was able to say that the manuscript was "off his hands" and publication was to begin in the October number of *The Cornhill*. "By that time I hope to have another ready." In the same release of creative energy, he took up his comedy, *The Sentimentalists*, which he had begun eight years earlier, and wrote two more scenes of it.

For the summer months it was planned that Marie should take the little boy to Normandy for their usual visit to her relatives, and that

Meredith should remain in England and work for three weeks before going over to bring them back. Arthur had been invited to stay with other Vulliamy relatives in Dauphiné, and his father sent him detailed instructions about money and places to visit, with special advice—in view of the strained relations between France and Prussia—not to get into arguments with the French officer who was to be his host. Beginning to feel hopeful about his elder son, Meredith told Hardman that the youth's letters "speak promisingly."

On July 14th, Meredith believed that war between France and Prussia would not occur immediately; but within a week hostilities commenced, and all plans were changed. Meredith had some hopes of being sent over to report for *The Morning Post*, but soon learned that no correspondents would be allowed at the front. His wife's brother-in-law was called to the colors and was soon in the thick of action, and before long the home of the French kinsfolk was in the path of German invasion. Arthur remained at school in Württemberg. Thus personally implicated with both the warring nations, Meredith was also exposed to the conflicting views of his friends. Cotter Morison was strongly pro-Prussian. Captain Maxse, who had enjoyed youthful affairs of the heart in France, was intensely pro-French. Meredith and Morley strove to keep a balanced position between these extremes. At first he said, "On the whole, I side with France, or so incline. The instinct of the people in seizing an opportunity to dispute the aggrandizement of Prussia is right." Within a week he was optimistically remarking, "If we are energetic and wise it may be the last of the great fights of Europe." Three months later, his sympathies had veered: "This war is chargeable upon France, and the Emperor is the knave of the pack . . . The Germans, on the contrary, reap the reward of a persistently honourable career of civic virtue . . . I admire and respect the Germans, and God knows my heart bleeds for the French."

Mrs Meredith's father died during the summer; and it was perhaps a consequence of this bereavement that Meredith paid a dutiful visit to his own father and stepmother in Southsea, on his way to stay with the Maxses at Southampton, where he spent a fortnight, chiefly in yachting. He then joined his wife at the home of friends in Kent, after which they stayed for a while in lodgings at Eastbourne, because funds were insufficient for traveling farther afield. Meredith had been having one of his digestive attacks, and the sea-bathing made him feel much better.

There was a good augury for his long-deferred success as a novelist in the fact that *Harry Richmond* was coming out in *The Cornhill Magazine*. This was the most widely read monthly, to which nearly all the leading authors contributed. The serial was provided with lively illustrations by the rising young George du Maurier. But the author's name was not attached to the story, and he began to fear that he would not reap his deserved credit. Few readers of *The Cornhill* were likely to be familiar enough with his previous work to notice any identifying touches; and besides, the story was a wide departure from his usual style. On hearing that some people were attributing it to the aging Irish novelist Charles Lever, Meredith wrote to Hardman to suggest that the secret should be divulged to Shirley Brooks, editor of *Punch*, in the hope that the true identification might thus leak out. "I shall have another to follow when *Richmond* ceases," he told Hardman, "and so by drumming may make the public hear me at last."

His letters throughout the autumn were full of comments on the war; and at the beginning of December, when it was obvious that Germany was winning, he wrote a moving "Ode to France," in which he expressed his sympathy for the vanquished nation and prophesied her recovery in purified grandeur. He had envied Swinburne's declamatory odes on public events, and now at last he had a theme that roused him to similar eloquence. Though difficult in places, through the packed wealth of metaphor, the ode was a monumental achievement in the grand manner.

Submitting it to Morley for *The Fortnightly Review*, Meredith explained, "Latterly I have felt poetically weakened by the pressure of philosophical reflection, but this is going, and a fuller strength comes of it, for I believe I am within the shadow of the Truth, and as it's my nature to sing I may now do well." He was so convinced of the poem's value and topical significance that if Morley could not bring it out at once, the poet would do so himself, "and O my poor purse!" It was accepted, however, and appeared in the next issue of *The Fortnightly*.

His opinion gradually crystallized into satisfaction that England had remained neutral and that both France and Germany might learn a needed lesson from the war. Chiding Maxse for his blind partisanship, he said bluntly, "What I wish is that you and I should look to the good future of men with some faith in it, and capacity to regard current phases of history without letting our sensations blind and bewilder us. I am neither German nor French, nor, unless the nation is attacked, English. I am European and Cosmopolitan—for humanity! The nation which shows most worth, is the nation I love and reverence."

His interest in international questions had been stimulated not only by the war on the Continent but also by the theme of *Harry Richmond,* which dealt largely with the relationships between people of two nationalities, English and German. The two *Emilia* books had touched upon the contrast of English temperament with Italian, and Meredith now extended his study of national traits.

His love of the scenery and mores of Germany glowed in this book as warmly as in *Farina*. He depicted a little princely court with as much affection as Thackeray had done, and with less satire. And his scenes of typical German life were contrasted with others as essentially English —Squire Beltham and his manor house, Farmer Sweetwinter and his lush meadows.

A conspicuous change in style resulted from his decision to write in the first person. Subtle allusions and devious indirections had to be abandoned, for the fictitious narrator, while he was a cultivated and sensitive young man, was displayed as essentially simple and straight-forward. In this assumed style Meredith was surprisingly successful; it was warm, natural, and lively. Glimpses of Meredithian ideas occur throughout, and the descriptions of scenery also reveal his predilections, but never obtrusively enough to spoil the plausibility of Harry Rich-mond's character. Some of the author's pet opinions, which would have been inappropriate if expressed by the young narrator, were in-geniously introduced as the remarks made to him by the enlightened Princess Ottilia or by her sardonic old tutor.

The story had already been told in many familiar fictitious biog-raphies—the slow, painful achievement of maturity by a youth who must conquer many illusions and suffer many miseries before he learns the truth about himself and the world. As such, it belongs with *David Copperfield* and *Great Expectations* and *Pendennis*. As in those novels, one of the young man's strongest adversaries is his own conceit; and as in them also, the contrasting power of unselfishness is symbolized by some of the feminine characters. Meredith, however, gave his own peculiar emphasis to both themes—the absolute necessity of conquer-ing egoism, and the superior nobility of women over men. Ottilia was the preternaturally wise and selfless young woman, far too perfect for human nature's daily food, who first came into his work as Noorna bin Noorka.

Not only was the style more natural than in his other novels, but the tempo also was more even and the plot more firmly built. The scenes proceeded in clear order and proportion; the few instances of fragmentary clues were fully justified by the limitations of the point of view. The basic outlines of the plot were almost mathematically regu-lar: Harry was perpetually divided between the claims of his father and his maternal grandfather; he fell in love with two splendid girls, one intellectual and gracious, the other practical and assertive; he had also felt youthful fancies for two other girls, even more violently contrasted —a passionate gypsy and a gentle country lass.

These structural mechanics of the book were richly overlaid with the irresistible charm of the events. There are gypsy episodes that have all the open-air freshness and picaresque vigor of Borrow. There are scenes of dynastic intrigue in a little German principality that set a model for the "Ruritanian" school of fiction. The early chapters re-create the unquestioning receptivity of childhood. And vitalizing the whole story is the unrivaled figure of an indomitable adventurer, Harry's father, Richmond Roy.

In depicting this personage, Meredith had to practice some discreet implication. Richmond Roy was a claimant to the throne of England, on the basis of an asserted secret marriage of a former royal personage (necessarily George IV or one of his brothers). In fact, the author made a composite out of the valid but childless marriage of George to Mrs Fitzherbert and the unhallowed but prolific union of William IV to the Irish actress Dorothy Jordan, which had contributed a tribe of Fitzclarences to English society. But in the heyday of Victoria's reign it would have been highly impolitic, if not positively treasonable, to base a novel openly upon a challenge to her tenure of the monarchy. Therefore the "great cause" of Richmond Roy was subtly indicated by small clues but never stated in positive terms. Furthermore, the authenticity of his claim was never brought to proof; and this element of unsolved mystery added greatly to the peculiar effect of the characterization. The reader is left with a fascinating array of alternatives. Was Richmond a legitimate royal scion, unjustly deprived of his rights? Or was he the bastard of a royal intrigue, inheriting some of the dynastic temperament? Or was he a sheer adventurer of lowly origin, making a supreme bid for power? And if this third alternative be accepted, there still remain two possibilities: he might be an unscrupulous rascal, dramatizing his impressive manners and magnetic personality, or he might be a fanatic who had convinced himself of the truth of his chimerical claim. The various possibilities are kept in such perfect balance throughout the book (though never openly discussed) that the reader is apt to end without reaching a decision. But instead of rendering Richmond's character indistinct or inconsistent, the uncertainty adds to his complex and compelling spell. He is akin to the great verbose misfits and lovable rogues of literature—to Falstaff and Micawber—but the aura of mystery adds a tragic overtone to the fantastic absurdity of his words and deeds. Always a bit larger than life in his eloquence, his opportunism, his sheer animal vitality and resilience, Richmond is yet a convincing personality and not a caricature. The reader shares the mixture of helpless exasperation and grudging respect with which Richmond's friends and enemies alike reacted to his compulsive energy.

Although the social milieu was widely different, *Harry Richmond* had remarkable and probably unconscious resemblances to *David Copperfield*. It is not merely that both books are exceptionally successful in starting with a child's earliest impressions and gradually advancing toward a mature outlook through school days and young manhood. The plot situation and some of the characters are also similar. In addition to Richmond Roy's resemblance to Micawber, there is a parallel between David's two friends, Traddles and Steerforth, and Harry's Temple and Heriot; and the story of Heriot and Kiomi, though less prominent in the plot, is identical with that of Steerforth and Em'ly. Moreover, Harry's own love story, with his idealized devotion to Princess Ottilia, while his appropriate mate, Janet, waits patiently in the background, repeats the relationship of David with Dora and Agnes.

The inner, emotional kinship, however, between Dickens's novel and Meredith's arises from the fact that both are intimately autobiographical. Not since *Evan Harrington* had Meredith put so much of his own experience into a book; and while the earlier one was closer to the facts in matters of detail, *Harry Richmond* was deeper in emotional identification. Some external facts of Meredith's early life, to be sure, can be seen in it. Rippinger's school is probably a faithful representation of the boarding school he attended, and the visits to Sarkeld are full of memories of the author's year at Neuwied. Janet Ilchester was as much a portrait of Janet Duff Gordon as Rose Jocelyn had been; and her dutiful decision to marry the worthless Lord Edbury—paralleling a similar episode in *Evan Harrington*—was Meredith's unconscious interpretation of the real Janet's marriage to the middle-aged Henry James Ross, with the compensation that the fictional Janet could be rescued from matrimony at the last moment and preserved for union with the autobiographic hero.

Though Mabel Sweetwinter plays a minor role in the book, this very insignificance is to be noted. She is the blond, buxom farm girl, to whom love is all of life, and who disastrously accepts a lover above her in station. But in contrast with Lucy Desborough and Dahlia Fleming, she is treated almost cavalierly, as nothing more than a seductive physical specimen, without endowment of either spiritual grace or even normal intelligence. Whatever private memory may have originated

Meredith's preoccupation with this type, the lapse of years had reduced it to a mild sweetness.

Her antitype, the ferociously independent Kiomi, was drawn from a more recent source. Her original was a gypsy model who sat for Sandys for a number of his paintings and was well known to the frequenters of his studio.

The fundamental personal element in the book, however, was in the relationship of Harry Richmond with his father, which was essentially that of George Meredith with Augustus, complicated with a few glimpses of Arthur Meredith's relationship with George. Richmond Roy had the aristocratic bearing and expansive schemes of Augustus Meredith, with some touches of old Melchizedek added. In both cases the improvident father met financial disaster (Augustus Meredith's bankruptcy and Richmond's term in the debtors' prison) and both tried to obtain the inheritance that was due to the son from the deceased wife. In both cases opportune aid came from the resources of the deceased wife's sister. Viewed impartially, of course, there is something ludicrous in comparing the vast wealth of the Belthams with the thousand pounds that descended to George Meredith from his mother and the nine hundred-odd pounds from his aunt Macnamara. But emotionally the situation was identical, and one is tempted to say that Harry Richmond is the final wish-fulfillment of Meredith's boyish dreams: he is the heir to vast wealth, and he is of putative royal descent, even if the legitimacy is doubtful. And the ambivalence in Harry's attitude toward his father, compounded equally of dazzled admiration and humiliated fury, must have approximated George Meredith's feeling toward Augustus. Even in such a detail as Harry's disapproval of his father's plan for a second marriage, there is a reflection of the actual circumstances.

In contrast with the overwhelming vigor of Richmond Roy, his son inevitably appeared to be a negative character. Some readers complained that he was little better than a cipher, dragged in the wake of the more forceful personalities who chose to take an interest in him. But this was consistent with Meredith's theory that the average young person is malleable, with capabilities of becoming either good or evil, depending on the blows he receives from the hammer of experience. Harry is the same sort of well-intentioned but undeveloped youth as Wilfrid Pole; he annoys the reader more, simply because he is central in the story and because he frankly records his own vacillations and apprehensions.

Sentimental readers protested also because Janet Ilchester was shown as a greedy, domineering little girl who yet developed into a generous adult. The author did not mean that her youthful assertiveness was selfish. Rather, she was a realist, who naturally clashed with Harry's romantic notions because she never accepted the genteel conventions, whether as an uninhibited child or as a candid woman. As a portrait of Janet Duff Gordon she was probably a more objective achievement than Rose Jocelyn had been.

Meredith's friendship with Dr Gordon and his family at Pixholme remained cordial, and he enjoyed the cheerful young people with their charades and dumb-crambo. Alice Brandreth found him endlessly entertaining:

*He would often out in the garden, or while we were walking over the hills, start a kind of comic dialogue in which he himself would represent both actors . . . He would invent love affairs and adventures for us, or for some of the visitors who were staying at Pixholme . . . I recall to mind one little gentleman, very plain, short, and bald, with a hesitating manner. Mr Meredith, as soon as ever he met him, started him on a series of gay and gallant adventures in pursuit of a fair heiress who lived on one of the hills round Dorking . . . Every time he came to Pixholme Mr Meredith would be ready with a new and fantastic suggestion as to the manner in which he should propose marriage to the lady, or some novel idea as to the way in which he might capture her affection . . . I wondered sometimes how the poor man could endure these constant caricatures of his hesitation and peculiarities.*

Whenever Miss Brandreth was staying at Pixholme she used to come over to Flint Cottage frequently to play duets with Mrs Meredith on the piano; and although Meredith was fond of his wife's music he "did not like either duets or practisings, and he used to make sarcastic comments on our performances, and excelled in weird and whimsical comparisons of our music to farmyard noises."

Visitors to the house were sometimes embarrassed by his mordant remarks to his wife, and their unanimous admiration of Mrs Meredith was apt to be touched with pity. She seems, however, to have understood her husband's temperament very well, confident of the affection that lurked behind his sarcasm, and she parried his ridicule with unruffled cheerfulness. He once described her as "a mud fort. You fire broadsides into her, and nothing happens."

Henry M. Hyndman, who renewed his friendship with Meredith upon joining the editorial staff of *The Pall Mall Gazette*, termed her "charming, clever, tactful, and handsome . . . a good musician, a pleasant conversationalist, a most considerate, attentive, and patient wife and an excellent mother."

*Her care of her husband was always thoughtful but never obtrusive, and Meredith with all his high qualities was not by any means an easy man to live with . . . This lovable lady was as humble as she was devoted. They were going out together to some grand party and she said to my wife, "It is not me they want to see, it is my clever husband." I remember, too, that once when dining with us a well-known man of that day made a vigorous attack on France and French life and French women. We were horrified and at a loss what to do or say. Mrs Meredith, however, in the most pleasing way took up the subject, showed, of course, in a few words that she knew a great deal more about it than the unfortunate critic, and without the least betraying that she was French herself put things right.*

Through their close association on *The Fortnightly Review,* Meredith had come to regard John Morley as one of his best-loved friends. Morley's moderate and long-sighted view of world affairs, his scholarly yet vigorous interpretation of history, his belief in the spiritual value of communion with Nature, accorded more nearly with Meredith's own ideas than did those of any other member of their circle. He was therefore delighted when the Morleys took a house near Guildford, thus moving into Meredith's region of Surrey. A young man named James Sully accompanied them as tutor to Morley's stepson. "Among the visitors that I met at Morley's," Sully says in his reminiscences, "was George Meredith, who held me spellbound by his brilliant table talk. Frederick Greenwood was another guest on this occasion. We had to listen as best we could while Meredith made merry in his deliciously extravagant manner over the unlucky attempts of some *nouveau riche* to spread a luxurious table and select choice wines. Our host, shaken by laughter to the verge of tears, had at last to plead for a pause in the Rabelaisian torrent." Sully then went for a long tramp across the hills with Meredith and Greenwood, and listened to their "piquant gossip from the realm of 'high life.' "

Meredith's habit of satirical exaggeration and his cocksure assertion of his opinions were apt to give offense to some hearers. It is a paradox of the novelist's mind that his insight into human character as a basis for his creative work is often unaccompanied by a quick perception of the feelings of those around him. Real people all too easily become identical with the figments of his imagination who lack independent sensibility outside of their creator's ken. Again and again Meredith hurt the feelings of his friends, sometimes to the extent of permanent rupture. Thus he had fallen out with Swinburne and Rossetti. Thus he had incurred squabbles with Wyse during their walking-tour together. If Captain Maxse had not been of uncommonly sweet disposition he, too, would have rebelled against Meredith's sarcastic diatribes. In December, 1870, for example, Maxse appealed to him to devote himself entirely to writing propaganda on behalf of his "genuine convictions." Meredith straightway improvised a burlesque plot for an opera "to popularize the Democratic movement," and he reported gleefully that Maxse had "savagely" accused him of "buffoonery" and that "the poor fellow danced with disgust."

Believing that he could always speak his mind freely to Morley, he had no suspicion that a streak of sensitive egoism made the younger man cringe under contradiction. He was shocked and wounded when he received in March a solemn letter in which Morley stated that for the past six months Meredith's conversation had conflicted so painfully with his "opinions, ideas, and likings" that he was always unhappy when they were together. Though admitting that they thought alike on all larger issues, he asserted that Meredith was the only friend in whose presence he did not feel that he was deriving new strength.

Casting back for a possible reason for the complaint, Meredith could only remember a discussion of Robert Buchanan's pretentious new poem, *The Book of Orm,* which he had ridiculed but which Morley admired. He composed a dignified and affectionate reply, expressing his surprise and regret, and proposing that they should see as little of each other as possible for the next two or three years, after which they might come together naturally and resume their intimacy.

Under Morley *The Fortnightly Review* had steadily become more outspoken in its championing of the Positivist philosophy. Cotter Morison was a leading disciple of that faith, and Maxse had been attracted by its "religion of humanity." Through these channels the ideas of Positivism had played a major part in Meredith's new intellectual alignment. After the break with Morley, two other energetic members of the coterie became influential with him.

One of these was Frederic Harrison, a noted authority on jurisprudence and a crusader in many progressive causes, particularly trade unionism. The other Positivist who was becoming a close friend of Meredith's was Leslie Stephen. Melancholy in temperament, shy and silent in manner, the lean, red-bearded Stephen was the antithesis of handsome, talkative Meredith. But after their first meeting in Austria they were often brought together by common interests and activities.

Both were contributors to *The Pall Mall Gazette*, and in 1871 Stephen became editor of *The Cornhill Magazine*, before *The Adventures of Harry Richmond* had finished appearing in its pages. A stronger bond between them was their shared love of long walks. Meredith learned to admire and respect the sincerity that underlay Stephen's awkward demeanor.

On June 10, 1871, Mrs Meredith gave birth to a daughter, who was given the name "Marie Eveleen." Alice Brandreth describes how Meredith came over to Pixholme the next morning "almost breathless with joy" to announce the news; but in his letters his allusions to the event were something less than enthusiastic. He was too painfully aware of his interminable bills, his inadequate house, and the tireless energy of small children, as exemplified in her five-year-old brother.

About the middle of August he went to the Continent for a six weeks' tour, which included eight days with Arthur. As the latter was now eighteen, his father tried to form a final estimate of his character and potentialities. He reported to the Jessopps:

*He is a short man, slightly moustached, having a touch of whisker; a good walker, a middling clear thinker, sensible, brilliant in nothing, tending in no direction, very near to what I predicted of him as a combatant in life, but with certain reserve qualities of mental vigour which may develop; and though he seems never likely to be intellectually an athlete, one may hope he may be manful . . . In a comparative examination of 50 he would be about 25th.*

Believing that the boy's power of thought was not being stimulated enough in the somewhat sluggish Swabian town, he considered transferring him to Berlin, where incentive to study would be stronger.

Having finished its serial run, *The Adventures of Harry Richmond* came out in three-volume form at the end of October, with the author's name attached. Meredith had been anxious that his friends should suspend their judgment until they could read it as a unit and thus discover the total effect. To Jessopp he said:

*Consider first my scheme as a workman. It is to show you the action of minds as well as of fortunes—and here and there men and women vitally animated by their brains at different periods of their lives—and of men and women with something of a look-out upon the world and its destinies . . . I dare say the novel won't be liked, but I know my plan, I do my work, and if I am kept very poor I hope to pay all in time. As for recognition of the stuff in my* writing, and the system it goes on, I care little for it now, and when I thrust myself into the Pillory by publishing, the smack in the face and the pat on the shoulder are things in the day's order.

Similarly he hoped that Hardman would "see that the conception was full and good, and was honestly worked out":

I resisted every temptation to produce great and startling effects (after the scene of the Statue, which was permissible in art, as coming from a boy and coloured by a boy's wonder). Note, as you read, the gradual changes of growing Harry, in his manner of regarding his father and the world. I have carried it so far as to make him perhaps dull towards adolescence and young manhood.

As usual, the first reports from the publishers threw cold water on his hopes. The book was not selling well, and Mudie's Library was too deluged with other novels to give it much circulation. Its reception from the critics was mixed. *The Examiner* declared that the author "indulges in the wildest vagaries of plot-making" and "writes with meaningless sententiousness," and that his characters "are only puppets." *The Athenaeum* also saw no merit in it. But *The Spectator* grudgingly conceded that it "shows originality, wealth of conception, genius and not a little detailed knowledge of the world . . . It would be far truer to say that it has the stuff for half-a-dozen first-rate novels in it, than that it is a first-rate novel itself." *The Daily News* lauded it as "a book in every sense remarkable"; *The Westminster Review* confessed that "whilst we are reading, we are fascinated and spell-bound"; and *Blackwood's Magazine* called it a "wild, half-mad, and wholly clever performance."

In the history of fiction, however, *Harry Richmond* has a significance beyond its immediate effect on the critics. It was published at a time when the English novel was showing signs of reverting toward the romantic. R. D. Blackmore's *Lorna Doone* appeared in 1869; William Black's first three successful novels in 1869, 1870, and 1871. Perhaps it was only chance that made Meredith's new novel much more romantic than his previous ones. He was trying out his talents by experimenting with a new atmosphere, as he had already done in *Rhoda Fleming*. When a younger generation of writers went further in romantic storytelling, this was the novel of Meredith's that charmed them most.

# Beauchamp's Career

IN NOVEMBER Meredith was hailed by a voice from the past. Richard H. Horne had recently come back to England after seventeen years in Australia. He had never lost interest in his young admirer: when his epic *Orion* was reprinted in Sydney he mentioned Meredith in the preface as one of the young English poets who had appreciated it; and long afterwards he had written to Meredith and enclosed his photograph, but had received no reply. His return to England was not triumphant, for he was in want of money and many former friends condemned him for having deserted his wife when he emigrated. Feeling hurt when Meredith made no move to welcome him home, Horne sent him one of his books, which elicited formal words of praise, a lame apology because no copy of a book by Meredith was available to be presented in return, and a few complaints about the critics. Horne had no means of realizing that this unaccountable chilliness was part of Meredith's pathological insistence upon severing every emotional link with the days of his early poetry and his first marriage.

About the end of the year he rendered one of his most questionable judgments on a manuscript submitted to Chapman & Hall. It was a queer work which began like a serious travel book and evolved into a satiric fantasy. The writer was an unknown young man who had formerly been a sheep-raiser in New Zealand, and the title was *Erewhon*. Meredith rejected it with a curt "will not do"; and thirty years later, in the preface to a revised edition, the author, Samuel Butler, remarked that the publishers had rejected it "under the advice of one who has attained the highest rank among living writers," and added, "I believe their reader advised them quite wisely. They told me he reported that it was a philosophical work, little likely to be popular with a wide circle of readers. I hope that if I had been their reader, and the book had been submitted to myself, I should have advised them to the same effect." In his private notebook Butler phrased this idea less politely: "I should probably have condemned his *Diana of the Crossways*, or indeed any other of his books, had it been submitted to myself. No wonder if his work repels me that mine should repel him."

Meredith's friendship with Alice Brandreth had extended to her parents. E. L. Brandreth was a learned philologist, and his wife pleased Meredith by her sense of humor and her outspoken prejudices. When he or Mrs Meredith went up to London they often stayed with the Brandreths in South Kensington. If he spent an evening at the theatre he would keep the breakfast table the next morning in roars of laughter with his burlesquing of the performers. The Brandreths were friends of Edward Dannreuther, a German pianist and musicologist, and when Meredith accompanied them to informal concerts at Dannreuther's house in Orme Square he would meet Browning, George Eliot, and other writers and musicians, with whom lively conversation, after the music, would last far into the night.

In spite of Meredith's sarcastic jokes, Alice as she grew up fell into the habit of confiding in him. He pleased her by always punctiliously calling her "Miss Brandreth" in public, he listened tolerantly to her naïve chatter about her literary tastes and her religious convictions (both strictly conventional), and he gave wise advice about the evil of selfishness and the spiritual rewards of misfortune and the error of mistaking sentimental flirtation for true love.

Arthur Meredith's problems were giving his father a good deal of anxiety. A year before, Jessopp had suggested that when the boy returned from abroad he might be able to try for a Taylorian Scholarship at Oxford, on the strength of his knowledge of German. In spite of the straitened family finances, Meredith and his wife agreed that they would try to support him at the University for a couple of years if he had any prospect of eventually gaining a fellowship. Arthur, however, was unenthusiastic. His only idea for the future was that he might become an author, and to this plan his father was anything but encouraging.

The correspondence between them had become strangely apathetic. Arthur submitted dutiful reports on his holidays, his health, his expenses, and his studies. The ponderous thoroughness of his letters was echoed in his father's replies, which were largely confined to pedantic literary discussion, on such subjects as the comparative merits of Ossian and Homer, and the moral excellences of Cicero and Socrates. Meredith's letters read like textbook essays, without a trace of his individual tone. Indeed, they had a touch of pomposity that suggested the manner of Sir Austin Feverel. When Arthur gave his opinions on religion, his father replied with conscientious solemnity:

*The Christian teaching is sound and good: the ecclesiastical dogma is an instance of the poverty of humanity's mind hitherto . . . Belief in the religion has done and does this good to the young; it floats them through the perilous sensual period when the animal appetites most need control and transmutation. If you have not the belief, set yourself to love virtue by understanding that it is your best guide both as to what is due to others and what is for your own positive personal good.*

For shy, sensitive Arthur, alone in a foreign country, these oracular counsels cannot have been very nourishing. But in writing to Maxse, just at the same time, Meredith revealed his thoroughly human anxiety and affection for his son. Maxse offered to nominate Arthur for an appointment in the foreign service, to go out to China and learn the language in order to become an official interpreter. No doubt with ironical recollections of his own father's scheme of sending him to Hong Kong when he was about the same age, Meredith apologetically stated many reasons for declining: the boy could not prepare in two months for the qualifying examination; he was interested in European affairs and was having a good opportunity of observing them; there would be little chance of promotion for him; "to him the East would seem like banishment"; and finally, "I shudder at the thought of losing sight of the boy altogether."

In the autumn of 1872 he paid Arthur another visit, in the course of a Continental trip. As usual, Mrs Meredith and the children were left with her relations in Normandy, while her husband went to Germany and Austria. He particularly enjoyed a stay at Salzburg, and drew his customary sustenance from sunrises over the Alps, before returning to spend the final days of the holiday with the Vulliamys.

Throughout the year he was working intermittently on his next novel and continuing to produce poetry. The September *Cornhill Magazine* contained his rather difficult "Song of Theodolinda," which told the story of the Iron Crown of Lombardy in an oblique and condensed manner, using it as a symbol of the temptation of spiritual pride.

A new journalistic venture engaged him at the end of the year— a series of dialogues on current topics, contributed to the weekly

*Graphic* under the title of "Up to Midnight." He described himself, in a letter to Greenwood, as "having some fun" with these sketches, and added that he "might by and by turn the Dialogues to good purpose, but I fear the grave commercial men sitting on it won't stand me long." He was right. The series ran for only five issues, from December 21 to January 28. In their brief career the dialogues were a faithful resuscitation of the method of Thomas Love Peacock. The interlocutors were a batch of ideological puppets straight out of *Headlong Hall* or *Crotchet Castle*. But their opinions about polar exploration, agricultural wages, and England's relations with France and Ireland and India were distinctly less exuberant than those Olympian conflicts of wit and prejudice had been.

Meredith's hopes for Arthur were encouraged when, in March, 1873, a street-rioting episode in Stuttgart provided the lad with material for a two-column article which was printed in *The Morning Post*. Perhaps, after all, Arthur would be able to make a career for himself as a writer.

The new novel was now well advanced. In the burlesque letter to Maxse seven years before, Meredith had imagined himself in 1870 making his friend the hero of a novel to be called "Sir Harry Firebrace of the Beacon, Knight Errant of the Nineteenth Century"; and now to some degree he was carrying out that notion in earnest. Nevil Beauchamp, his hero, was a full-length portrait of Maxse; and the Southampton election in which Meredith had helped to campaign supplied the central action of the story.

The manuscript had been promised to the publisher for the end of May, but in April he realized that an additional month would be needed for completing it. He told Jessopp that he was so busy with the book that he could not even spend a day in London. The letter included a perceptive analysis of his own idiosyncrasy as a novelist:

'The world is too much with me' when I write. I cannot go on with a story and not feel that to treat of flesh and blood is to touch the sacredest; and so it usually ends in my putting the destinies of the world about it—like an atmosphere, out of which it cannot subsist. So my work fails. I see it. But the pressure is on me with every new work. I fear that Beauchamp is worse than the foregoing in this respect. The centre idea catches hold of the ring of the Universe; the dialogues are the delivery of creatures of this world, and the writing goodish. But altogether it will only appeal (so I fear) to them that have a taste for me; it won't catch the gudgeon World, and I, though I never write for money, want it—and there is a state of stultification for you.

As usual, he took much longer to finish the work than he had confidently predicted. And when it was eventually turned in, a disappointment ensued. George Smith, as publisher of *The Cornhill Magazine*, had held out hopes of serialization; but after reading the manuscript he regretfully told the author that it would not suit the taste of his readers.

Having already suspected the story's lack of popular appeal, Meredith knew that it was better suited to the more intellectual clientele of *The Fortnightly Review*, though unluckily the fitness of this audience and their consequent fewness meant that the rate of payment would be much lower than what *The Cornhill* would have paid. A further difficulty was that Morley was still editor of *The Fortnightly* and Meredith was not on speaking terms with him.

Meredith's unhappiness over the broken friendship was discernible in a letter to Greenwood a year before. Referring to "a famous case known to us" in which "a formal editorial letter" had notified him of his having given offense, he remarked cynically:

*All states of life have their privileges, and mine is to be behind the scenes of many illustrious and ringing names, and to laugh. How truly wise is so and so! I hear, and I bow. The aim of the pretenders must be but to have this homage of the public, and who would rob them of it because he happens to be behind them on the stage and peruses a dead blank instead of the pretty picture confronting the praiser?*

In May, 1874, when the problem of *Beauchamp's Career* developed, Greenwood and Maxse took it upon themselves to act as mediators. They described the book glowingly to Morley, who by this time was feeling ashamed of his peevishness; and he asked them to inform Meredith that he would be happy to accept the story if it could be reasonably condensed for serial publication. Meredith replied in a friendly—though constrained—letter, and in the subsequent months of correspondence about the revision of the novel he repeatedly included warm praise of Morley's current articles. Within a year they were back on their old footing of intimacy; and when Morley wrote his *Recollections*, forty years later, he ingeniously recorded his contrition by telling the episode in a manner favorable to Meredith, though not revealing that "the friend to whom [Meredith] was much attached" was none other than Morley himself. "We may be quite sure," Morley concluded, "that the breach, though its causes were not wholly superficial, quickly ended in loyal oblivion."

When Morley asked him to shorten the novel for serialization, Meredith consented without forebodings. He thought he could easily omit the letters, part of Beauchamp's amorous adventures in France, "the heavier of the electioneering passages," many bits of discursive conversation, and some of the author's comments at the beginnings of chapters. The central theme, which he must retain, was "the personal abnegation coming, in spite of errors here and there (and as it were in spite of the man himself), of a noble devotion to politics from the roots up"; but this might even be made more effective by "the exclusion of a host of my own reflections." As Chapman & Hall were willing to bring out the novel in three-volume form, the omitted material could then be restored.

He soon found that to reduce the manuscript by at least one third was not so easy as it sounded. Two months after agreeing to the attempt he had done nothing more than read it over and make mental notes for cuts, lulled by Chapman's report that Morley was in no hurry to begin. In mid-July came a peremptory demand for the first instalment, and Meredith hastily sent off three chapters, with only slight excisions. As the publication started in the August number of *The Fortnightly*, he was committed to the task and had to continue doggedly, soon discovering that practically the whole book had to be rewritten in order to make the necessary condensation.

Meanwhile an inquiry about the American rights came to him from Moncure D. Conway, a popular preacher and lecturer, formerly editor of liberal periodicals in Cincinnati and Boston, and now minister of the South Place Chapel in London. Having heard that Conway had mentioned his books favorably in lectures, Meredith replied with thanks for the praise but with a warning that the new book was "not likely to please the greater number of readers." He gave Conway a good summary of its theme:

It is philosophical-political, with no powerful stream of adventure: an attempt to show the forces round a young man of the present day, in England, who would move them, and finds them unutterably solid, though it is seen in the end that he does not altogether fail, has not lived quite in vain . . . A certain drama of self-conquest is gone through, for the hero is not perfect. He is born of the upper class, and is scarcely believed in by any class, except when he vexes his own, and it is then to be hated. At the same time the mild spirit of a prosperous middle class, that is not extremely alarmed, is shown to be above persecuting; so that the unfortunate young man is in danger of being thought dull save by those who can enter into his idea of the advancement of Human-

*ity and his passion for it . . . I think his History a picture of the time—taking its mental action, and material ease and indifference, to be a necessary element of the picture.*

The idea of an American edition persisted for several months, Chapman using it as an added reason for demanding speed with the revision, as advance sheets were to be sent off to the United States as soon as they were ready. Meredith's forebodings, however, were justified, as no American publisher accepted the book at that time.

Captain Maxse was in Austria for his health, and Meredith was longing to join him in an Alpine walking-tour, but the dull job of condensation kept him at his desk through a rainy summer. As an interlude, he wrote a long poem, "The Nuptials of Attila," derived from the same era of history as his recent "Theodolinda." At the end of the year he was still slaving over the revision of *Beauchamp* and petitioning his friends for comments on the published instalments, to guide him in the task. He sent proofs of each monthly portion to Maxse, thus submitting his hero's behavior to the authoritative opinion of the young man's prototype, just as he had formerly read *Evan Harrington* to the Duff Gordons to test the authenticity of the Jocelyn family.

Another job of revision was undertaken about this time. The Leipzig firm of Tauchnitz offered to bring out *The Ordeal of Richard Feverel* in their series of British authors. Meredith had told Jessopp not long before that upon looking through the book he had felt "a sharp distaste. The lumpy style is offensive." He therefore decided to make some changes. To have remedied the style, however, he would have had to rewrite every page of it, a task far beyond his patience. Instead, he merely changed a few words here and there, and at two or three points cut out large gobbets and crudely stitched up the incisions. The first four chapters were condensed into one, completely omitting a caricature of a group of agitators for "women's rights," written in the manner of Peacock. Another discarded chapter was one in which Sir Austin interviewed his feminine counterpart, Mrs Grandison, in the hope of selecting one of her daughters as a mate for his son. Meredith's judgment was sound enough in regard to both excisions; but unfortunately he did not take the trouble to salvage some details which deserved to survive, and of which more than one was actually needed for clear comprehension of the story. The role of Benson the butler in subsequent events lost much plausibility with the cancellation of his preliminary portrait. The whole of Richard's seventh-birthday scene, and its parallel seven years later when he refused to strip for his physical examination, were a lamentable loss, both for their comedy and for their psychological foreshadowing. By the disappearance of another paragraph, even the "ordeal" in the title was deprived of some significance. Worst of all, the basic principles of the great System were largely deleted. Apart from making some later references unduly cryptic, the net effect of the revision was to diminish the satire and proportionately to increase the emotional element.

On into 1875 his letters complained of overwork and the impossibility of snatching even two days "for pleasure." In April he told Morley that "I go nowhere, see, hear, know nothing." His life, however, was not quite so drab as these complaints imply. We hear of his seeing Irving in *Hamlet* and Salvini in *Othello*; and at the end of the year, after his work on *Beauchamp* was terminated, he was inveigled into a series of amateur Shakespearian readings. Alice Brandreth, now a lively girl of twenty, was ambitious to become an actress, and her strait-laced mother consented to let her perform several Shakespearian plays, so long as no scenery or special costumes were used and no young men were allowed to read the lovers' parts. Meredith received the parental approval for these romantic roles, because "he was always so good to Allie, as he understands girls so well."

Rehearsals were held both at Pixholme and at the Brandreths' London house, with Meredith as an exacting but patient coach. He was amused by the cast that the imperious young lady had recruited, for most of the men were elderly pedants from her father's circle. They included A. J. Ellis, phonetician and apostle of simplified spelling, F. J. Furnivall, the pugnacious Shakespearian scholar, James Joseph Sylvester, the originator of algebraic invariants, Dr Isaac Burney Yeo, an authority on health resorts and diet, John Palgrave Simpson, a minor dramatist and novelist, and Charles Kegan Paul, who was just then publishing his biography of William Godwin and had recently given up his holy orders in the Church of England because he had long been a Positivist and a Unitarian. Incidental music was provided by Dannreuther.

This grey-headed phalanx being interspersed with some of Alice's contemporaries, Meredith felt that censorship was included among his duties. When a young reader launched innocently into one of the bawdier speeches he would reach for the book, draw a pencil through the lines, and say mildly, "Don't read that." His chief pupil recounts how "he took much pains in teaching the various readers to manage the tone of their voice properly, and would often point out to us how varied were the possibilities of inflection, and how much speech gained by placing the voice in different ways according to the emotions that we wished to convey." Occasionally his patience gave out and he relapsed into caricaturing of their ineptitudes.

Meredith was obliged to read the principal role in each play, opposite to Alice as the heroine. In rapid succession he was Benedick in *Much Ado About Nothing*, Petruchio in *The Taming of the Shrew*, Orlando in *As You Like It*, Malvolio in *Twelfth Night* (a welcome change from heroism), and Bassanio in *The Merchant of Venice*. "He had a resonant and beautiful voice," Alice testified, "but it must be recorded that he was not himself a good reader . . . He would be so busy observing the other readers that, when his own turn came, he lost his place and muddled his lines, and when he read the lover's part he employed a sort of contemptuous tone that made it exasperatingly difficult for anyone reading the heroine's part with him to imagine for a moment he was even interested in her . . . His reading of Petruchio gave him fairer scope, and Malvolio was extremely good, the words of which he trolled forth in the gayest, most infectious manner. We all laughed so much that it was difficult to continue our reading." He even let himself be wheedled into promising to write a play specially for the group to read.

While these pastimes were being concocted, *Beauchamp's Career* came out in book form, and was not very warmly received. The ending, with the utterly fortuitous death of the hero, displeased many readers; and indeed Meredith's wife had pleaded vainly with him to remove this wantonly cruel stroke of fate. To all her appeals he replied that there was no other possible end for Nevil Beauchamp.

The identification of Captain Maxse as the model for Beauchamp was obvious to anyone who knew him; but Meredith thereby involved himself in a delicate situation as far as his hero's private affairs were concerned. He must have been aware that Maxse's married life, which had begun in a romantic fervor fifteen years before, had lapsed into incompatibility, and that a separation was imminent. Mrs Maxse, a charming and beautiful woman, was devoted to London, and her chosen friends were sophisticated artists; she had no sympathy with her husband's love of country life and his political crusading. Meredith avoided portraying her in either of the two women whom Nevil Beauchamp unsuccessfully wooed. One of them, it is true, had the same name as Mrs Maxse (Cecilia) and, like her, was the daughter of a retired colonel; but there was little further resemblance. Some of Alice Brandreth's friends claimed to recognize her as the original of Cecilia Halkett, and wrote playful rhymes about it. She asked Meredith whether they were right, and he answered that no character in fiction ought to be regarded as derived from a single real person, but that Cecilia's conventional upbringing as the only child of devoted parents was like Alice's, and that Alice would undoubtedly behave similarly in rejecting a suitor if her parents did not approve of him. When Alice hotly contradicted him, he shrugged and changed the subject.

The other woman in Beauchamp's life, Renée de Croisnel, was suggested by a French interlude early in Maxse's career, long before his marriage. Renée's Gallic mixture of emotional impulsiveness and family loyalty gained plausibility through Meredith's acquaintance with his own Norman relatives, their home territory being affectionately described as the estate of the Croisnels. Some of Meredith's other happy foreign days, in Venice and among the Alps, also contributed to the romantic atmosphere in which Renée moved, and helped to create the personal enchantment that the novelist felt in his fictional character. He remarked twenty years later to Marcel Schwob, "Wasn't she a sweet girl? I think I am a little in love with her yet." And he told another friend that he liked this the best of his novels: "Sometimes *Harry Richmond* is my favourite, but I am inclined to give the palm to *Beauchamp's Career*. There is a breezy, human interest about it, and the plot has a consistency and logical evolution which *Richard Feverel* lacks. Then, a thing that weighs with me, the French critics liked it; they said that Renée is true to life."

The personal element in the story was strengthened by the fact that Blackburn Tuckham, Beauchamp's favored rival for Cecilia's hand, was an equally precise portrait of Meredith's other closest friend, William Hardman. Tuckham's heavy physique, his North Country common sense, and his imperturbable Toryism were alike drawn from Hardman. In the eight years since Meredith's removal from Kingston to Box Hill they had seen little of each other, though their affection remained alive. Hardman was busy with practical affairs, and in 1872 had become editor of the Conservative *Morning Post*, while Meredith's associations were more and more exclusively with Radicals and freethinkers.

The identity between Maxse and Beauchamp extended to their respective uncles. The Hon Everard Romfrey, the irascible old Whig in the novel, was taken straight from the Hon Grantley Berkeley, brother of Maxse's mother and a character celebrated for his quarrels and his fads. Even the ugliest episode in the book, when Romfrey horsewhips an elderly political adversary, paralleled Berkeley's flogging of the publisher of *Fraser's Magazine* because of personal insults in a review of a novel Berkeley had written. It was characteristic of Meredith to make Romfrey one of the most likable characters in the story. He embodied all the reactionary prejudices that Meredith despised; he behaved selfishly and violently toward everyone around him; and his original, Grantley Berkeley, was a bully and a good deal of a fool. Yet the aristocratic self-confidence and gruff English patriotism of Romfrey, his innate chivalry and his penchant for direct action, found a deep affinity in Meredith's heart. The horsewhipping was not motivated by vanity, as in the actual event, but by his fantastic notions of chivalry, as the victim had been reported as slandering a woman he admired. Meredith's love of fair play functioned in the realm of ideas: the novel must not give all the noble sentiments to Dr Shrapnel and all the generous actions to Nevil. Therefore Nevil was shown to have faults as conspicuous as his virtues; and the party of reaction was shown to include jolly Tuckham and magnanimous Romfrey as well as contemptible Cecil Baskelet.

The victim of Romfrey's assault, Dr Shrapnel, has evoked contradictory identifications. This philosophical Radical, with his unworldliness, his obstinacy, and his elaborate rhetoric, is delineated with unmistakable sympathy, and according to Meredith's custom he serves as mouthpiece for some of the author's own most provocative ideas. One critic has seen in him even a physical resemblance to Meredith himself. Others suggest his kinship with Carlyle. The letter he wrote to Beauchamp calls to mind one that was written to Maxse by Ruskin. Something of all these ingredients may have gone into his composition, but his immediate prototype was an actual Southampton resident, Dr Edwin Hearne, who had been one of Maxse's chief supporters in the election. Hearne's penchant for controversy is indicated by the titles of two of his pamphlets: *Cholera Non-contagious, and the Absurdity of Quarantine Restrictions* and *Thoughts on Medical Education, and the Importance of Relieving Mental Labour from Legal Restrictions.* Meredith portrayed this indomitable old rebel as a lovable and exasperating visionary.

Though Meredith regarded *Beauchamp's Career* as his favorite among his novels, many readers find it a depressing and disillusioned book. It contains many passages of his most effective writing and he had reached a mature mastery of his art by the time he came to compose it; therefore the inference must be that its effect of disillusionment was no accident, but was consciously intended. Perhaps Meredith felt that the richly romantic tone of *Harry Richmond* might have exposed him to the despicable charge of sentimentality, and to right the balance he offered a view of life that was unequivocally astringent.

True, it includes some elements that recall the preceding novel. As in that book, the hero stands indecisively between two beautiful women who both love him, and of whom one represents an English and the other a Continental type. And as in *Harry Richmond*, the hero is a candidate in a parliamentary election. But even in the handling of these parallel materials the difference is conspicuous. Harry Richmond's campaign for Parliament was a minor episode in which his friends obtained a seat for him with practically no effort, whereas in *Beauchamp's Career* the political theme dominates the book. And Harry Richmond's two beautiful ladies were both more positive characters than their counterparts. Renée de Rouaillout, like Princess Ottilia, defies convention and imperils her reputation by coming to England in pursuit of the man she loves; but Ottilia hurried to Harry's bedside because she believed he was dying, whereas Renée turns up on Nevil Beauchamp's doorstep because she can no longer endure her elderly husband. Similarly, whereas Janet Ilchester frankly admitted her love for Harry and resolutely compelled him to marry her and accept her wealth, the inarticulate Cecilia Halkett can reveal her feelings only by frequent blushes and secret tears, and she temporizes until filial duty forces her to accept a husband she does not love.

The book is almost too persistent in repeating the theme of loveless marriage. At the beginning, the young Renée de Croisnel obeys her father in rejecting Beauchamp and marrying the repulsive Marquis de Rouaillout. Later in the story Cecilia Halkett performs a similar sacrifice. At the end Jenny Denham, a very minor character until this point, is rushed into a loveless wedding with Beauchamp only because it is the cherished wish of the adored guardian to whom she owes much kindness. Alongside of these examples, the other important woman in the book, Rosamund Culling, feels such strong (if partly maternal) affection for Beauchamp that she marries his uncle with no other purpose than to try to mollify the old man and save Beauchamp's inheritance for him.

Against this background of the "conflict of love and duty" Nevil Beauchamp is portrayed as the fanatical idealist who will let nothing stand in the way of his vision of honor and justice. When he is first introduced, his fanaticism is patriotic, and carries him to the point where he becomes a national hero through his exploits in the Crimean War. Upon his meeting with Renée, he is equally idealistic in his love for her. He attempts a Quixotic abduction and is reluctantly brought to realize that she really insists on carrying out the marriage with the middle-aged Marquis that has already been determined by family negotiation. These boyish escapades of Nevil's prepare the way for the real theme of the book: his intense conversion to political Radicalism.

Meredith set the stage carefully to bring his hero into the center of the fiercest conflict of loyalties. Nevil's family background was aristocratic and reactionary. His professional training was in the Royal Navy with its rigid tradition of unquestioning duty to King and country. And being a penniless orphan nephew, with two cousins who stood in equally close relationship to the rich and dogmatic old Everard Romfrey, Nevil could inherit a competence only by remaining in favor with that uncompromising antagonist to all ideas of reform.

Meredith shows Nevil's valiant and yet infuriating persistence in championing his new convictions against all these obstacles. The young man's candid obstinacy reveals his kinship with his equally candid and obstinate uncle. But the situation has to be carried further if his unflinching devotion is to be fully proved; and in this later development the romantic-minded reader is apt to suffer. For Nevil, just as for the women in his life, the conflict of love and duty eventually comes to a head; and in his case it is duty to "the cause" that prevails. When Renée flees from her intolerable husband and offers herself to Nevil, his haste to summon a chaperon and then to hand Renée back to her family is due only partly (if at all) to his delicate concern for her reputation; it is much more for his own, since he knows that in puritanical England his political prospects will be ruined forever by a scandal. And when, after being thus finally freed from the long enchantment in which Renée has held him, he brings himself to propose to the rich and beautiful Cecilia who has silently worshiped him all the while, it is frankly to obtain her fortune so that he can finance a newspaper for the unpopular Radical party.

Thus does Meredith cynically demonstrate how the purest ideals can motivate acts that are conventionally branded selfish or dishonorable. And in spite of all Nevil's noble efforts, as things eventually work out, the emphasis on his "career" in the title is sharply ironic. Futility, if not absurdity, dogs his steps. Through a thoughtless impulse of jealousy on the part of Rosamund Culling, the woman who loves him most unselfishly, a bitter feud develops between Romfrey and Nevil's demigod, Dr Shrapnel. For months all Nevil's energy is devoted to the petty purpose of making his uncle apologize to the injured doctor. When this empty formality is finally achieved, it results from circumstances over which Nevil has no control: his own near-fatal illness and his uncle's anxiety over his new wife's pregnancy. Once this ironical climax of Beauchamp's career is accomplished, the author ends the story with two events that are so abrupt and fortuitous that they can only be regarded as intentional flouting of the reader's sympathies: in two brief chapters Nevil marries the unwilling Jennie out of grati- tude to her for nursing him back to life; a son is born to them; and then Nevil is drowned in a last act of his impetuous courage, saving the life of an unidentified child.

By constructing his story on a frame that emphasized the irony of fate and the bitterly absurd contrast between Beauchamp's visions and his accomplishment, Meredith also cast a sardonic light upon the social ideals that Beauchamp championed. There is no doubt as to where Meredith's own political sympathies lay. By taking his beloved Maxse as the model for Beauchamp and by aiming many shafts of wit at the stubbornness of the Tories and the complacency of the Whigs, the author indicated his approval of the troublemaking Radicals. One of his own formative influences is recalled by passages that describe Beau- champ's admiration for the works of Carlyle. Dr Shrapnel's visionary dithyrambs and allegories are full of phrases and symbols that Mere- dith used in his poems to express his own theories. Most Meredithian of all is the contempt for bourgeois smugness. Both Radicals and reac- tionaries might often be ludicrous in their extremes, but whether aristocrats or laborers, they deserved respect; whereas the money- grubbing shopkeepers, the "passive fleshpot class" and its "religion of Comfort," evoked nothing but unmitigated disdain.

But Meredith was too much of the ironist to be a good propagan- dist. He understood human nature too well to assume that all social virtue was on one side of a party fence and all political sin on the other. And it was as the ironist, too, rather than as the social reformer, that he loosed his most telling shafts against the whole structure of modern politics. He showed startling prophetic insight in incidental remarks. Here is Dr Shrapnel's forecast for the English Liberal party, at a time when Gladstone was at the height of his power:

"Compromise begat them. Once let them leave sucking the teats of com- promise, yea, once put on the air of men who fight and die for a cause, they fly to pieces. And whither the fragments? Chiefly, my friend, into the Tory party. You between future and past are all for the present—but with the hunted look behind of all godless livers in the present. You Liberals are Tories with foresight, Radicals without faith. You start, in fear of Toryism, on an errand of Radicalism, and in fear of Radicalism to Toryism you draw back."

And here is the Doctor on imperialism:

*"If India is to be held for the good of India, throw open India to the civilized nations, that they help us in a task that overstrains us. At present India means utter perversion of the policy of England. Adrift India! rather than England red-coated."*

Meredith's brilliant picture of the parliamentary campaign, with its plots and publicity schemes and subtle bribery; his sarcastic discussion of how handicapped a parliamentary democracy must be in international relations, with its technique of alternately frightening the public so that sufficient funds will be voted for defense, and then soothing it so that foreign nations will not be wantonly antagonized; his cynical delineation of the role played by the newspapers in political intrigue and capitalistic dominance; all these passages about England in the sixties are amazingly applicable not only to England but also to the United States and other democratic countries, ninety years afterwards.

The protection of his impartial irony enabled Meredith to convey opinions that would have been censorable without that disguise. Just as he had used a fantastic situation in *Harry Richmond* to imply a disrespectful attitude toward the British monarchy, so now he used the extremist orations of Shrapnel and his pupil Beauchamp to condemn the aristocracy, the church, and the throne. The half-caricatured figure of the old firebrand was merely speaking in character when he declared that the English middle class had reduced the monarch to "a rickety ornament like that you see on a confectioner's twelfth-cake." And his hatred for organized religion was chiefly illustrated by a pleasantly comic situation in the last chapter, when he and Nevil had to overcome their "natural repugnance" and consent to his ward's marriage to Nevil being a conventional church service. "Must we still be grinning subserviently to ancient usages and stale forms, because of a baggage that it is, woe to us! too true, we cannot cut ourselves loose from?" This outburst was full of Meredithian ideas, and yet its tone was that of a burlesque upon Shrapnel's prejudices.

Many features of *Beauchamp's Career* harked all the way back to *The Ordeal of Richard Feverel.* Like Richard, Nevil is a Quixotic young aristocrat who shatters the rigid traditions of his family and who thereby brings tragedy upon himself and those who love him. The platoon of elegant gentlemen who come and go throughout the story, with little individual characterization and even less connection with the plot, are similar in the two books. This is a distinct defect in *Beauchamp's Career*. Seymour Austin, Grancey Lespel, Stukely Culbrett, and Lydiard (who does not even receive the identification of a Christian name) are little more than wraiths, whom the reader keeps vainly expecting to play some role in the story. Other loose ends are also baffling, such as the allusions to Jenny Denham's dead father, a noted poet to whom Dr Shrapnel owes some special gratitude. A reader accustomed to tightly planned novels, in which every character and episode is eventually fitted into the tidy structure, finds it hard to realize that Meredith included these dim personages and irrelevant details simply because real life is like that.

Aware of these peculiarities, the author could not resist sometimes sneering at his critics and defending his literary experiments. An analysis of Renée's unconventional fascination ended with the remark:

*The writer in this country will, however, be made safest, and the excellent body of self-appointed thongmen, who walk up and down our ranks flapping their leathern straps to terrorize us from experiments in imagery, will best be satisfied, by the statement that she was indescribable: a term that exacts no labour of mind from him or from them, for it flows off the pen as readily as it fills a vacuum.*

This passage was no more than a passing gibe at the reviewers; but elsewhere he broke into the very middle of an episode with an irrelevant and highly personal vindication of his technique in fiction. All the boredom of his daily task of reading trite manuscripts for Chapman & Hall, all his jealousy of the formula novelists who won fame while he remained obscure, burst forth in this querulous and remarkably intimate digression:

*We will make no mystery about it. I would I could. Those happy tales of mystery are as much my envy as the popular narratives of the deeds of bread and cheese people, for they both create a tide-way in the attentive mind; the mysterious pricking our credulous flesh to creep, the familiar urging our obese imagination to constitutional exercise. And oh, the refreshment there is in dealing with characters either contemptibly beneath us or supernaturally above! My way is like a Rhone island in the summer drought, stony, unattractive and difficult between the two forceful streams of the unreal and the over-real, which delight mankind—honour to the conjurers! My people conquer nothing, win none; they are actual, yet uncommon. It is the clock-work of the brain that they are directed to set in motion, and—poor troop of ac-*

*tors to vacant benches!—the conscience residing in thoughtfulness which
they would appeal to; and if you are there impervious to them, we are lost:
back I go to my wilderness, where, as you perceive, I have contracted the habit
of listening to my own voice more than is good.*

Thus with a sort of muttered apology he brought his diatribe to an end;
but it still rumbled in his mind, and a few pages later he briefly returned
to his charge against "the fictitious romances which mark out a plot
and measure their characters to fit into it."

The comparison of *Beauchamp's Career* with *Richard Feverel*
shows how far Meredith had traveled in fifteen years. The exuberant
high spirits and poetic rapture of the earlier book had vanished. Richard
Feverel's bemused project of rehabilitating prostitutes was totally different from Beauchamp's political campaign for remaking society. Near
the beginning of *Beauchamp's Career*, when the hero was in his boyish
ardor of love, there were two or three of the old lavish nature scenes,
especially the view of the Alps from a fishing-boat in the Adriatic; and
later occur a few brief glimpses of the English Channel from a yacht,
and of the Downs that Meredith loved so keenly in all moods; there
are even allusions to the southwest wind. But these seem to obtrude almost perversely into the atmosphere of intellectual detachment that
the author had cultivated until it pervaded every chapter of the book.

His technical tricks and basic doctrines had not wholly changed.
He retained his habit of sometimes omitting a *scène à faire*. The account of Nevil's visit to Renée's château, for instance, breaks off short
at the point where he has been challenged to a duel by one of her admirers; only much later the fact casually emerges that her brother fought
the duel in his stead. As for the Meredithian doctrines, there is his persistent feminism, chiefly voiced by Seymour Austin, who believed that
women ought to be admitted to political councils and allowed to earn
their living in the professions. And Nevil Beauchamp, who did not
share this creed of political equality for the sex, went further in advocating free standards of sexual morality: "Love is to be the test: and
if a lady ceases to love her husband . . . if she sets her fancy elsewhere,
she's bound to leave him. The laws are tyrannical, our objections are
cowardly."

Even deeper than feminism at the heart of Meredith's system was
the hatred of egoism. Dr Shrapnel's manifesto contained a memorable
paragraph on "the stench of the trail of Ego in our History." And in
the last chapter Meredith went out of his way to insist that Beau-

champ's career had not, in a spiritual sense, been a failure, but had been a triumphant defeat of Ego.

*Beauchamp's Career* did not go entirely unacclaimed. Henry Duff Traill was one important critic who wrote favorably about it, in *The Pall Mall Gazette*. Meredith was so well pleased with the review that he asked Hyndman who had written it, and consequently Hyndman arranged a dinner party for the author to meet the critic. An invitation to Traill to visit Box Hill was then extended and accepted. Joseph Comyns Carr contributed a favorable notice of the novel to *The Saturday Review*, and about the same time made Meredith's acquaintance at the house of Frederick Jameson, a genial architect who was always hospitable to writers, musicians, and artists. Justin M'Carthy, now the author of successful novels, read the book with enjoyment; later he declared in his *Reminiscences* that "I find much in *Beauchamp's Career* which seems to lift me higher in thought and soul and in hope than any other of Meredith's novels has done; and I do not know where, in fiction, one can find love scenes more beautiful than those which are pictured in what I may call the Venetian pages of the story." The most enthusiastic reviews appeared in two obscure journals, *The Secularist* and *Cope's Tobacco Plant*, and both were written by a half-starving Scottish poet, James Thomson, who affirmed that Meredith was "quite unappreciated by the general public, ranked with the very highest by a select few."

The writers of these praises were all younger than Meredith, and a few other tokens also indicate that a new generation was beginning to respond to his work. Frederick York Powell, who took his degree in 1874, later declared that "we read Meredith in the early seventies at Oxford; I remember reading both poems and novels in 1870." Though Meredith in his increasing bitterness was conscious only of being "tied up to be lashed" every time he brought out a book, he was imperceptibly enlisting a few partisans.

For some months after the publication of *Beauchamp's Career* Meredith allowed himself the luxury of writing poetry. In March he described himself as "idly busy with verse: unable to let go forth that which ought not to have so much time wasted on it, therefore discontented with the work and myself." Five months later he confessed that "pecks of poetry had been coming from me." One of the poems was "A Ballad of Past Meridian," a brief and austere but yea-saying allegory of middle age. Soon afterwards came a longer and sprightlier piece, more in the vein of his novels, "A Ballad of Fair Ladies in Revolt"; it was a somewhat prosy argument between a conventional gentleman and a bevy of devotees of "women's rights." Perhaps Meredith intended it as a more sympathetic substitute for the satire on the same theme that he had recently eliminated from the opening chapter of *Richard Feverel*. The poem ran to almost three hundred lines and in apologizing to Morley for its length Meredith added that he "had to exercise restraint to keep back more verses."

All the conflicts and frustrations of his youth must have been brought back to memory when he was summoned down to Southsea to attend the funeral of his father, who died on June 18. No conventional display of filial grief can have been expected from him. Even his resentment had grown dim. Nearly forty years had passed since they had ceased living together; the shop in Portsmouth High Street was in a different existence from the writers and intellectuals who had absorbed him into their world.

In June Frederic Harrison encountered him at a meeting of the Metaphysical Society, which had been formed some years before for the discussion of philosophical problems by leading writers, scientists, and thinkers of all stripes. It was "a most pleasant party round Gladstone," Harrison reported. "I was greatly charmed by the brilliance of Meredith. He is indeed a talker." About this time Harrison took a house at Cobham, not far from Box Hill, and Morley advised him that "to see Meredith in the country is to see Leviathan in his bath. Pray seek him out."

Consequently he and Harrison saw a good deal of each other during the next few months. In his autobiography, Harrison says of Meredith: "A man of original genius, a hearty friend, a brilliant talker if ever there was one in our time, he bore hard times and bright times with equal courage and self-respect. I would meet him in London society, in a country house, in his own rural home on Box Hill—and always found him the same imcomparable companion and stalwart spirit."

Now that the Maxse household had been broken up, Meredith was invited from time to time to stay at Effingham Hill, the home of the Captain's mother, Lady Caroline Maxse. She had much of the arrogance and pugnacity of her family, the Berkeleys, and was uninhibited in expressing her aristocratic prejudices. Through her anecdotes Meredith was carried back in imagination into the days of the Regency.

The Brandreths went to Russia in the summer, Mr Brandreth being a delegate to a congress of Orientalists in St Petersburg, and Meredith excelled himself in comic inventions about the adventures awaiting Alice among the passionate Slavic pundits. Professor Sylvester, one of their play-reading group, had just left for America to become Professor of Mathematics at Johns Hopkins University, and had declared his intention of recommending Meredith for appointment as lecturer on poetry and rhetoric there. Though Meredith's allusion to the scheme was in his customary tone of mockery, it carried a hint of genuine interest, and one wonders what his response would have been if the post had ever been offered to him.

For his next piece of prose he took up a story that he had left unfinished fifteen years before. In the spring of 1876 the town of Seaford suffered from a disastrous storm, which partially wrecked the carpenter shop of Meredith's old friend and landlord, Richard Ockenden. Thus reminded of his visits twenty years earlier, Meredith was also provided with a suitably melodramatic climax for *Van Diemen Smith*, a story he had begun in 1861. An even more important element was brought into it at this time, too, derived from his friend Hardman's comic anecdotes about a pompous civic official at Kingston, one Busby, whom Meredith transformed into Martin Tinman, the ambitious bailiff of Crikswich. Without either Tinman or the hurricane, the original version can have been little more than an embryo.

In its completed form, as published in *The New Quarterly Magazine* in January, 1877, entitled "The House on the Beach," it was a departure for Meredith in being of the dimensions that can only be described by the unfortunate word "novelette." Under 40,000 words in length, it had a plot almost as simple as that of a short story; and while scene and characters were presented with something of the amplitude of a novel, they were kept within the rigid bounds of a three-act play— five characters, a small chorus of townspeople in the background, and a single setting.

The manner of telling was free of Meredith's idiosyncrasies. The whole texture is much more reminiscent of Trollope in its mildly satiric picture of commonplace people and a shabby small town. The heroine, Annette Smith, is just such an ordinary sensible girl as Trollope enjoyed portraying. Both she and her admirer, Herbert Fellingham, are far from certain that they are in love with each other, and neither of them is permitted one moment of romantic emotion. Fellingham is chiefly interesting from his resemblance to Meredith at the same stage of his career—a rather rootless young journalist, fond of good wine and long walks, and incurably addicted to ridiculing everyone he met, though sometimes chiding himself for his intolerance.

The theme of the story resided chiefly in the two older men, of

whom one, Van Diemen Smith, must have been the original inspiration for the whole thing, but the other, Martin Tinman, finally usurped
the limelight by being a burlesque version of two types that deeply
concerned Meredith in more serious studies also—the egoist and the
snobbish tradesman. Like Mel Harrington, Tinman is a shopkeeper
who has grown rich enough to dream of acceptance into good society;
but in the sterile dullness of Crikswich his ambition can shape itself
only in the silliness of posturing in a court suit and delivering a florid
patriotic proclamation to the Queen.

Even in this buffoonery Meredith's fascination with the theme of
social climbing is unmistakable. Just as in *Harry Richmond* he had
ventured perilously close to the taboo act of introducing the current
royal family in his pages, so here the comic scene of Tinman's performance in Victoria's audience chamber is conveyed without being
actually described, by Meredith's usual tactics of implication, preparation, and retrospect. One cannot help feeling that his pitiless gibing
at Tinman as the snob and climber is partly to exorcise some suspected
trace of the same impulse in the author himself.

In pleasant contrast with Tinman, Van Diemen Smith is likably
blunt and impulsive, with a hasty temper and an inexhaustible fund
of affection. Here Meredith firmly withstood the temptation of melodrama. Though Smith had not actually been transported to Botany
Bay, he had fled to the sanctuary of the new colony after deserting from
the Army, and therefore he was risking punishment by his return to
England. This reproduces the central situation of *Great Expectations*,
which was published in the very year when Meredith first talked of
his "Van Diemen Smith" story. But instead of the terror and suspense
of the Dickens novel, Meredith offers a mild study of the half-
inarticulate love of home which draws the exile back with his newly
gained wealth and his naïve daughter, and which does not prevent him
from exasperating his English friends with his extravagant praises of
everything Australian.

As the setting, Meredith draws the drab, boresome, sewage-smelling
little seaside resort with full conviction; and in the minor characters
he shows the affectionate perception of small-town and rustic humor
that had cropped out in *Evan Harrington* and *Rhoda Fleming*. His
Seaford friends the Ockendens were drawn to the life as Mr and Mrs
Crickledon.

Faithful to the technique of an effective play, the whole story fore-
shadows the exciting final scene, which not only supplies the denoue-
ment but also symbolizes the central theme, when all Tinman's wealth

is swept away by a single upheaval of Nature. In order to emphasize the symbolism, Meredith resorted to some improbability so that Tinman might be actually garbed in his precious court suit at the time when he was rescued from his collapsing house. But the tale does not end on this symbolic note. In the closing paragraph, all Annette's anxieties with regard to her enforced engagement to Tinman are dissolved when she realizes how irresistibly ludicrous he is. True to Meredith's favorite doctrine of the revelatory power of laughter, Annette succumbs to helpless peals.

*It rolled her heart and senses in a headlong surge, shook her to burning tears, and seemed to her ideas the most wonderful running together of opposite things ever known on this earth. The young lady was ashamed of her laughter, but she was deeply indebted to it, for never was mind made so clear by that beneficent exercise.*

# CHAPTER

## XI

# *The Comic Spirit*

THROUGHOUT the nine years of occupancy of Flint Cottage, Meredith had been irked by two deficiencies of "the Hat-box," as he nicknamed the house. There was no spare bedroom where guests could be accommodated, and there was no separate room for him to write in. He had to do all his work in a corner of his bedroom, with domestic turmoil constantly within earshot. Even though young Willie, now eleven years old, was sent this autumn to boarding-school for the first time, the overcrowding was not relieved, for his room was too small to serve for a visitor. A little wooden chalet was therefore built for Meredith up at the top of the steep garden behind the house, in the shadow of the fir wood that covered the crown of the hill. It consisted of two tiny rooms, one equipped with a writing-desk and bookshelves, the other with a narrow "hammock cot" and simple dressing-table. Thus he was provided with a workplace that suited him admirably. "It is the prettiest to be found," he told Morley; "the view is without a match in Surrey. The interior is full of light, which can be moderated; and while surrounded by firs, I look over the slope of our green hill to the ridges of Leith, round to Ranmore, and the half of Norbury."

Upon the completion of this refuge, he settled into a permanent routine. Getting up at dawn he could go for a walk or sit down to his writing without disturbing the household. When he was busy, meals were sent up to him and neither family nor visitors were allowed to intrude. In 1874 Maxse had given him a dachshund, which immediately became a favorite and proved to be the first of a long series of the same breed. Meredith's sinewy figure, striding along lanes or up hill slopes, with Jacob scouting for rabbits, was as familiar a sight to his neighbors as the natural features of the landscape.

The new year of 1877 found him in the midst of a fresh task which gave him some anxiety. He had undertaken to deliver a lecture at the London Institution, choosing as his topic "The Idea of Comedy and the Uses of the Comic Spirit." Several of the older novelists, notably Thackeray, had gained substantial profits through lecturing, but Meredith had never previously considered doing so. Perhaps a faint chimera of the appointment at an American university flitted in the back of his mind when he agreed to the assignment. The lecture was delivered on February 1, 1877, and with characteristic pride he avoided any implication that he expected his friends to attend. "The hour is unearthly," he told Hardman; "so I ask none to come." He was relieved to find the "audience very attentive and indulgent." Hoping to be clearly heard, he held himself to a moderate pace, and occupied almost an hour and a half. "No one left the hall, so that I may imagine there was interest." Cotter Morison was enthusiastic about it, and praised the speaker's distinctness of articulation.

The lecture was published in *The New Quarterly Magazine* in April, with many misprints, for some of which Meredith had to confess that he was himself to blame, as he was never good at correcting his own proofs. Though it received little attention at the time, it gradually gained recognition as one of the pre-eminent critical essays of the Victorian age, and a notable example of a creative writer's analysis of his own genre.

The lecture brought into focus a theory that he had held throughout his writing—the value of laughter as a form of intellectual clarification and emotional therapy. He conceived it as neither satire nor burlesque, but a dispassionate and clear-sighted perception of folly, sentimentality, and conceit. His own adoption of this attitude in his novels has been partly responsible for the disfavor they evoke in some readers. He holds himself aloof from his characters and observes them with Olympian mockery at moments when the reader would prefer an illusion of sympathetic identification.

In the course of the lecture he introduced several of his pet doctrines. Pure comedy can flourish only, he asserted, in a society which permits mental equality between the sexes. His basic assumption was that the Comic Spirit can promote true human progress by destroying inflated self-importance and providing a sane sense of proportion: it functions only when the senses are under the complete control of the intellect. In the emphasis upon reason and the avoidance of excesses the argument aligned itself with the classical tradition, and so there is nothing surprising in his choice of Molière as the best exemplar of it.

The style of the lecture was appropriate to its subject, being clear, graceful, and lively. Though some portions threaten to become bafflingly abstract, Meredith usually rescued them by virtue of a clever metaphor or a poetically apt phrase. The personification of the Comic Spirit in the concluding paragraph—with the sage's brows and the faun's smile, looking humanely malign and casting an oblique light on human self-deception and disproportion, "followed by volleys of silvery laughter"—forms an unforgettable epitome of the whole theory.

The comfort of his new working-quarters encouraged him to fresh projects. He described his enjoyment to Morley jubilantly:

*Anything grander than the days and nights at my porch you will not find away from the Alps: for the dark line of my hill runs up to the stars, the valley below is a soundless gulf. There I pace like a shipman before turning in. In the day, with the S. West blowing, I have a brilliant universe rolling up to me . . . In this room of mine I should have no excuse for idleness.*

He gave a formidable list of the different works he had in hand. One was "a 5-act comedy in verse," presumably the one he had promised to Alice Brandreth. It may have been a play with a Spanish setting, of which a few fragments of manuscript survive. He spoke also of "tales," and one of these, "The Case of General Ople and Lady Camper," came out in *The New Quarterly Magazine* in July. Only about two-thirds as long as "The House on the Beach," it was another borrowing from Hardman's fund of anecdotes about his Kingston neighbors. A certain General Hopkins, a retired officer living at Norbiton, had been persecuted by his erratic next-door neighbor, Lady Eleanor Cathcart, who persisted in sending him unflattering caricatures of himself until he felt obliged to bring a legal action against her. Adopting the whole episode, Meredith depicted his own former home, Kingston Lodge, as the General's house and Hardman's Norbiton Hall as the lady's.

General Ople is a perfect specimen of the half-pay officer, with his well-scrubbed appearance, his stock phrases, his routine-stifled mind, and his passion for gardening. Lady Camper, in contrast, remains an enigmatical figure until almost the end of the story. Her campaign against the General appears to be actuated by sheer malicious mischief, if not actually by pathological sadism. She reduces him to helpless stuttering by constantly interrupting his remarks with gibes at his clichés, and when she starts sending him her drawings her diabolical insight into his weaknesses drives him to the verge of insanity.

Meredith made the General such a harmless and even likable variety of the egoist that the lady's perpetual puncturing of his self-respect resembles a boy's motiveless tormenting of a bewildered animal. It is true that the General in his innocent conceit started with the mistaken notion that Lady Camper had taken a fancy to him; and that his snobbish respect for her rank was also partly responsible for his asking her to marry him. It is true also that Lady Camper's nephew has fallen in love with the General's self-effacing daughter (a well-drawn sketch of the inarticulate out-door girl), and that the General is too self-centered to realize that she is grown up and deserves a life of her own. But Lady Camper's interest in this affair is made to seem only a mercenary insistence on a larger dowry than the General can afford to pay.

Unless the reader knows enough about Meredith's predilections to observe the incidental detail that Lady Camper is a Welshwoman, she is likely to be accepted as the unjustified aggressor against an inoffensive victim; and therefore the climax comes as a surprise. Lady Camper suddenly asks the General to renew his proposal of marriage, and in a long lecture she explains that his selfishness has now been suitably chastened by humiliation. In short, Lady Camper emerges as a feminine counterpart of Meredith himself, sharing his view of the therapeutic value of comedy and using her skill with the caricaturist's pencil in the same spirit as he used his with the novelist's pen. The undertone of undeniable cruelty in Meredith's social satire was never more clearly revealed; and he tacitly admits as much when Lady Camper asks for the General's forgiveness and attributes her conduct to her Welsh ancestry: "You English have the smallest experience of humanity. I mean this: to strike so hard that, in the end, you soften your heart to the victim. Well, that is my weakness. And we of our blood put no restraint on the blows we strike when we think them wanted, so we are always overdoing it."

Among all his other undertakings, Meredith was helping his wife with a translation. Chapman & Hall had commissioned her to translate Charles de Mazade's *Vie de Cavour* into English, and it was duly published late in 1877. In addition, he was writing poems and "touches of a novel." Though he had not taken a trip away from home for five years, he felt that he must withstand the temptation to run over to the Continent to join either Morley or Maxse, who were both summering abroad. In August he wrote despondently to Maxse (now promoted to rear-admiral):

*As for me, I fear I am again condemned to trot round my circle, like an old horse at a well, everlastingly pulling up the same buckets full of similar fluid. I may be precipitated abroad by incapacity to continue writing; and once or twice the case has looked like it, though I have recovered in a middling fashion: but not to do the work I call good—rather the character of work one is glad to leave behind, however glad to have accomplished.*

Two months later, reporting no holiday except a couple of short visits to friends a few miles away, he grumbled, "I am consequently dull, unrubbed, no reflector. I write, and not perfectly to my satisfaction." In November an invitation to give another lecture, this time at the august Royal Society, merely caused him discomfort: "I hate it, and it does not pay me, it makes me nervous, and I have to give up my inner mind's work to it. But I have the question going on, whether I ought to decline anything, I, unlucky, portionless, ill-paid!" He rejected the offer, and a fortnight later described himself as "happily cut off from all ambition."

Slight encouragement came in a proposal for a new edition of his first novel. The sanguine Kegan Paul, his confrere in the Shakespeare readings, had now set up in business as a publisher, and wanted to reissue *Richard Feverel*, with the revisions that had been made for the Continental edition.

About the same time Meredith disinterred "Love in the Valley" from his long-obliterated first volume of poems, and revised it drastically, enlarging it from eleven stanzas to twenty-six, omitting several of the original stanzas, and changing the others almost beyond recognition. It was bought by *Macmillan's Magazine* for sixteen guineas.

All his miscellaneous writing was secondary to the new novel that was steadily growing under his hand. It was called *The Egoist* and in some ways it was an outgrowth of his recent shorter pieces. Both Tinman, in "The House on the Beach," and General Ople, in the other novelette, had been studies in egoism, and Meredith had drawn them with the same ruthless contempt that he now directed toward Sir Willoughby Patterne. Even the plot of *The Egoist* was essentially that of "The House on the Beach": an unsophisticated girl gets engaged to a wealthy man who has brought pressure to bear on her father; she gradually discovers her fiancé's intolerable conceit; and she finally wins her freedom—and her emotional maturity—through perceiving that he is ineffably comic. Meanwhile, a thoroughly suitable young man waits inconspicuously in the background.

Yet in spite of these similarities, *The Egoist* was utterly different in its total effect. In the two tales the comedy had bordered on farce and the plot had been roughly manipulated. The more extensive canvas of the novel enabled the author to develop action out of motive, to probe subtleties of character, and to reveal the complex ironies in the interplay of personalities. His inquiry into the art of comedy as crystallized in his lecture, was applied to every scene of the new book.

*The Egoist* is also comparable in many ways to *Evan Harrington*. Meredith's original allusion to "the Comic Muse" in that novel was now expanded into a full chapter discussing the Muse's functions. Unity of time and place, already notable in the earlier comedy, was now more strictly applied, and the focus was made clearer by reduction in the number of supernumerary characters. Sir Willoughby was a masculine counterpart of the Countess de Saldar—charming, confident, unscrupulous in self-defense; but he was a far more subtle study because the Countess had lived a whole life of social pretense, and was fully armed for the battle, whereas Sir Willoughby—born to rank and wealth —believed implicitly in his own perfection and was confronted with unrecognized weaknesses of a wholly psychological kind.

Meredith's new friend, Henry Duff Traill, visited him at Flint Cottage when the book was at an early stage, and the introductory chapter was read to him. Noticing a look of incomprehension on Traill's face, Meredith broke off to demand, "You don't understand all that?"

"No," replied Traill, "I'll be damned if I do."

"Well, I suppose it is rather hard," Meredith agreed, with a cheerful laugh. Traill averred that the style was made simpler before the book was published; but in his opinion it still remained indefensibly obscure.

In April, 1878, Alice Brandreth was married to her cousin, Jim Gordon, and they came to live at Pixholme. Their publisher friend, Kegan Paul, wrote to tell them that a young Scottish author, Robert Louis Stevenson, whose first book his firm was about to issue, was staying for a week at the Burford Bridge Inn, accompanied by his parents, and that Stevenson was eager to meet Meredith. Leslie Stephen was a friend of both; and a few months previously another of Stevenson's friends, W. E. Henley, had uttered appreciation of Meredith's work in an article in *London*, a Conservative weekly.

The two writers were introduced to each other in the Gordons' garden, and Alice always remembered how eagerly the lean, pale, young Stevenson listened to Meredith's conversation "with rapt attention and appreciative smiles . . . He was an inspiring listener, and had the art of drawing out the best of Mr. Meredith's brilliant powers of conversation." Before the week was over, Stevenson had announced that thereafter he was permanently enrolled as "a true-blue Meredith man." In his turn, Stevenson won favor by his lively retorts to Meredith's customary chaffing. After his departure, when someone at the Gordons' house expressed surprise at Kegan Paul's confidence in the young man's future career, "Meredith trumpeted down our feeble utterances by informing us that some day he felt sure we should all be proud to have known him, and prophesied success and fame for him."

As soon as Stevenson's *Inland Voyage* was published, Meredith received a presentation copy, and replied in a long letter that began with warm praise and went on to shrewd criticism of a few details of phrasing. A message to Henley was included, expressing Meredith's "sense of the honour he does me by giving so much attention to my work":

*His praise is high indeed, but happily he fetches me a good lusty clout o' the head now and again, by which I am surprisingly well braced and my balance is restored. Otherwise praise like that might operate as the strong waters do upon the lonely savage unused to such a rapture.*

The unwonted sensation of having disciples recurred several times during the summer. One was George William Foote, an aggressive young freethinker and a friend of James Thomson, whose review of *Beauchamp's Career* had been contributed to Foote's anti-religious magazine, *The Secularist*. Foote wrote to inquire why cheap editions of Meredith's novels were not in the market; and Meredith replied that he thought there would be no sale for them. "The English cure one early of a desire for applause, and as well as I could do, I have worked without thought of that and the profit coming of it." To Foote's further demand for the publication of a volume of Meredith's poems, the answer was that "the conditions of sale which frown on collections of verse not offering themselves as appropriate gift-books for the innumerable nuptial curate and his bride are, I fear, adverse. Poetry in England is required to have a function of a practical kind, and to exercise it." When Comyns Carr sent a similar inquiry, the explanation was still blunter: "I have paid heavily for that audacity twice in pounds sterling. I had for audience the bull, the donkey, and the barking cur. He that pays to come before them a third time—we will not give him his name."

Carr and his wife had been added to the regular visitors to Flint Cottage. Carr's recollections provide a record of the routine:

Our long rambles filled the afternoon, and were preceded by a simple but thoughtfully chosen lunch, which, when the weather allowed, was set out upon a gravel walk in front of the cottage . . . Meredith attached no small importance to the details of these little feasts. He prided himself not a little on his gastronomic knowledge . . .

When he had only a single companion to listen there was no man whose talk was more penetrating or more sincere; and he was at his best, I used to think, in those long rambles . . . The active exercise in which he delighted seemed to steady and concentrate those intellectual forces that sometimes ran riot when he felt himself called upon to dominate the mixed assembly of a dinner table . . .

No one, assuredly, ever possessed a more genuine or a more exalted delight in nature . . . He would break away on a sudden from some long-drawn legend of a half-imaginary character that was often set in the frame of burlesque, to note, with a swift change to a graver tone, some passing aspect of the scene that challenged his admiration afresh. And then, when he had quietly added this last specimen to his cabinet, he would as quickly turn again, with boisterous mirth, to complete the caricature portrait of some common friend, which he loved to embellish with every detail of imagined embroidery.

In a mixed company Meredith did not often lean to the discussion of literature. He inclined rather, if an expert on any subject was present, to press the conversation in that direction, exhibiting nearly always a surprising knowledge of the specialist's theme . . . But in those long rambles when we were alone he loved to consider and discuss the claims of the professors of his own art, rejecting scornfully enough the current standards of his own time, but approaching with entire humility the work of masters whom he acknowledged . . .

When I was able to stay the night our evenings would be spent in the little chalet . . . Of talk he never tired, and it was often far into the night before we parted. He loved also, when he found an appreciative listener, to read aloud long passages from his poems. Once I remember he recited to me during a single evening the whole of "Modern Love." On occasion—but not, perhaps, quite so willingly—he might be tempted to anticipate publication by reading a chapter or two from an uncompleted story.

Mrs Carr, who also wrote her memoirs, admits that her husband, being a noted conversationalist himself, was sometimes irked by Meredith's invariable domination of an after-dinner group. Whenever Meredith found himself at a loss for a word, Mrs Carr observed, "he would always contrive to busy himself with his handkerchief or hold the situation with a prolonged 'Ah—' in order to prevent anyone else from taking the floor." She also quoted passages from one of the "serial stories" in which his humor found vent:

Around a not too intellectual worshipping devotee of his whom he had nick-named Benedetto he wove an elaborate romance, piling rhetoric upon rhetoric as he outlined to his friends the fairy tale of Benedetto's love affair. According to Meredith's fancy, the young man was hopelessly attached to a certain lady who was known to be very kindly disposed toward a well-known scientist. Benedetto was tall and handsome, and the scientific man was almost a dwarf, so Meredith made much play of this fact . . .

This kind of banter was a convenient mask for the despondency in which he was toiling through *The Egoist*. "I have been nowhere," he told Maxse in October, "but on my weekly hack-cab-horse expeditions, and it is doubtful that I shall ever go anywhere except on that tramroad, until I proceed in mute accompaniment to my last March. Life under these conditions is not so seductive as it appeared in youth, though in youth I looked out under a hail of blows. I don't complain, you see, of inconsistency in my career. If I could quit England, hold off from paper, and simply look on for the remainder of my term—mountains near—I would ask for no better. To be mixed up with them is hard, these English are so astonishing to my ideas of dignity and valour."

He showed an increasing tendency to talk about "these English" with contempt, from the altitude of his Celtic ancestry. Primarily, no doubt, the reason was the public's disregard for his writings; but he found many targets for scorn in current political events and social attitudes—bungling imperialism in India, lack of firmness toward Russian aggression in Turkey, reliance on volunteer troops instead of conscription. His Celtic descent was coming to be the explanation that he offered for all his departures from current opinions and conventional behavior. He claimed that even his inveterate habit of humming tunes was an infallible proof of Welsh blood.

The reason for his concentrated work on *The Egoist* was explained later in a letter to Foote: "As it comes mainly from the head and has nothing to kindle imagination, I thirsted to be rid of it soon after conception." In this mood of repugnance, he sat up late every night to work on it during the winter, and managed to finish it by the middle of February, 1879, at a heavy cost to his health. For several months afterwards he suffered from a racking cough, which did not yield to "my customary specific of hard exercise, with which I generally sweat out all attacks." He described it as "what is called catarrh of the stomach . . . The effect is a sort of 'old man's cough' . . . To be wakened up at night by a seizure is akin to the dark archangel's intimation to you to prepare for immediate flight." Later he became convinced that he had had whooping cough.

His weakened condition left him without confidence in the new book. "I don't think you will like it," he warned Stevenson; "I doubt if those who care for my work will take to it at all . . . It is a Comedy, with only half of me in it, unlikely therefore to take either the public or my friends."

In spite of this pessimism, he had started vigorously to work upon another novel, to be entitled *The Amazing Marriage* and to include a portrait of his new young friend Stevenson as a leading character. Within two months of finishing *The Egoist* he had written a quarter of the new story; but thereafter his illness put an end to all writing for many weeks. A novelette, "The Tale of Chloe," which was printed in the July number of *The New Quarterly Magazine*, must have been written at some earlier time.

This brief story was a departure from all his previous work. It is his only experiment with historical fiction, in the sense of being an attempt to re-create the atmosphere of an earlier epoch. Set in the elegant frivolity of an eighteenth-century fashionable watering-place, it sought to build an illusion of authenticity by pretending to quote from contemporary lampoons and from the memoirs of Beau Beamish, the social dictator of the Wells. These artifices helped Meredith to fabricate the needful mood of chilly wit, mannered grace, and cynical sophistication. But the story, oddly enough, which he chose for displaying in this environment was his nearest approach to tragedy, with more than a modicum of both the melodramatic and the sentimental.

His aloof, allusive manner was well suited to the artificial society that he was delineating. For the figure of Beamish, with his ruthless tactics in polishing the crude manners and customs of the wealthy barbarians who patronized the resort, Meredith drew details from Beau Nash, the famous master of ceremonies in Georgian Bath. The central character, however, was less convincingly portrayed. Chloe, who was intended to be a paragon of feminine charm and altruism, is a well-born young lady (Welsh, of course) who has been despoiled of her reputation and her patrimony by an obviously scoundrelly lover. In her humiliation she has fled from her relatives and taken up residence at the Wells, where she repels all admirers and divides her time between writing poetry and giving wise counsel to the autocratic Beau. He assigns her the task of chaperoning a beautiful young duchess, a former milkmaid, whose senile husband has ventured to let her come for a glimpse of gaiety. At the same moment Chloe's scamp of a lover reappears, and it is soon patent to everyone that he is clandestinely wooing the Duchess. After resolutely ignoring the intrigue, Chloe prevents the elopement by hanging herself in the doorway through which the Duchess must emerge.

The reader's sympathy is unfortunately deflected, partly because Chloe is incomprehensible both in her attachment to the worthless Caseldy and in her morbid act of immolation, but also because the Duchess, in her naïve candor and bumpkin charm, comes more vigorously to life. She is a belated reappearance of the girl who haunted his earlier novels—the blond, buxom, and seducible daughter of the farmyard. In contrast with Lucy Desborough, Dahlia Fleming, and Mabel Sweetwinter, Duchess Susan is a robustly comic figure, but she inherits some of the author's affection for them.

The character of Chloe was suggested by Miss Fanny Braddock, who at Bath in 1731 lost heavily in gambling and hanged herself with a knotted silk girdle in a doorway. Thirty years later, when Goldsmith wrote *The Life of Richard Nash* he elaborated this event into the pathetic story of "Miss Sylvia S——," an heiress from the North of England, who spent all her money in paying the debts of her faithless lover, a notorious roué, and was then persuaded by Beau Nash to seek solace at Bath, where she became immensely popular for several years but finally gave way to her melancholia and hanged herself. Meredith combined this with another eighteenth-century scandal, the same one from which Tennyson derived "The Lord of Burleigh"—the marriage of Henry Cecil, Earl of Exeter, in 1791, to Sarah Hoggins, a Shropshire farm wench. But the climax may have been suggested from his own circle of acquaintances. Violet Hunt states that he told her "The Tale of Chloe" was based on an episode in the life of Christina Rossetti. According to this report, Christina's former fiancé, John Collinson, whom she had rejected when he joined the Church of Rome, re-entered her life after he had married another woman, and persuaded her to elope with him. Her devoted elder sister Maria suspected the scheme and thwarted it by lying on the mat inside the front door every night for a week.

Should this legend be true, Christina's poem "Goblin Market" can be regarded as a symbolic confession of the experience; and Meredith's tale certainly offers a similar picture of one woman's devotion to another. If this was its basis, however, there was a violent transference of characterization. Chloe herself bears some resemblance to Christina Rossetti, with her verse-writing, her melancholy playfulness, and her renunciation of love. But the role of Christina in the situation is actually given to the Duchess, who could not be a more utterly different personality. Meredith may have felt that this extreme unlikeness was needful to disguise the source of the plot; and it may be responsible for the lack of convincingness that pervades the story. He worked hard to prepare for the climax, with use of ominous foreshadowing, such as the silken rope that Chloe was constantly plaiting; and the final scene undeniably possesses macabre vividness. But the reader cannot be brought quite to believe that the character Meredith had drawn would have behaved as Chloe did.

Meanwhile, the republication of *Richard Feverel* evoked another enthusiastic article by James Thomson. Meredith, he declared,

*may be termed, accurately enough, for a brief indication, the Robert Browning of our novelists; and his day is bound to come, as Browning's at length has come. The flaccid and feeble folk, who want literature and art that can be inhaled as idly as the perfume of a flower, must naturally shrink from two such earnestly strenuous spirits, swifter than eagles, stronger than lions.*

In the same month that this paean was published, it happened by coincidence that Meredith had a talk with Browning when they both attended a private view at the Grosvenor Gallery. Browning's new book, *Dramatic Idylls*, contained his poem on Pheidippides, and Meredith told him that Cotter Morison had previously suggested this subject to him as suitable for a poem, but that he had hesitated to attempt it. The next week Robert Louis Stevenson came and stayed for several days at Box Hill; for the first part of the visit the two authors were alone together, until Mrs Meredith and little Mariette returned from a holiday at Eastbourne. These friendly conversations with Browning and Stevenson within the span of a week typify the remarkable way in which Meredith's literary associations ranged across the Victorian era. And the range can be extended to the middle of the twentieth century by the fact that it was in this same year, 1879, that a wordy and opinionated novel, entitled *Immaturity*, was submitted to Chapman & Hall by George Bernard Shaw, and was rejected on the basis of Meredith's comment, which was the monosyllable "no." A year or two later he was equally unfavorable toward *Cashel Byron's Profession*, by the same author.

At the beginning of July, Meredith was "not perfectly re-established,

anaemic, vacuous, adust, songless, fountainless." Later in the month
Morley persuaded him to come on a walking-tour in the Lake District.
The weather was wet, and Meredith had to admit that in his debili-
tated condition he felt stiff after a climb "up and down crags of a
sufficient slope for brooks and kids." Toward the end of August he and
his family set off on a two months' visit to France, which he enjoyed
all the more intensely because of the seven-year interval since his last
foreign travel. Leaving Mrs Meredith and the children with her brother
in Normandy, he took a comprehensive tour, from Dreux through Char-
tres, Orléans, Blois, Tours, Bourges, Clermont-Ferrand and the Cé-
vennes to Nîmes, a spot that especially charmed him. Then he went on
southward to Arles, Marseilles, and Nice, as far as Bordighera. Returning to Marseilles by water, he proceeded to Lyons and then to Pont de
Beauvoisin, where he had some mountaineering with his wife's brother-
in-law. His final stay at the Vulliamy home on the banks of the Avre
brought him pleasant social intercourse with agreeable neighbors.

After seven delightful weeks of Continental sunshine and courtesy,
the return to England was dismal. On the Channel steamer the cabin
was "redolent of beer and stale crumbs and brandy-breathing steward."
A chilly fog enveloped them the minute they stepped ashore at Dover,
bringing on coughs in all four of them; whenever they asked for information they were "driven straight back by blasts of the stench of
liquors"; and on the train their luggage was broken open by pilferers.
Parents and children were equally depressed by having to settle down
again in "old galley-slave England."

The new publisher was not wholly satisfactory. *The Egoist* remained in Kegan Paul's hands for eight months before it came out
in three-volume form; and meanwhile Meredith was annoyed to discover that without any authorization Paul had released it to run as a
serial in a newspaper, *The Glasgow Weekly Herald*, and had even permitted a change of the title to *Sir Willoughby Patterne, the Egoist*.

When Paul finally brought out the book, at the beginning of
November, Meredith was prepared for another failure; he told Hardman that "the whole cast of it is against the modern style." The opening chapter, virtually a summary of his lecture on comedy, was indeed
a tough morsel of abstract theorizing that was likely to repel any casual reader; and thereafter the story assumed the qualities of a well-
organized play of the type that he had extolled in the lecture. The
ironic attitude of "the Comic Spirit" was maintained throughout. The
action all took place on Sir Willoughby Patterne's estate or in its immediate vicinity; after a few necessary preliminaries in the first four

chapters, it occupied no more than a few weeks; and there were only seven important characters and less than a dozen supernumeraries. Even the chapter titles read like stage directions, naming the persons who are to participate in the scene. In theme, too, it obeyed the classical unities, resembling a Racine tragedy in its conflict of emotion versus duty. At a climactic point, when Clara Middleton was torn between her repugnance for Sir Willoughby and her obedience to her father's insistence upon their marriage, the conflict was stated like a summary of a Racinian scene.

With this tight dramatic structure, Meredith could less often indulge in his trick of dodging a key scene; but he did it at a few points, notably Clara's confession to Whitford that she had begun to hate her fiancé, her first major appeal to Sir Willoughby for release from their engagement, and Sir Willoughby's final self-abasement in beseeching Laetitia Dale to accept him. In the latter instance Meredith sardonically defended his own evasion:

We cannot be abettors of the tribes of imps whose revelry is in the frailties of our poor human constitution . . . If in these festival hours under the beams of Hecate they are uncontrollable by the Comic Muse, she will not flatter them with her presence during the course of their insane and impious hilarities . . . And indeed not without reason do the multitudes of the servants of the Muse in this land of social policy avoid scenes of an inordinate wantonness, which detract from the dignity of our leaders and menace human nature with confusion. Sagacious are they who conduct the individual on broad lines, over familiar tracks, under well-known characteristics. What men will do, and amorously minded men will do, is less the question than what it is politic that they should be shown to do.

As one of the devices for maintaining the mood of high comedy, Meredith altered some features of his style. Superficially the abundance of allusions and metaphors and epigrams produces the same impression as in earlier books; but the self-conscious elaborateness has given place to a sort of prose which—for all its ornateness—is essentially conversational. By the use of incomplete sentences and recurrent phrases, he was trying to suggest the implications that a fluent talker achieves by gesture and tone of voice while gleefully embroidering some stimulating topic. This arose partly from Meredith's increasing habit of improvising oral stories for the amusement of his friends, and partly perhaps from his other habit of reading his unpublished chapters aloud to visitors with all his declamatory skill applied to the interpretation of his text.

In the actual dialogue among the characters, he carried further than ever the fragmentary effect of real conversation—the irrelevancies, digressions, and revertings through which people contrive to communicate with each other. In Sir Willoughby, particularly, he reproduced the phenomenon of "delayed reaction": after someone else has made a remark, the speaker goes on expressing his own train of thought, apparently oblivious of the interruption; and then a few moments later he responds to what was said. These effects are baffling to a reader accustomed to logical rhetoric, but Meredith was approximating actual human speech more closely than any previous English novelist had done.

For the central theme of the novel he went squarely back to the one that stemmed from his own marital disaster. Sir Willoughby Patterne had much in common with Sir Austin Feverel, but now Meredith plainly asserted what he had tacitly implied in the earlier novel—that the ineffable possessiveness and complacency of such a man made it impossible for any self-respecting woman to endure him as a mate. Behind the façade of elegant comedy, the novel was a grim exploration of the horrors of incompatibility, the nightmare sense of frustration felt by a woman caught in the respectable trap of matrimony and realizing that a lifetime under this yoke would be literally a fate worse than death. As a concession to convention, and to keep the situation in the comic sphere, Meredith depicted a couple who were not yet married: Clara Middleton was merely trying to break an engagement, not to desert a husband. To the late-Victorian English upper class, however, a betrothal was so formal a contract that the girl who jilted her fiancé incurred a stigma only one degree less reprehensible than the wife who eloped with a lover.

For Clara's dilemma to be sufficiently acute, she had to be alone in her agony, with no one to understand her point of view and no definable reasons to justify it. Therefore Sir Willoughby had to be portrayed with all advantages in his favor. He was rich, handsome, athletic, aristocratic, and urbane. His conversation was intelligent and well informed, and not more opinionated than his hearers expected. He fulfilled the duties of his rank conscientiously. Even in his idealization of women he conformed exactly with the accepted model of the hero of romance. As the reader (seeing through Clara's eyes) steadily grows more aware of Sir Willoughby's inner defect there is danger of losing sight of the fact that his continued popularity with everyone except his fiancée was due not to willful blindness in his friends and kinsfolk but to the conventionally admirable qualities that formed his external personality. This was essential to Meredith's theme: Sir Willoughby had not a single flaw by any accepted ethical standard, and yet he must be pitilessly revealed as a very incarnation of evil because he represented the quality that Meredith had come to regard with loathing—the possessive, aggressive trait that he summed up as "egoism."

So strong was Meredith's hatred of the trait that it broke through the novel's surface of elegant irony and occasionally hissed in savage, contemptuous epithets such as "fatuous." The portrayal would have been more devastating if Sir Willoughby had always stood self-condemned without these manifestations of his creator's bias. Yet by the time the story is over Meredith has grudgingly done justice to his victim: Sir Willoughby eventually emerges as a truly pathetic figure, helpless and baffled in the face of consequences which, while resulting from his own behavior, nevertheless show that his nature has been wholly shaped by forces of the culture and the class into which he was born. His martyr's conviction of his own rectitude is one of his most infuriating traits and yet it has to be accepted as his vindication from personal guilt.

The positively spiteful tone suggests that Sir Willoughby had a model in the author's own experience, and Meredith admitted as much. A few of the baronet's traits seem like touches of actual portraiture, such as his scorn toward poets and poetry. To be sure, Meredith was inclined to attribute this attitude to the English race in general, and particularly to the English aristocrat; but some of these comments are dragged in so gratuitously that Meredith seems to be avenging some rankling slight.

The author combined two of his abiding bugbears by insisting that Sir Willoughby was not only an egoist but also a sentimentalist. As well as uttering sentimental platitudes, he devoutly believed them. His inability to comprehend Clara's point of view arose from his habit of regarding her as the pure, innocent, mindless creature that the young maiden was traditionally supposed to be. With a characteristic gibe at popular fiction, Meredith showed that Sir Willoughby was an avid reader of current novels and accepted them as a true depiction of life. Chapter thirty-three included a delicious parody of their style when Sir Willoughby was visualizing a grand reconciliation scene between him and Clara in the remote future.

Sir Willoughby is so effective an embodiment of a type that he was probably drawn from several sources, including the author himself. Meredith can scarcely have been unaware that in Sir Willoughby, Doctor Middleton, and his daughter there were close parallels with

George Meredith, Thomas Love Peacock, and Mary Ellen Nicolls. The identification of Middleton with Peacock, in his pedantic hobbies, his dogmatic prejudices, his puns, and his love of vintage port, was unmistakable. Even in appearance they were alike. Mrs Nicolls, like Clara Middleton, tried repeatedly to discourage her persistent wooer. While the inexperienced Clara, still in her teens, cannot be likened to the disillusioned widow whom Meredith married, they have some resemblance in being scholarly, outspoken, and erratic, as the result of their upbringing by a pedantic father. And Colonel de Craye's summary of the satirical essay he meant to write about marital disillusionment, which becomes significant to Clara in her growing dread of marriage to Sir Willoughby, sounds like a burlesque of Meredith's own *Modern Love*:

"*Our poor couple are staring wide awake. All their dreaming's done. They've emptied their bottle of elixir, or broken it; and she has a thirst for the use of the tongue, and he to yawn with a crony; and they may converse, they're not aware of it, more than the desert that has drunk a shower. So as soon as possible she's away to the ladies, and he puts on his Club.*"

The whole book is thus tinged with a penitential overtone that makes it a sequel to *Richard Feverel*: in that novel, written at the very time of his wife's elopement, Meredith depicted the unfaithful woman with angry contempt; now he made amends by imagining how the whole miserable imbroglio might have been avoided if she had clearly recognized the first symptoms of incompatibility and had rescued herself in time.

The characterization of both Sir Willoughby and Clara sometimes anticipated later psychological theories. In chapter six, for instance, Sir Willoughby was unmistakably provided with a mother fixation: the widowed Lady Patterne had become mortally ill shortly after his engagement, and he was at once filled with morbid forebodings about his own death, and jealously entreated Clara never to marry anyone else. It was this psychopathically sentimental interview that first warned Clara of the abnormal strain in her impressive lover. Slighter, but equally prescient of later techniques, was the device for showing Clara's suppressed desire for a new lover who might rescue her from Sir Willoughby. She had recently heard the story of his previous engagement to Constantia Durham, who escaped by eloping with a certain Captain Harry Oxford. Sir Willoughby's reticent secretary was named Vernon Whitford. Clara caught herself thinking of Constantia's lover as "Harry Whitford," and several times during a subsequent conversation she half uttered the name "Oxford" when she meant to refer to the other man. When conveying the wishes and fears of his central characters, Meredith often used a technique not unlike that which in the twentieth century came to be called the "stream of consciousness." He showed that the process of thinking was a confused sequence of images and almost formless concepts, rather than the organized reasoning that previous novelists had chronicled.

The book marked a new stage in Meredith's thinking about the relations between the sexes. Most of his earlier heroes—Richard Feverel, Harry Richmond, Nevil Beauchamp—had been like Sir Willoughby in regarding women with the traditional romantic idealization. Though Meredith had shown in each case that the women could be more realistic and more indomitable than the men, he had exhibited the idealistic youths in a favorable light. Now he recognized clearly that the heart of the problem was woman's need of emotional freedom. In *The Egoist* he insisted that the over-possessive attitude of the male was bound to arouse repulsion in the wife. He kept pointing out that the masculine demand for absolute purity in women was a survival of primitive arrogance, and that the result was hypocrisy on the part of women, who could conform to the false ideal only by pretending to be utterly chaste not only in actions but in thoughts, and who thus were obliged to comport themselves like something little better than imbeciles. In the previous novels Meredith had apparently shared something of the idealization of feminine innocence that he was now assailing, and had indicated that a woman's strength of character arose from her very lack of sophistication—from her intuitive kinship with the genuine natural forces that have become inhibited by artificial conventions. In *The Egoist* for the first time he asserted the essential claim for "women's rights"—not as an issue of political or social legislation but as the need for psychological and spiritual independence.

Being the character in the novel who was to vindicate this claim in the face of ingrained prejudices on the part of most of his readers, Clara Middleton had to be delineated with tact. That her determination to discard her fiancé should not seem too capricious, she was represented as having accepted his proposal while she was too young and naïve to realize anything about the facts of life. A motherless only child, she had been trained by an unworldly father who was more interested in teaching her Greek than in leading her toward emotional maturity. Thus her intellectual background was beyond that of the average young lady, and her impulses had not been schooled in the strict pattern of Victorian propriety; but she had no foreboding about her relations with the opposite sex. Early marriage being assumed to be every girl's destiny, and Sir Willoughby being the embodiment of the perfect husband, she plighted herself to him without any visualization of what matrimony would mean. When she and her father went on their visit to his estate, her first initiation came from her distaste for his frequent hugs and kisses. This physical repulsion was soon rationalized, as she brought her rapidly expanding intelligence to bear upon the motives that governed all his actions. Finally, when she was fully convinced of the enormity of his egoism, the most horrifying feature of his company was utter boredom: "Women can bear revelations—they are exciting: but the monotonousness. He slew imagination." An immoral fiancé would have been preferable.

Thus, on a level that could be regarded as high comedy, Meredith presented once again a crisis such as had been suffered by the heroines of his previous books in terms of real physical and emotional torment—the disillusionment that followed upon their discovery of the truth about men. For Lucy Feverel it was the period of loneliness and illness leading to her death; for Sandra Belloni it was the black days and nights of wandering through the underworld of London and contemplating suicide from the bridges; for Dahlia Fleming it was months of wasting disease and mental collapse. The vivacious young Clara, guest in a luxurious mansion, and engaged to a handsome nobleman, could not be reduced to such straits; but her mental agony as she struggled for an exit from the trap was essentially just as tragic as theirs. Her only natural ally—her father—being wholly on the other side, she searched for a confidante, in Laetitia Dale, in Colonel de Craye, in Vernon Whitford. Since apparently the only way to convince the obstinate Willoughby of her rejection was to put some other man in his place, she was soon analyzing both de Craye and Whitford as possible lovers. In these thoroughly human impulses, she horrified conventional readers by her lack of fidelity and of maidenly reticence.

The characters of de Craye and Whitford reveal a weakening in Meredith's pro-Celtic and anti-Saxon prejudice. De Craye, to be sure, was Irish, not Welsh; and he was given a full measure of the Irishman's wit, charm, and fluency. But in him, as in no previous Celtic character of Meredith's, there was an element of shallowness and of moral instability. In spite of all his grace and kindliness, he did not allow the code of gentlemanly conduct to hamper his hopes of stealing his best friend's fiancée; and therefore the reader was not too deeply distressed when he was the victim of Sir Willoughby's outrageous deception.

Whitford, on the other hand, who embodied the traditional English traits of taciturnity and self-restraint, emerged as the hero of the book. Closely modeled upon Leslie Stephen, in his mountaineering, his devotion to research, and his disillusioned irony, "the sunken brilliance of the lean long-walker and scholar," he offset the other Anglo-Saxon traits of smugness and lack of imagination that were unsparingly portrayed in Sir Willoughby. Like Stephen, Whitford was an adherent of Comte's Positivism, with its emphasis upon the welfare of the race and the expendibility of the individual. His endurance of Sir Willoughby's arrogance sometimes made him seem inert, but this was a concomitant of his unspectacular merits. Meredith was depicting the Christian virtues of humility and altruism that he had first embodied in Austin Wentworth in *Richard Feverel*; but whereas Wentworth was the "muscular Christian" of good impulses and slow wits, Whitford was the intellectual freethinker and therefore a person whom Meredith could treat much more affectionately. Indeed, he became the very personification of "the Comic Spirit":

*His mouth shut rigidly, and there was a springing increase of the luminous wavering of his eyes . . . Yet, as he was perfectly sedate, none could have suspected his blood to be chasing wild with laughter, and his frame strung to the utmost to keep it from volleying.*

The resemblance between Whitford and Austin Wentworth was sharpened by the peculiar and unnecessary detail that both men were handicapped from a rash early marriage to a vulgar and drunken woman. In view of the obvious identification of Whitford with Leslie Stephen, the references to the fortunate demise of a former spouse were peculiarly tactless, as Stephen's first wife, the younger daughter of Thackeray, had died tragically, only two years before Meredith began writing this book, and Stephen married a young widow during the very months when Meredith was betrothing his fictional counterpart to Clara.

Meredith's kinsfolk, the Ellises, already offended by his caricature of his aunt's husband as Major Strike in *Evan Harrington*, suspected a further insult in the portrayal of Captain Crossjaye Patterne of the Royal Marines. Actually the gallant officer was sympathetically displayed, his quiet devotion to duty being the antithesis of his cousin Willoughby's vanity. His son, one of the most natural and likable twelve-year-old boys in fiction, is said to have been suggested by Captain Ellis's son George, whom Meredith had known in boyhood; but probably many of his traits came from young Will Meredith, who was now just at that age.

The concluding chapters, written under stress of illness, were the weakest part of the novel. Logically the situation was valid enough. When Sir Willoughby realized that there was an actual prospect of his being jilted by a second girl, his pathological dread of ridicule forced him to decide that the only way to save face was to make it seem that he had jilted her. And this action, in turn, had to be attributable to noble motives. He therefore concocted two reasons: first, that he had begun to suspect Clara of unseemly partiality for Vernon Whitford; and second, that he himself had always unwittingly been in love with his earliest admirer, Laetitia Dale. Therefore he planned to repel public malice with a *fait accompli* by announcing his own engagement to Laetitia while Clara was magnanimously handed over to the despised Whitford. Ironically, this was the best possible arrangement for everyone concerned; but Meredith could not let Sir Willoughby off without the final humiliation of rejection by a third woman—the one whose devotion he had always complacently taken for granted. In maintaining the suspense of this crisis, the author failed to make Laetitia's behavior convincing. The involved series of misunderstandings became tedious, and the ladies of the neighborhood who personified the voice of gossip were crudely caricatured.

Throughout the book Meredith's enhanced technical skill can be seen in his handling of symbols to heighten emotional effects. The double-blossomed cherry tree, the lofty Alpine peaks, the destructible beauty of porcelain—these and other images are subtly interwoven to suggest the theme of Clara's fight for independence.

The reception of *The Egoist* is generally regarded as being the turning-point in Meredith's fame. His predictions of the book's failure were by no means fulfilled. Henley acclaimed it in at least four papers —*The Pall Mall Gazette, The Athenaeum, The Academy,* and *The Teacher.* James Thomson's praises were again confined to the obscure pages of *Cope's Tobacco Plant.* But other reviewers joined the favorable chorus. *The Daily News* speculated upon how the "honest English mind" would respond to the "highly seasoned dish which Mr Meredith has placed before it. Will the plain palates relish the exquisite savours of so delicate a wit? Will they appreciate the subtle essences he has cunningly distilled into the dish?" And Henley asserted thunderously:

He is a companion for Balzac and Richardson, an intimate for Fielding and Cervantes . . . In the world of man's creation his people are citizens to match the noblest; they are of the aristocracy of the imagination . . . There is no question but The Egoist is a piece of imaginative work as solid and rich as any that the century has seen, and that it is not only one of its author's masterpieces, but one of the strongest and most individual performances of modern literature.

When Thomson read the series of appreciative reviews expressing opinions that he had been announcing unheeded for several years, he noted sardonically in his diary:

At length! Encouraging! A man of wonderful genius and a splendid writer may hope to obtain something like recognition after working hard for thirty years, dating from his majority!

Meredith himself, however, had become so pathologically antagonistic to reviewers that even their praise irritated him. Having toiled heroically on behalf of *The Egoist*, Henley was annoyed by the discovery that the author was unappreciative. "It is curious," he grumbled to Sidney Colvin, "that Meredith should have winced under my articles as he seems to have done. I go and worry my guts out and try to teach the blasted public something of the author's meaning and games, and the author repudiates me on all hands, and says that he 'should have preferred to have been criticised'!" Shortly afterwards, while begging Colvin to write a long review of the novel for *The Times*, Henley summed up his ambivalent feelings toward the book and its author: "It is an attempt at art by an elderly apprentice of genius. It is the material for a perfect comedy—not of intrigue; d——n intrigue; intrigue is not comic—but of character—the missing link between Art and Nonsense. An Inorganic 'Misanthrope.' The devil will surely damn him hot and deep. I hate and admire him."

# CHAPTER

## XII

# *Collapse of Health*

FOR more than fifteen years Meredith had faithfully sustained his duties as one of the "gentleman readers" to Mrs Wood, the rich widow of Eltham. A niece of hers, Mrs O'Shea, who was unhappy in her marriage, had recently found refuge there for herself and her children; Meredith's visits proved to be a slight break in the tedium, and the sprightly Kitty O'Shea was diverted by the formalized banter that passed between the old lady and her entertainer:

Before he began to read to my aunt, the following dialogue invariably took place:—

"Now, my dear lady, I will read you something of my own."

"Indeed, my dear Mr Meredith, I cannot comprehend your works."

"I will explain my meaning, dear Mrs Wood."

"You are prodigiously kind, dear Mr Meredith, but I should prefer Molière today." . . .

To Aunt Ben, Meredith appeared to be a very young man indeed, and in her gentle, high-bred way she loved to tease him about his very great appreciation of his own work—and person. Meredith took her gentle raillery absolutely in good part and would hold forth upon what the literary world "of all time" owed him in his books, and also upon what Lady This-or-that had said in admiration of his good looks at such-and-such a gathering. My aunt used to delight in these tales, which were delivered in the mock-serious manner of a boy telling his mother of his prowess, real or imagined; and after a time of listening to him, with only her gently modulated little bursts of laughter to encourage him, she would say, "Oh, my dear Mr Meredith, your conceit is as wonderful as your genius!"—bringing forth from him the protest, "My dear lady, no! But it is a pleasure to you to hear of my successes and to me to tell you of them."

A similar impression was formed by Julian Hawthorne, a young American writer who met Meredith at this time at the home of Baron Trübner, a partner in Kegan Paul's firm:

*I saw a handsome man with wavy grey hair and short grey beard, in talk with a group of women with low necks and adoring looks. The man's profile was clear as a cameo, and his face had an intellectual refinement that was almost excessive, and not typically English . . . Meredith wore the polite smile of an eighteenth-century preux chevalier, and was responding to the ladies' questions with witty little apothegms and paradoxes . . . But his manner had not the ease of the man-of-the-world, profound though was his insight into the world. He was not awkward or ungraceful; he was as quick and precise as a beautiful bird; but his self-possession was, I thought, assumed; he was really shy and embarrassed, and trying to act up to what the ladies expected of him . . . Self-consciousness is contagious; the ladies became uneasy, rearranged their bracelets; a stray lock of hair; lifted themselves in their bodices; smiled unreally; they didn't know what was the matter. Their demigod was only too demigodlike . . . He would have been happier as a beautiful and brilliant woman, the queen of a salon. He played at masculinity and extolled it, but masculine men don't do that.*

Though naturally gratified by occasional appreciation from fashionable ladies, Meredith derived his chief pleasure from having friends visit him at Flint Cottage, free from the tension of social occasions in London. Leslie Stephen had organized an informal walking-club known as "The Sunday Tramps," and several times a year Box Hill was chosen as their rendezvous. The members were picked for their intellectual interests as well as for pedestrian endurance; the original group included Sir Frederick Pollock (authority on jurisprudence), G. Croom Robertson and James Sully (psychologists), and Cotter Morison. Whenever they were to go to Box Hill, the party would be limited, so that Meredith's hospitality should not be overtaxed. He would join them for a walk of ten or twelve miles, escorted by his dachshund and sometimes by one of his children or Maxse's. "Here," says Julian Hawthorne, an early recruit of the club, "Meredith was at his best—simple, natural, happy, full of golden thoughts and emotions freely and humanly scattered; better than his books, quite other than the Meredith of drawing-rooms and of encircling ladies."

On their return, Mrs Meredith would have a bountiful tea ready for them. Afterwards Meredith might lead them in a stroll to see some favorite view; a select few would stay for dinner, followed by adjournment to the chalet for cigars and talk. James Sully describes these sessions:

*His utterances were spontaneous and flowed with a wonderful continuity. It was the rarest thing to catch him hesitating for a word. The maintenance of such a smooth current of speech implied, in his case, a tense form of intellectual concentration. His hearers were for the most part aware of this, and wisely made no attempt to interrupt the flow of ideas. If one of the unwary did venture on a word, Meredith had an effective way of chastening the hardihood . . . Yet, impatient as he was of interruption when primed for discourse, Meredith would now and again graciously give not only our chief, but even less important members of the fraternity a chance to join in the talk . . .*

*The most brilliant, if not also the most stimulating, passages in his talk were expressions of the comic spirit, ranging from the playful antics of a boyish "larkishness" up to the mature and artfully adjusted attack of wit and irony. Extravagance of statement, caricature, a touch now and again of Rabelaisian eagerness to leap the barriers of conventional propriety—these were some of the more salient features of his utterance . . .*

*When the comic mood was well set, Meredith's hearers might now and again observe him as he glimpsed the crest of a new billow of mirth approaching. One could watch the play of the mouth, the underlip lowered and the tip of the tongue exposed for a second, as some new aspect of his comic quarry disclosed itself . . . Meredith would sometimes join in the laughter he was provoking; yet only so as to secure a moment's relief from the intellectual strain.*

*The finely moulded head, sometimes described as Greek, was in itself arresting, whether fully exposed within doors or half hidden out of doors by a sort of deerstalker's cap; and it acquired a new dignity when the talker graciously leaned forward as if to mark a special intimacy of accost. The bright, truth-loving eyes doubled the hold of the speech; while the voice, always mellow and finely modulated, riveted the attention by a musical link. Among other striking features in his appearance were the easy yet perfectly fitting brownish-grey suit which set off the ruddy tints of cheek and necktie, and the easy and gracious movements, which had nothing of the Frenchman's quick, energetic gestures.*

The memoirs of Hawthorne and Sully and Mr and Mrs Comyns Carr, along with others of similar import, show that by the time Meredith reached the age of fifty he had completely molded himself in a dramatic personality. Some of its components dated back to his childhood admiration of his aunt's Continental elegance, and to his nonage under the tuition of the erudite Dr Charnock; other arts of fluency and epigram had come from foreign travel and from friendship with some of the best minds of the time. It was a flawless structure which had become his second nature; impenetrably screened behind it lurked the Portsmouth tailor shop, the bankrupt father, and the dreadful decade of his first marriage.

Hence came a peculiar element in the attitude of his more recent friends. They enjoyed his company; most of them admired and respected him; some positively idolized him; but none of them felt any genuine intimacy. It was not that he seemed either aloof or insincere; but he created the effect of a perpetual and consummate theatrical performance, and the pilgrims to Box Hill were not so much consorting with a friend as they were appreciating a unique work of art.

His holiday in the autumn of 1879 did not fully restore his health. In the winter he found himself able to work both morning and afternoon as long as the weather was frosty, but "when the soft winds came I broke down, the stomach lost all power, and since then I have worked badly and waked continually." At the end of April he reported that he had "been pensioned off all work of any worth of late." An outing with the "Tramps" put him in better fettle.

His personal acquaintance with James Thomson began that summer. A friendly correspondence had been maintained between them for two years, and now the publication of Thomson's book of poems, *The City of Dreadful Night,* evoked a letter of unstinted praise for "such rarely equalled good work . . . many pages that no other English poet could have written." Meredith asked Morley to let him review the book for *The Fortnightly,* but learned that it had already been assigned to another critic. An invitation to Box Hill brought Thomson down on June 29—"a day to be marked with a white stone," as he described it, "a real red-letter day in all respects. He is one of those personalities who need fear no comparisons with their best writings."

Two weeks after gaining this new friend Meredith was grieved by the loss of an old one. The death of Tom Taylor ended the sole literary friendship that had lasted without interruption for thirty years, since the very beginning of Meredith's career. Only eight months earlier Taylor and his family had spent a happy day at Flint Cottage, enjoying the glowing woods of the Indian summer. Meredith wrote a moving sonnet in his friend's memory.

A longer poem, "Phoebus with Admetus," which was published some months later in *Macmillan's Magazine*, showed that his revision of "Love in the Valley" had reawakened his taste for its syncopated melody; and in it he expressed his love of Nature in a more ecstatic tone than in anything he had written for many years.

Meanwhile, he was busy with another novel. Not resuming work on *The Amazing Marriage* after the interruption caused by his illness, he had turned to a subject that made the least possible demand upon his creative power. While all his other novels had derived some characters and episodes from real life—through his own observation or the anecdotes of friends—he now borrowed a complete plot and cast of characters from a single published source.

A new German book, *Meine Beziehungen zu Ferdinand Lassalle*, by Countess Racowitza, *geboren* Helene von Dönniges, had fascinated him by the author's unintentional revelation of her vanity and shallowness. A beautiful young woman of fashion, she had fallen in love with Ferdinand Lassalle, the idolized leader of German Socialism, and her family's disapproval had led to Lassalle's death in a duel. The story contained several elements in which Meredith was keenly interested—the egoism which was the tragic flaw in both protagonists, the barrier of social caste which wrecked their love affair, the woman's problem in seeking freedom to live her own life and play some part in public affairs. Besides, Meredith took recent Continental politics seriously, and the story provided intimate glimpses of international and governmental events.

As he announced repeatedly, both in the foreword and at intervals through the book, that his narrative was based scrupulously on fact, one wonders why he troubled to create fictitious names for the performers. Presumably he felt that this flimsy veil of fiction was needed to justify his invention of dialogue and other slight liberties that he took with his source. The real events had occurred only fifteen years before; and as his attitude toward all the participants was far from flattering, he may have considered that good taste, or even legal immunity, demanded the fictitious disguise. Only about half as long as his other novels, *The Tragic Comedians* was printed in five instalments in *The Fortnightly Review* between October, 1880, and February, 1881, and Chapman & Hall published it in two volumes on December 15, 1880. For the serial issue it was arbitrarily shortened by the omission of paragraphs here and there.

This novel went further than *The Egoist* in using the techniques of the drama: it was concentrated upon a single line of plot, the characters were kept to a minimum, and attention was never deflected from the two principals. Even the title proclaimed the dramatic theme, and other phrases of theatrical connotation were used, as when the author remarked, "It is here the place of the Chorus to state that . . ." The Chorus, of course, was the philosophizing novelist.

With dramatic perfection the original events conformed to the familiar Romeo-and-Juliet pattern—the lovers whose elective affinity is thwarted by every obstacle that social prejudice can interpose. Ferdinand Lassalle was forty, a freethinker, a political Radical, and a Jew. Furthermore, his personal reputation was sullied by his long-standing alliance with the Countess Sophie von Hatzfeldt, whose alimony suit against her husband he had prosecuted for eleven years. Helene von Dönniges was eighteen; her family was Catholic, conservative, and aristocratic; and she was engaged to the eminently suitable Count Racowitz. Under the names of Sigismund Alvan and Clotilde von Rüdiger, Meredith accurately depicted the two lovers, while the elderly Countess von Hatzfeldt became Lucie, Baroness von Crefeldt, and Count Racowitz was Prince Marko.

Meredith had already used the Romeo-and-Juliet situation for its full tragic value in his earliest novel, and there had been traces of it in practically all his subsequent plots, for the problem of social barriers was one that concerned him deeply. But in this story, as its title emphasized, he refused to treat it as a theme for high tragedy, even though it culminated in a violent death. Meredith felt that the Comic Spirit could legitimately preside over this narrative because of the self-deception and conceit which in his view controlled every action of the couple and which vitiated any genuine nobility in their doom. The best-loved romantic theme was here subjected to a rigorously anti-romantic analysis.

The two brought inevitable disaster upon themselves because they were both egoists, less obnoxious than Sir Willoughby Patterne only because they had a Continental flair for dramatizing their emotions, in place of his English smugness. Clotilde was the perfect coquette, the female egoist whose one concept of love is that the man must become her slave while she remains undisturbed. She laid a calculated plan of campaign to conquer the notorious political leader because no one else seemed worthy of her mettle; and she always felt inwardly justified by her own emotional sanctions, no matter how inconsistently or deceitfully she might behave under the pressure of external forces. Like Sir

Willoughby, she had been conditioned by her addiction to sentimental fiction:

*Clotilde's imagination drew on her reading for the knots it tied and untied, and its ideas of grandeur. Her reading was an interfusion of philosophy skimmed, and realistic romances deep-sounded.*

Meredith had taken such a strong dislike to the Countess Racowitza on the basis of her self-revealing memoirs that his portrayal of Clotilde was generally colored with sarcasm.

Sigismund Alvan was the histrionic demagogue, handsome, eloquent, and self-assured, who cannot conceive the possibility of failure, whether in his public career or in his affairs with women. He had something of the hypnotic strength of self-dramatization that Meredith had previously displayed strikingly in Richmond Roy. While his intellect warned him clearly of Clotilde's defects, his passion for her had become so mingled with his self-esteem that he was determined to defeat her family and to establish his social acceptability by their marriage. She was the symbol of the conventions that he had always flouted, and for that very reason he must conform with them in acquiring her as his wife. It was a valid psychological study; and while Meredith never minimized Alvan's faults, his attitude toward him was more lenient than toward Clotilde. He remarked, with his customary gibe at the unrealities of fiction, that Alvan "was not heroic, but hugely man," and "out of romances, [man] is not melodiously composed." Even Alvan's boastfulness was tolerable in its frank ebullience.

One of the ancient dramatic devices, the peripeteia, was exploited to the full, with its concomitant *hubris*. Alvan's almost insane self-confidence carried the prophecy of catastrophe throughout, and devices of tragic foreshadowing were heavily interspersed, such as the emphasis on Alvan's campaign for abolition of dueling and the symbolic blighted tree which seemed to pursue the lovers during their ramble in the forest at the moment of their fullest accord and which recurred in Alvan's dreams as the crisis approached.

These tragic accoutrements are bound to rouse the reader's sympathy for the lovers caught in destiny's trap; and at many points their pattern of behavior is so natural in its mixture of strength and weakness, insight and folly, that they earn a full measure of pity. But whenever pathos threatens to dominate, Meredith grimly alienates sympathy by pointing to some trait of selfishness or conceit. The novel is ineffectual in the very degree of its success in carrying out the author's purpose.

Through being kept ironically conscious of the inherent flaws in both the central characters, the reader is denied the satisfaction of identifying himself wholeheartedly with either of them.

In other respects, too, the author's intellectual and artistic control of the novel militates against its effectiveness. The condensation and the undeviating focus on the central couple divest it of the illusion of reality that comes with richness of incidental detail. Though the two chief characters are analyzed minutely as to their moods and motives, some important events in which they participated are given in mere summaries. The secondary characters are firmly prevented from assuming independent existence; the Baroness, for instance, is merely a name until almost the end of the novel, where she appears briefly and at once reveals a more definite personality than any of the others.

In style, as well, Meredith seemed to be restraining his idiosyncrasies. Neither the narrative nor the dialogue often became epigrammatic or elliptical. The unusually direct and concise manner was combined with rhythmic movement and lyrical similes to produce an effect like poetic drama. The setting was laid in regions that he had previously described with enthusiasm—the German courts of *Harry Richmond* and the Alpine resorts where again and again he had brought his characters for their most exalted moments; but he allowed himself only an occasional paragraph of rapture over a mountain sunrise or a tramp through the forest.

Equally self-denying was his avoidance of the political and social implications of his theme. As a study of the European turmoil in the sixties, it could have been a companion piece to *Vittoria*. But whereas that novel lost some of its structural unity by its detailed presentation of riots and secret negotiations, *The Tragic Comedians* seldom gives more than passing allusions to political events. The theme of anti-Semitism lurks in the background of the story; but while revealing his awareness of the ominous problem, Meredith nowhere let it assume major proportions. He did, however, introduce two unequivocal expressions of his own respect for the talents and achievements of the Jewish people. A couple of pages offered a vivid glimpse of an interview between Alvan and Bismarck, but it was reported in Alvan's words as a specimen of his ineffable self-confidence. Since Alvan was a champion of democracy against royalist despotism, he embodied Meredith's own political ideals, and might have been portrayed, like Sandra Belloni or Nevil Beauchamp, as an incorruptible visionary. But this again would have distorted the strictly psychological focus. Only in a few paragraphs was Alvan's ideology summarized, in terms that revealed

Meredith's approval of it. The longest such exposition was in chapter fifteen, and it forms as brief and clear a statement of Meredith's brand of evolutionary Radicalism as can be found anywhere.

Written in about six months, this novel was the hastiest of Meredith's productions and seems to have aroused none of the excitement that he usually felt about a work in progress. Its painful effect arises from something more than the foredoomed tragedy or the author's lack of sympathy toward the characters. The second half, in particular, has a sense of strain and misery not wholly attributable to the chronicle of Alvan's long mental agony. This intangible gloom must be an emanation of the illness and depression of spirits in which the book was written.

His concentrated work upon *The Tragic Comedians* led to a grave relapse in health. He reported to Wyse at the beginning of January, 1881, that "I am slightly coming round to be able to write, but for several months I have been incapable: and I loathe the pen so much that I shun the plain duty of immediately replying to letters. The malady, as of old, is bradypepsy, influenced by the nervous excitement of composition continued too long." During February and March "the dreadful curse of Verse" was on him. One consequence was his ecstatic poem, "The Lark Ascending," which came out in *The Fortnightly* in May, a technical *tour de force* in its imitation of the bird's sustained song.

His son Will was at Westminster School, and Meredith was pleased to see signs that the boy was being "manlified." His concern over Will's training was intensified by a revival of difficulties in connection with his elder son. During the nine years since they had seen each other, correspondence between Arthur and his father had gradually lapsed. Harried with overwork and illness, Meredith neglected to write letters, and Arthur—always touchy—inferred that his father wanted nothing more to do with him.

Upon completion of his studies at Stuttgart he was employed by the de Koninck firm in Le Havre. Neighbors of Meredith's at Mickleham, the Beneckes, then helped him to obtain a position in a linseed warehouse at Lille. Having inherited a little money from his mother's family, he did not ask for funds from home to eke out his salary. His father was disturbed by reports that the youth was eager to give up his job and to try to make a living by writing. Then in June, 1881, Meredith was shocked when Lionel Robinson brought news that Arthur had suffered a hemorrhage of the lungs, with the further implication that bad working conditions and poverty might have caused the decline in his health. In a long, remorseful letter Meredith advised him to give up his employment and take a year's rest in Devonshire or Switzerland; he offered to contribute to Arthur's income, and he added a warm invitation to come for a visit to Flint Cottage and make the acquaintance of his brother and sister. He further suggested that Arthur might share the chalet and receive help with his experiments in authorship. "I am allowed the reputation of a tolerable guide in writing and style," Meredith said, "and I can certainly help you to produce clear English." It was a boast that might have surprised his critics.

Arthur's reply was somewhat reassuring. He had decided to live in the mountains, and he thought his income would be adequate. Being unwilling to visit England, Arthur begged his father to come and see him abroad. This request, however, had to be rejected. "I am in difficulty with the work I am doing just now," Meredith explained, "and behindhand with it." The tone of his letter was stoic: "I have failed, and I find little to make the end undesirable. While I can be of service to my children, I would stay, but no longer. There is nothing saddening about death to a man of my age . . . . Part of me has become torpid. The quality of my work does not degenerate; I can say no more. Only in my branch of the profession of letters the better the work the worse the pay, and also, it seems, the lower the esteem in which one is held for it."

His sense of pressure was due to his having two novels in hand, with some prospect that one of them might be accepted as a serial for *The Cornhill*, if he could turn in an adequate portion of it by October. He worked so hard during the summer that another bout of illness came on in September. After several short visits to counteract "the sameness of our animal life" at Box Hill, which he blamed for his slowness of recovery, he was able to resume some writing, chiefly poetry, but only in brief stints, with rests between.

Some solace came in indications that his influence was increasing. James Thomson on September 13 spent another day with him. "We had a fine stroll over Mickleham Downs," Thomson reported to a friend. "We had some good long chat . . . M. read me an unpublished poem of considerable length, which, so far as I can judge by a single hearing (not like reading at one's leisure), is very fine, and ought to be understood even by that laziest and haziest of animals, the general reader. He says that, having suspended work on a novel, poems begin to spring up in his mind, and I am glad that he thinks of bringing out a new collection."

In the midst of his own anxieties, Meredith did not overlook the signs of poverty and depression in Thomson, who was at a crisis in his affairs. Meredith introduced him to Morley, who was then editing the daily *Pall Mall Gazette* as well as *The Fortnightly Review*; but Thomson was too far gone in illness and drink to take advantage of the opportunity, and he died eight months later.

A new admirer was added to Meredith's circle in the person of Grant Allen, a versatile Canadian-born writer who was best known as a popularizer of scientific ideas. His latest book, *An Evolutionist at Large*, was arousing controversy in 1881 when he and his wife settled in Dorking, their house, The Nook, being just a convenient walking distance from Flint Cottage. One of Allen's current theories was the predominance of the Celtic strain in the English race, a notion close to Meredith's heart, and their friendship ripened quickly.

Abroad, too, he was gaining adherents. A young poet and critic, André Raffalovich, son of a Russian banker in Paris, wrote to him so ecstatically that at first Meredith suspected a practical joke, until Raffalovich sent copies of *Le Journal de St Petersbourg* and *Le Gaulois*, containing articles praising his books. Even his Portuguese cousin, the Marqueza de Thomar, whose husband was now Ambassador to the Vatican, got wind of his literary achievements and commanded her brother to write and establish friendly relations.

In December he felt improved after a visit to Brighton, where he stayed out in the sea breeze every day and did no writing; but he was becoming aware of a disquieting new symptom. Until now his attacks had all been the old digestive trouble, but just after Christmas he informed Maxse that "the malady seems to be nervous, affecting the spine, and I begin to feel my legs labouring after an hour of motion." It was the worst affliction that could conceivably have befallen this tireless walker.

The first week of March, 1882, he and his wife spent with friends in London, where he saw Irving in *Romeo and Juliet* and Lily Langtry in *Ours*, and did not think much of either of them. The change invigorated him, but as soon as he went home and resumed work he had a relapse. Under doctor's orders he confined his writing to a few hours in the mornings only. Eager to try a "water cure," he was struggling to finish the book that he was working on, so that he could go to Evian-les-Bains in the summer, and perhaps regain his "ancient talent for walking."

Robert Louis Stevenson came again to stay at the Burford Bridge Inn in May, escorted not only by his father and mother but also by the wife he had brought back from California. Stevenson's enthusiasm for

Meredith's books had continued to wax. A month previously he wrote to Henley:

*I have just re-read for the third and fourth time The Egoist. When I shall have read it the sixth or seventh, I begin to see I shall know about it. You will be astonished when you come to re-read it; I had no idea of the matter— human, red matter he has contrived to plug and pack into that strange and admirable book. Willoughby is, of course, a pure discovery; a complete set of nerves not heretofore examined, and yet running all over the human body —a suit of nerves. Clara is the best girl ever I saw anywhere. Vernon is almost as good. The manner and the faults of the book greatly justify themselves on further study . . . I see more and more that Meredith is built for immortality.*

He dined several times at Flint Cottage during his stay in the valley, astonishing the Meredith family with his black shirt and velvet jacket. His praises of *The Egoist* must have evoked from his host an anecdote that he retailed five years later when discussing this novel in his essay on "Books Which Have Influenced Me":

*It is yourself that is hunted down; these are your faults that are dragged into the day and numbered, with lingering relish, with cruel cunning and precision. A young friend of Mr Meredith's (as I have the story) came to him in an agony. "This is too bad of you," he cried. "Willoughby is me!" "No, my dear fellow," said the author; "he is all of us." I have read The Egoist five or six times myself, and I mean to read it again; for I am like the young friend of the anecdote—I think Willoughby an unmanly but a very serviceable exposure of myself.*

A few months after this visit to Box Hill, Stevenson published his essay "A Gossip on Romance," with its famous description of the imaginative response aroused in him by the Burford Bridge Inn, where "some further business smoulders, waiting for its hour"; and in it he paid a handsome compliment to Meredith's first novel:

*The last interview between Lucy and Richard Feverel is pure drama; more than that, it is the strongest scene, since Shakespeare, in the English tongue. Their first meeting by the river, on the other hand, is pure romance . . .*

By such avowals, Stevenson identified himself squarely as a Meredithian devotee. When he wrote *Prince Otto* three years later, he was so obviously emulating the style and atmosphere of *Harry Richmond* that Edmund Gosse scolded him for making "a wilful and monstrous sacrifice on the altar of George Meredith, whose errors you should be the last to imitate and exaggerate." Henry James, too, was of this opinion. *Prince Otto* was, he said in an essay on Stevenson, "more than anything else, an experiment in style, conceived one summer's day, when the author had given the reins to his high appreciation of Mr George Meredith." After declaring that Dumas ranked next to Meredith as Stevenson's favorite author, James added, "I should go so far as to suspect that his ideal of the delightful work of fiction would be the adventures of Monte Cristo related by the author of *Richard Feverel*."

Before the end of the eighties, Stevenson infected an entire new generation of young novelists with his creed of romantic fiction. Between 1885 and 1889 came *King Solomon's Mines, Dead Man's Rock, Micah Clark, The House of the Wolf*. As filtered through Stevenson's more lucid pages, the Meredithian influence lost its peculiarities of phrase and manner. Nevertheless, Meredith can be nominated as principal begetter of this school of romanticism which opposed the apostles of French and Russian realism through the last twenty years of the nineteenth century. The line of descent from *Harry Richmond* through *Prince Otto* to *The Prisoner of Zenda*, the most arrant romance of them all, is as plain as daylight.

Meredith's direct relationship with young authors was by no means confined to the romancers. About the time of Stevenson's visit to Burford Bridge, the reader for Chapman & Hall was brought into touch with a remarkable new writer of a different type. A manuscript entitled *Saints and Sinners* had been submitted a year previously, the author's name being given as "Ralph Iron." Meredith noted, "Plot silly. Early part well written." In April, 1882, the same writer sent in a new manuscript, *The Story of an African Farm*, and on this one his comment was, "Return to author for revision." On June 1, in response to a request from the publisher, the author called at the office, and turned out to be a dark-eyed young woman from Cape Town, named Olive Schreiner. Chapman was encouraging, and said that his reader would like to see her. The introduction was so perfunctory that she thought the name of the courteous, grey-bearded gentleman was "Merithett." He did not talk to her about her book, but asked questions concerning South Africa; when she championed the rights of the Boers he agreed with her warmly, and called them "the only race of gentlemen left." He also gave her one piece of practical advice, saying that he always offered it to young authors: "never to make an agreement with a publisher without putting down everything in black and white, and always to get some friend who was a competent business man to make the arrangements for them." Meredith's own experiences echoed wryly in the remark.

Chapman told the young author that the British public would consider the book wicked, and the railway bookstalls would ban it, unless she inserted a few sentences to show that her heroine was really secretly married to the man she ran away with. Here can be seen the exaggerated fear of offending the prudery of readers which Meredith had derived from his brush with Mudie's more than twenty years before. Miss Schreiner, an ardent feminist, angrily refused to make any such change. "I told him he could leave the book alone, and I would take it elsewhere. He climbed down at once. . . ." After the book became a phenomenal success, she learned that George Meredith was the reader she had talked to; and a few years later the newspaper columnists began to say that under Meredith's guidance she made various revisions in the book. In a fury she denied that "I ever let anyone touch my work . . . I am sure Mr Meredith would be as sorry as I am such a thing should be said . . . He is the only man in England who has given a blind, life-long devotion to his art, careless where it leads."

As she grew older, her war against the legend became almost psychopathic. Each time she retold the episode, her conversation with Meredith was described as shorter and more casual, and she maintained that she had made absolutely no changes in her manuscript. On the other hand, her own journal indicates that two months elapsed between her interview with Chapman on June 1 and her resubmitting of the manuscript. When she talked to Chapman again on July 29 he told her a decision would be rendered in a week. The records of the firm show that the book was accepted on August 10. Furthermore, B. W. Matz, who was a clerk in the office at the time, says, "I remember Miss Schreiner calling at our office by appointment to see Mr Meredith on more than one occasion in connection with the book. . . . As was his custom with beginners, [he] took unusual pains to give Miss Schreiner his help and advice; and she readily and graciously accepted them." In view of her pronounced egomania, the violence of her denials of any revision, uttered in years when her later writings had failed to duplicate the success of her first book, suggests some suppression of unpalatable facts.

Though sometimes championing an unknown young writer even if the proffered manuscript was off the beaten track, Meredith was usually cautious in his recommendations. H. M. Hyndman had recently been converted to Socialism and, resigning from *The Pall Mall Gazette*, had founded the Democratic Federation to propagate the doctrines of Marx. Meredith listened sympathetically to his theories, but when he proposed to translate Stepniak's sensational book, *Underground Russia*, Meredith refused it for Chapman & Hall. It was brought out by the rival firm of Smith, Elder, and went through several editions.

Work on his novel came almost to a standstill, though he "found no difficulty in verse." Late in August he went to Switzerland to take the waters at Evian, and was joined by Arthur, who was greatly improved in health after three months of mountain-climbing in the Dolomites. Together they went on to Northern Italy—Lugano, Rovio, and Milan—plagued by heavy rain most of the time. The reconciliation of father and son was thus ratified, and during the next few years Arthur came over more than once for brief visits to Flint Cottage, where he got along well with his half brother and sister.

At the end of the Italian trip Arthur went on to Sannico, where he intended to live for a while, but his father fled from the rain and returned by way of the Riviera to the Vulliamy home in Normandy. To Leslie Stephen, who was worrying about the story that had been promised for *The Cornhill* and was already a year late, he wrote that "I begin rather to feel that I shall write when I try . . . I am a bit stronger, less nerve-shaken after holding the pen for a couple of hours. If things go well I shall have the story ready by the Spring, but I dare not forecast very hopefully."

Though his recovery continued through the winter, he seems to have neglected the novel in favor of preparing a volume of poems. He revealed this news to Maxse with embarrassment: "At heart, it is plain, I must have a remainder of esteem for our public; or I have now the habit of composition, which precipitates to publishing. I scorn myself for my folly. Where he can get no audience a spouting Homer would merit the Cap and Bells."

Entitled *Poems and Lyrics of the Joy of Earth*, the volume was brought out by Macmillan & Co. in June, 1883. Its acceptance may be attributed to the fact that Morley had become literary adviser to the firm; but, even so, the author once again sustained the costs of publication. In addition to some poems that had appeared in magazines it contained many others, including long and important ones. There were also twenty-five sonnets, revealing a variable skill in that medium; the first of them, "Lucifer in Starlight," was one of the great English sonnets of all time, and "Earth's Secret" and "The Spirit of Shakespeare" were also notable, but some of the others were cramped in thought and harsh in movement, though all of them—even those with twists of satiric humor—expressed the very essence of Meredith's philosophy.

Among the long poems were four magnificent ones that had not been printed elsewhere. "Melampus" was a companion picture to "Phoebus with Admetus," in the same melodious, Swinburnian lines and with an even intenser utterance of love for living creatures. "The Day of the Daughter of Hades" narrated in more than six hundred nervous, triple-stress lines a brief return of Persephone from the Underworld to visit her mother, Demeter, accompanied by her daughter, Skiageneia, who reveled in her single day of life in the realm of mortals. The hurrying movement of the poem, with its long sentences and its run-on lines, almost painfully reproduced the sense of fleeting time. In old age Meredith named this as his most important poem, because it uttered his doctrine of defying life's sorrow and brevity; but at the time the book was published he preferred "Earth and Man," a poem in gnomic quatrains which expounded his evolutionary concept of the relationship between human life and the natural forces that produced it. It was a didactic poem, seeking to embody vast abstractions in simple terms, and the images had to be tightly packed if an epitome of the author's faith were to be conveyed in some seven hundred words. The words themselves were familiar enough—mainly monosyllabic—but the sequence of the argument and the full interpretation of the condensed metaphors require thoughtful reading.

The fourth of the big new poems, "The Woods of Westermain," was more imaginatively evocative in presenting one of the author's key doctrines—that fear is an inevitable outcome of egoism and that only the person who has mastered selfish desires can enjoy the rapture of communing with Nature. Trees and woods had become one of Meredith's recurrent symbols, and this long poem used them to illustrate the contrast between selfish terrors and undemanding serenity. The hundreds of quick-moving lines vividly suggested the beauty and eeriness of the woodland; but the reader is apt to be overwhelmed by the involutions of the allegory and the elusive melting of one metaphor into another, especially as the poet often used nouns as adjectives and verbs as nouns, and dispensed with such helpful adjuncts as prepositions and articles.

These new major poems were conjoined with those reprinted from periodicals, notably "The Lark Ascending," "A Ballad of Fair Ladies in Revolt," and above all the expanded version of "Love in the Valley," to form the most powerful and original volume of poetry that had appeared in a decade. Ten days after publication the publishers told him that the book was "moving," but this satisfactory news did not reconcile him to the shocking number of misprints in it, which resulted in Macmillan's making a new printing at their own expense.

The book received a fair amount of attention. Alice Meynell, in her husband's paper, *Merry England,* said that "Mr Meredith is to be congratulated on having faults, and not limitations," the principal fault being obscurity. Theodore Watts-Dunton, principal critic for *The Athenaeum,* objected that "there are lines which strike upon the ear like flints," but conceded that "manliness and intellectual vigour combined with remarkable picturesqueness are the most noticeable qualities." Mark Pattison, an influential Oxford don, hailed it in *The Academy* as "one of the most remarkable, perhaps the most remarkable, of the volumes of verse which have been put out during the last few years." Charging "Love in the Valley" and "The Day of the Daughter of Hades" with diffuseness, he praised "The Woods of Westermain" but went on to complain that "unfortunately Mr Meredith's healthy wisdom is veiled in the obscurity of a peculiar language which makes even his general drift doubtful, and the meaning of many score lines absolute darkness." W. P. Ker gave high and perceptive praise in *The Contemporary Review;* but W. L. Courtney, in *The Fortnightly,* condemned all the poems except "Love in the Valley" and "The Lark Ascending."

Sure that his genius was primarily poetical, Meredith regarded his first book of verse in twenty years as an event of literary moment. The qualified and impercipient praise that it received seemed to him no better than an insult, and he became convinced that no critic was willing to recognize the merits of his poetry. From this time onward the surest way to gain his good graces was to declare his poems superior to his novels.

In the summer Meredith had recovered his health sufficiently to be able to enjoy moderate walks; and he attributed his improvement partly to a diet of milk and fruit, recommended by Cotter Morison, with strict abstinence from meat and wine. By doctor's orders he was restricted to two meals a day—breakfast at eleven and dinner at seven. He went up to London for various theatrical and musical events and for dinner parties, including one especially arranged for him and Browning, at the latter's request. But at large gatherings he found it strangely difficult to understand what was being said. Reporting to Maxse on a "roaring gabble-gobble at Morison's, a dinner of sixteen," he admitted that "it was full half an hour before my ears could distinguish an articulation at the table." He was not ready to acknowledge any symptoms of impaired hearing.

At the end of October he informed Morison that his friend Dr Burney Yeo was "positive as to the spinal cord as the seat of the malady . . . I can't walk much. A mile beyond the right distance cripples me. And as soon as I feel better I fall in the old ways and am lamed again." But ever since his change of diet he had been "working at a splendid pace . . . producing rapidly." A teetotal and vegetarian regime was sad austerity for such an epicure, but for a while Meredith lauded it fervently. His friend Hyndman gives an amusing account of it, distorted by the fact that Hyndman was not aware of Meredith's ailment, and mistakenly believed that his paralysis was entirely subsequent to the dicting.

*Poor Mrs Meredith had a hard time during this bread and roots period. She saw her husband gradually going down hill and becoming every day more gaunt and hungry-eyed and skeletonic; yet if she or any one else ventured to suggest that this meagre diet was unsuited to a man of his habit of life and work, and that—this very gently—his increasing acerbity was caused by sheer lack of sustenance and his energy consequently sawing into his exposed nerves—well, it was a case of "stand from under" very quickly. Mrs Meredith tried every conceivable device to arrest the nerve weakness she saw coming upon Meredith. She boiled his vegetables in strong broth, introduced shredded meat as far as she dared into his bread in connivance with the baker, and tried various other estimable frauds upon him. All to no purpose.*

*She begged me as one of his oldest friends to try what I could do. I did try and, metaphorically speaking, fled for my life. Really, I thought my old friend would die, so determined did he seem to commit suicide in this unpleasant way. At last things got so bad and he was so weak that he recognized the truth himself . . . So Meredith took to meat-eating again and all went well.*

At the end of 1883 he "discovered" another new writer for Chapman & Hall. When the manuscript of a novel entitled *The Unclassed* was submitted he was so strongly impressed by its uncompromisingly grim picture of poverty that he summoned the author for an interview. George Gissing was a high-strung, eager young man with a background of instability, who was struggling to establish himself as a writer and had already published one novel at his own expense. In the tall, emaciated figure, burning dark eyes, and sensitive features, Meredith recognized genius and suffering. He had perhaps already heard something about Gissing from Frederic Harrison, who had recently rescued the young man from indigence by hiring him as tutor for his sons.

As usual, the identity of the publisher's reader was not disclosed. Gissing had read and admired most of Meredith's novels, but he had no idea that their author was the man who gave him such unprecedented encouragement and such detailed suggestions. Only when his book was on the eve of publication did he learn the truth. "It is an excellent thing to have got his good word," he wrote to his sister. "His own novels are of the superlatively tough species." And when his sister worried about how the public would take the book's frankness, he told her, "Do not lose sight of the fact that a man like Meredith can wholly praise this book, a man whose own writing has nothing whatever 'offensive' in it, but yet is deeply intellectual."

# CHAPTER

# XIII

# *Grief and Fame*

MEREDITH's "hot fit of composition" had effected good progress with his next novel. This may have been one of the two that he had had in hand more than two years earlier, or it may have been a fresh undertaking. Whichever may have been the case, the prospect of publication in *The Cornhill* had evaporated during the long interval. In January, 1884, while complaining about the "galley-oar of work," he was able to predict that the story would begin as a serial in *The Fortnightly* in March or April. It was "partly based on a real instance," and its title was *Diana of the Crossways*. He admitted in February that *Diana* was "rather in the Doldrums," and he now set the date for its first instalment as "April or May." A letter to Stevenson on March 24 said that he was "just finishing at a great pace a two-volume novel . . . partly modelled upon Mrs Norton. But this is between ourselves. I have had to endow her with brains and make them evidence to the discerning. I think she lives." The date for the serial's commencement was now "May or June." When he wrote to Mrs Leslie Stephen the same day, regretfully declining an invitation to a dinner for James Russell Lowell, "whom I love," he explained: "I am now writing daily very hard, and though the work flows to its end in full view, my health at present is of a kind hardly to bear the strain. If I come to London I lose the next morning for work; I am besides but a tottering dummy at the festal board . . . Meanwhile I hope to finish with the delivery of the terrible woman afflicting me (a positive heroine with brains, with real blood, and demanding utterance of the former, tender direction of the latter) by the end of April."

On May 19, however, the news was that *"Diana of the Crossways* keeps me still on her sad last way to wedlock. I could have killed her merrily, with my compliments to the public; and that was my intention. But the marrying of her sets me traversing feminine labyrinths, and you know that the why of it never can be accounted for."

Clearly he was aware of the difficulties he incurred. It was not the first time he had taken a woman for the central figure in a novel; but the previous ones had been comparatively simple in their psychology —Rhoda Fleming, the country girl governed by an inflexible will, and Sandra Belloni, endowed with the intuition and the emotional naïveté of the artist. Diana Warwick presented a different problem. The novel must convincingly portray her as brilliant and charming, must involve her in compromising situations without alienating the reader's sympathy, must insist that she was intelligent even though she made catastrophic mistakes.

His troubles were increased by the fact that the source of the story was unmistakable. In *The Tragic Comedians* he had felt no scruples about taking his whole plot directly from real events, because they had happened in a foreign country and furthermore had been openly printed by one of the chief participants. But the Honorable Caroline Norton was a distinguished English lady who had died barely seven years before; she had been the beloved friend of some of Meredith's own closest intimates; and several events of her life were topics of angry partisan dispute.

Mrs Norton, granddaughter of Richard Brinsley Sheridan, was famous for beauty and wit, and her poems and novels had been widely read. In 1836, when she was twenty-eight, her reputation was shadowed by a lawsuit brought by her husband against the fifty-seven-year-old Prime Minister, Lord Melbourne, accusing him of seducing her. After a celebrated trial, which is supposed to have been burlesqued by Dickens as the Bardell-Pickwick case, Melbourne was acquitted. Seventeen years later she brought an unsuccessful suit against her husband to force him to pay her separation allowance and to prevent him from receiving a share of her personal income. In this connection she printed two pamphlets, appealing for financial independence for women and a liberalizing of the divorce laws.

Meanwhile in the forties it had been generally believed that Sidney Herbert, a handsome young bachelor Cabinet minister, was her lover. When the secret of the Cabinet's decision to repeal the Corn Laws was betrayed to *The Times* in December, 1845, causing a political crisis in which Peel resigned as Prime Minister, Mrs Norton was widely suspected of having learned the news from Herbert and having allowed it to leak out to the editor. Herbert shortly afterwards married a young heiress who had loved him for years; and after the Hon George Norton finally died, his widow, at the age of sixty-nine, married a devoted admirer.

Meredith followed all these events and rumors of events with entire fidelity, merely telescoping fifty years into about five. His heroine resembled Mrs Norton even in minor mannerisms, and he included equally recognizable glimpses of many of her friends, such as Henry and Charles Greville, Samuel Rogers, and Alexander Kinglake. He put in also a sketch of his own youthful self in the person of Arthur Rhodes, a London law clerk with literary ambitions who fell under Diana's spell.

He had indeed met her once or twice, when she was already over fifty, and had been fascinated by her beauty, though she was not greatly impressed by the still gauche young man. The encounter had been at the Duff Gordons' at Esher, for Lady Duff Gordon was her dearest friend and most ardent defender. The Duff Gordons therefore appeared in his novel also, in the guise of Sir Lukin and Lady Dunstane. As compared with his previous picture of Lady Duff Gordon as Lady Jocelyn, this one showed less of her ferocity and more of her kindliness. Her health had given way in her later years, and so Lady Dunstane was depicted as an invalid. Sir Lukin was a less exact portrait of Sir Alexander. To heighten the dramatic situation, Meredith had Sir Lukin succumb once to the temptation of making love to Diana; and in view of the otherwise close adherence to the real facts about Mrs Norton's friendship with the Duff Gordons, he was guilty of seeming to attribute this scandalous conduct to his old friend without justification.

His interest in the Norton affair may possibly have been sharpened by rumors at the time he was writing the book, concerning Mrs O'Shea, whom he had come to know well at the home of her aunt, Mrs Wood. Living apart from her husband, she had become the confidante of the Irish nationalist leader Charles Stewart Parnell, and was suspected of being his mistress. O'Shea had already challenged Parnell to a duel over the situation, but had been dissuaded by his wife's appeal. The parallel with the Norton-Melbourne case was patent.

While writing the later part of the story Meredith discussed it in detail with a remarkable woman, Flora Louise Shaw, one of the first lady journalists, who became head of the colonial department of *The Times*. Of a good Irish family, with an admixture of French blood—an ideal breed, in Meredith's view—the tall, handsome Miss Shaw was a strong imperialist and enjoyed visiting Meredith to discuss the affairs of the world. She embodied his ideal of the emancipated woman, who had gained intellectual grasp without sacrifice of charm; to know her, he said, "is to look through an Eyelet on the Promised Land . . . In matters of abstract thought as well as in warm feeling for the poor muddy fry of this world, you will find her unmatched." He told her about his dilemma as to whether Diana should die at the end or marry her faithful Redworth; and Miss Shaw used to claim that it was her impassioned appeals that persuaded him to take the latter alternative.

In June, when the novel was almost finished and the first instalment had appeared in *The Fortnightly*, Mrs Meredith underwent an operation for cancer. She remained in London for several weeks of convalescence, and at first Meredith spent all his spare hours with her; but as her recovery continued he was obliged to devote some time to accepting unwonted tributes to his increasing fame. He reported to his daughter that "Papa still suffers from the persecution of invitations to dinner, which is becoming intense; mixed with summonses to be a Vice-president of strange societies . . . As for work, it is treated as the whiff of a cigar. No sooner do I take pen in hand than a telegram arrives, bags are packed . . . and away I fly."

As a result of these interruptions, he confessed at the end of August that he had not yet been able to write the final chapter. "The coupling of such a woman and her man is a delicate business. She has no puppet-pliancy. The truth being, that she is a mother of Experience, and gives that dreadful baby suck to brains. I have therefore a feeble hold of her; none of the novelist's winding-up arts avail; it is she who leads me." Not until October could he inform Stevenson that "my Diana is out of hand, leaving her mother rather inanimate." And by that time he had found that the editor of *The Fortnightly*, T. H. Sweet Escott, who had succeeded Morley two years earlier, was unaccommodating. The story had been limited to eight instalments of eighteen pages each, and Meredith begged Stevenson not to read the serial version, as "the poor girl has to be mutilated horribly." A dozen chapters were omitted, and the others were reduced to skeletons. He had probably made revisions also since June, for the resemblance between Lady Dunstane's dangerous operation and Mrs Meredith's seems too close to be coincidence, and Sir Lukin's desperate anxiety over his wife's peril is very like what Meredith had felt.

His letter to Stevenson was in acknowledgment of a request that he would accept the dedication of *Beau Austin*, a play written in collaboration by Stevenson and Henley. Meredith warned them that their choice of his name for the distinction would "do the book no good before the public." In spite of this ungracious reply, he cannot have been unaware that their public profession of "admiration and respect" was a token of the honor in which he was now held by some of the most acclaimed younger writers.

His wife was recuperating with her sisters at Eastbourne, but Meredith could spare himself only half a week at Ramsgate "for bracing air" between the ending of *Diana* and the beginning of his next task. He was hoping to resume *The Amazing Marriage* after five years' interruption, but he was "not quite certain, as the question of Life presses on me more seriously in other works. It seems an absurdity that I should be writing on but such must have been the decree at my birth."

The serial came to an abrupt end in the December number of *The Fortnightly*, after only seven instalments instead of the promised eight, leaving the seven final chapters unprinted. A note announced that "those who care for more of Diana of the Crossways will find it in the extended chronicle." When published by Chapman & Hall in three volumes in February, 1885, the book had forty-three chapters, whereas the serial version had only twenty-six.

The novel opened with an elaborate attempt to establish Diana in historical perspective as a figure in English society at the beginning of Victoria's reign. The first chapter was made up of citations from supposed diaries and memoirs of the period—a device already used in *The Tale of Chloe*. Meredith thus tried to convince his readers of Diana's wit and charm before undertaking the harder task of showing those traits at first hand. And through several more chapters she was presented through her impact on others, prior to the first revelation of her inward personality. Intending to portray a complex and paradoxical character, the author made his approach circumspectly.

Like Sandra Belloni, Diana is the spiritually pure woman who can move through equivocal situations and can impulsively commit indiscretions without being sullied in the act. There are even closer resemblances to Clara Middleton, the only difference being that Diana's efforts to find a way of escape from marriage occur after the event. In order to create this situation without too much discredit to Diana's intelligence, Meredith had to pass over the whole episode of her marriage hastily and almost evasively. The resemblance of her story to Clara's is particularly close in the scene when she is on the verge of open flight and is challenged by the argument that it would be a coward's trick. Like Clara, too, she has a physical revulsion against amatory caresses.

As in *The Egoist*, Meredith chose a thoroughly English type for his hero, and contrasted him with the blatant absurdity of a race-proud

Celt who was another admirer of Diana's. Redworth was an unimpressive hero, with his cautious deliberation and his practical concern for finances; and indeed it was these traits that precipitated the whole chain of events by delaying his proposal to Diana until after she had accepted Warwick.

Another parallel with *The Egoist* was in Percy Dacier's hasty recourse to the adoring and neglected Constance Asper, after Diana rejected his final suggestion of elopement, just as Sir Willoughby turned to Laetitia Dale when he was jilted by Clara.

Though Meredith delineated himself objectively in the story as Arthur Rhodes, there are indications that he subconsciously identified himself in many respects with Diana. She was Celtic; she was haunted by the consequences of an incompatible marriage; she was a witty talker who led dinner-table conversation and sometimes hurt sensitive feelings by her sarcasm; she was a novelist struggling to earn a living in the face of critical disfavor. One of her novels, like one of Meredith's, dealt with a prima donna; and like Meredith she used her own acquaintances as models for her fictional characters.

The readers who grumble because Diana is often impetuous or unreasonable are ignoring her resemblance to the central characters in Meredith's previous books. Like Richard Feverel and Evan Harrington and Sandra Belloni and Nevil Beauchamp, she was undergoing an ordeal. All these were young men and women with defects, particularly impatience, intolerance, self-assertion. But they all had in them an inherent strength and nobility that could be brought out only by agonizing experience. As a theologian would phrase it, when they had "crucified the Old Adam" they achieved salvation. In each book this marked the end of the story, whether the actual outcome of the events was happy or tragic. Diana's long-delayed marriage to Redworth was merely the symbol of her having mastered her lower nature and learned to live on sane terms with the world.

The weakest spots in the novel are the points where the author was awkwardly suspended between fact and fiction. The great political secret never becomes clear in the reader's mind because Meredith could not openly identify it as Peel's abandonment of the Corn Laws, and no equally momentous substitute could be invented. Peel had to remain an unnamed specter, much as Mazzini was in *Vittoria*, Bismarck in *The Tragic Comedians*, and Queen Victoria in *Harry Richmond*. Because Meredith believed the legend that Mrs Norton had betrayed the Cabinet secret to Delane, editor of *The Times*, he felt obliged to make Diana—half deranged by financial and emotional stresses—carry the mysterious tidings to Tonans; but he shirked the actual interview between them. As in all his other novels, he here offered a crucial scene by implication, bringing the characters to the very threshold of the event and then showing its after-effects.

His use of recurrent metaphors was noteworthy throughout. The most persistent was that of hounds or wolves pursuing a defenseless quarry, as symbol for the persecution of Diana through gossip and envy. And from the opening chapter onward, the book contained his usual flings against popular sentimental fiction for its shoddy style and its misrepresentation of life.

Meredith's admirers were delighted with the book. Cosmo Monkhouse, discussing it in *The Saturday Review*, said that "amongst all his intellectual and literary feats, Mr Meredith has, perhaps, never accomplished one more striking than in making us feel that his Diana justified her reputation. He has made her move and speak before us as a living woman." Henley, in *The Athenaeum*, declared it to be "one of the best of all Mr Meredith's books":

*It is a study of character, and it is also a study of emotion; it is a picture of fact and the world, and it is touched with generous romance; it is rich in kindly comedy, and it abounds in natural passion; it sets forth a selection of many human elements, and is joyful and sorrowful, wholesome with laughter and fruitful of tears, as life itself. In one word, it is a common novel, as* Amelia *is, and* Vanity Fair.

George Gissing advised his brother, "By hook or crook, get hold of *Diana of the Crossways*. The book is right glorious. Shakespeare in modern English, but, mind you, to be read twice, or if need be, thrice. There is a preface, which is a plea for philosophic fiction, an admirable piece of writing, the English alone rendering it worthy of the carefullest pondering. More 'brain stuff' in the book than many I have read for long."

Not only the dedicated band of disciples, however, acclaimed the new book; the public also showed interest. In part, this was because Meredith was no longer alone in writing novels that dealt with complex social and psychological relationships or suggested dissent from accepted conventions. Half a dozen of Henry James's novels had now been published in England. *A Modern Lover* and *A Mummer's Wife*, the startling first novels of George Moore, appeared in 1883 and 1885.

People were talking about the outspoken French realists, Flaubert and Zola, as well as about the plays of Ibsen, with their themes of social analysis.

A stronger appeal to public curiosity, however, was in the hint that the book told the full story of Mrs Norton's political and amatory adventures. The success of a *roman à clef* is usually in direct ratio to the recent fame of its characters and the questionableness of their morals. Most people had heard enough about her involvements with Lord Melbourne and Sidney Herbert to be avid for scandal. Among those who considered it "smart" to know the latest gossip, *Diana of the Crossways* became the vogue.

It is ironical that the feature of the book which contributed most to its popularity was also accused of being its main defect. The Duff Gordon family were angry that it gave new currency to the report that their beloved Mrs Norton had betrayed a state secret to the press, and her own relatives were also annoyed. Ten years later her nephew, the Marquess of Dufferin, requested Meredith to issue a public refutation of the slander, and accordingly subsequent editions of the novel were prefaced with a statement that the "calumny . . . has latterly been examined and exposed as baseless. The story of Diana of the Crossways is to be read as fiction."

Meredith's adherence to the supposed facts, however, had laid him open also to condemnation on artistic grounds. The reviewers of the book, and other critics discussing it later, have said that Diana's behavior, both in her marriage to the contemptible Augustus Warwick and in her secret interview with the editor, was inconsistent with her character and intelligence, even though Meredith tried hard to show motives for both actions. The objection is based on a misconception of his purpose. Because he was successful in depicting Diana's wit and courage, readers idealize her as a character of perfect wisdom and integrity, and proceed to assume that the author also was her unquestioning admirer. On the contrary, he showed her as a prime illustration of the theory that he advanced whenever he discussed the relationship of the sexes: that women have been so conditioned to be the playthings and chattels of men that even the most intelligent woman cannot avoid behaving impulsively and irrationally if exposed to a difficult ethical decision. His novel was not only a protest against the social taboos by which Diana's reputation was sullied when she separated from her husband and lived as the friend and equal of men; it was also a condemnation of the system that forced women to be shallow hypocrites and denied them any opportunity to develop sound judgment.

Hence emerged another reason for the sudden rise in Meredith's fame. Hitherto it had been assumed that his novels were not suitable for feminine readers, who were supposed to like sentimental and refined fiction that made no demand upon their brains. In his novels he himself insistently maintained the tone of a man writing for men. But a vast change was now in process. "The New Woman" had appeared on the scene. The fashion for aesthetic sensibility, which had prevailed for twenty years under Pre-Raphaelite leadership and which Meredith had satirized in the Pole sisters in *Emilia in England,* was giving place to a fashion of frankness, intellectualism, and political awareness. Women's colleges had been opened at Oxford and Cambridge. Women were admitted to medical practice in 1876. The epoch-making Married Women's Property Act, redressing some of Mrs Norton's prime grievances, was passed in 1882, and many other legislative acts were affecting women's status. Indeed, women's suffragists almost succeeded in having the vote accorded to them in the Reform Bill of 1884, and suffrage in local elections was granted in 1888. In this sudden flush of independence, women had been delighted when they discovered how *The Egoist* punctured male complacency; and they decided that Diana Warwick, who retained all her feminine charms and yet consorted with men on their own ground, was the embodiment of their dreams. From that hour, Meredith was the chosen novelist of the "emancipated" woman.

*Diana* went through three editions before the end of 1885, and the upsurge of his popularity was also conveyed to his publishers in an unprecedented demand for his earlier novels, most of which had gone out of print. At the end of May *The Athenaeum* reported a rumor that Chapman & Hall were considering a uniform edition of his books, and this was formally advertised in July. It was a triumph for which he had waited through many years; but it came at a time when he had no heart for gloating.

In the previous year, during the agonizing days of his wife's operation, he had pondered stoically on the mystery of existence:

*I live on hope; a condition resembling a midway station across the abyss, and depending on the winds as well as power of heart; for now that she has failed, my sense of stability takes wing. However, in footing the tight-rope, one must not look ahead—nor under—nor up; but steadily at the present support.*

Thus he wrote to Mrs Leslie Stephen; and to Maxse, more profoundly:

*The soul's one road is forward. Dreams of sensational desires drown it. But as to the soul, we get the conception of that, by contrast with the sensations. We go and are unmade. Could elective reason wish for the reconstruction? And yet it is quite certain that the best of us is in the state of survival. We live in what we have done—in the idea: which seems to me the parent fountain of life, as opposed to that of perishable blood. I see all round me how much Idea governs; and therein see the Creator; that other life to which we are drawn: not conscious, as our sensations demand, but possibly cognizant, as the brain may now sometimes, when the blood is not too forcefully pressing on it, dimly apprehend. Consciousness excites human felicity to kill it. Past consciousness, there may be a felicity eternal. These are not words, they are my excruciated thoughts—out of bloody sweat of mind, and now peaceful, imaging life, accepting whatever is there.*

This credo puts him firmly in the camp of the idealists, deriving through Carlyle and Coleridge from Kant and Hegel, in opposition to the mechanistic determinists who dominated current philosophy and were on the verge of invading fiction under the banner of naturalism. In the great debate over the evolutionary hypothesis, it aligns him with the creative evolutionists, from Lamarck to Samuel Butler and Bergson, in contradistinction to the Darwinist believers in blind chance. In the dark days of the subsequent winter his creed was reaffirmed in one of his most characteristic poems, "The Thrush in February," written in the tight, metaphoric style that his verse had now assumed. After an introductory description of his chalet and its vista, he gave a glance back to his "young time" and his undeviating allegiance to the goodness of Earth:

> *Imbedded in a land of greed,*
> *Of mammon-quakings dire as Earth's,*
> *My care was but to soothe my need;*
> *At peace among the littleworths.*
>
> *To light and song my yearning aimed;*
> *To that deep breast of song and light*
> *Which men have barrenest proclaimed;*
> *As 'tis to senses pricked with fright.*
>
> *So mine are these new fruitings rich*
> *The simple to the common brings;*

*I keep the youth of souls who pitch*
*Their joy in this old heart of things:*

*Who feel the Coming young as aye,*
*Thrice hopeful on the ground we plough;*
*Alive for life, awake to die;*
*One voice to cheer the seedling Now.*

*Full lasting is the song, though he,*
*The singer, passes; lasting too,*
*For souls not lent in usury,*
*The rapture of the forward view.*

The poem went on to glorify the "warriors of the sighting brain" who "scorned the ventral dream of peace" and led humanity toward the serene and loving knowledge of Earth's "mystic secret" enabling us to "fall, or view our treasures fall, unclouded."

For six months after Mrs Meredith's operation she seemed to be recovering, but at the end of January further surgery was found to be necessary. She assured him that it was not to be so severe, but his forebodings were dark. More than two months after the operation she was removed to Eastbourne, still totally helpless and unable to speak. Meredith was by now certain that there was no hope of recovery, and he spent as much time as possible at her side, though returning to Box Hill at intervals to do his regular work.

One of his tasks with Chapman & Hall at the moment was the advising of Gissing in his next novel. A departure from scenes of poverty, it was a study of temperament among people of higher station, and upon Meredith's suggestion the manuscript was shortened to two-volume length and the book was retitled *Isabel Clarendon*. Gissing followed it with another manuscript in a similar setting, *A Life's Morning*, and he records that "Meredith tells me I am making a great mistake in leaving the low-life scenes; says I might take a foremost place in fiction if I pursued that." The warning influenced him in his choice of theme for his next book, *Demos*.

Meanwhile, Meredith was busy with revision of his own novels for the new edition. Following the precedent that he had set with the reissue of *Richard Feverel* ten years before, he cut down the texts, though not so drastically. In both *Evan Harrington* and *Harry Richmond* a number of fairly long passages were deleted, but the others suffered merely verbal changes. The title of *Emilia in England* became

*Sandra Belloni,* for no apparent reason, and to the confusion of bibliographers.

Coming out in nine volumes at monthly intervals, at a reasonable price, the edition made his work available to many readers. Gissing reread the whole series as they appeared. "It is incomprehensible that Meredith is so neglected," he averred. "George Eliot never did such work, and Thackeray is shallow in comparison." And again, "For the last thirty years he has been producing work unspeakably above the best of any living writer and yet no one reads him outside a small circle of highly cultured people." The edition served as occasion for a number of articles in prominent periodicals, discussing Meredith's work as a whole—one by H. D. Traill on "The Novel of Manners" in *The Nineteenth Century,* one by W. L. Courtney in *The Fortnightly Review,* one by the indefatigable Henley in a weekly called *The State;* other articles came out in *The Pall Mall Gazette, The Saturday Review,* and *The Spectator.*

The Uniform Edition was brought out by Roberts Brothers in Boston simultaneously with the English publication, and thus Meredith was introduced to the American public virtually for the first time. Apart from several paper-bound pirated volumes there had only been the Harper edition of *Evan Harrington,* a quarter of a century before.

Meanwhile, week after week Meredith suffered the torture of knowing his dying wife's dumb endurance—the tears in her eyes when she looked at her son and daughter, the heroic effort to hide her hopelessness. During the spring, whenever he was not with her at Eastbourne, he spent all his hours alone in the chalet at Box Hill, scarcely allowing himself ten minutes, morning and evening, to go down to the cottage for his solitary meal.

The nation was going through anguish of frustration and suspense very like his own, with General Gordon besieged in Khartoum and the Tory press clamoring for an all-out war to rescue him. Horrified at the weakness of the politicians in the crisis, Meredith told Maxse that "these are times when I feel the curse of an impotent voice"; and he sent to *The Pall Mall Gazette* a sonnet "On the Danger of War" which was so earnest that it took the form of a prayer.

About the same time he wrote his long and intensely personal poem, "A Faith on Trial," contrasting his wife's hopeless struggle for life with the lavish fecundity of the English spring. On top of his beloved hill, feeling the south wind and hearing the skylark, he reviewed his wife's noble character and the happy visits to Normandy that he had shared with her; and he reaffirmed his lifelong doctrine that nature knows nothing of grief—that Earth seems cruel and terrifying only to the self-centered people who demand certainties and have not learned her lesson of unquestioning acceptance.

The dying woman was brought home from Eastbourne early in June, with a first-rate nurse to tend her. Fourteen-year-old Riette won her father's praise as "a little Angel" by her devotion in helping to care for her mother, cooking, and managing the household accounts. "We know not how long the hunted bit of life will last," Meredith told Morley on June 21; but as late as the beginning of September she was able to enjoy being taken out for drives, and to be brought downstairs so that she could lie on a sofa in the family circle. On September 17, when Meredith had been in London for his usual weekly duties, he came home in the evening to learn that she had died in her sister's arms forty minutes before.

For weeks he was in a daze of grief and poignant memories, clinging only to the certainty that "with me she lives till I go out." His son Will went to Normandy to be with his uncles and cousins, and Riette was staying with Mr and Mrs Morley. Meredith's friends were prompt with invitations, but, as he told one of them, "I am wretched when I quit this neighborhood despite the misery of the associations. They are my cup." His daughter's future was his immediate concern. He would have liked to keep her at home, with a governess; but he realized that a young governess in a widower's house might inspire gossip, and an old one, he was sure, would not get on with Riette's mercurial temperament. Besides, when his friends introduced candidates he was likely to intimidate them by his positive and strict ideas as to how a young lady ought to be brought up. In spite of the sympathy expressed in his novels for women's greater social freedom, he was determined that Riette must learn to observe the *convenances* in every detail. After one interview the bewildered applicant confided to Alice Gordon, "He talked to me for a long time, and skipped across the centuries for examples of female education, but really I don't know if he will engage me or not, and I am rather frightened at the many things he will not permit his daughter to do." Baffled by the complexities, Meredith began to consider the alternative of finding a boarding-school near enough to enable Riette to come home for frequent week-ends.

Grief and anxiety brought on a stomach attack, and in October he mentioned that he was "living chiefly on Dr Nichols' Food of Health." Arthur had come over from the Continent to see him. Gradually he was piecing a way of life together, but it was a life devoid of much solace. As his children would be finding more and more of their concerns beyond

his orbit, he must reconcile himself to soltitude. Deafness was beginning to set a barrier to easy conversation. And he could not hope that
he would ever again enjoy the rapture of tramping. "I can't walk any
of my old strides," he told Stevenson, "am no longer the lord of territory."

By the end of the autumn a governess had been found for his daughter, and so he had human companionship when he emerged from the
chalet at dinner time. The publishers reported good sales of the Uniform Edition. He learned that a group of friends were planning to get
up a subscription to have his portrait painted, and he firmly vetoed
the scheme on the ground that it was a waste of money. As a compromise it was suggested that he should have his photograph taken by
Frederick Hollyer, and he replied grumpily, "I have never shared the
enthusiasm of certain acquaintances for a sight of themselves on the
carte. The human waves roll like the seas, with a momentary difference
in the features, and that small, and not distinctly significant. I like to
see the portraits of our greatest, and of beautiful women. Not being
the one or the other, I fancy it will require accident or the police to
subject me to the operation."

More and more he had to depend on the stimulation of visitors
who enjoyed hearing him talk. Among them were the scientific ration-
alists who congregated at the home of his neighbor, Grant Allen. One
of these was Edward Clodd, an affable soul who earned his living as
Secretary of the London Joint Stock Bank but found his real career in
writing books to popularize evolutionary and agnostic theories—*The
Childhood of the World, The Childhood of Religions, Jesus of Naza-
reth.* Clodd first met Meredith at a dinner at Cotter Morison's house,
where another guest was the physiologist George John Romanes, also a
popularizer of Darwinism. Clodd reported himself "agreeably surprised" to find Meredith "very chatty, more coherent and less fantastic
than his novels. Happily I struck a responding chord in saying that I
assessed his poem 'Earth and Man' as the highest in worth in the new
volume of his verse . . . He himself thinks it the best in the book."
As they were thus in agreement in their philosophy of life, Meredith
adopted Clodd as a cherished friend to whom he eventually talked
about his early life with unwonted candor. Clodd recorded many of
his remarks in the *Memories* that he wrote after Meredith's death,
though commenting that, "lacking the sonorous voice that rolled from
the cavernous mouth and the resounding laugh that came from the
heart; the animated face and gestures; the words, Pactolian in their
flow, now set down in rigid type, are lifeless."

A less cordial impression of his talk was formed by Henry Sidgwick, Professor of Moral Philosophy at Cambridge, who met him at dinner at Leslie Stephen's in 1886, and liked him, "but was somewhat disappointed in his conversation. He was not affected or conceited and talked fluently, but not exactly with ease, nor did his phrases seem to me often to have any peculiar aptness; once or twice there was an amusing stroke of humourous fancy, as when he talked of an unhappy singer's voice being 'like the soul of a lemon in purgatory'; but these things did not come often."

Other friendships reflected Meredith's increasing concern over contemporary politics. John Morley had become an M.P. in 1883; and when Gladstone was returned to power in February, 1886, pledged to grant Irish Home Rule, Morley was appointed to the key position of Chief Secretary for Ireland. All Meredith's pride in his Celtic heritage and his contempt for Saxon insensitivity made him ardently support the Irish cause. Admiral Maxse, on the other hand, having been schooled in the Navy's patriotic tradition, opposed Home Rule so bitterly that he gave up his Radicalism and became a strong Unionist, as the Conservative party now began to call itself. The strength of the affection between Maxse and Meredith was proved by its survival unimpaired through this period of heated controversy.

Another old acquaintance, Justin M'Carthy, was also a prominent Home Rule M.P., and through him and Morley, Meredith met some of the promising young Nationalist and Liberal politicians, such as John Dillon, who had been arrested several times for boycotting, and Richard Burdon Haldane, the brilliant young Scottish lawyer and philosopher. When men like these journeyed down to Box Hill in the intervals of parliamentary sessions, to listen to his opinions, Meredith could believe that he was exerting a kind of influence in the affairs of the nation.

Literary pilgrims also were welcome at Box Hill. James M. Barrie was a young Scots journalist who had just come to London to work for Greenwood on *The St James's Gazette*. As an admirer of Stevenson, he belonged to the Meredithian cult, as he tells in his autobiography, wherein he names himself "James Anon" and makes much sport over the monumental silk hat with which he tried to lend dignity to his little figure:

[Meredith] *was royalty at its most august to Anon, whose very first railway journey on coming to London was to Box Hill to gaze at the shrine . . . There is a grassy bank opposite the gate, and the little royal residence is only* some twenty yards away. Even to Anon that day it seemed small but very royal. He sat on the grassy bank and quivered. Presently he saw a face at the window of a little sitting-room he was to be very familiar with in the hereafter. He knew whose face it was. Then the figure stood in the doorway, an amazing handsome man in grey clothes and a red necktie. He came slowly down the path towards the gate. It was too awful for Anon. He ran away. If the Hat was with him, it must have been in his hand; he could not have run with it on his head. Meredith knew of this affair afterwards, and also of the store I set by the Hat, which made him throw back his head and laugh uproariously. He always insisted afterwards that I was wearing the Hat on that pilgrimage, and that what brought him down the path was to have a closer look at it and not at Anon. After his wont he paraphrased the incident into vast proportions, and maintained that he thought I was the first arrival at his funeral.

An odd feature of this story is that in a letter of Meredith's, written at about the same time, he mentions an almost identical incident, save that the timid pilgrim was a "youngster" who worked in the Post Office Savings Bank and came down on bank holiday, later writing Meredith a twelve-page letter. Unless this is a remarkable coincidence, Barrie must be suspected of adopting a good story and applying it to himself. At any rate, the acquaintance was soon established through a more normal channel. Meredith's attention was drawn by an article in *The St James's Gazette*, and when he wrote to ask who was the author of it, Greenwood sent Barrie down with an introduction. The shy and ardent little Scot won immediate favor.

In May, 1886, Meredith sat near James Russell Lowell at a performance of Shelley's *Cenci*, "and left at the close of the so-called 5th act, with him and Mr Henry James." The next month, at a dinner of the Rabelais Club in London, the guests included Meredith, Oliver Wendell Holmes, Henry James, and Thomas Hardy. In consequence, Meredith wrote to Hardy a few days later, inviting him and his wife to come down for a day at Flint Cottage. A friendship between Meredith and James also developed, though it never became very intimate. James had been familiar with Meredith's work for a quarter of a century. When he was seventeen he read *Evan Harrington* as it came out serially in *Once a Week*, and it served as a catalyst to make him conscious of his own nascent impulse to be a writer.

In characteristic phrases, James has described "my very limited, even though extremely delightful to me, active intercourse with him. I had with him no sense of reciprocity; he remained for me always a charming, a quite splendid and rather strange, Exhibition, so content itself to *be* one, all genially and glitteringly, but all exclusively, that I simply sat before him till the curtain fell, and then came again when I felt I should find it up. But I never *rang* it up, never felt any charge on me to challenge him by invitation or letter." It has been suggested that no less than three of James's stories, "The Pattern in the Carpet," "John Delavoy," and "The Death of the Lion," contain some traces of Meredith's personality and career.

Early in August, Robert Louis Stevenson and his wife came for a four-day visit. Both the young Merediths being away in France, there was ample room for guests in Flint Cottage. Meredith asked the Stevensons to bring their friend Sidney Colvin; and when he did not come Flora Shaw was invited down for a night, to listen entranced to the conversation of the two lively talkers. Stevenson, whose health was very frail, felt so much better than he was reluctant to leave the stimulating breezes of Box Hill.

As the crisis of Meredith's grief abated, he began to feel a revived interest in pretty and sympathetic women. In the autumn of 1886 the Grant Allens were visited by a cousin, Hilda de Longueuil, aged twenty-four, a member of a distinguished Canadian family. Her present home was in the South of France, whither she had withdrawn to nurse her misery after a disastrous love affair. Meredith was touched by her sad beauty, her habitual shyness, and the naïve enthusiasm that sometimes enabled her to express her ideas with wit and animation. From her glances he inferred that the interest was mutual, and the Allens soon told him that she admired him deeply.

As long as she remained a guest at The Nook his visits there were more frequent than usual; and when she was about to leave he half-seriously suggested accompanying her across the Channel to shield her from the abrasions of travel. This offer being declined, he consoled himself during the next few months by writing long letters to her to convey solicitude, gallant compliments, and expositions of his doctrines about thinking for oneself and facing life with fortitude. It was her request that finally impelled him to submit himself to Hollyer's lens. There were several poses, and his friends were pleased with two of them, but Meredith was scornful. "A supercilious grey beast," he scoffed, "commenting within himself disdainfully on a rival poet's verse."

He was determined to rescue Miss de Longueuil from her obsession that she had forfeited all normal human relationships. He sent her a long poem, entitled "Hilda's Morning and Evening Dose of Rhyme," which assured her that she would find a new lover far nobler than the unworthy one who had broken her heart. He proposed to address to her a fortnightly series of "Letters to a Lady, on the Art of Fiction," for the double purpose of preventing her from brooding and of enabling him to crystallize his opinions on his vocation. He insisted that she must write comments in reply so that the book could then be published as a collaboration under their joint names. As nothing came of the scheme, her diffidence must have restrained her from aspiring to this eminence in company with the man she admired. Instead, Meredith was offered an embarrassing substitute: Miss de Longueuil's sister, who fancied herself as a writer of fiction, sent him a manuscript of "Tales of Provençe" in expectation that he could get it published by Chapman & Hall. Professional ethics overcame personal sympathy, and he had to advise against the acceptance of the book.

During the autumn and winter he was actively writing poems, including a long one, "The Appeasement of Demeter," which showed that he still turned to Greek myth for a symbology suited to his philosophy of Earth. Tokens of fame continued to be received without enthusiasm. When young Arthur Symons proposed to dedicate his *Introduction to the Study of Robert Browning* to Meredith as "the greatest of living novelists," Meredith's consent was delayed until Symons cut out the laudatory phrase. Havelock Ellis wrote to him in December with a proposal for publishing the lecture on comedy, but Meredith withheld permission, saying, "it requires extension and filling-in. At present the style is lumpy. I purpose to write it over again some day, that it may be more generally intelligible."

His domestic circumstances were much improved by the coming of a new governess for his daughter. An ebullient, kindly Irishwoman, whose husband had been French, Mme Ponsard was a sister of the charming Mrs Sitwell who was loved by Stevenson and who eventually married Stevenson's friend Colvin. She loaded Meredith with thoughtful little attentions, as well as responding merrily to his teasing. His son Will had left school and was apprenticed to the profession of engineering, through the influence of Jim Gordon, Alice Brandreth's husband. Will was a sturdy, blond youth, good-humored rather than quick-witted. Showing some talent for drawing, he made a picture to accompany a poem of his father's in Comyns Carr's new *English Illustrated Magazine*.

The news of Meredith's elder son was not good. Arthur had lived for several years on Lake Garda, contributing occasional articles to magazines and working desultorily on a pretentious book about English style. But in the autumn of 1886 he had a serious collapse in health, and was confined to a hospital in London. Meredith visited him there as often as possible; but Arthur was more inclined to show affection toward his half-sister, Edith Nicolls, now Mrs Charles Clarke, who was living in London and always welcomed him into her home.

The publication of Meredith's novels in Boston resulted in a chorus of praise. To one American, William Morton Fullerton, who wrote a letter of appreciation, Meredith replied gratefully, "Americans appear to have received my work very generously. Since their most noble closing of the Civil War, I have looked on them as the hope of our civilization . . . They have the spirit to excel in classics and belles lettres. Therefore I am justly flattered by their praise, if I win it; their censure, if they deal it to me, I meditate on." Even in this mellow mood, however, he could not exclude a touch of bitterness:

*I am, I trust, to the full as modest a person as I am bound to be. In origin I am what is called here a nobody, and my pretensions to that rank have always received due encouragement by which, added to a turn of my mind, I am inclined to Democracy, even in Letters, and tend to think of the claims of others when I find myself exalted. This is the advantage I have gained from sharp schooling. Good work is the main object. Mine I know to be faulty. I can only say generally that I have done my best to make it worthy. On the other hand, simple appreciation, without comparisons of me with contemporaries, is welcome to my heart.*

*The New Princeton Review* published an article by his friend Flora Shaw, who not only praised his writings but ecstatically described the delights of walking and talking with him on Box Hill. Soon Americans were knocking at his door. Gratification was but thinly veiled by satire when he wrote to Hilda de Longueuil in the summer of 1887:

*Latterly I have really been kept in employment by Americans: was interviewed by an American lady the other day: "her one object in England was to meet me &c., and now that it was gratified she &c." But she was at least able to quote from the books, and I was drenched from my dead fountains. Articles in American reviews are sent, followed by the writers' request that I will kindly inform them whether they are in accord with my views of my work, and I have to write, and further work is retarded by the exercise of courtesy. It is curious to think that a writer despised in England should have struck the American mind; and of course the said writer inclines to think that it is because there is a mind.*

These remarks were occasioned by an article in *The Harvard Monthly* by young George Pierce Baker, who prophesied with twenty-year-old assurance that Meredith would be the cause of a permanent change in public taste. Meredith's reply gave a notable manifesto of his literary aims:

*Close knowledge of our fellows, discernment of the laws of existence, these lead to great civilization. I have supposed that the novel, exposing and illustrating the natural history of man, may help us to such sustaining roadside gifts. But I have never started on a novel to pursue the theory it developed. The dominant idea in my mind took up the characters and the story midway.*

*. . . My method has been to prepare my readers for a crucial exhibition of the personae, and then to give the scene in the fullest of their blood and brain under stress of a fiery situation.*

*Concerning style, thought is tough, and dealing with thought produces toughness. Or when strong emotion is in tide against the active mind, there is perforce confusion. Have you found that scenes of simple emotion or plain narrative were hard to view? . . .*

*In the Comedies, and here and there where a concentrated presentment is in design, you will find a "pitch" considerably above our common human; and purposely, for only in such a manner could so much be shown. Those high notes and condensings are abandoned when the strong human call is heard.*

It was not only in the United States that Meredith's fame was spreading. The English battalion of admirers was gaining recruits. Mrs Crawford, the Paris correspondent of *The Daily News*, was introduced to him by her friend Admiral Maxse, and received the usual invitation to stay at Flint Cottage. She saw the aspect of her host which had uttered itself in his poem "Melampus":

*After an early lunch Meredith took me over his little domain, and then for a long walk in the neighbouring woodlands. He led the party, holding in one hand a long pole, with the help of which he could bound over wide watercourses. He called attention to particular trees, to junipers on the hill, to the cedars at Mickleham, and along the hedgehog-haunted Mole. [He talked] about hedgehogs, badgers, ants, humblebees, moles, magpies, and other denizens of the woodland . . . I could not see in him anything of the conscious lion. A good child could not have been more frankly natural, transparent, and engaging.*

CHAPTER XIII *Grief and Fame* 273

Another new admirer was William Sharp, who was editing an anthology of English sonnets and asked permission to use some of Meredith's. Sharp thought highly of *Modern Love* but doubted whether its component parts could properly be admitted as sonnets. After some correspondence, he compromised by printing "Lucifer in Starlight" in the body of his collection, and five of the *Modern Love* sequence in the appendix with high praise. Thus auspiciously begun, the friendship was improved when Meredith met Sharp and found him to be a tall and romantically handsome young poet who was proud of the Celtic strain in his ancestry.

Other young poets of Sharp's generation were also recognizing Meredith's poetic power. William Butler Yeats was reading many of his poems at this time, and found that "they are certainly very beautiful, and have far more serenity and suavity than I had expected . . . 'Love in the Valley' . . . is full of a curious, intricate richness." Stevenson, in a letter to Yeats several years later, described the "spell" that was cast on him by "Love in the Valley" when he first read it in Meredith's 1883 book: "The stanzas beginning 'When her mother tends her' haunted me and made me drunk like wine, and I remember waking with them all the echoes of the hills about Hyères."

The most dazzling meteor in the literary sky just then was Oscar Wilde, who treated Meredith to a complimentary garland of epigrams in his brilliant essay on "The Decay of Lying," published in January, 1888:

Ah! Meredith! Who can define him? His style is chaos illumined by flashes of lightning. As a writer he has mastered everything except language: as a novelist he can do everything except tell a story: as an artist he is everything except articulate. Somebody in Shakespeare—Touchstone, I think—talks about a man who is always breaking his shins over his own wit, and it seems to me that this might serve as the basis for a criticism of Meredith's method. But whatever he is, he is not a realist. Or rather I would say that he is a child of realism who is not on speaking terms with his father. By deliberate choice he has made himself a romanticist. He has refused to bow the knee to Baal, and after all, even if the man's fine spirit did not revolt against the noisy assertions of realism, his style would be quite sufficient of itself to keep life at a respectful distance. By its means he has planted round his garden a hedge full of thorns, and red with wonderful roses.

Wilde's essay, like Stevenson's "Gossip on Romance" five years before, was a militant attack on the current vogue of naturalism in fiction, and it is significant that both men singled Meredith out as one of the paladins of their cause.

In the bitter uproar over the Irish question, Meredith's political interest remained acute. He made his views on the subject public in October, 1886, in an article in *The Fortnightly*. In April, 1887, he was a guest at the Eighty Club, a select political group, and was introduced to Gladstone, "who favoured me with the pleased grimace of the amiable public man in the greeting of an unknown," and who impressed him as being "very much of an actor." He met one of the Irish firebrands, Barry O'Brien, at a dinner party in his neighborhood, preceding a lecture by O'Brien on Home Rule. Haldane and John Dillon came down several times for long political discussions and Meredith was deeply impressed with Dillon's sincerity and strength—"this man has a head and eyes for poets to study."

During the winter Meredith had put together a number of his uncollected poems to form a volume entitled *Ballads and Poems of Tragic Life*, which was published by Macmillan & Company in May. He told a correspondent that "there will be another to follow, of a more spiritual flavour." He talked also of other projects:

> Perhaps, if I am not driven to the novel, I shall be at a Poem treating of all the Explosives in the modern mind and manufactories: *The Anarchiad*. What do you say?—The hero, Karl Onyx, has as many adventures as Odysseus. I am at times moved strongly by the theme. On the other hand I have a Knight of Perfectibility in prose, who is very seductive to my pen. Neither would fill the purse, and so I look at them as a lean lover looks at damsels that sit gazing over his uncrowned pate upon the wreathed and portly. The novel is my brawny scullery Jill.

Neither of the seductive schemes was ever undertaken, and even the novel was suspended; in April he reported that "latterly I have been forced to discontinue prose, owing to evil digestion and nerves. Verse does not tax me so heavily. Even letters have to be postponed."

The new book of poems was not widely or warmly reviewed; in thanking Foote for a favorable notice in his magazine *Progress*, Meredith said that "the verses . . . seem to have violently offended very many." *The Spectator* remarked that "the greater part of his verse is inarticulate. It is in no sense meaningless; it is simply unable to say what it desires . . . Yet what pleasure do they miss who are repelled, who never learn to know the noble chords of music he sometimes strikes!" Henley reviewed the book in both *The Saturday Review* and

*The Athenaeum*, but without the enthusiasm he had lavished on the novels. While giving Meredith credit for "intellectual passion," he said that "there is genius, but there is not felicity. We clap for Harlequin and we kneel to Apollo. Mr Meredith doubles the part, and is irresistible in both . . . His aim in art (it would appear) is . . . to vanquish by congestion, clottedness, an anxious and determined 'dandyism' of style."

This review of Henley's gave Meredith peculiar annoyance. He sent it to Miss de Longueuil with querulous complaints about "the kind of stuff I call down on myself by publishing":

*It is because I do not pass among reviewers that they treat one who is little a favourite with the public, and who courts no favour, with this form of politeness. I am termed a harlequin, a performer of antics. I choose, when I write, the expression seeming to my imagination just, and as it is not conventional they denounce it . . . So they pursue their course, treating each new book of mine to blows, and me to a reluctantly lessening contempt confirmed in dislike, while gradually the submerged volume comes back to the surface, is demanded, and spoken of respectfully . . . Believe me, it is only the bad manners which I complain of. I know my faults. I know too that all writers have some. The unfairness consists in reviewing favourites on the line of their good things, and the unfavoured in examples of their weak or unappreciated.*

The remark about "a harlequin and a performer of antics" rankled, and he quoted it to G. P. Baker, remarking, "I am accustomed to that kind of writing, as our hustings orator is to the dead cat and the brickbat flung in his face—at which he smiles politely; and I too; but after many years of it my mind looks elsewhere." His suspicion of a critical conspiracy against his books threatened to become obsessive.

# CHAPTER

# XIV

# *Pilgrims to the Shrine*

MEREDITH had been urged by Janet Ross to join her in Florence in May, 1887, and go with her to Tarentum for the summer; but though tempted he declined, as likewise an invitation to the Scottish Highlands. For the month of August he rented a house at St Ives, Cornwall, close to the summer home of the Stephens, whose children were his favorites as friends for his daughter. Here he enjoyed long days in the open air, bathing and walking with Riette and a young woman companion, niece of her governess. His "impeded peptics" prevented his settling down to steady writing, though he mentioned that "verse comes in a spout by fits." After his return home he was distracted with domestic worries over an incompetent cook and a sickly housemaid, and with seeking a new governess to replace the kindly but overmercurial Mme Ponsard. Even letter-writing became a nerve-racking task, and before the close of the year his correspondence with Hilda de Longueuil came to an end.

In January, 1888, when his daughter was away in London having her first glimpses of Society, he was still incapacitated, and informed Maxse dolefully that "for this 'dilation' there seems to be no remedy—unless it be, to avoid all liquids, and the pen. After a turn of writing I stir a roarful mob within, so that there is a positive diversion in a cough, and a sneeze bears promise of a new chapter. Living so much alone as I do, I am at the mercy of the haunting demonry."

News of his continued illness was conveyed by Henry James to Stevenson, who was seeking health in the Adirondacks, and Stevenson replied, "I wish I could go and see him; as it is I will try to write; and yet (do you understand me?) there is something in that potent, *genialisch* affectation that puts one on the strain even to address him in a letter. He is not an easy man to be yourself with; there is so much of him, and the veracity and the high athletic intellectual humbug are so inter-mixed."

Stevenson's admiration for his books was as keen as ever; a few months later, passing through San Francisco on his way to the South Seas, he astonished a newspaper interviewer by asserting:

*I think George Meredith out and away the greatest force in English letters . . . It is enough to disgust a man with the whole trade of letters that such a book as Rhoda Fleming should have fallen flat; it is the strongest thing in English letters since Shakespeare died, and if Shakespeare could have read it he would have jumped and cried, "Here's a fellow!" No other living writer of English fiction can be compared to Meredith . . . I serve under Meredith's banner always.*

One of Meredith's strongest friendships was ended in February, 1888, by the death of Cotter Morison. After the funeral Meredith took Edward Clodd to lunch at the Garrick Club, where "he talked of the mockery of the Burial Service which had been read in full over the remains of a man who lived and died an unbeliever, and whose last book was a trenchant attack on Christianity. And he said that if we did not give directions to the contrary, words, all unmeaning to those who die outside the Christian pale, will be spoken at our graveside."

In addition to his literary friends Meredith enjoyed a circle of con-genial neighbors in Surrey, to whose houses he often went to dinner. There was Colonel Lewin, a retired army officer and amateur author, whose house was on Leith Hill. There was John C. Deverell, a lawyer who shared Meredith's interest in nature and in sport. There was Sir Trevor Lawrence, Member of Parliament for the constituency. Sir Trevor's two spinster sisters, Misses Mary and Louisa Lawrence, had a London flat in Whitehall Place where they loved to entertain Mere-dith whenever he came to town. Before Mrs Meredith's death, their unconcealed adulation of her husband had aroused her exasperated amusement. Newer friends were Mr and Mrs Walter Palmer, who soon gained his affection. Mr Palmer was a wealthy biscuit-manufacturer of Reading, and his beautiful young wife loved to assemble literary and artistic celebrities both at their country mansion and at their town house. Another and unrelated Mrs Palmer, wife of General William Jackson Palmer of Colorado Springs, an American railway builder, invited him to house parties at a lovely thirteenth-century manor that she was renting near Sevenoaks, where his fellow-guests sometimes included Henry James, the American painters John S. Sargent and Edwin A. Abbey, and Fred Jameson, the architect and translator of the Wagner librettos.

Meredith's fabulous narratives in after-dinner conversation were becoming famous. Some of his auditors recognized them as pure improvisation, while others apparently assumed that they had some basis of fact. Henry Murray, a minor novelist and journalist, dining at Flint Cottage after the customary afternoon of rambling and conversation, tells how

one of the guests would drink nothing but mineral water, and Mr Meredith warned him against that habit with an intense, and even tragic, solemnity, illustrating its dangers by an horrific story about a fellow-collegian at Düsseldorf—"when I was studying medicine there"—who had fallen a victim to an unbridled thirst for that class of beverage. The unfortunate youth had died suddenly and in inexpressible agony, leaving behind him a solemn request that the autopsy should be performed by his friend, George Meredith. "When I made the first incision," said the narrator, suiting the action to the word with a horrible pantomimic gusto on the joint of mutton he was carving, "the glitter of the stalactites in the poor fellow's gastric cavity positively blinded me—I had to wear blue glasses for months after."

Richard Le Gallienne, on a similar occasion a couple of years later, listened to one of his impromptu rhapsodies occasioned by the fact that the wine bottle was empty. "Waving toward the bottle with a magnificent gesture," he addressed the parlor maid:

"Mary, you behold here a body from which the soul is departed. A body without a soul! Mark it there empty and useless, of no value to gods or men. Once full of genial fire, golden warmth for heart and brain, alive with inspiring ichor, the Hymettian fount of noble talk and soaring thought, the elixir vitae of wit, making of man's dull brain a thing of magic and dreams, lifting our dull mortality into the highest heaven of invention! But behold it now, a hollow echoing shell, a forlorn cadaver, its divine life all poured out of it, no laughter in it, no wisdom, no human kindness in it, any more for ever. What shall be done with it, Mary? A body from which the soul is departed! What do we do with such? What is there to be done, but to hurry it out of sight of gods and men—mournful reminder of feasts that are at an end, and dimming candles . . ." And so for some minutes he went on, piling fancy on fancy, till, with a final gesture of dismissal, he concluded with "Mary! remove this bottle!"

His acquaintances knew better than to interrupt one of his mono-logues, and transgressors learned a harsh lesson. His young Franco-Russian admirer, André Raffalovich, was now established in a handsome flat in Albert Hall Mansions; at a luncheon there, one of Meredith's auditors was a fledgling humorist, T. Anstey Guthrie, who reports:

*He had begun to speak when one of the party, a girl, broke in with some re-mark. On which Meredith observed: "I had just launched a conversational barque for which I had ventured to anticipate a favourable voyage, and it had scarcely left port before foundering untimely—sunk by this young lady's comment. Precisely why she should have chosen to submerge it I can but conjecture. It may be that the sails or the rigging did not meet with her ap-proval. Or possibly the Captain had—ah—a red nose. Or perhaps—" and here he invented a number of similar explanations before concluding with— "But, whatever her reasons, my unfortunate vessel is—ah—irrecoverably lost." It was quite good-humouredly said, but it was a rebuke notwithstand-ing, and was intended to be one.*

His adoption into Liberal party councils was progressing. In May, 1888, he attended a dinner of the Eighty Club in honor of Charles Stuart Parnell, and sat between Morley and Haldane, who was on the Irish leader's left. A few weeks later he sat between Morley and Arthur Balfour at a dinner given by Haldane and Herbert Henry Asquith at the Blue Posts. Asquith, one of the brightest young lights of Liberal-ism, says that Meredith "was a regular guest for years at our annual symposium at the Blue Posts and more than held his own in the most exacting company." From time to time Asquith went down on Sun-days with Haldane to visit Meredith, and he expresses the usual opinion that "as a charming companion and arresting talker I put him among the first I had known . . . Nothing could be more exhilarating than to watch him, with his splendid head and his eyes aflame, stamping up and down the room, while he extemporized at the top of his resonant voice a sonnet in perfect form on the governess's walking costume, or a dozen lines, in the blankest of Wordsworthian verse, in elucidation of Haldane's philosophy."

No longer able to write steadily for many hours a day, he devoted more of his solitary time to reading. He became so keenly interested in studying Greek that until the very end of his life a visitor, if ushered into his room unexpectedly, was likely to see a Greek grammar in his hand. His greatest devotion, however, was to French literature. Visitors to the chalet were struck by the quantity of yellow-paper-backed French books on his desk and shelves. The history of war was another favorite subject, and his conversation often turned to episodes in the lives of great commanders. This interest was increased through his editing of a series of "Military Biographies" as part of his duties with Chapman & Hall. His opinions on English politics came to be dominated by concern over the country's lack of adequate defense and need of a large permanent army.

Clear evidence of his widening fame was the attention paid him by newspaper columnists, such as Clement K. Shorter, literary editor of *The Star*, a new Radical daily. Shorter was a brash young man, confident in knowing all the literary gossip, and he saw the advantage of enlisting with the Meredithians. "My most fanatical hero-worship," he says, "was devoted to George Meredith. I read his novels with the wildest enthusiasm, and his poetry with little less delight. My rhapsodies over Meredith's work were often printed in my weekly column in *The Star*."

The growth of his reputation he regarded with a mixture of incredulity and embarrassment. When his first royalty cheque arrived from Boston he called it "a startler": "I had heard of large sales over there, and a man of experience wrote, through the publishers, to tell me that it is nothing to what it will be. But I confess the touch of American money has impressed me with concrete ideas of fame." In reply to a complimentary letter, he protested: "It must be a predisposition of yours in my favour, that ranks me among the celebrities; for I am not one; and let me add, I entertain a dread of the honours befalling them. They, however, have the consciousness of worth which enables men to support their load. In my case, there would not be such sustainment." When Roberts Brothers commissioned Mrs Mary Rebecca Foster Gilman, of Concord, to compile a book of extracts from his prose and verse under the title *The Pilgrim's Scrip: or, Wit and Wisdom of George Meredith*, he told her, "I speak honestly in saying I could wish you were more worthily engaged. Over here I have not encouraged the collecting of extracts from my books."

Trying to compel himself to resume writing, he said in a letter to an admirer, "I must soon be doing, or the trick will quit me. Without placing myself high—or anywhere,—I am, I moan to think, disdainful of an English public, and am beset by the devils of satire when I look on it. That is not a good state for composition, although I have pressing matter, many themes to work out before I take the flight."

His son Will was now employed by an engineering firm in South Wales, and was eager to have the family with him for the summer. Riette welcomed the prospect of good sea-bathing; her father, merely stipulating for high land and bracing air, relinquished some visions of the Highlands or the Continent, with the wry comment that "now I am a father—a secondary being." It seems to have been his first visit to the country from which he was proud to have derived his blood. He admired the scenery and the historic ruins and he learned a few phrases of Welsh; but the weather and the uncomfortable accommodations caused him to call it "a term of extreme probation." Unable to find a suitable house to rent, they had to put up at hotels, "and it was English hotel cookery. Rain usually at night, walks not possible except in penitence. No places of amusement. I had in desperation to go to bed at half-past nine, and scientifically dawdle, do massage, pugilism, to reach ten o'clock before I jumped in. Not a chair gave repose for reading or writing."

Those who encountered him were amazed at his energy and his talk. One evening at dinner, when his daughter and her friend were to go to a ball, they discussed the possibility of having Will supply their costumes with electric lights; and Meredith improvised a cautionary tale of a short-circuit that would instantaneously reduce all the dancers to a little heap of ashes on the floor. The hotel guests at other tables, instead of leaving the room at the end of the meal, sat eavesdropping on the conversation till half past ten. Another night, when the party strolled out to the deserted beach at midnight, Meredith launched into a poetic rhapsody upon the setting moon and the phosphorescent water, which inspired one lady ("who had spent years in Italy") to a wild impromptu dance on the sand.

After seventeen days at Tenby they went on to Llanelly, where Will was employed, and at a steel mill there Meredith was fascinated by the fantastic lurid flashes from the furnaces. The tour then took them to Llandilo, to Llandrindod, to Brecon, and finally to Ferndale for another glimpse of modern industrialism—this time a colliery. The party went down one pit, a quarter of a mile deep; and while the others walked all the way to the coal face, Meredith remained behind to squat down for an hour's chat with a grimy old miner. After the long, tiring day at Ferndale, they did not reach Merthyr till late at night. A local candidate for Parliament was addressing a crowd in front of the hotel, and Meredith's companions had trouble in preventing him from stopping to heckle the speaker.

Though his closest friends were aware that he was suffering the gradual inroads of paralysis, a stranger could not yet notice any trace of decline in his physical vigor. During the autumn he was visited at Box Hill by his American disciple William Morton Fullerton, who sent a full report to *The Boston Advertiser*:

*Mr Meredith met me with his nervous little dachshund at the station . . . A bright eye, a straight nose, a compact, lithe, broad-shouldered figure, a person with fine breeziness in all his movements, and a strong step upon the earth without a touch of uncertainty in it—that was Mr Meredith as I first saw him . . .*

*[I made] some wholly obvious reference to the changing leaves, and the sombreness of their color in comparison with that of our American foliage; and I finished with a platitude about the English hues being more pleasing, as they were less obtrusive and suggestive of the dying year . . .*

*Mr Meredith had no place for sentimentality of that sort. What was there in the thought of the passing years that should be sad? It was life, more life and fuller, for which men should be ever seeking, to be sure. But life was not to be had by whining into a past that had turned tail and fled. Rather, men must look up bravely, planted on the honest present, to the problems of the pressing future, never content to live in a fool's paradise, but always courting activity, and making use of moments as they came, so bravely, so well, that such moments would be quite transformed into the energy of character, not left behind to haunt you like sloughed chrysalises of vanished butterfly hopes and impulses. How eloquently did he crush my poor thought . . .*

*We got upon the subject of Mr James and Mr Stevenson. For Mr James, both as man and writer, Mr Meredith has a very warm regard; but Mr Stevenson, who was undoubtedly a sort of protégé of Meredith, he thinks a very great artist. "I knew Stevenson," he said, "long before he was known to you all. I saw what was in him and knew that he would do good work."*

At the very end of 1888 Meredith's next volume of poetry, *A Reading of Earth*, was published by Macmillan & Company. It contained some of the finest of the poems in which he set forth his matured philosophy of Nature, the confidence and joy that man can derive from obeying Earth's dictates and abandoning selfish illusions. The poems included "The Thrush in February," "Earth and a Wedded Woman," "Meditation under Stars," "A Faith on Trial," and the magnificent

"Hymn to Colour," which used some of his most difficult symbolism to formulate the core of his metaphysic. Unable to endure the thought of insensitive critical strictures upon these most intimate utterances, he forbade the issue of any review copies. The only notices, therefore, were two or three written voluntarily by admirers. One was in *The Scots Observer*, probably by Barrie, one in *The Scottish Art Review*, by Sharp, and one in *The National Reformer*, by Foote.

Arthur Meredith's health had now reached a state of collapse, and a voyage to Australia was decided upon. When Meredith saw him in February, 1889, he was shocked by the young man's obvious feebleness. He wanted to contribute toward the cost of the Australian journey; but knowing how obstinately his son had rejected every offer of financial aid in the past, he did not propose it directly, but begged Edith Clarke to use her influence in persuading Arthur to accept the gift. "Tell him it will be the one pleasure left to me when I think of his going . . . Tell him that I now receive money from America—and there is promise of increase. And I live so simply that without additions to income I could well afford myself this one pleasure." Arthur, however, denied himself the luxury of a first-class cabin, and when he sent a letter home en route he described uncomfortable conditions on the boat—especially that his cabin-mate was an alcholic, whereat his father was horrified, having always an inordinate disgust toward drunkenness. In June he was relieved to receive news that Arthur had reached Sydney in improved health.

Meredith's determination to continue with his writing, in defiance of illness and discouragement, was fanatical. "My work," he wrote to his old friend Mrs Jessopp, "holds me to it with rigour; and I have much to say; and my time on the surface of our sphere is short. I can rarely get away for shortest excursions." And to Janet Ross, declining another invitation to visit her in Florence: "Why do I work? I am not obliged, and might survey mankind from the top of Fiesole. But the habit is on me. I have besides things to say which friends would forget."

There were several projects in various stages of completion. He was still confident about *The Amazing Marriage*, and read chapters of it to various visitors. At one time he had made a good start on a novel called *Celt and Saxon*, which was to illustrate his theories on the traits of the two races. He talked much about writing *The Journalist*, in which he intended to depict Greenwood, Morley, and W. T. Stead among its main characters; as a rumor of this reached the newspapers, columnists began to announce that it was scheduled for early publication. He told Henry Murray, however, that it was not to be published until after his death; and there is a story to the effect that he eventually made his friend Dr Plimmer burn it in his presence.

The novel on which he was actively engaged was one provisionally named *A Conqueror in Our Times*. He told the whole plot of it to Alice Gordon one day during a walk on Box Hill, when he had scarcely begun to write it; and she felt sure that it would prove to be one of the world's greatest novels. "Hard at work with my *Conqueror*, who has me for the first of his victims," he told Sharp in November, 1889. Being convinced at last that the general public would never acknowledge his merit, he assured himself that he was writing solely to please himself. Refusing to contribute to some controversial symposium of Edmund Gosse's, he said, "I am hopeless of our public. The English have hardened me outside, and there has been a consequent process within. I do my work to the best of my ability, expecting the small result for the same, which I get." And in his annual New Year letter to Greenwood, he remarked, "As to me, there seems a chance in America, where perhaps I may come to my end—not among our good English, to whom I am odious and nauseous (I quote them)." It was the final irony of his career that his name had eventually become known only by being identified with obscurity and willful distortion of syntax. At least, he could shield himself against further disappointment by persuading himself that his purpose was (as he said later) "to serve these critics a strong dose of my most indigestible production."

In this mood he wrote a baffling poem, "Jump-to-Glory Jane," which appeared in *The Universal Review* in October, 1889. He was interested in the Salvation Army and other current revivalist movements, and ostensibly the poem was a grotesque account of the death of a woman enthusiast, much in the vein of his early "Roadside" pieces. But there were undertones of symbolism; and in a letter to Harry Quilter, editor of the magazine, mentioning the example of Mrs Girling, founder of the Shakers, Meredith insisted that the poem was "a satire, but one of the pictures of our England as well."

To his annoyance, Quilter insisted on republishing the poem as a separate volume, handsomely illustrated. Meredith could only insist that the illustrator "should be warned against giving burlesque outlines." Two popular artists, Lindley Sambourne and Bernard Partridge, declined the task, which then fell to Laurence Housman. Quilter's preface told how

when this poem first appeared . . . demands for explanation flowed in upon me by every post; clergymen remonstrated . . . The very artist I wished *to illustrate the poem . . . confessed that he could not do justice to the verses, and would rather not undertake them. Somehow this got abroad, and certain journalists made themselves merry over the artist's incapacity to understand the text submitted to him . . . "Forced, feeble, and vulgar" was this "tedious doggerel" according to one authority; "silly and incomprehensible," growled a second; "scarcely likely to add to the author's reputation," sighed a third; and so on throughout the list . . . My very publisher asked me privately what it meant.*

Meredith had gained the degree of notoriety that made him "newsworthy" in journalistic eyes; but with it a stigma that proved more exasperating than neglect had ever been.

The devotion of his friends was his compensation. He delighted in James Barrie's rapid climb to success and was active in ensuring his election to the Garrick Club. William Sharp and his wife were now among the privileged few invited to spend week-ends at Flint Cottage. On their first visit, Meredith read aloud to them in the evening from the novel in hand; "the reader's enjoyment," says Mrs Sharp, "seemed as great as that of his audience." On the Sunday afternoon he took them deep into the Deerleap Woods near Wotton—"my Woods of Westermain," he explained—to enable Mrs Sharp to hear a nightingale for the first time.

Clement Shorter, after a year or two of worshiping at a distance, was introduced at Box Hill and soon established a footing. On his becoming editor of *The Illustrated London News*, his column in *The Star* had been taken over by Richard Le Gallienne, another fanatical Meredithian. A young poet with flowing locks, Le Gallienne had written a book about Meredith while still a clerk in Liverpool, and brought it with him when he came to London to enter journalism. He enlisted the interest of John Lane, who had started a publishing house that specialized in the new "aesthetic" works; and Lane went to a good deal of trouble to compile an exhaustive bibliography for the book. "I suppose there is nothing to be done to dissuade you," Meredith wrote to him. "Do not think me indifferent to kind attentions. But . . . my writings are very verjuice to the critics." In response to Lane's persistent inquiries he even supplied a few details about his early publications.

Le Gallienne describes his first visit to Flint Cottage:

*Me he received with a quite fatherly sympathy and soon put me at my ease, though, as his talk was exactly like his books, elaborately fanciful yet knotted*

*with thought, one had to snatch at what one could, magnetized by the rush
and verve of his resonant voice, and dominated by his lordly manner. It was
a manner, it seemed to me, slightly theatrical, almost affectedly bravura . . .*

*Seated at the table were Mr Meredith's beautiful young daughter, and
his son, really a very modest and wholesome young Englishman, whom he
had a rather cruel way of teasing and addressing as the "Sagamore." With a
kingly wave of his hand towards him he would say: "Behold the Sagamore!
Mark that lofty brow! Stand in awe with me before the wisdom that sits
there enthroned . . ." and so he would proceed mercilessly to improvise on
the sublime serenity of Wise Youth, seated there so confidently at the top of
the world, till the poor tortured Sagamore would blush to the roots of his hair.*

The devoutest idolators were two spinsters, aunt and niece, Kath-
erine Bradley and Edith Cooper, who wrote passionate lyric poems
and poetic dramas under the pseudonym of "Michael Field." Living
at Reigate, only a few miles away, they had sent Meredith copies of
several of their books, and had received courtly replies expressing high
praise. One day early in 1890, when they got into a train for London,
the compartment was occupied by a gentleman who politely pushed
the footwarmer along so that they could share it. By the time he retired
behind his newspaper the two poetic ladies were exchanging excited
glances, for both identified him from the published photograph of
Meredith: "the iron-grey hair and beard, the forward sweep of the
moustache, the large, beautifully-modelled eyelids, the unusual shape
of the ear's 'porch.' Only the eyes were new—for in the portrait they
are covered—quick, much the colour of nuts at Christmastide; yet,
with all their rapidity, a certain profound languor emerges, and slow
recluse smiles, that send their ripples no further than the orbs themselves."

Apparently he became aware of their interest, "for every now and
then the fulgent eyes swept us in survey," and after getting out at Cannon Street he "doubled back a minute's space to throw an uncertain
glance into our carriage." Meanwhile, Miss Cooper had purloined an
envelope that he had dropped, and found that it was his daughter's
shopping-list. On the return journey in the afternoon, he again got
into their compartment, and soon observed who his companions were:

*He laid the paper on his knees, and his hands on it, and turned full round
to watch and receive. I was obliged to read closely, for his eyes were full prepared for my least look in his direction. Sim [Miss Bradley], who could see
his hands, says they were folded, determinedly observant. Soon after, she*

came to sit by me, and we talked vividly each to each. Sometimes his lids covered his eyes as in the portrait; but if we took the moment for a study of his features, the brave lights were upon us, like a tiger's through the jungle. We actually went on to Reigate to give him a clue to what he, I am sure, more than guessed: it had a strong effect on him . . . Shortly, he is fascinating—O strange allure!—all that is Meredithian is in his wonderful glance and the compass of expression in his mustily hazel eyes; the rest of his face is full of studious wear and unobtrusive dignity.

A few days later Miss Bradley traveled with him again, and was still enchanted by his eyes, "dusk as bloom on purple grapes, yet generative of fire and at moments with the alert brilliancy of lighted wine at a festival. Why does heaven play with us like this? It is trouble merely to see this being and not to know him as a friend." Nowhere in Meredith's novels are the subtly comic interplay of egos and the fine shades of proper deportment better chronicled.

William Sharp met the two ladies at this time, and told them all about Meredith's habits: his getting up before sunrise, his preference for working on two novels at once, his reclusiveness—"coming to London not more than once in three months"—and his love of the southwest wind—"he will throw up an engagement in town when it blows, rather than miss it on his hills." Also, said Sharp, he was "endowed with the strongest magnetism." The ladies hopefully impressed upon Sharp how eager they were to meet their idol.

In the spring of 1890 Arthur Meredith came back from the Antipodes, obviously in weaker health than when he went away. His half-sister, Edith Clarke, took him into her home and nursed him devotedly.

Meredith's long-anticipated visit to Scotland was made in August. He stayed in Glasgow with Mr and Mrs George Stevenson, admirers who had kept him supplied with woodcock in season for several years; then he went on to Cloan, the Highland home of Richard Haldane and his mother and sister. "It was quite unnecessary to entertain him," says Miss Haldane, "for the wonderful sentences poured from his mouth and we had but to listen. The little burn that passed our house attracted him greatly, and he loved to walk by it in the early morning and to talk of the sound of the stream tumbling down among the stones as one of the sweetest in nature." He made great friends with the aged minister of the parish, and announced his intention of using him as a character in a novel. His departure was in typical style: "He marched up and down the platform of our little station at Auchterarder, while waiting for a much-delayed train, declaiming to the astonished station-master and porter sentence after sentence of Meredithian eloquence on everything on earth and above the earth, not one word of which did they comprehend." Afterwards he was delighted when Miss Haldane sent him a plaid and he was careful to wear it the next time she saw him; she comments upon "how gracefully he wound his plaid over his shoulders, and how it fell over his spare form in folds."

Shortly after his return home, his son Arthur died on September 3. It had to be recognized as a release from incurable illness, but it combined with other deaths to invoke thoughts of mortality. Meredith had attended the funeral of his friend Browning in Westminster Abbey on the last day of the previous year, and had pondered, "sweeter the green grass turf than Abbey pavements." Now he wrote to Morley, "With all the dues to life, I am ready for my day of darkness." And just a week after his son's death, he lost a beloved friend of thirty years, William Hardman. Their ways of life had diverged widely, as Meredith had confined himself more and more to the country while Hardman was winning a knighthood as editor of *The Morning Post*; but the affection between them had survived.

It was inevitable that Meredith's mind should dwell at times upon the closing of his life, for he could not ignore the insidious encroachment of locomotor ataxia. He had succeeded in concealing it for a decade from all but his closest friends, but the symptoms were becoming patent. His obstinate fight against it is described by James Sully, a stalwart of the "Sunday Tramps":

*He never seemed to tire of talking: on a visit I paid him in 1890 he kept the ball going with only a few short pauses for two or three hours, one half of the time sitting in the garden and the other climbing the hill . . . It was at this visit that I became aware of his weakness. As he moved awkwardly down the steep grassy slope of the hill, I instinctively stretched out my hand to help him. He gently but firmly put away the proffered aid. Later on, at the Cottage, I made another attempt to assist him as he lifted himself out of a low chair, and again the offer was declined. Then, on a still later occasion, when Leslie Stephen and I were lunching with him, he made a sign to me as Stephen was leaving the drawing-room, and invited me to lend him my arm. He had remembered, and was far from bearing me any ill will.*

The American singer David Bispham, when invited to meet him at dinner at the home of the Beneckes in Dorking, was astonished by his demeanor:

*After what seemed an interminable time Meredith came in, or rather stum-*
*bled in, after walking across the half mile of meadowland between the two*
*houses. He apologized for his tardiness, speaking very fast and very loud, and*
*holding himself steady by means of a chair, a table, the mantelpiece, or*
*whatever he chanced to be near. With all his reputation for abstemiousness*
*I feared the eminent author was under the influence of liquor.*

Concurrent with his lameness, his increasing deafness was making
him the more prone to monopolize conversation and disregard other
people's remarks. The perpetual strain of concealing his disabilities
produced the note of tension that many people observed in his social
animation during those years; and it was responsible also for a tendency
toward impatience and arrogance.

His daughter Mariette acted as hostess for his visitors at Flint
Cottage, and played the piano to him in the evenings, as her mother had
done. A duller task was the copying of all his manuscript as soon as it
was written, so that the duplicates could be kept in her dressing-case,
as a safeguard against loss by fire. Sir John Pollock describes her as an
"enchanting vision to the eyes, the perfect embodiment of every man's
imagination of the perfect Dresden China shepherdess"; and her father
treated her like a precious piece of porcelain. She complained to Miss
Haldane that even in the garden of the cottage she was expected to have
a chaperon. Of course, she had to endure his strenuous teasing; all
through a dinner party his jokes might be aimed at her, while she—like
her mother before her—listened with a cheerful smile, and occasionally
murmured, "Oh, Papa!" But along with her dainty beauty she had a will
of her own. A lady who had been a visitor at the house next door to
Flint Cottage told Michael Field that she overheard through the hedge
"a high resonant masculine voice say, 'My dear daughter, I have heard
you declare several times of late—"My dear father, unless you dress
better, I shall not be able to acknowledge you in society"—you seem
to think you are a queen and we are only here to do you service.' "

His prudishness was by no means confined to his daughter's conduct. When he went to French plays in London with the Gordons
he was horrified to see young girls in the audience laughing at the
*risqué* jokes. "How can their mothers let them stay and listen?" he
groaned. Even his own novels fell under his ban: when a schoolgirl, in
a letter asking for his autograph, told him she was enjoying *Diana of the*
*Crossways,* he replied severely that she was too young for it: "Bear in
mind that Nature abhors precociousness, and has the habit of punish-

ing it; so in the meantime give a good part of your leisure to healthy walks and games." This was Sir Austin Feverel's "System" with a vengeance.

In contrast with his old-fashioned firmness toward his own women-folk and his old-fashioned punctilio toward all other ladies, his opinions about the rights of the feminine sex were steadily growing more liberal. An important poem of this time, "The Sage Enamoured and the Honest Lady," proclaims his belief in total freedom of discussion and judgment for intelligent women in matters of sex. The poem depicts a grey-headed celebrity, not unlike Meredith himself, in love with a beautiful woman who has been willingly seduced in a passionate love affair of her earlier years. In an effort to cure his unseasonable ardor, she tells him her story, first trying to condone her behavior, until she realizes that his icy silence is a condemnation. She momentarily hates him as one of the intolerant male persecutors; then she recognizes her own self-deception and frankly admits having been an adulteress. In gratitude for her generosity and courage, the Sage subjects her to a long lecture on the right relationship of the sexes, counseling a due allowance for sensual passion, but also a rational concern for the welfare of future generations. As Tennyson had done fifty years before in *The Princess*, he forecasts a time when sexual conflict and inequality will be at an end, when men and women will mate in wise acceptance of Nature's law. The lady is thus restored to self-respect and human kinship, and the Sage's love for her becomes more spiritual through his respect for "Soul's chastity in honesty."

The poem can be considered tedious in its didactic wordiness; but it was intensely sincere, originating largely in Meredith's temporary captivation with Hilda de Longueuil. A new edition of "Modern Love" was about to be published, and he added "The Sage Enamoured" to it, as a sequel to that earlier heart-searching on the same subject.

Similar frankness and tolerance in treating a breach of conventional morality was displayed in his new novel, now entitled *One of Our Conquerors*. When he told Jessopp at the end of May that he was just finishing the novel, he added that he was "a bit strained, as I have condemned myself both to a broad and a close observation of the modern world in it, throwing beams both upon its rat-tides and its upper streams." It ran as a serial in *The Fortnightly* from October, 1890, until May, 1891, and was also printed in *The New York Sun* and *The Australasian*.

The title, of course, was ironical, being applied to a wealthy financier; but the treatment of the "conqueror," Victor Radnor, was surprisingly kindly. Though Radnor becomes revealed as essentially an egoist, who brings disaster upon everyone around him in spite of his genuine affection and lavish generosity toward them, the author displays no trace of the contempt that weakened his dissection of Sir Willoughby Patterne. But this restraint adds all the more emphasis to the theme of the novel, which is the same as that of "The Sage Enamoured": although Radnor's bigamous union with Nataly wins sympathy on every emotional ground, it is nevertheless a sin because of the resultant blight upon their daughter's happiness.

This novel marked a further step in the freedom with which Meredith felt he could discuss unconventional marriage relationships. Clara Middleton had merely tried to break an engagement; Diana Warwick, though separated from her husband and eager for a divorce, had not become another man's mistress; but Victor Radnor and Nataly Dreighton lived together for twenty years without a legal marriage. In order to avoid shocking his readers or alienating their sympathy, Meredith presented the situation circumspectly; he began by showing the couple's happiness and affection, and only gradually revealed that Victor had a legal wife living.

Victor's character was drawn with skill. He was a new social phenomenon—a self-made capitalist who was not a vulgarian but a man of culture, dignity, and charming manners. The reader slowly perceives that behind his impressive façade there is a perpetual strain, coming from two sources—the uncertainty of his financial speculations and the menace of his legal wife's precipitating an open scandal. His strenuous activity, his boundless hospitality, his over-genial friendships are all unconscious efforts to obliterate these anxieties from his mind.

The full facts about his wife, when finally supplied, give the first inkling of his essential selfishness. As a very young man he married a wealthy older woman, obviously with the sole motive of furthering his career. As in the case of Diana, it could be argued that he was too inexperienced to realize the gravity of the step. It is implied that Mrs Burman almost bullied him into it. Besides, Meredith gives him some of the self-dramatizing imagination and irresistible resilience of Richmond Roy, so that one is unable to condemn him as a scoundrel, for he could not be so likable unless he had hypnotized himself into a genuine belief in his own virtue and wisdom.

In contrast with Radnor's self-centered complacency, the author endowed the two women of the household with every virtue. Nataly is a paragon of patience and unselfishness. Their daughter, Nesta, is one of Meredith's most captivating girl characters—impulsive, candid, clever, with inherent strength that responds to a crisis. The legal wife, who is kept ominously out of the picture until almost the end, arouses the reader's interest by this very invisibility; and when she finally takes the limelight, though only for her death scene, she is a convincing and pathetic figure. The description of her drawing-room must have derived its details from Mrs Wood's sepulchrally handsome mansion at Eltham, and it is possible that something of Radnor's original relations with her was suggested to Meredith by his own connection with his aged employer, who had died a year or so before he began writing this book.

Most of the other characters were types that Meredith had already been using ever since his first novel: Colney Durance, the cynical, epigrammatic onlooker, a mouthpiece for the author's own bitterest comments; Mrs Marsett, the ostracized "fast" woman; Dartrey Fenellan, the man of fine character shackled to a degenerate wife. As in *Richard Feverel* and *Evan Harrington*, he employed Dickensian exaggeration in his main comic character, Skepsey. But it was characteristic of his oblique methods that he made this absurd little man a fanatic for the pet Meredithian dogmas of physical fitness and national defense. The author's permanent grudge against orthodox churchmen was shown in the caricatures of the two unctuous preachers of Tunbridge Wells. His new interest in revivalism caused the inclusion of Priscilla Graves. Such other contemporary fads as vegetarianism and total abstinence came in for their share of ridicule.

The plot was ably constructed to emphasize its central theme. Irony was strongly introduced when Nesta, in her turn, fell in love with a man who was unhappily married. Even the comic-relief character, Skepsey, was mismated and was longing for escape in order to marry a more congenial woman. The tragic climax was foreshadowed by the heart-attacks that Nataly suffered and heroically tried to conceal; and Victor's eventual insanity was also prepared for from the outset.

The backgrounds were consistently vivid, especially the views of metropolitan London in its strangeness and beauty. As in his other novels, the Surrey countryside and the Alps received lyrical description; and there were amusing glimpses of the smug narrowness of Tunbridge Wells. The Radnors' love of music led to the inclusion of pleasant amateur musical interludes, reflecting the happy hours that Meredith spent with various friends who shared this taste with him.

When Alice Gordon read the book she was disappointed to find scarcely a trace of the beauty and passion that had thrilled her when he told her the story in advance; they were "obscured by the whirl of words." The opening chapter, as usual in Meredith's later novels, was particularly baffling—a fifty-page stream of consciousness in Radnor's mind, dealing with dilemmas and events which the reader has no clue to understanding. In this connection Meredith told Lionel Johnson that he always wrote his first chapters last. Throughout the book long passages were devoted to allusive philosophizing about the major conflicts of modern society, not only in sex relations but in religion, finance, politics, and international affairs. Nor are the difficulties in reading the novel confined to the subtlety of its psychological analysis or the complexity of its problems. As well as resorting at intervals to the stream-of-consciousness device, Meredith carried his cryptic style to an extreme. He seemed incapable of using a straightforward word or phrase if an ingenious metaphor could be substituted. Reading becomes a continuous process of solving riddles.

While the basic plot-line was clear and powerful, there were irrelevant and sometimes freakish digressions. Radnor's ambulatory house party, when he took a group of friends on a tour of Northern France, served no function beyond illustrating his prodigality; one feels that it was introduced chiefly to display the author's familiarity with French scenes. Durance's serial story, *The Rival Tongues*, is both tedious and confusing when it is forcibly injected into the narrative at intervals. It was a close reproduction of the impromptu fantasies that Meredith made up about his friends—in fact, it was essentially his story about Alice Brandreth's trip to the philological congress in Russia. The most impertinent of all the digressions is the whole chapter about the misconduct of the Misses Duvidney's lapdog. It is undeniably comic, but on a schoolboy's level of humor, grotesquely enwrapped in Meredith's figurative phrases. Not only the dog but also its adoring owners are minor characters with no claim whatsoever to such detailed portrayal.

Nevertheless, with all due allowance for its oddities, *One of Our Conquerors* has merits that rank it among Meredith's greatest novels. Once the special technique of reading is acquired—no difficult task for anyone inured to some twentieth-century fiction—the characters are found to be warmly human and the plot takes a firm grip. As a social and psychological study it has good claim to be called the richest fulfillment of Meredith's peculiar powers. It is overcrowded because he tried to include too many facets of contemporary life; but no other novelist would have had the temerity to undertake so much, or the energy to cram so many original and stimulating ideas into his pages.

The obscurities and vagaries of the book provided a field day for the critics; but Meredith was fortified with his conviction that he had maliciously intended to torment them. The reviewer in *The Daily Chronicle* perceived this attitude:

Mr Meredith grows more and more trying. He seems to take a Satanic delight in wrapping simplicity in as many fantastic coverings as he can devise. Of course he doesn't mind your being cross; he enjoys it. You may take him or leave him; all's one to him.

*The Daily Telegraph* acknowledged that "at the cost of infinite patience we appreciate that here we have the last word of triumphantly analytic science, dividing with merciless scalpel the living tissues of our common humanity." Both *The Saturday Review* and *The Athenaeum* were infuriated. The former declared that "the whole book is a puzzle . . . The author's usual faults of incoherence, prolixity, straining after epigram, seeking after the uncommon, lack of firmness in character-drawing, and allusiveness are intensified . . . This surely is not the way to write." *The Athenaeum*, terming the story "slight, shapeless, and very unattractive," the narration "clumsily managed," and the style "affectedly grotesque," announced a judicial decision:

It is becoming a common experience to meet cultivated persons who gravely assure us that Mr Meredith is our greatest living novelist . . . To us this vogue is inexplicable . . . So far from being a great novelist, he does not seem to us to possess the qualifications which go to the making of a capable novelist of even the second rank, and, even if those qualifications were his, their effect would be ruined by a literary manner which even in these days of affectation and strain is of unique perversity.

Lionel Johnson was almost alone in defending it. His review in *The Academy* declared that "read three or four times, the book grows upon the reader, the apparent confusion disappears, the intricacies of style become intelligible, and the whole greatness of design is evident." Echoing Meredith's own claims, he justified the style by arguing that "in proportion as the subject is simple, or idyllic, or tragic, or humourous, or rapid, so does the style assume those qualities." Few readers, however, were likely to read it three or four times. Writing in *The Yellow Book* five years later, J. M. Robertson declared that "with the exception of Zola's *La Terre*—hard reading for a different reason— *One of Our Conquerors* was the hardest novel to read that I ever met with."

In spite of such complaints, the tide of Meredith's fame was flowing strongly. Le Gallienne's book added impetus to it. Within a few months another book about him was published, this one being by a young Irish writer named Hannah Lynch, a symptom of the increasing interest in Meredith on the part of women. Oscar Wilde reaffirmed his respect in his essay on "The Soul of Man Under Socialism":

*One incomparable novelist we have now in England, Mr George Meredith. There are better artists in France, but France has no one whose view of life is so large, so varied, so imaginatively true. There are tellers of stories in Russia who have a more vivid sense of what pain in fiction may be. But to him belongs philosophy in fiction. His people not merely live, they live in thought. One can see them from myriad points of view. They are suggestive. There is soul in them and around them. They are interpretative and symbolic. And he who made them, those wonderful quick-moving figures, made them for his own pleasure, and has never asked the public what they wanted, has never cared to know what they wanted, has never allowed the public to dictate to him or influence him in any way, but has gone on intensifying his own personality, and producing his own individual work.*

His most unexpected convert was Frank Harris, a bumptious egomaniac who seldom saw merit in anybody's work but his own. A friend of Wilde's, he was at this time editor of *The Fortnightly* in succession to Escott. Grant Allen advised him to send some of his short stories to Meredith, and the reply was so complimentary that Harris asked Frederic Chapman's permission to print a couple of the stories in *The Fortnightly*. The second one, "A Modern Idyll," incurred such accusations of moral laxity that the directors of the publishing house insisted that Harris resign the editorship. A few days later Chapman notified him that the resignation need not take effect, as Meredith had interviewed the directors and persuaded them to withdraw their command.

When Harris visited the office for further instructions, Meredith happened to be there, and Chapman brought the young editor in to meet him. "No one who did not see it," Harris says, "can imagine the extraordinary quickness and speed of the face: the most expressive face in the world, I think; a mirror to every momentary change of expression":

*He was more than kindly, cordial indeed, and irresistibly frank. He had heard from his friend Chapman what the silly directors had done, and had therefore come up to see them. "Couldn't allow them to be so long-eared, blind* to their own interest, as business men generally are. Admirable stories, as he had written to me; the public will want more of them."

All this came to me as a consecration—such understanding, such genial, sure appreciation; the hot blood flew to my cheeks, prickled behind my eyes. The unconsciousness of the man was superb, no suspicion of his own kindness or what it meant to the beginner, or perhaps those keen eyes of his did see even that . . .

All the while, Meredith was shouting, at least talking in a very loud voice, with fine accent and appreciation of the words, and while the volume of it roared and rung in my ears, the keen eyes flitted everywhere . . . For the first time in my life I allowed myself to be completely overwhelmed and talked down. When I went away, we had arranged to meet again.

Not for long, however, was Harris content to be the silent partner in conversation. Anstey Guthrie describes a dinner party at which "Meredith began to lead as usual, but was never permitted to finish. Frank Harris interrupted by disagreeing with him, and expounding his own views with vigour and eloquence. For a time Meredith seemed a little restive under what must have been, for him, an unprecedented experience, but gradually he became spell-bound by Harris's undoubted power, and ended by evidently admiring his antagonist." When Meredith's hostess teased him the next morning about his capitulation, he answered placidly, "But I was sober, my dear."

All these young adherents, whether they regarded Meredith as an avatar or as a museum exhibit, were a sorry substitute for the glorious friends of his prime. Among the few who survived, John Morley was too busy in the councils of the nation to spare time for private visits, and Leslie Stephen was getting so frail and deaf that he had to resign the leadership of the "Sunday Tramps." Admiral Maxse alone remained faithful; whenever he was at Dunley Hill he would walk over often to see Meredith, usually bringing his daughter Violet and any guest who might be staying with him. One of these was Margot Tennant, a brilliant specimen of the sophisticated young circle in London society. She told Meredith all about a plan of hers for founding a magazine, *Tomorrow*, and recited the list of celebrities who had promised to contribute. "At any rate," she declared, "I think it will have a *succès d'estime*." Meredith gave her one of his sharp glances. "A *succès de snob* would be more likely," he observed.

One of Maxse's ardent admirers was Alfred Austin, the prosperous and complacent poet; and Meredith never tired of ridiculing his tiny stature, his conceit, and his Tory fervor. "The Admiral's Ancient" was

Meredith's nickname for him; and when Austin confided that he "had a cult" for the beautiful young Miss Maxse, Meredith found a perfect target for his ridicule. For months he tirelessly composed burlesque odes that he attributed to Austin; and he embroidered a legendary wooing with such details as Austin's standing on a chair to kiss the tall lady. He was somewhat abashed when Austin requested him to accept the dedication of his book, *Fortunatus the Pessimist*. His response was the customary warning that the venom of the critics might be incurred by an author who thus associated himself with their chosen victim.

In December, 1891, the general public and even most of the literary profession learned for the first time that Meredith was the reader for Chapman & Hall. The occasion was a libel suit in which he was summoned to testify. An author whose books he had consistently recommended for publication was Colonel Alfred Burden Ellis, who was a stepcousin of his own, being a son of General Sir Samuel B. Ellis, whose first wife had been Meredith's Aunt Catherine. There had been no communication between the families for half a century, and if Meredith was aware of the connection it certainly did not influence his judgment. Ellis was a recognized authority on West African native lore, and since 1883 Chapman & Hall had published several of his works.

In advising the acceptance of a volume of fiction, *West African Stories*, Meredith insisted on the omission of one lurid tale about a murder and a loose woman, but he raised no objection to one that gave a detailed portrait of an unscrupulous Gold Coast trader named James Peacock. The libel action was brought by a retired trader named James Pinnock who could prove that Colonel Ellis was acquainted with him. Both parties engaged brilliant counsel: the plaintiff had Sir Charles Russell, later Lord Chief Justice, and the defendants had H. H. Asquith, later Prime Minister.

The author's deposition cited various sources for the events and names in his story, none of them connected with Peacock; but as he was away on foreign service the brunt of the cross-examination fell on Meredith, as spokesman for the publishers. "He had, I think," Asquith said later, "to stand the most severe ordeal that any witness could be exposed to—cross-examination by Sir Charles Russell, the greatest of advocates; and he came out well."

He testified that the story called "Mrs Fitzgibbon" had been excised at his request because it dealt with an adventuress and was not in good taste. Some parts of "James Peacock," he admitted, were in questionable taste also: the description of Peacock's mother was "the attempt of a serious man to be humourous—a sort of elephantine humour," and he objected to it personally, "but it went down with the public, and so he had to pass it." He had regarded the whole story as pure fiction, and had not previously known that any elements in it were derived from facts.

"Can you swear," demanded Russell, "that you have never heard the name of Pinnock?"

"Not since the days of my youth," was the imperturbable reply, "when I learnt his catechism."

Meredith's well-phrased answers aroused several bursts of laughter in the court, and the whole performance must have gratified his histrionic sense, even though his employers lost the case, Pinnock being awarded damages of £200. Meredith's participation drew inordinate attention to the trial. In the next issue of *Punch* it figured in two articles and a cartoon, and *The Times* hailed the verdict in a leading article that sounded like a gibe at Meredith's own methods in fiction: "We are grateful to Mr Pinnock for putting limits to the right claimed by certain novelists to mash into literary pulp their friends, acquaintances, and the world in general." The sting of this comment would have been all the sharper if any readers had known the ironical fact that the Ellis family had twice been outraged by Meredith's portrayal of Colonel Ellis's father as a character in his books.

# CHAPTER

# XV

# *Prosperity*

ANNOUNCEMENT of a revised edition of *The Tragic Comedians*, in September, 1891, touched off a lively dispute over Meredith's importance, in the correspondence column of *The Star*, including a letter from George Bernard Shaw, which Meredith termed "good criticism." In later years, Shaw asserted that he was never able to read any other novel by Meredith because "I disliked upper-ten ladies and gentlemen so much (they bore me)." The reprint of "Modern Love," with its sequel, "The Sage Enamoured," came out in the same month, no review copies being issued, though Meredith expressed his expectation that the new piece would "provoke our social Conservatives' thunder."

His Scottish friend George Stevenson served as an intermediary for the University of St Andrews in proposing that the honorary degree of LL.D. should be conferred on him. As he was seriously unwell he declined the honor on the ground that he probably could not be present at the ceremony. Stevenson wrote again to assure him that the degree could be conferred *in absentia,* and it was consequently accepted, with the customary protestations of unworthiness.

He was immobilized by illness throughout the spring, and had to submit to giving up his Spartan cot in the chalet and moving to the house, where he could be more easily tended. But he always rallied to the challenge of visitors. One day in March, Barrie brought down two young novelists who were leaders in the Stevenson-inspired school of romance—Arthur Conan Doyle and Arthur Quiller-Couch. Meredith managed to hobble to the gate to meet them with eloquent words of welcome. To Doyle's surprise, his chief topic of discourse was the memoirs of General Marbot, from which he retailed many anecdotes. Doyle could not make up his mind whether he liked Meredith or not.

Correspondence with Miss Bradley and Miss Cooper had continued, and they received further enthusiastic descriptions of him from Lionel Johnson, the tiny, fragile poet, who was one of his new devotees. When Meredith sent them a copy of the new *Modern Love* they brazenly inquired whether they might call on him. He replied that he did not want them to see him when he was not at his best: "I feel wintry, and with the knowledge of looking so, which pinches and contracts us, as when cocks are made conscious by their moulting." Before long they met his daughter at an art exhibition and decided that "she is frank, cold, spoiled, shallow. Her complexion is very fair, her eyes steel-blue, blonde hair in masses, deep lips with lovely curves . . . She is elegant, she bears herself haughtily—has no graciousness in the eyes." As she told them her father was feeling better, their hopes were revived; soon afterwards, standing in their garden, they held out clenched fists in the direction of Box Hill, while trying "to *will* with power that he be moved to ask us to lunch."

Sure enough, the invitation arrived the next day. But the reality of their visit fell short of the ineffable anticipation. When they rang the doorbell at Flint Cottage, according to Miss Cooper's record, "suddenly a grey figure jerks out of the door—I see a knot of vermilion under the throat, a grizzledness, brown skin beaten by life . . . From the indistinct vision I am instantaneously conscious of disappointment, that is a sorrowing pain. 'I must come forth to bid you welcome,' says a voice highly artificial, measured in pronunciation and rather rigid in timbre."

Mr and Mrs Le Gallienne were there for the week-end, and the occasion is described in Le Gallienne's reminiscences as well as in Miss Cooper's diary. He had already spent the morning in the chalet, listening to his host's latest poem, "The Empty Purse," and some chapters of *The Amazing Marriage*. "As he read sonorously and rapidly," says Le Gallienne, "with an eye alert for intelligent comprehension in his listener, it was a scrambling business to follow his drift." When they were walking down to the house the young man was emboldened to ask whether Meredith would some day let him have a piece of his manuscript, and the promise was genially given.

Miss Cooper found the young poet attractive, but eyed his wife with feminine ruthlessness. As Meredith did not eat lunch at the normal time, he vanished as soon as he had greeted the two ladies, and his daughter was left with the full burden of entertaining the guests. Miss

Cooper revised her impression of the girl, who proved to be merely "a little spoiled, and only distant through awe, which soon melts away."

Not until the meal was half over did the host join them in the dining-room. He asked Miss Cooper if she enjoyed old Hock, and she intrepidly said yes. "Then one of the oldest bottles in my cellar shall be brought for you." She felt that there was "a sense of fuss as host and housemaid disappear." On his return he delivered "a Dionysic homily on the rich power in wine of improvement."

Near the end of the meal Le Gallienne provided a painful diversion:

*Keeping Meredith's promise of a page of his manuscript in mind, I ventured to remind him of it, and with well-meant diffidence I said, "Of course, Mr Meredith, I don't expect anything important, I don't expect—I don't expect —the manuscript of* The Egoist *or* Richard Feverel"*—and then, in an evil moment, I added, "only a little poem!"*

*The ignominy of the moment is with me yet. The air seemed to grow still as with imminent thunder, and then, with merciless sarcasm, he let loose his lightnings upon me.*

*"Oh, I see," he said, turning to my fellow-guests. "Mark you that. He wants nothing important. Only a little poem! How truly, after all, he speaks. Everyone knows the unimportance of my poor poems—'poetical matter, not poems,' as some person of insight has acutely said. Yes! nothing important— only a little poem!"*

*So he went on, while I expostulated in vain, humbled to the dust. The two kindly ladies came staunchly to my rescue, but the damage was done. There was no mending the matter that day—and I never got my manuscript.*

After the Le Galliennes left, Miss Cooper had a chance to examine Meredith's appearance more exhaustively than by furtive glances in a train:

*[His eyes] are worn hazel—there is a little nervous difference in their focus— about them something of that piteous old-dog decrepitude one sees in portraits of Carlyle. The hair is in tint stone colour, what there is of it curls. The mouth is gaunt with suffering, the nose fierce and withered, the brow rather narrow, much lined, the laugh a brilliant contradiction to the features. —Tragic life written over them—a certain distinction in his look and manner, that of county society; solitude looming above every other record on the face —solitude that has embittered. With humour his voice becomes more pliant, even imitative, so that he gives a reed-like key to a woman's words—his movements have Celtic suggestiveness.*

At three o'clock he had to withdraw to eat his solitary lunch. "Food is nothing to me," he explained; "I shall be with you again in a few minutes." Then, punctilious as ever, he escorted them in a rain-drenched tour of the garden and chalet, talked over the teacups, orated on women's rights, expecting that the unconventional pair of she-poets would share his advanced doctrine; but he did not mention their plays, and he ignored the subtle repartees and oblique allusions that they strove to interject. When they were at the door to leave, Miss Cooper turned to say good-bye and he nervously blurted out, "How do you do?" As their cab trundled them away, they agreed that "we had been in contact with greatness that astonishes, irritates, pursues—that has nothing of breadth, peace, or geniality in it."

Another literary lady, a former neighbor, published her opinions of him at that time. The chubby little Mary Mackay had burgeoned into Marie Corelli, darling of the circulating libraries, and her insatiable egomania impelled her to bring out an anonymous book, *The Silver Domino*, shrewishly satirizing all the critics and authors of the day. Meredith, having once praised her piano-playing, came off comparatively easily: her sarcasm was aimed chiefly at the style of *One of Our Conquerors*, and she termed him "an Eccentricity—a bit of genius gone mad—an Intellectual Faculty broken loose from the moorings of Common Sense and therefore a hopelessly obstinate fixture in the 'groove' of literary delirium." She added a caricature of his behavior:

Whether he be haranguing to the verge of deafness some stray acquaintance at the Garrick Club; whether he be met, a greybeard solitary, stalking up the slopes of Box Hill; whether he be inveighing against the "porkers"—i.e., the Public—within the precincts of a certain small and extortionate but rigidly pious bookseller's shop in the town of Dorking; or whether he be visited in his own small literary chalet, which he built for himself in order to escape from "domesticity" and the ways of the "women" he is supposed to understand—in each and all of these positions he is distinctly amusing—and never more so than when he thinks he is impressive.

Persistent pain finally forced him in June to make an appointment with a London specialist, George Buckston Browne, who describes how he came into the consulting-room and "plumped himself down" in a chair. Because of his ataxic condition he "literally threw himself into chairs or onto couches with alarming precipitancy." "Mr Browne," he announced, "I am a writer." Being an admirer of his novels, the surgeon answered, "Mr Meredith, you need no introduction here," and opened the door of a bookcase which contained a complete set of his works.

An operation followed promptly, and a large gall-stone was removed from his bladder. By this time he and the surgeon were fast friends. "He gave me his entire confidence," says Browne, "and although extremely sensitive in every possible way, he proved an excellent patient. I never had to waste my energies in combating his whims and fancies." The surgeon was reluctant to accept a fee, but Meredith insisted upon paying it.

He made a good recovery, and his experiences under the anaesthetic provided him with a new fantasy for the entertainment of his friends. By the end of the summer he was able to resume his social life. In September, at a house party of the Walter Palmers, he met Oscar Wilde, and uttered his impression, with unwonted terseness, in two words—that Wilde was "good company." It was unlikely that two such stars of conversation should feel congenial, especially in a group that included other celebrities—Johnston Forbes-Robertson, H. B. Irving, David Bispham, and the artist Louise Jopling.

A new volume of Meredith's poems came out in the autumn, grimly named *The Empty Purse*. One poem in it, "A Night of Frost in May," was in the loveliest mood of his nature verse, describing a favorite theme, the song of the nightingale in a wood; but all the others displayed his gnarled didacticism. The faults of his poetry and of his prose at this epoch were in paradoxical opposition. *One of Our Conquerors* was difficult reading because its method was essentially poetic—an elusive accumulation of metaphors and emotional symbols; *The Empty Purse* was equally difficult because its method was prosaic—the discussion of general principles in abstract terms and with the logical pattern of dialectic. Fifteen years later he admitted that the title poem was "not poetry. But I had to convey certain ideas that could not find place in the novels."

The poems in the volume undeniably presented some of his most vital ideas. The "Ode to the Comic Spirit" was a final development of the theory that he had announced in the lecture on comedy and in the first chapter of *The Egoist*. The "Ode to Youth in Memory" expounded his philosophy of acceptance in relation to the new ordeal of being old and crippled, and his insistence upon loving and trusting the young, whose companionship can bring inner serenity. The title poem turned to public and social problems, and admonished "Our Later Prodigal Son" to disregard the frenzy of the demagogues and

the prejudices of rich reactionaries and to find the true wisdom of
Earth, which teaches adaptation to changing conditions and eternal
concern for the welfare of posterity—

> *The cry of the conscience of Life:*
> Keep the young generation in hail,
> And bequeath them no tumbled house!

In spite of austere title and forbidding style, the book sold better
than its predecessors. Shortly after publication, when Meredith wanted
to give a copy to a friend, he found that the supply of the first issue
was already exhausted.

Will Meredith had become engaged to Margaret Elliot, a stepdaughter of his father's friend Colonel Lewin, of Leith Hill. As she
was a charming, pretty girl, with musical ability, her future father-in-
law was well pleased, and attended the wedding in October. In the
same month he was present also at a different sort of ceremony, the
funeral of Tennyson in Westminster Abbey. He cannot have avoided
thinking about his own forty years of neglected poetry, the earnestness
of his sense of poetic mission; he must have compared himself mentally with the leading poets of the day and wondered sardonically
which of them would inherit the laureateship.

Another of Tennyson's offices did indeed devolve upon him. Tennyson had been the first holder of the presidency of the Society of
Authors, and Meredith was elected to succeed him. The action implied that the literary profession considered him the most distinguished
writer of his generation.

It occurred opportunely in respect to his personal affairs, for the
Society had been founded for defending the rights of authors in their
relations with publishers, and Meredith was belatedly realizing that his
fame in both England and America ought to bring him better material returns. The profession of literary agent having recently emerged,
Meredith engaged one of its earliest practitioners, W. Morris Colles,
to handle his interests. Colles took one look at the evidence and went
vigorously to work.

Roberts Brothers were a conservative Boston firm, and Meredith
had been so pleased by receiving royalties from them that he had not
dreamed of the more aggressive and profitable methods of New York
houses. But for five years Charles Scribner's Sons had kept an eye on
him. In December, 1887, a representative of the firm interviewed Chapman in London, obtaining exact figures on the number of copies that

Roberts imported in sheets, and the price paid. Meredith "has a ro-
bust and rugged way of expressing himself," the scout reported, "and
I should think his novels good property."

Meredith was visited on New Year's Day, 1890, by S. S. McClure,
the American syndicate proprietor, who had been converted by Stevenson to enthusiasm for Meredith's novels, and who wanted to buy reprint rights on some of the short tales. They sat talking by the fireside
in the chalet till two in the morning, and Meredith as usual read
some chapters of *The Amazing Marriage* aloud. On returning to London McClure assured a Scribner representative that Meredith was on
the verge of wide popularity. As McClure's instinct for best sellers
was legendary, his opinion carried weight.

Edward L. Burlingame, a Scribner official, cabled to his home office
from London in the spring of 1891: "INTERESTED IN MEREDITH BUT
REGARD READING NECESSARY." He soon added that while a new *Feverel*
or *Beauchamp* would be welcomed, "we should be worse off than
nothing with one of his vagaries." In a fuller dispatch he spoke of the
storm of criticism that was sure to be stirred up by *One of Our Conquerors*. "Lang and Colvin both condemn it. We are safe in having
nothing of his to take unread."

By December, 1892, Colles entered the picture: "Barrie tells Colles
that Meredith has a remarkable new novel nearly ready, for which he
(Barrie) can negotiate." Shortly afterwards, on instructions from
Scribner's, Colles visited Flint Cottage and Meredith read him part
of *The Amazing Marriage*. The agent reported to New York that "he
is right in believing it to be by far the most popular of any of his
stories . . . Mr Meredith is loath to let it go out of his hands until
it is thoroughly revised." A sample would be sent to Scribner's as soon
as it could be typed.

The situation with regard to his English publishers was more complicated. His work as reader for Chapman & Hall had gone on mo-
notonously for more than thirty years, and naturally the firm had
brought out most of his novels. After 1880, when it became a limited
company, he and Fred Chapman were the sole survivors from the old
regime and shared the chief burden of determining policy. B. W.
Matz, then a junior clerk in the office, says that "to every member
of the firm he was a great man, respected and almost reverenced as a
personality of an unusual order, and his presence in the office created
an impression such as the King's would do on entering a shop."

There was no real reason why Meredith should continue the drudg-
ery of reading several manuscripts a week at a meager salary, for his

royalties were now sufficient for the modest way of life that he preferred. He must have derived satisfaction from the sense of power conferred by his secret authority to make or mar the hopes of writers.

His strongest enthusiasm was likely to be for books on current
Continental affairs, on travel, and on Nature. He approved W. H.
Hudson's nature books, but not his two novels, though one of them
(*Fan*) was accepted. It is interesting to find him praising a book on
Whitman by a young South African graduate of Cambridge, Jan
Christian Smuts. Inconsistently enough, he was always hard upon the
works by intellectual women, who might seem to embody his own
ideals for the sex. The belligerent Eliza Lynn Linton never won his approval, and he was dubious even of several brilliant younger women,
such as Sarah Grand and "John Oliver Hobbes," who were sometimes
labeled by the critics as his own disciples in fiction. His rejection of
*The Heavenly Twins*, by Mme Grand, in 1892, was comparable to
that of *East Lynne* thirty years earlier, for the book became a monstrous success. His objections to the manuscript were exactly those
that were perpetually lodged against his own novels:

*The author is a clever woman, and has ideas: for which reason she is ham-
pered at present in the effort to be a novelist . . . The writer should be advised to put this MS aside until she has got the art of driving a story.*

The bulk of his judgments, naturally, were flat rejections, and as he
grew older he became more scornful in the gibes that caused his weekly
reports to be read by the office staff with unholy glee.

The publicity of the Pinnock trial had invaded his cherished secrecy, but he retained the position for three years longer. The firm
was no longer as strong financially as when he entered it; new competitors were using more energetic methods to capture the market. Meredith's request for an increase in stipend was rejected, and Colles had
no trouble in proving to him that he was not being fairly treated in
the matter of his own books. For the Uniform Edition the publishers
leased the copyrights for seven years, by a flat payment of £100 for
each book. Now more than a year had passed since the end of the con-
tractual period, but no new arrangement had been made. On *Diana
of the Crossways* the firm's rights had been for five years only, and
therefore they had been selling it for two additional years without
authority. The original plates of the Uniform Edition continued in
use, in defiance of Meredith's pleas for correction of many "scandalous
printer's errors." In spite of repeated requests he had not even been

given a receipt for the fee he had paid to redeem the copyright of *Evan Harrington* from Bradbury & Evans. Marshaling these complaints to Fred Chapman in righteous indignation, Meredith informed him that Colles would thereafter deal on his behalf. The old friendly understanding was defunct.

On March 23 Colles handed Burlingame a rough typescript of the first three chapters of *The Amazing Marriage*, and the latter reported to Scribner's that he could not tell yet whether "it is going to develop into a great, vigorous, human kind of a story, or whether Meredith is going to ride a hobby hard in his most fantastic fashion." He explained that if the novel were accepted as a serial for *Scribner's Magazine*, the firm would have the right of taking Meredith's next two books: one would be a much-revised edition of the three stories that he had contributed to *The New Quarterly Magazine* fifteen years before; the other had been described to Burlingame as a story of fifty to eighty thousand words on a subject of "rather a questionable sort, treated with the greatest boldness and realism." Burlingame added that he did not feel "very hot" about all this if Meredith's earlier books were to remain in the hands of another American publisher.

On April 7 Burlingame cabled the New York office: "MEREDITH DESIRABLE SERIAL WANTS TWELVE HUNDRED POUNDS ALL SERIAL RIGHTS PERHAPS COMPROMISE ELEVEN SHALL I SECURE BOOK ALSO FIFTEEN ROYALTY." In reply Scribner set his maximum figure at one thousand pounds, and this was promptly accepted. Burlingame cabled triumphantly on April 13: "MEREDITH SECURED SAIL ETRURIA SATURDAY."

While these negotiations were going on, the proposal that Meredith should sit for his portrait was renewed, this time by George Frederick Watts, whom he had known thirty years before, when they were both in Lady Duff Gordon's circle at Esher. Having become the best-loved painter of the time, Watts had put most of the contemporary celebrities on canvas, with the intention of presenting the series to the nation. "It is distressing," Meredith lamented, "for I could not consent to absorb any of his precious time, or to sit for such a purpose. I am ashamed to say I have no ambition to provoke an English posterity's question, Who is he? and my grizzled mug may be left to vanish . . . It is really painful to meet the dear and noble fellow's offer in such a manner."

Pressure was exerted. The American Mrs Palmer, now living at Guildford, near Watts's house, invited Meredith on a visit in the spring of 1893, and brought him over to see Watts in his studio. Thus trapped, he could no longer refuse, and for five mornings he posed for the picture, while talking copiously to the painter and his wife. Watts's serene kindliness was an antidote to Meredith's usual tincture of satire, and he discussed his contemporaries positively favorably. After he and Watts had agreed about the beauty of Mrs Norton's flexible nostrils, Meredith launched into his theories on human progress:

"We have the rise and dip of the wave, but mankind goes forward . . . We want to be stripped of conventionalities—women more so than men . . . I believe that this age will be ranked as the most heroically striving of any time." He attributed much of this earnestness to the work of Carlyle . . . "He has taught all earnest people today that they have to take life seriously and do some work for the world—that there is a yea and a nay, and they must make choice of one or other." . . . They then spoke of Tennyson, Mr Meredith saying that he was the most natural, the most spontaneously natural, of human beings . . . Talking of Mrs Leslie Stephen, Mr Meredith said, "I want to make a portrait of her when I get her more by heart." Signor [Watts] mentioned that George Eliot had said that she did not draw from life. "Oh, I do," Meredith answered emphatically, "but never till I know them by heart."

The painting faithfully reproduced Meredith's features, but recorded the worn and anxious look resulting from his illness rather than the lively play of expression that impressed those who saw him in conversational action. When he was told it was a good likeness, he merely grumbled, "Once and in truth there was a presentable phiz, when no one cared for it."

Jim Gordon had been killed in a riding-accident in February, and the widow came two months later to spend a few days at Flint Cottage. Characteristically, Meredith behaved, she says, as "a wise surgeon friend." His affection for her did not impel him to any conventional utterance of sympathy. Instead, he administered "bracing" advice, devoid of sentiment: "You have now been given the opportunity of your life—and will you sink beneath the waters? You have a mind; use it, or it will bite you . . . You have had the advantage of a very good and careful education, but the great disadvantage of seeing life from only one point of view."

The glittering thousand pounds from Scribner's sent him desperately to work, and he wrote every day from half past ten till six, and felt tired in the evenings. The mere physical effort of guiding a pen was now agonizingly hard; his formerly beautiful, clear handwriting had become spasmodic and shaky. He had been forced into his old predicament of working on two novels at once: he was determined to revise the early chapters of *The Amazing Marriage*, written a dozen years before, as well as to push the story on to its conclusion; and meanwhile he had not finished *Lord Ormont and His Aminta*, the novel which he had been writing for many months and which presumably was the one on a "rather questionable" subject that Burlingame heard about.

He entertained hopes that both books might be liked, for he was avoiding the eccentricities that had disfigured *One of Our Conquerors*. When Clement Shorter inquired about the book then being written, hoping that it might be available for him to use in *The Illustrated London News*, he was told, "It seems that literary playfulness in description is antipathetic to our present taste. I should not imagine my present novel to contain any of it." A little later Meredith wrote to H. S. Salt, "One fancies that a cultivated man might perceive in a writer a turn for literary playfulness, when strong human emotion is not upon him. To find this taken seriously, as an example of my 'style,' is quaint. But we will admit that there is too much of it." The forthcoming novels were narrated in a more straightforward manner.

Better health and financial prospects improved his spirits. When Miss Bradley and Miss Cooper were invited to dinner at Flint Cottage in the autumn, they found him "far more vigorous" and more congenial than on their first visit. He talked appreciatively about Michael Field's plays, showing that he had read them thoroughly. "He, the Euphuist in language, rallied us on our tendency not to use the vernacular . . . His talk foamed before us and we had good draughts. There is great magnetism in his eyes."

Conan Doyle was lecturing on Meredith that year in various English, Scottish, and Continental cities, proclaiming him the foremost living English novelist. When he paid another visit to Flint Cottage he was treated to lively comments on contemporaries, such as "Rudyard Kipling has no refinement," and "When the Prince of Wales laughs, he laughs from the tip of his beard to his bald head, and he laughs all around his neck." After lunch Meredith asked his guest to come up to the chalet and hear a few chapters of *The Amazing Marriage*. Doyle, in front as they climbed the steep path, heard a scramble and a thud which indicated that the crippled man had stumbled and fallen. With an intuition of Meredith's painful pride, he pretended to notice nothing amiss, and walked steadily on till his host overtook him and resumed the conversation where it had been interrupted.

Meanwhile the news of Scribner's contract for *The Amazing Marriage* was received with dismay by Roberts Brothers. In response to their angry protests, Burlingame rejected any charge of infringement of their rights, and denied their allegation that Scribner's had craftily seduced Meredith away from them. On the contrary, Meredith had offered the manuscript voluntarily. The Boston firm then lodged a formal demand for the book rights, and met with a flat negative. Accordingly, they notified Meredith that the issue of his book by another publisher would break the continuity of their set of his works, and that they would accept nothing of his in the future if they could not have the present novel.

Meredith felt the pleasurable embarrassment of an aging spinster suddenly courted by two suitors. He wrote to Burlingame in perturbation, emphasizing the smallness of the royalty that the other firm had been paying, but blaming his agent for persuading him to grant the book rights of *The Amazing Marriage* to anyone else, and requesting Scribner's to release him from that portion of the contract and to let Roberts bring out the book. "As for me, whether I am a loser or not, I do not care."

Scribner's in reply detailed their legal position and refused to compromise. Anxiety and overwork having brought on an attack of illness, Meredith could not make up his mind for two months, but then he repeated his conviction that Roberts Brothers' application ought to be approved. He would willingly "pay a fine to a reasonable amount" to Scribner's for the redemption of the book rights. Once more Scribner's rejected the proposal; and about the same time Roberts informed him that they would pay royalties of only 10 per cent, not the 15 per cent that Scribner's offered. This put an abrupt end to his scruples. Perhaps as a reward for his compliance, Scribner's at the same time agreed to bring out the American edition of *Lord Ormont and His Aminta,* then in the midst of its serial publication in England.

Distressing predicaments like this had never happened in the old carefree days before he had committed himself to the aggressive mercies of an agent. Besides, he was suffering under the tyranny of a definite date on which the manuscript must be ready. His habit of interminable rewriting was seriously restricted. "I have to go the round of a work-horse daily," he complained at the beginning of January; and three months later he said that the "press of work to meet an Agreement" was "wearing me to threads." An attack of ulcerated eyelids for a time prevented work on the manuscript. In his April letter to

Scribner's he warned them that he might need a six weeks' postpone-
ment of the date when the book was to reach them. Terming himself
"dreadful busy" at the end of June, he remarked that "a novelist's
prolonged delivery is a terrible matter"; and he confessed to Sharp
that he was "not too happy" about the book. He said on August 7
that it would "want a chapter or two for finish at the end of the
month . . . I have had to drive two dozen characters as two, making
all run together to one end."

He was not too preoccupied to maintain his political interest.
When Lord Rosebery became Prime Minister that spring, Sir Edward
Grey noted that "George Meredith and Rosebery met some time ago
and took a mutual dislike to each other. Rosebery would naturally
resent being explored by Meredith's critical faculty and Meredith
would be huffed at his resenting it. Meredith is said to be very keen
on politics just now: he was too lame to go to the great anti-Lords
demonstration in the Park on Sunday, but he sent his gardener to
represent him."

Literary interviews also broke in upon his writing. In June he
was visited by Wilfrid Scawen Blunt, the poet and traveler, whose
gratitude he had earned on two counts. On his advice Chapman &
Hall had rejected Blunt's first book in 1867, and, Blunt says, "I bear
him the reverse of a grudge. He was entirely right, for the book, except for a few sonnets, was worthless. It was a fortunate refusal." In
1892, on the other hand, Meredith and York Powell were the only two
people who wrote to Blunt in praise of his narrative poem, *Esther*,
when even his friends condemned it. On his side, Blunt was fascinated
with *Modern Love*—some critics claimed that his best-known work,
the *Love-Sonnets of Proteus*, was an imitation of it. They held a good
many radical social views in common, and Meredith regarded Blunt
as "one of the few honest men in public life." Blunt's diary tells how
he managed to manipulate his four-horse coach into the tiny drive-
way in front of Meredith's house.

*He is terribly deaf and afflicted with creeping paralysis, so that he staggers
from time to time, and once today nearly fell. It does not, however, affect his
mind, and he has a novel on hand which keeps him writing six hours a day.
He is a queer, voluble creature, with a play-acting voice, and his conversation
like one dictating to a secretary, constant search for epigrams. I took the bull
by the horns at once about his novels, said I never read prose and looked upon
him only as a poet. This pleased him, and he gave me two volumes, recommending especially the piece called "Attila." . . . During our talk a lunch-*

eon was brought to him on a tray, as he said he was too busy to sit down to a regular meal, and could not write after one o'clock, so I left him to his work and drove on.

John Morley, visiting him in the same week, after a long interval, felt he would probably not live much longer:

*His disabilities of movement were painful, and he is very deaf. Otherwise he was less altered than I had expected. One or two splendid expressions fell from him, but on the whole he was less turbulent and strained than he used to be . . . Melancholy can never be absent from the last days of a disappearing orb; but this was less melancholy than some. Meredith's lifelong view of nature and human days fits in with the evening, as with the noonday hour. He has shunned the world, and so it costs him less to leave it.*

He was well enough to don frock coat and silk hat on June 18 for Violet Maxse's wedding to Lord Edward Cecil, a son of Lord Salisbury, a former and future Prime Minister. Meredith signed the register as one of the bride's witnesses, along with Morley, Asquith, and Joseph Chamberlain, the groom's witnesses being Lord Selborne and Arthur Balfour.

Just a month later, Meredith's own daughter was married to Henry Parkman Sturgis, a son of a well-known American-born London financier. As his house was at Leatherhead, she was not going far away from home; but her departure marked the end of family life at Flint Cottage. Thereafter Meredith's only companions were his devoted gardener, Frank Cole, the women of the household staff, and his idolized dachshunds. "It was very amusing," says Mrs Gordon, "to watch him talking to his dogs. He would speak to them exactly as if they were human beings, only with more intonation of the voice, and with more gestures; and they seemed to understand everything he said, and on their part conversed with him in doggy fashion, with movements of ears, tail, and paws." When children visited the cottage, his favorite entertainment for them was to make the dachshunds "sing."

*Lord Ormont and His Aminta*, after appearing as a serial in *The Pall Mall Magazine* during the first half of 1894, was brought out in three volumes by Chapman & Hall. It was another study of an incompatible marriage (this time because of disparity in age); and it showed the final stage of emancipation in Meredith's handling of the theme. Though Diana had been on the verge of elopement with Dacier, chance intervened to preserve her honor; though the saintly

Nataly had lived bigamously with Radnor, their union was shown to produce tragic consequences; but now Matthew Weyburn and Aminta were portrayed as ideal characters, and after she left her husband and lived with Weyburn their illicit union was pictured as blissful and socially unimpeached.

This outcome was made possible by the exceptional nobility of everybody concerned. No longer does Meredith show bias, as he did against Sir Willoughby Patterne, or even pity, as toward Victor Radnor. To all the characters the author's attitude is sympathetic to the verge of sentimentality. Matey Weyburn, the visionary schoolmaster, is cut in the pattern of the paragons of "muscular Christianity" and runs the inevitable risk of being labeled a prig. Aminta is equally perfect in her beauty, her athletic prowess, her dignity, and her intuitive judgments. Lord Ormont, the "strong, silent" military man, gains the reader's respect in spite of his stupid conduct. He is a more gracious version of the choleric old aristocrat previously drawn as Everard Romfrey in *Beauchamp's Career*. Even the villain, Morsfield, is allowed to be vain and Byronically emotional, rather than evil.

The author's unwonted mellowness is responsible for a pervasive weakness in the story. He cannot bring himself to inflict much real suffering on any of his characters. Morsfield is kept in a subordinate position and is conveniently killed off by a minor character before he can wreak much mischief. The conflict is confined to an affectionate dispute between Lord Ormont and his domineering sister and to Aminta's own internal problem as to whether she should desert her husband. The characters being so admirable, the reader has little doubt that they will always do the right thing.

The gracious charm extends also to the style. Vanished are Meredith's allusive references and tortured syntax. Though there is a continual flashing of metaphor, the short and urbane novel glides effortlessly throughout.

The author let it be known that he had found the central situation for his story in the life of the Earl of Peterborough, a brilliant general of the time of Queen Anne and a headstrong, tactless man who was repeatedly in disgrace with the government. Late in his life Peterborough secretly married a lovely young actress, Anastasia Robinson, and the public believed her to be his mistress until he acknowledged her as his wife, not long before he died. There seems to be no doubt, however, that Meredith also drew largely from a more recent story, that of the Earl of Cardigan, leader of the Light Brigade in the famous charge at the Battle of Balaklava. Indeed, Meredith described that charge quite accurately in listing Lord Ormont's exploits, but transferred it to the Peninsular War. Though a hero with the public for his courage, Cardigan was an unpopular martinet in the service, and was also notorious as a duelist. At the age of sixty-three he was married to a beautiful young lady at Gibraltar in circumstances that provoked some gossip. Lord Cardigan had been dead for twenty-five years when this book was written, but the widow was still conspicuous in London society and therefore the identification had to be disguised.

Meredith shifted the date to the opening years of Victoria's reign, and depicted the girl as a young hero-worshiper just out of school. The hardest problem lay in accounting for the Earl's concealment of the wedding. Meredith attributed it to his contemptuous withdrawal from English society after he had been retired from active duty as punishment for conducting a successful campaign in India too high-handedly. A secondary reason was his unacknowledged fear of his sister, who was fanatical in the matter of family pride.

The author's other difficulty was to establish his readers' sympathy with the adultery between Aminta and Weyburn. Her husband's advanced years and his refusal to treat her as an intelligent adult were scarcely sufficient reasons. The novel was therefore started with a boy-and-girl attachment between them. The opening chapters depicted young love with the same idyllic freshness as in *Richard Feverel*, though without the passionate intensity.

As usual, he drew much from personal experience. Lord Ormont's disdain for the English public which slighted his military prowess derived validity from Meredith's similar feeling in regard to the lack of recognition for his books. Into the General's mouth he could also put some of his own strong convictions about how England's prestige and old-time warlike valor had been destroyed by pusillanimous bourgeois pacifism. And his own physical helplessness echoed in the grumbling of the Earl's sister against old age and ill health. This character, the indomitable Lady Charlotte Eglett, was a faithful and loving portrait of Admiral Maxse's quarrelsome, candid mother. In both the brother and the sister Meredith was at his best in displaying the mingled defects and merits of the English aristocratic tradition.

The preliminary scenes at Cupar's school, like the school scenes in *Harry Richmond*, recalled Meredith's year at a small boarding-school, when he had been so much imbued with loyalty to an idolized head-boy. But more important was the tribute to the Moravian school at Neuwied, which was embodied in the description of Weyburn's establishment in Switzerland, combined with some features of the "objective" school that Arthur attended in Hófwyl. The international make-up of the personnel, the easy confidence and affection between boys and masters, the wholesome open-air life with long walking-trips across the mountains, all showed how gratefully Meredith cherished the memory of his German institution, and throughout the novel these principles of education were zealously proclaimed.

The joy of healthy physical exercise dominated the book; and the climactic episode, in which Weyburn wooed Aminta while they were swimming together half a mile from shore, provoked lively argument among critics as to whether it was humanly possible. The whole story was carried along by a quality of sheer gusto that had never been sustained as consistently in the novels that Meredith wrote in the days of his muscular vigor.

The reviewers greeted the book with a tone of relief in the discovery that he had emerged from the wilderness of its predecessor. He was termed by *The Athenaeum* "a rather flippant Zeus, hurling thunderbolts with his right hand and letting off squibs with his left." Lionel Johnson was again enthusiastic, especially about the description of movement: "His style in such places has the brilliance of rippling and sparkling waves, laughing and dancing shoreward, with a kind of delighted waywardness, a grace upon their strength. It is joyous writing, cordial and entrancing; it clears the air to an exulting serenity." But while Johnson, as a poet, enjoyed the emotional charm, Henry James, as an analytical novelist, fumed at the lack of solidity. He declared in a letter that "the unspeakable Lord Ormont has roused me to critical rage. Not a difficulty met, not a figure presented, not a scene constituted—not a dim shadow condensing once into audible or visible reality—making you hear for an instant the tap of its feet on the earth."

Meanwhile, the completion of *The Amazing Marriage* was beset with hardship. Meredith was accustomed to the easygoing system of English periodicals, for which an author could write the later chapters after serial publication had begun, and he was nonplused by discovering that the whole manuscript was expected in New York well in advance of January, the scheduled date for its commencement in *Scribner's Magazine*. On September 27 he managed to send off a "large instalment" of the typescript, promising that the rest would follow "at the earliest possible moment." Replying to a protest from Burlingame, Will Meredith admitted that his father had not yet finished the work, "although he has been occupied with absolutely nothing else for the last three months." With emphasis on his father's bad health, he pleaded that "it would not be wise to prejudice the conclusion of a work such as the one which you have been so fortunate as to obtain."

Burlingame was unimpressed. Upon finding that the first batch of material was thousands of words longer than what had been allowed for, he demanded permission to have it cut for the serial publication. Will Meredith took a firm stand: "It would be most detrimental to the story to curtail it in any degree and surely having a story of this kind you can make arrangements to let it run for a slightly longer time than your usual term . . . If Mr Meredith undertakes to go through the entire work again cutting down and curtailing you will have to wait a very considerable time, this work for you having already taken very much longer than he anticipated. Moreover, Mr Meredith has other matters to which he desires to give his attention." The day after posting this letter, he received a peremptory cable repeating that condensation was essential, and in his reply he acceded to the demand and requested that the shortening should be done by an experienced member of the Scribner staff, "cutting reflections, retaining story." Having thus capitulated, Meredith in his confirmatory letter insisted that the subsequent book-publication should present the full text. Prompt payment of the first half of the purchase price and also of substantial royalties on *Lord Ormont and His Aminta* salved the author's pride, and relations with the house of Scribner became serene. Just before Christmas he was able to tell friends that he had finished the novel, "but the latter part has worn me—owing to my state of health more than the task."

With his daughter auspiciously wedded and his American editions flourishing, Meredith was ready for the final break with Chapman & Hall. Fred Chapman's resignation as chairman of the company signalized the end of an era. Meredith relinquished his employment as reader, and made arrangements with another firm for the issuing of his next book. It was a volume made up of "The Tale of Chloe" and the two other stories that had appeared in *The New Quarterly Magazine* nearly twenty years before, and it was brought out in January, 1895, by Ward, Locke, & Bowen. This was only an intermediate relationship, for a minor volume. William Maxse Meredith, having given up the electrical-engineering profession, replaced Colles as his father's business representative, and about this time he took a position with a major publishing house, Constable & Company. Negotiations were set afoot for the transference to them of the Meredith copyrights.

His fame in Britain and the United States attracted the attention of some French critics, notably Marcel Schwob. He established a cordial acquaintance by letter, and in 1894 gave a note of introduction to his friend Paul Valéry, who received the usual invitation to dinner at Flint Cottage, with the warning that "the cookery is unfortunately English but the wines are true French." Valéry was impressed by Meredith's accurate knowledge about Napoleon and his empire, and remarked that "he loved France almost violently."

Schwob himself visited the cottage soon afterwards. He had been warned by Oscar Wilde that Meredith was sensitive about his paralysis and would announce that his lameness was the temporary result of a fall that very morning. Schwob refused to credit the prediction; but to his amusement this proved to be one of Meredith's first remarks to him. The subject was therefore left unmentioned in the article that Schwob wrote about his visit. Meredith had come straight from his writing-desk to greet the guest, and "his eyes, during the first minutes while he was talking to me, were literally *drunk with thought.*"

While leading me to his little cell, Meredith said, "They claim that the brain gets tired. Don't believe it. The brain never gets tired. It is the stomach that conquers one. And I was born with a bad stomach," he added with a smile . . .

His language is like that of his characters who translate into English what they have thought in Italian, in German, or in French. One feels strongly that Meredith is translating what he says and that his metaphors are the result of a transposition of symbols . . . He does not think in English or in any known language, but in Meredith . . .

"Death?" Meredith said to me. "I have lived enough. I am not afraid of it: it is only the inside and the outside of a door."

Léon Daudet came to see him at the same time, and he, too, described his host with Gallic intensity:

Meredith was beautiful, with a strange, high-strung, painful beauty, the result of sorrow and thought. Long curling hair, a high, white, open brow, a pointed white beard, frosty blue eyes glowing with a watchful flame, a straight nose, a deep strong voice, nervous hands, and ataxic legs, gave him the appearance and the fascination of a modern sorcerer, a Celtic Mephistopheles.

A few months later Daudet came again, accompanied by his father Alphonse and by Henry James. The famous French writer was equally paralytic, and when Meredith met their train and limped along the station platform beside him, Daudet was struck with "a sense of fraternal irony—these two novelists dragging a wing like two wounded seagulls, crippled, these birds of storm, punished for defying the gods: an episode worthy of Swift."

Meredith welcomed his visitor like an old friend. "Let me tell you how fond of you I am. For ten years I've been keeping for you some bottles of Côtes-Rôties wine." He extolled the poetry of Mistral and asked Daudet to explain a few of its baffling Provençal idioms. "I live here among barbarians. You understand, don't you, Daudet? You must pardon me."

Admiral Maxse was also in the party, and tried to console the two lame novelists by telling how disabled he had been for months after spraining his ankle.

*"Oh, I remember," said Meredith. "Just think, that sprain swelled till it was the size of a child's head, and then to that of someone with water on the brain. It became an object of curiosity. People came from all around the neighbourhood to look at it and feel it." Thereupon he burst out into joyous and terrifying laughter, while poor Maxse did not dare to contradict . . .*

*He disliked being pitied for his chronic illness, and always spoke of it as something that had occurred the day before or at least very recently. "You have been a doctor, my dear Léon Daudet. That means you don't understand a bit about what people feel who are in pain. Ah, you don't even listen to them any more. It's better it should be like that. It encourages the invalid if the doctor never pays any attention to his complaints."*

Before the Daudets left London, they and Henry James gave an evening reception in Meredith's honor. Léon described how "he received homage and thanked his admirers with a smile. Civilization attains its highest expression on such occasions, when female beauty surrounds and salutes subtle creative intelligence. The reception became a discreet apotheosis, which seemed to please the great man."

Meredith even hobbled down the long platform of Victoria Station to see his new friends off for Paris. R. H. Sherard, also present to say good-bye, reported that the farewell handclasp was so prolonged that the sudden starting of the train almost dragged Meredith off his legs before the two crippled authors could disengage their fingers.

The Daudet-James reception for him was soon followed by another tribute of respect. His friend Clodd was serving as president of the Omar Khayyám Club, which included a number of well-known authors and journalists among its members. In August, 1895, it held a dinner at the Burford Bridge Hotel. In response to a special invitation Meredith explained that his simple diet prevented his going out to large dinners, but he consented to join the company afterwards on condition that he should not be asked to speak, as he had never made a public speech in his life. At the proper time Shorter went up to Flint Cottage and provided an arm to aid Meredith in the short walk to the hotel. When they entered the dining-room all the members rose to their feet and stood until Meredith was seated. Clodd expressed the Club's sense of the honor that his presence conferred upon them, and Meredith's courtesy impelled him to render thanks. With a hand on the chairman's shoulder he chaffed him about his cunning device to make him break his silence: "Clodd is the most amiable of chairmen but the most dastardly of deceivers. Never in my life before have I been on my legs to make a speech. Now, before I know it, I am bustled over the first fence and find myself overrunning the hounds. I have my hands on the fellow at this moment, and I could turn on him and rend him; but I spare him." He went on with a few sentences that sounded more natural and sincere than his usual conversational style.

Responding to the toast to "The Guests," Hardy and Gissing in turn got up and told how much Meredith's kind advice had helped them in their first efforts at authorship. Meredith was particularly glad to see Gissing, after the lapse of a decade, and his cordiality encouraged Gissing to come to Flint Cottage several times in subsequent months for tea or dinner. The whole affair of the speech amused Meredith inordinately, and thereafter his nickname for Clodd was always "Sir Reynard."

No previous novel of Meredith's had been awaited with such lively anticipation as *The Amazing Marriage*. Most of his friends had been listening to sample chapters of it for years. Stevenson, far away in Samoa, wrote to Meredith repeatedly during 1893 and 1894 to ask about the progress of the story that would show him his own youthful self depicted in the character of Gower Woodseer. "It will be a brave day for me when I get hold of it," he said; but he died just a month before the first instalment appeared in *Scribner's Magazine*. "It is I who should go," exclaimed Meredith, when he heard the news, "not he, who is young and loved."

A final fillip of curiosity about the new novel was added by rumors about friction with the publishers. A columnist in *The Pall Mall Gazette* wrote in October, 1895, "Mr George Meredith is changing publishers again. His latest work met with a somewhat wintry welcome from the house which he had previously favored, whereupon he repaired to an opposition press, where, it is said, he promptly obtained £1000 down, plus royalty rights." This evoked an angry statement from Meredith, branding the paragraph "inimical by implication and false in statement, evidently inspired by the person interested to make things appear so before the public." The new chairman of Chapman & Hall then felt obliged to announce in his turn that his company did not have "any hand in any such nonsense" as the columnist's gossip. The fact, he said, was that "I made Mr Meredith a commercial offer for his coming book. I offered him the market value, and perhaps a little over, basing my offer on the experience of the firm in the case of previous novels by Mr Meredith. Much as I admire Mr Meredith's work and himself personally, I could not, in the interests of our share-holders, afford to publish his works at a loss. Mr Meredith was surely quite right and wise to accept the best offer he could get elsewhere." The display of soiled linen must have galled Meredith's pride to the quick, but at least it settled the finality of his break with Chapman & Hall.

*The Amazing Marriage* was published by Constable & Company in two volumes. Starting off with a typical stratagem, Meredith cast the first three chapters as a monologue by "Dame Gossip," and suc-ceeded marvelously in imitating the intonation of a garrulous old woman. Like the opening of *Diana,* this was intended to produce an illusion of historical authenticity for the story. These opening chapters formed a complete short story in themselves, narrating events that preceded the main action by twenty years. The runaway marriage of "the Old Buccaneer" and the beautiful young heiress was told with a verve that re-created the very spirit of the Regency-Byronic period. The personality of the fabulous Captain Kirby was based upon the friend of Byron and Shelley, Edward John Trelawny, several details being taken from his autobiography; and there was an admixture of Lord Cochrane, the fiery admiral who was cashiered through political in-trigue and thereafter commanded the navies of Brazil and Greece. The portrait of an aged but indomitable adventurer, love-maker, and scorner of convention carried an affectionate note suggesting a certain degree of self-identification, or wish-fulfillment, on the author's part.

Thereafter the story began over again in the early-Victorian era that had been the setting for several of Meredith's other novels. Kirby's son and daughter, brought up in his highly unorthodox style in a re-mote German castle, are suddenly flung into the midst of sophisticated high society. Through them and the cheerful vagabond Woodseer, Meredith could draw strong contrasts between natural emotional behavior and artificial formalities. The arrogant Lord Fleetwood amazes his sycophants when he is fascinated by Woodseer's frank scorn of his wealth and rank. The central thesis of the book, however, as of the preceding one, was that a wife is absolved of all duty toward a husband too egoistic to accept her as an equal partner.

Fleetwood's marriage to Carinthia was loveless on his part, at least. He courted her out of wounded vanity when another woman rejected him, and then he was forced to marry her by her miserly guardian who saw a chance of getting rid of a penniless ward. Fleetwood was little short of a maniac in his overweening pride and his demand for absolute obedience. But he possessed intellectual gifts, artistic sensibility, and a haughty candor that win the reader's unwilling admiration, and it is only by the greater strength in the character of Carinthia that sympathy remains centered in her. Like Sandra Belloni, she expressed her feelings and followed her impulses with utter naïveté, so that Fleetwood could not decide whether his bride was an imbecile or a subtle schemer. But when he deserted her on the wedding day and then subjected her to prolonged indignities, all the nobility of her character emerged, and he was slowly won to respect her and then to desire her. Up to this point the author used the "patient Griselda" theme, as he did in *Richard Feverel* and *Rhoda Fleming*. But the ending flouted sentimental expectations: Carinthia scorned her repentant husband and went off with her brother on a quixotic mission to aid the rebellion in Spain.

Some episodes of the story were melodramatic to the verge of fantasy. The birth of Carinthia's child was so unexplained that a wit said the title ought to be *The Amazing Baby*. Fleetwood's final withdrawal to a monastery also was not made plausible. Meredith must have realized his mishandling of these events too late, for a copy of the book is in existence in which he has written additional paragraphs to suggest explanations.

The book was an epitome of Meredith's enthusiasms. Not only Woodseer but several other prominent characters were Welsh, and for the first time he actually laid some of the action in Wales. His love of mountain scenery was never more passionately displayed than in the magnificent descriptions of Alpine landscapes. And Gower Woodseer, modeled upon Stevenson in his careless dress and his light-hearted rambling over Europe, was also in many respects a portrait of

Meredith himself in youthful days—a tradesman's son teaching himself to think and to write without the benefit of public school or university.

Viewed objectively the book has its inequalities and its implausible spots. But for the first time since *Harry Richmond* Meredith created an atmosphere of sheer romance, casting over the whole book a glamor that captivates the reader's imagination strongly enough to create a spell utterly disproportionate to the actual details of the narrative. *Richard Feverel* had made much use of references to Ferdinand, Miranda, and the magic island; but it was in *The Amazing Marriage* that Meredith came nearest to the rich sunset glow that suffuses *The Tempest*. His last novel was his tenderest, his least worldly, his most poetic.

# CHAPTER

## XVI

# *The End of Action*

ONE of the reviews of *The Amazing Marriage* led Meredith into a new friendship. He had formed a high opinion of a weekly column called "The Wares of Autolycus" in *The Pall Mall Gazette*. At the Omar Khayyám Club dinner, declaring that a recent column about Eleanora Duse "reached the high-water mark of literary criticism of our time," he asked who the writer was, and the editor of the paper disclosed the identity of Alice Meynell. Meredith's compliment to her was promptly printed by Shorter in his column in *The Illustrated London News*. Meredith was probably not aware that Mrs Meynell had already reviewed his work in *Merry England* a decade earlier or that the Meynells had christened their youngest son "Francis Meredith" in his honor; but he sent her a copy of *The Amazing Marriage* inscribed "in homage."

Her review of it in her column was ecstatic: "Poetry is the conspicuous secret of the book. As in this great book, so in life, poetry is not hidden. It is unrevealed." Comparing Carinthia to Shakespeare's Helena, she went on to talk about the glorious descriptions of Nature and the skillful linking of them with the heroine's moods: "Always secret, always accessible, always present, nature is the simplest thing in the most intimate book in the world."

Meredith asked Clodd and Shorter to tell Mrs Meynell that one of his few remaining wishes was to "lure" her acquaintance. When she agreed to come to Box Hill, he promised to receive her and her husband "as among the most beloved of my friends . . . I have long been attached to you in the spirit, and am indebted past payment." On their arrival he accompanied Mrs Meynell in the cab from the station to his house, leaving her husband to walk up. Never talkative, she was speechless in this crisis. Meredith asked her if she had written a certain anonymous book, and she said "No." He expressed disappointment, and then—knowing that her name had been Thompson—he asked if Francis Thompson was her brother. Again she said "No," and he expressed double disappointment. In spite of this inauspicious beginning, he was completely charmed by her grave and fragile beauty, her subtle wit, and her serene silences. When she protested that she was not a talker, he wrote in reply, "Your plea in excuse makes me ashamed of my prattle. Let me tell you that my mind is not always with my tongue in the act. I do it for the sake of sociability, and I am well disposed either to listen or to worship the modest lips that have such golden reserves."

Discovering that she liked double violets, he arranged to have them growing perpetually under glass in his garden, so that he could send them to her periodically. His own favorite flower, the pale-blue iris, he dedicated to her and renamed "Alicia Coerulia" in her honor. He extended his affection to her little girls, to whom he wrote playful letters. His infrequent visits to London were made endurable by the possibility of his having tea at Mrs Meynell's house or by his stipulating that she should sit beside him at a "crush" at Mrs Palmer's. Whenever there was fine weather he tried to persuade her to bring her children down for a holiday at Box Hill. He discussed poetry and her "deeper thoughts of Earth and Life" with her, tempering his skepticism slightly in deference to her Catholic faith but not hesitating to argue with her about her literary preferences or to find fault with some of her poems. When Henry James visited him in May, Meredith extolled her new book of essays, *The Rhythm of Life*, and was so gratified by James's concurrence that he gave him a copy of the book. And he placed his admiration for her essays on public record in a critique of them in *The National Review* in August, 1896—his first book-review in twenty-seven years.

By that time he was calling her his "sweet sister in the muse" and had begun composing a series of sonnets to her. He talked of publishing them under the title "The Lady of the Time," but this was never done, and only one of them survives. He once told her that she could have made him what he should have been and what he could not be without her; and he compared dates to find out whether she had still been unmarried at the time he became a widower—what she called "a retrospective offer."

Her even more aged adorer, Coventry Patmore, soon showed signs of acute jealousy toward this intruder at the shrine. As the Victorian laureate of connubial love, Patmore could feel little enthusiasm for Meredith as an author, remarking, "I should think it cowardly to know women as well as he does." He fumed at the very thought of his gentle lady showing favor to such a satirical analyst.

A permanent protégé of the Meynells was Francis Thompson, the visionary poet whom they had rescued from semi-starvation. Thompson was not a wholehearted devotee of Meredith's work. His biographer says cautiously that "of Meredith's poetry his admiration was of the established sort that needs no questioning"; but in 1892 he had sent to Katharine Tynan a detailed condemnation of "Love in the Valley" as "the most utter and unmusical misconception" of the *tempo rubato* principle: "that triple accent is iterated with clockwork precision in every line, till it becomes a horror." Everard Meynell describes Thompson sitting in a teashop reading a Meredith novel and ignoring the bagful of books he was supposed to be reading for *The Academy*; and in a letter of 1895 Thompson said that he held Meredith "the most unquestionable genius among living novelists," but this opinion was based on acquaintance with only five of the novels.

Now that all the Meynell household were Meredith's dear friends, he naturally insisted that Thompson must come to Flint Cottage for an overnight visit. The resulting comedy of incompatibility is well described by Everard Meynell:

*To dine and sleep and wake in that small cottage was to be at very close quarters with nature and a man. With birds at the window, trees bowing and rustling at the back door, and at the front the vivid grass ready for his feet, Francis was thrust into the presence of a showy bit of nature, and was hardly more easy than if he had been thrust at the theatre into a box directly adjoining the crowded stage. He would pull at his necktie, and smooth his coat, and be most warily conscious of his companion's eye, microscopic, like a blackbird's, for defect. The singing of Meredith's blackbirds would be no less confusing than the stream of Meredith's talk; the nodding flowers and the thousand shadows, like sunshine and the talker, were too strange for him. For years he had evaded nature and an eye; here he was forced to be seen and to see in the unclouded atmosphere of this garden on a hill, and during a long drive. Talk and caviar for breakfast were alike foreign to him, who never breakfasted even on toast. To be on tremendously good terms with nature for her own sake, with talk for its own sake, with French literature, with the Celt, was Meredith's triumph; Thompson was shy of all these. Meredith's method was one of acceptance, of birds' song and Burgundy.*

*Thompson's method was of refusal because he was not hardy enough for one*
*or the other.*

Blissfully unaware of his guest's exposed nerves, Meredith chaffed
him about misprinted words in his poems, and completed his discomfiture by quoting—in Mrs Meynell's hearing—the most ardent lines
from "Love in Dian's Lap," the poem in which Thompson had poured
out his bashful adoration of her.

While Meredith's friendship with the lovely Meynells blossomed,
that with "Michael Field" was withering. The two captious ladies
spent an afternoon with him in September, 1895, and nothing pleased
them. His courteous welcome at the window of their cab seemed to
Miss Cooper to be "not a breath, but an emphasis—not an encouragement, but a declaration of itself." His soothing endearments to his
excited dachshund were "somehow an artificial offence against his aggressive courtesy." Through more than two hours of his best monologue she eyed him pitilessly:

*His head is of Elgin marble perfection . . . A same perfection haunts the*
*eyelids . . . With these two features, nobility is at an end—the nose is*
*shrewish, lacking in generosity, breadth of inspiration, flutter of sensitiveness*
*—a not ill-shaped, but poor nose. The mouth is sunk, grim—the words form*
*in the brain and are emitted; they do not rise fresh on the lips. There is no*
*eloquence, no magic on those lips of almost parallel lines; under the beard*
*one has a prophetic sense that the chin is peaked like the nose. Those eyes*
*. . . have no lightnings, no prehensile power, no malice . . . I can never*
*be sure they move together, but even this does not make them interesting—*
*their colour is a mere vagueness between brown and indigo . . . One goes*
*away chill—one's being unexercised—the conversation one has heard is like*
*marvellous conjuring.*

He was settling into a patriarchal position both in private life and
in the literary world. His first grandchild was a son born to the Will
Merediths in November, 1894, and christened "George" in his honor.
His daughter gave birth to a girl the next August. With his son super-
vising his business interests and his daughter coming over from Leatherhead several times a week to write his letters or entertain his visitors,
he was relieved of tedious responsibilities. His sufferings in finishing
*The Amazing Marriage* had convinced him that novel-writing was no
longer feasible, and so he abandoned two or three half-written stories.
Talking to Gissing in September, 1895, he dwelt upon the hardships

of his early life and declared that he intended to give up writing and to rest for the remainder of his days.

A circle of considerate friends made existence agreeable for him. The Walter Palmers were probably the most generous, their town house in Upper Brook Street being usually his quarters when he came to London. He treated "Queen Jean"—as he called Mrs Palmer—with an affectionate make-believe of feudal devotion and ornate flattery. Whenever he attended one of her glittering receptions he was a first-rate "lion," though his gentle roaring was necessarily interspersed with the performances of other celebrities—perhaps French recitations by Coquelin and Réjane, or violin solos by Johannes Wolff. Other intimate friends were Mr and Mrs Seymour Trower, at whose house at Weybridge he could enjoy boating on a familiar stretch of the river. He was perhaps most at ease when he visited Dr and Mrs H. G. Plimmer in Sydenham; Dr Plimmer, a bacteriologist and Fellow of the Royal Society, and his wife, a cultivated, kindly German, were both lovers of music, particularly devoted to Wagner, and Meredith enjoyed going to concerts with them or listening to recitals at their house. The Plimmers moreover had mastered the technique of giving him presents without offending his touchy pride. To all these friends he assigned nicknames and addressed impromptu rhymes, and he knew that all of them understood his peculiar blend of fantasy and ridicule.

He was receiving attentions also in a more exalted social sphere. In October, 1896, Viscount Battersea invited him to The Pleasaunce, his luxurious country place at Overstrand, near Cromer, in Norfolk. Meredith enjoyed the sea air, and Lady Battersea took him for daily drives in her Victoria, during which he confided to her many anecdotes of his early struggles and later triumphs. He was delighted to have an opportunity for long chats by the fireside with his old friend Augustus Jessopp, now a canon of Norwich, while Lady Battersea listened eagerly to their "racy talk" and tried to decide which of the two handsome old men looked the more distinguished.

Fellow-guests at one point in the visit were Prince Pierre Troubetzkoi and his bride, the sensational American novelist Amélie Rives. To Lady Battersea's amusement, Meredith chose this juncture for declaring that no woman had ever written a first-rate novel. Jane Austen, Charlotte Brontë, and George Eliot were demolished in turn, while the American lady sighed deeply to express her injured feelings.

During this summer also he was persuaded by Sir Trevor and Lady Lawrence to sit for his portrait to the most fashionable artist of the day, Sargent. On seeing the result, he was disgusted to find himself depicted as an old man. "I beheld," he told "Michael Field," "a face of gruel in which floated balls like the eyes of a codfish kept for three days in ice. There were also brown concaves in the gruel. The nose was a reed shaken in the wind; the grim mouth was packed full of savage teeth—and this was an Impressionist's impression of me. One eye was completely dead. Sargent made me an amiable Shade."

He must have been aware that with the growth of his fame a cluster of legend was attaching itself to him. Except to trusted friends, he remained reticent about his birth and parentage. As late as 1901 he would not give these details even for a census. Clodd was staying with him at the time and undertook to save him the trouble of filling out the forms in his distorted handwriting. When Clodd got to the question, "Place of birth," Meredith demanded, "Is that necessary?" "Yes." "Well, put Hampshire." "That's too vague; you'll have the paper returned for more definite answer." "Then say near Petersfield." And in the space for "occupation" Meredith would not allow "author" and insisted on "has private means."

In the absence of facts, literary columnists were driven back upon surmise. The coincidence in the choice of pen name by Bulwer-Lytton's son, "Owen Meredith," which had long caused confusion between the identities of the two writers, was seized upon as a clue to some relationship. Grant Allen used to say they were so much alike that they must be half-brothers. Other quidnuncs used *Harry Richmond* as a source for the suggestion that its author was an offspring of royalty.

A different chapter of the legend was devoted to his prowess as a talker. When Bernard Shaw had exceeded even his own record of loquacity by preaching Socialism at an open-air meeting on a rainy Sunday at Trafford Bridge, Manchester, for four hours, his friends Henry Salt and Clement Shorter hatched a scheme to bring him to Box Hill to meet Meredith. Shaw was to start talking the moment he entered the door and to continue for four hours without letting Meredith interject a word. This is Shaw's version of the story. Salt protests that the proposal was entirely Shaw's own, "and much too reckless to have any other source." However it originated, the plan was not carried out; but the idea was so fascinating that it passed into literary folk-lore, and more than one contemporary memoir contains a circumstantial narrative of the encounter.

His withdrawal from authorship did not extend to poetry. Instead, he embarked upon his most ambitious undertaking, a series of odes on French history, expressing his exalted admiration for the spirit of France. He finished the one on "The French Revolution" before the end of September, 1896, and started work upon "Napoleon." They had to share his attention, however, with the duller work of revising his novels for a new collected edition that was to be brought out by Constable & Company. Gissing was perturbed when Meredith told him that he was "slashing at them"; and certainly some of the changes seem merely capricious. The first volume, *Richard Feverel*, now subjected to revision for the second time, was brought out in the autumn. Sargent's portrait was used as frontispiece for the edition de luxe; contrary to Meredith's opinion, it showed all the bristling vigor of his defiant old age.

This project led to the final round in the combat between the American houses of Roberts and Scribner. On a visit to New York, Otto Kyllman of Constable & Company discussed with Charles Scribner the desirability of issuing the collected edition concurrently in the United States. The obstacle was Roberts' possession of the rights for the earlier novels. After returning to London, Kyllman proposed that Scribner's could take out a fresh copyright on all the books, in view of the changes that had been made in the text. Meredith wished "some friendly arrangement" with Roberts Brothers by which they would consent to discontinue their edition; but if they rejected "a reasonable proposal" Scribner's would be legally justified in bringing out the revised volumes.

Scribner's replied cautiously that they would like to issue the revised edition, but that it would be difficult for them to purchase the rights from Roberts and that Meredith had better make the arrangement himself. "So far as my father and myself are aware," Will Meredith protested, "they have no claim whatever upon those works of his which they have published . . . I do not feel that we need consider them further in the matter." He proceeded to send Scribner's the proofs of the revised *Richard Feverel* so that their edition could be set up immediately.

Charles Scribner refused to run the risk of infringing the rights of the rival firm. Roberts Brothers reasserted their claim through advertisements warning purchasers against the "mutilated" new edition, and they notified Scribner's that they were prepared to embark upon a price-cutting war if necessary. Will Meredith began to realize with dismay that the whole American copyright of his father's works might be lost in the struggle, for the revised edition was on the eve of appearing in England, with no agreement for its protection in the United

States. He suggested desperately that Scribner's and Roberts should enter into a joint agreement for the issuing of uniform complete sets. When this fantastic scheme was rejected, Kyllman managed to persuade Roberts Brothers to surrender their plates and stock of the Meredith novels for the comfortable sum of $6000.

The outlook for the collected edition in England was good: half of the de luxe sets were subscribed for even before a prospectus was issued. Separately from it the *Essay on Comedy* was brought out in November, somewhat revised from its first printing in *The New Quarterly Magazine*. William Archer greeted it as "one of the subtlest, wittiest, and most luminous pieces of criticism in the English language"; and even the captious Bernard Shaw, discussing it in *The Saturday Review*, called it "an excellent, even superfine, essay by perhaps the highest living English authority on its subject." These other tasks conflicted so gravely with the French odes that Meredith was only midway in the second one at the beginning of December, though full of confidence in them: "It is History—my view; and I make History sing! Clio in Calliope."

On a somber day in early winter Miss Bradley and Miss Cooper paid their last visit. They were greeted with the news that a female journalist from London would also be present—self-invited, Meredith hastened to add, for otherwise the poetic ladies would have felt "angered through every bristle at such an unhonoured guest being asked to share our few hours at Flint Cottage." Meredith talked first about the intense pressure under which he was writing the French odes. Then he praised Mrs Meynell at tactless length. The newspaper woman, arriving late for lunch, proved to have "a fleshy face—all the features flesh, as an uncooked pie is paste—eyes that are points in the unmeaning knobbiness, a laugh that sibilantly flatters, stiff body and chestnut clothes." Miss Bradley expressed surprise when he offered cigarettes—did he really approve of ladies' smoking? Even his after-lunch cigar was a subject for Miss Cooper's petulance; he looked, she said, "remarkably fine with the delicate gyration of the smoke-circles round his sinuous face—not a prophet but a god of snarls and irony in Pythian comradeship."

The newspaper woman took possession of the chair at Meredith's better ear and produced a parcel from her string bag. "Not a gift, I trust," he protested. "Only a little thing to amuse you," the lady warbled, unwrapping a model of the Dresden bridal cup. "You see, dear friend, it is only a toy." After an unseemly argument, he compelled the visitor to retain the cup to give it to his son and daughter-in-law, with Miss Cooper's silent approbation—"the gift is indelicate from a widow to a widower."

Miss Cooper was reduced to playing with the dog in a corner of the room, while the stronger-minded "Michael" (Miss Bradley) invaded the conversation from time to time with contradictions of Meredith's remarks, but did not rouse him to scintillate. At long last the cab for the lady poets was due and they went to put on their wraps. On their return they found him intently autographing the new edition of *Richard Feverel*.

*With the absorption of age he hardly notices Michael's hand with a touch —he says to me carelessly, "You will excuse my rising." I am silent and bow like a snow-laden tree, while Michael's voice rings out as if a challenge were thrown down, "Good-bye, Mr Meredith,"—an alarmed, hurrying "God bless you"—and we are in the cab with seething hearts.*

Recurrence of his bladder trouble was making him feel miserable. He explained to Maxse that "the work I am doing pushed to write at night, and that, I suppose, must be the cause of my breakdown." He consulted Buckston Browne on Christmas eve and learned that he must undergo another operation. Frank Harris, on hearing the news, went anxiously to the hospital "and found him in bed laughing and chatting with friends who had come to see him. 'Science has abolished pain,' he said gaily, 'and with pain even the need of steeling oneself; the doctors have made the ford easy, we can't even feel the chill of the water.'" The operation was performed on December 30 and recovery was rapid. Before the end of January he could tell Mrs Meynell that he was "just able to think of the Napoleon." The editor of a magazine called *Cosmopolis* visited him and obtained permission to print all three of the odes.

Through his friendship with William Sharp, Meredith was now involved, without knowing it, in a strange mystification. In 1894 Sharp wrote a book of Highland lore in poetic prose, entitled *Pharais*. It was so utterly different from either his literary criticism or his conventional poetry that he published it under a feminine and Gaelic pen name, "Fiona Macleod." The book was received more cordially than any of his acknowledged work, Meredith being among its admirers; he called it "pure Celtic salt," a book "to fly sure to its mark."

So much curiosity was aroused by this unknown genius that Sharp had difficulty in maintaining his disguise. Two or three of his most intimate friends shared his secret, but to everyone else he explained that she was his cousin, a shy recluse who seldom left her remote Scottish home; and he persuaded an actual cousin to deal with the correspondence that was addressed to "Miss Macleod."

The fame of the book encouraged Sharp to write others in the same style. A copy of the second one was sent to Meredith with a letter in which Miss Macleod called herself "one of your most loyal readers" and dubbed him "Prince of Celtland." Naturally he responded warmly: in both books he found a "thrill . . . as of the bard of the three-stringed harp, and the wild western colour over sea and isles; true spirit of the mountains. How rare this is. I do not know it elsewhere. Be sure that I am among those readers of yours whom you kindle."

Sharp, too deeply involved for escape, especially dreaded the possibility of Meredith's discovering the imposture. When the Celto-phile Grant Allen expressed an intention of writing an essay on Miss Macleod's work, he received an anxious letter from her: "I trust you will not hint playfully at any other authorship having suggested itself to you—or, indeed, at my name being a pseudonym. And, sure, it will be for pleasure to me if you will be as scrupulous with Mr Meredith or anyone else in private, as in public, if chance should ever bring my insignificant self into any chit-chat." Whatever suspicions the keen-witted Allen may have entertained, he did not convey them to Meredith, who bestirred himself the next year to recommend Miss Macleod's latest book, *Green Fire*, to Scribner's for American publication.

By 1897, the mystery deepened. The official biography of Sharp, written by his wife, implies that the impersonation was always confined to correspondence, and that no one ever saw the elusive Highland lady. This seems to be confirmed by Le Gallienne, who states, "Sharp further mystified me by saying that 'Fiona Macleod' was shortly coming to London, and that he intended to introduce her to three people only—George Meredith, W. B. Yeats, and myself. These introductions were never made." On the other hand, there is positive evidence that she was taken to visit Meredith. Katharine Tynan says that Meredith was the only person who was "supposed to have seen Fiona in the flesh." Sharp himself declared in a letter to Ernest Rhys, "I took her to see George Meredith, at his own earnest request, and he was enchanted by her dark Highland beauty." And Meredith's own report of the visit is to be found in a letter to Alice Meynell: "Miss Fiona Macleod was here on a day of last week: a handsome person, who would not give me her eyes for a time. One fears she was not playing at abashment. Even after I had brought her to laugh, the eyelids drooped." Mrs Sharp in her book merely says that on June 10 her husband "went for a night to Burford Bridge to have some talks with George Meredith." The only explanation can be that he took the dangerous step of getting his Scottish cousin to represent Fiona for once in the flesh as well as in letters; the lady's averted eyes would be natural enough as she listened to the great man's compliments and Celtic rhapsodies.

He was steadily losing the fight against helplessness. The Brandreths and their now widowed daughter had continued to have him as an overnight guest from time to time at their house in Elvaston Square; but his increasing difficulty with the steep stairs culminated in a fall which painfully hurt his leg, and so it was decided that he should not come again. When Lord and Lady Battersea invited him for a second visit to Overstrand, he was loath to accept, and almost for the first time he acknowledged his disabilities. "Why do they want a cripple, deafish of one ear?" he asked Mrs Meynell. "My one satisfaction is being the least possible burden to others, not exposed to compassion." His daughter, however, had taken a house there for September, and the temptation of being near her and her two baby girls overcame his reluctance. Lady Battersea was impressed by his affection for the grandchildren, with whom he spent much of his time every day.

The French odes were slowly completed. "Napoleon" was sent to Mrs Meynell for her opinion in the middle of June, with some misgiving: "I have been tempted by the rhetorical—History's pitfall for the Muse. I have avoided it as much as I could, even in the Portrait, where antithesis invited strongly and was not always to be shunned." Six months later, when he had finished the third one, "Alsace-Lorraine," he did not send it to her because he was sure it would not really appeal to her sensitive taste—"these historic themes insist on an amount of rhetoric unless one vaporizes and symbolizes." And to Greenwood he wrote defensively, "You will think the Odes are long. But they do not dawdle, for the tussle between the soul of France and the Napoleonic grip has to be shown." After their magazine publication they were brought out in a volume, along with the "France, December, 1870," reprinted from a previous book. The title was *Odes in Contribution to the Song of French History.*

Rhetorical they undeniably were, but it was noble and sincere rhetoric, appropriate to the vastitude of the subject. Only Swinburne's odes on contemporary European events can be compared with them, and Swinburne's eloquence sometimes sounds shrill beside Meredith's rugged grandeur. On the other hand, his emphasis was often abrupt and violent, and the symbolism had all his usual obscurity. Most of the reviewers condemned them for these faults. Even Mrs Meynell, writing in *The Bookman*, said, "It is, indeed, a strange irony of fate that the lucid genius of France should be sung in such desperately tortured and turgid strain"; she deplored that there was "a defective expression and a carelessness of beauty," but added that parts of them were "marvels of brilliant energy, genuine kindling fires lighting the sky." And Francis Thompson, discussing the first ode upon its magazine publication, declared, "I am in tune with most audacity, but Mr Meredith leaves me gasping . . . The Ode is wonderful, though an unlawful wonder . . . The poem has a devil in it . . . No youth could rival the nether furnaces of this production of age." Experts testify to the deep insight into historical processes that the odes displayed; but as the subject matter of them was more remote from general interest than that of his other poetry had been, their effect was to reinforce the opinion that his work was impenetrably cryptic and willfully uncouth.

His friends knew that his seventieth birthday would occur in February, 1898, and decided to make it the occasion of a testimonial. Edmund Gosse records that "the idea of this congratulation originated with Leslie Stephen, who associated Thomas Hardy and myself with him in carrying out the scheme. But in the midst of the preparation, Stephen suggested that our exertions would probably be in vain, since 'it was hardly to be hoped, or perhaps feared,' that Meredith would reach his seventieth birthday."

In spite of these misgivings, the committee collected signatures to an address from "some comrades in letters who have long valued your work"; it declared that "you have attained the first rank in literature after many years of inadequate recognition. From first to last you have been true to yourself and have always aimed at the highest mark." The thirty signatories ranged from some of his oldest friends—Swinburne, Morley, and Stephen—to such unexpected names as the Bishop of London and Field Marshal Viscount Wolseley.

"The recognition," he wrote sincerely to Stephen, "touches me deeply. Pray let it be known to them how much they encourage and support me." But he was equally sincere when he commented to Clodd, "I know what they mean, kindly enough. Poor old devil, he *will* go on writing; let us cheer him up. The old fire isn't quite out; a stir of the poker may bring out a shoot of gas."

At the beginning of 1898 Alfred Sutro, a rising young playwright, became eager to dramatize *The Egoist*, and persuaded Forbes-Robertson that the part of Sir Willoughby would be ideal for him. Sutro was brought down to Box Hill by William Archer, the dramatic critic, to broach the scheme. Maxse and Clodd were also dining there, and Meredith's choicest wines were served with the courses. As Archer was a prim and abstemious man, there was eventually a platoon of full glasses in front of him. Meredith's clearest tones suddenly rang out, "I am afraid, Mr Archer, you don't like my wine." "Oh, yes, Mr Meredith, indeed I do," gasped the abashed critic, and he took a gulp out of each glass in turn.

To Sutro's relief, Meredith was gracious to him and gave him permission to prepare an outline of the play. They worked on it for almost a year, and the young dramatist's periodical visits to Flint Cottage elicited some of Meredith's good anecdotes and his customary gibes against the critics. All suggestions of making plays from his novels had previously been rejected on the ground that no one else could put words into the mouths of his characters. Sutro therefore adhered religiously to the existing conversations while Meredith himself wrote many pages of additional dialogue, in his most sprightly style; the collaborator sometimes had the difficult task of suggesting that it was too long. When the play was finished, there were only two sentences that Sutro had dared to insert, and he "positively swelled with glory" when the author approved them.

Gissing, who visited Meredith with Clodd on November 13, found him "far from well." He was sitting with the typescript of the dramatization on his knees, and said he had little faith in it. Two weeks later his son notified Scribner's that the play was ready and that Forbes-Robertson was under contract to produce it before the end of February. "My father has written the whole of the dialogue practically . . . It is pure comedy of the highest order and will take rank among the work of my father." Forbes-Robertson and the leading lady were entertained along with Sutro at Box Hill, for the final discussion of details.

After all these high expectations, the production never occurred. The financial backers decided that it would cost too much; the leading lady had a tantrum and quarreled with the manager. Forbes-Robertson took advantage of a flaw in the contract to avoid paying any indemnity.

It was probably Meredith's interest in this venture that stimulated him to return to his comedy, *The Sentimentalists*, which had been started in 1862, resumed briefly in 1870, and advertised in 1883 among his "Forthcoming Publications." He now rewrote the first five scenes, but got no further. After his death the various drafts were woven into a graceful but flimsy play by Barrie, and achieved a production— mainly as a gesture of respect—at a London theatre. The influence of Peacock was manifest in the group of character types who talk their way through it.

The walls were closing in. During the summer of 1898 Meredith declined the Batterseas' invitation for a third visit to Overstrand; and he admitted to "Portia"—as he now called Alice Meynell—that "I could rejoice to see you, and at the same time hate to be seen." He underwent another bladder operation the following March, and this one effected a lasting cure. The offer of an honorary degree by Oxford University was regretfully declined because of his inability to come to an Encaenia to receive it.

Now that he was a celebrity his uncurbed conversation could be dangerous. In September, 1898, he received a French journalist, Charles Legras, who was writing a series of "Visits to our English Contemporaries" for *Le Journal des Débats*. Meredith's remarks, as frank as usual, included a sneer at Alfred Austin's appointment as Poet Laureate. When the interview appeared in Paris, the titbits were picked up by London papers, to his embarrassment. *The Daily Chronicle* (obviously at his request) announced that he had not known Legras was interviewing him for publication, and that anyhow he had not uttered any of the quoted comments. Legras flatly contradicted both assertions.

The latest admirer was the Marchioness of Granby (subsequently Duchess of Rutland), who was an amateur artist of some ability. She not only drew his portrait but also presented him with sketches of several beautiful young women, including her own daughters and Lady Ulrica Duncombe, daughter of the Earl of Feversham. Lady Ulrica proved to resemble the ideal heroines of his novels, combining beauty and social distinction with the serious interests that had been fostered when she was an undergraduate at Girton. He decided that she was one who might profit by his garnered wisdom: for several years he gave her books and wrote long letters to her on literature, politics, and social problems, garnished occasionally with a compliment or a playful gibe at her lack of interest in young men.

Paying court to attractive women was one of the few pastimes that he could still engage in, and he made the most of it. "He spoke to them all," says Morley Roberts, "as if he loved them at first sight and would willingly kneel at their feet. I had seen this first when I had occasion to take down to Box Hill a lady whom he had desired to meet. In his most charming way—and he could be inexpressibly charming—he made delightful love to her with words so appropriate to an old man adoring beauty for the last time, that I was filled with admiration for his delicate intimation of a sudden sorrowful and hopeless passion . . . When I saw him later I asked him if he had been able to recognize the beauty of this particular lady's voice . . . 'Her voice? her voice?' said Meredith. 'Ah, no, I could not really hear her. But oh, her eyes, her eyes!' "

The amatory fervor in his letters to beautiful ladies shocked some of his friends when a selection of his correspondence was published after his death. "Haldane is slightly scandalized at the revelation of Meredith as a philanderer," Gosse wrote to Henry James. "Really, some of those last letters to ladies are a little excessive, are they not? Anacreon, with vine leaves askew in his grey curls, astride a cask of sherry."

In public affairs his chief concern was the South African War, which he bitterly condemned from the time of the Jameson Raid onward. As he had told Olive Schreiner twenty years earlier, he admired the sturdy Boer farmers; and he felt that England was guilty of disastrous bungling in allowing hostilities to develop. Frank Harris, who was an out-and-out pro-Boer, fell out with him for refusing to discredit every allegation of brutality laid against the Boers; but this was consistent with his avoidance of extreme positions.

Admiral Maxse died on July 1, 1900. For forty years Meredith had loved him with a sense of absolute trust, and had never faltered in admiration for his quixotic idealism, even while tirelessly teasing him. The tinge of schoolboy hero-worship in Meredith had concentrated itself in this one friendship. He told Alice Meynell that the bereavement had "shaken my stoic philosophy for the moment. I would so willingly have gone in his place, had there been the choice. I have lived so close to the dead that we converse, *he*, in his tones as I know them, and so patient of my rallyings, with the reluctant laugh."

Meredith's last collection of verse, *A Reading of Life*, was published in 1901. Its most remarkable item was "Fragments of the Iliad in English Hexameter Verse," which he had written ten years before and had discussed eagerly with his visitors at that time. The rest of the poems suffered from his habit of abstract and didactic philosophizing, except two that were poignant records of his immobilized but vital old age: a tiny lyric, "Song in the Songless," which symbolized all his spiritual pertinacity in forty-four words, and "A Night Walk," which recalled the glory of energy and the confidence of youth as felt in some moonlight expedition with a friend long ago.

One of the young writers brought down to be introduced to him was Desmond MacCarthy. In a proper spirit of hero-worship he arrived at Flint Cottage on a December afternoon in 1901, and while still in the narrow passage he could hear "the resonant rumble of a voice. The great man was talking to his dog."

Old age had blurred his eyelids, and his eyes, once blue, were faded and full of "the empty untragic sadness of old age"; but that vitality which had inspired many a packed page still vibrated in his powerful voice, and told in the impetuosity of his greeting. His talk was full of flourishes and his enunciation grandiose, as though he loved the sound of his own words . . . He talked with a kind of swagger . . . The eagerness with which he would now and again curve a hand round his ear and stoop forward to catch an interjection, showed that he was not a born monologist, and that he missed the give and take.

My Irish name set him off upon the theme of Celt and Saxon. The English were not in favour with him just then; the Boer War (he detested it) was dragging lamely on, and he belaboured the English with the vigour and bitterness of a disillusioned patriot . . . He accused the English of lack of imagination in statecraft, and abused their manners and their unsociability, their oafish contempt of friendly liveliness and wit, the sluggish casual rudeness that passed among the wealthy for good form; mouthing out sentences he had used, I felt, before, and throwing himself back, before a burst of laughter, with the air of one saying, "There, what do you think of that?" to watch upon our faces the effect of some fantastic, hammered phrase . . .

There was still such a fund of invincible vitality in him that it was incongruous to hear him bemoaning himself as one already dead and better buried: "Nature cares not a pin for the individual; I am content to be shoved into the ditch." . . . A nurse appeared and stood over him, with a graduated glass containing some dismal fluid in her hand; and we, who had forgotten we had been listening for two hours to an old invalid, took our leave. I looked from the door. He had sunk back in his chair, and with a wave of his hand he sketched an Oriental salaam.

Through Clodd's conniving he had been made an honorary member of the Whitefriars Club, in which London journalists kept up a determined effort to be jolly and Bohemian. The consequence was that the Club twice—in 1900 and 1902—held its summer meeting at Burford Bridge, lunching at the hotel and then spending the afternoon in the garden at Flint Cottage. There was a faint air of a royal levee as the "Friars" and their ladies filed past Meredith in his chair, to shake hands and hear a few words of greeting, after which they rambled among the flower beds and tiptoed reverently into the now dust-strewn chalet. During the second visit an address of homage was read, and Meredith spoke a few sentences in response: "I have no words to thank you. But look at the tops of those trees. From that short height the measure of all of us is seen to be pretty equal. Each does his work in his own way. I find so many people in different walks who can do what I cannot do. Respect is a very great thing, but I think we are in the habit of falling into a kind of delirium in regard to men who after seventy or more have made a name. We take them as brandy; it is better to make a kind of dilution, and therefore I mix a considerable amount of water with your compliments . . ."

His unwillingness to accept awards was now attributable to physical disability as well as to his inherent dislike of ceremonies. The University of Wales, in March, 1902, voted to confer upon him the honorary degree of D. Litt., but the distinction had to be declined, as the one from Oxford had been.

A new visitor to Box Hill about this time was Henry W. Nevinson, a war correspondent and critic who pleased Meredith with his bold support of unpopular causes. Nevinson described him rhapsodically:

*The great mouth opens almost foursquare. It is an Attic mask, a magician's cave. A spirit seems to be speaking, not with it, but through it, and on a broad scale of sound comes the voice, full, unhesitating, and distinct to the last letter, like the voice of one who has spoken much among the waves . . . There is no effort about the language; the great sentences are thrown out with lavish opulence—the careless opulence of Nature at her kindest. There is no pausing for figures, wit, or epigrams; they come of themselves, as water follows water from a spring.*

Meredith had hitherto refused to grant press interviews on the ground that an author should be known only through his writings. In February, 1903, however, he made an exception in favor of Harold Owen, of *The Manchester Guardian*, because of his respect for that paper's sturdy Liberalism. His remarks on "the present position of the Liberal party" occupied three full columns. He spoke frankly and forcibly. Britain, he said, had become an imperial power without formulating any coherent imperial policy. "We have a Parliament that is brought together too much on the old lines . . . The Australians and the Canadians are moving ahead of us in certain directions." He wanted to see the English working classes abandon their political apathy and take "a livelier, steady, and constant interest in the affairs of the country." A major cause of weakness, he believed, was that education was still too much in the hands of the clergy, "who are very good and honourable men as regards conduct, but who have no large view of the necessities of the national and political situations." He regretted that the South African republics had not been left independent, and he advocated immediate Home Rule for Ireland as the only way to forestall violence there. After commenting bluntly on the merits and defects of various party leaders, he stated that the Liberal party "will have no chance with the country unless it opens its arms to the Radicals."

The article stirred up amazing excitement. Most of the chief London and provincial papers reprinted long passages and many of them discussed it editorially. The Liberals hailed it as courageous and stimulating, the Conservatives smothered it in ridicule. At last Meredith received nation-wide recognition—not as an author but as a political pundit.

In the spring of 1903 he was laid up for weeks, and he was still being denied to most visitors late in June when Sharp came to see him. After a decade of writing mainly in the guise of Fiona Macleod, Sharp seemed almost to believe that his personality had been absorbed into that of the Highland woman. Finding Meredith frail and weak, he had a premonition that they would never meet again, and he felt that Meredith believed so too. The visitor was both flattered and embarrassed to realize that Meredith admired Fiona as warmly as ever. Mrs Gordon claims that he told her that he knew Fiona Macleod to be actually William Sharp, "but he sincerely hoped that Mr Sharp would never know that he had penetrated the secret of his pseudonym. He admired his work, and had the deepest comprehension of and sympathy with his wish to 'hide his journalistic appearance under a veil.' " If this had ever been so, however, he must have forgotten it by the time Sharp came to see him. In a detailed record of the visit, Sharp wrote:

*I could have (selfishly) wished that he had known a certain secret: but it is better not, and now it is in every way as undesirable as indeed impossible . . . What I did tell him before has absolutely passed from his mind: had, indeed, never taken root, and perhaps I had nurtured rather than denied what had taken root . . . At the end he spoke in a way he might not otherwise have done, and in words I shall never forget. I had risen, and was about to lean forward and take his hands in farewell, to prevent his half-rising, when suddenly he exclaimed, "Tell me something of her—of Fiona. I call her so always, and think of her so, to myself. Is she well? Is she at work? Is she true to herself and her ideal? No, that I know! She is a woman of genius. That is rare, so rare anywhere, in women, or in men. Some few women 'have genius,' but she is more than that. Yes, she is a woman of genius: the genius, too, that is rarest, that* drives deep thoughts before it. Tell her I think often of her, and of the deep thoughts in all she has written of late. Tell her I hope great things of her yet. And now . . . we'll go, since it must be so. Good-bye, my dear fellow, and God bless you."

It was, in truth, their farewell interview, for Sharp went abroad, and died two and a half years later. Subsequently the secret of Fiona's identity leaked out, and Meredith wrote to Alice Meynell in distress:

*He brought her to me, and she accepted my praises. A letter came to me saying that it was to be delivered when his breath was gone, and that it was "a mystery," but that he was the author. In none of his printed work, verse or prose, was there a sign of imagination or of simple fluency; and the Fiona papers have both. I am puzzled.*

In the whole strange story, one of the most pathetic touches is this quirk of conscience that drove Sharp to leave a posthumous confession for the man he had revered most deeply and deceived most ingeniously.

Dangerous illness kept Meredith helpless during the later months of 1903. When newspapers reported him in a critical condition, with only brief intervals of partial consciousness, he issued a bulletin:

*Report of me incorrect; though why my name should be blown about, whether I am well or ill, I do not know. The difficulty with me is to obtain unconsciousness; but sleep, on the whole, comes fairly. I am going on well enough. This for friends who will have been distressed by the report.*

It was true, nevertheless, that he had been close to death. He grumbled that "a meddlesome fellow thought himself professionally bound to practice an injection on my arm, and the heart was roused to resume its labours." For nearly six months he was kept at his daughter's house at Leatherhead, barely strong enough to sign his name. In February he received a letter from Stephen, written virtually on his deathbed, conveying his "satisfaction and pride in thinking of your affection"; and in reply Meredith wrote, "We who have loved the motion of legs and the sweep of the winds, we come to this. But for myself, I will own that it is the Natural order. There is no irony in Nature." Stephen died a few days later.

Surviving friends were all the more cherished. Morley was visiting him more frequently than for many years past, and Meredith reveled in their discussions of books and history. Telling Haldane to bring anyone he liked whenever he came to Box Hill, he added, "But don't bring Morley, for he and I have evenings together which we must have alone, because we have a past which is outside the time of you young men." Greenwood was another of the faithful. When the super-journalist, W. T. Stead, came down, Meredith was "so simple-minded" that he "took it for a friendly visit" from an old *Pall Mall Gazette* colleague; but a few months afterwards, in March, 1904, he found his remarks printed in *The Review of Reviews.*

Stead quoted some of his provocative views, notably a comic suggestion that he had once made to a Cabinet minister, that some English defects could be remedied only by sending a liner over to raid the coast of France and bring back a cargo of women as wives for English rustics. There was a note of defiance in his description of himself:

*People talk about me as if I were an old man. I do not feel old in the least. On the contrary, I do not believe in growing old, and I do not see any reason why we should ever die. I take as keen an interest in the movement of life as ever, and I enter into the passions of youth, and I watch political affairs and intrigues of parties, with the same keen interest as of old. I have seen the illusion of it all, but it does not dull the zest with which I enter into it, and I hold more firmly than ever to my faith in the constant advancement of the race.*

Publication of this article led other journalists to ask his opinions on various matters, and in the summer Clodd persuaded him to grant an authorized interview to Nevinson, for *The Daily Chronicle.* The only proviso was a ban on shorthand. Among his pronouncements, these were the most notable: "The English people have little real love for Nature . . . Forty years ago I had to give up going to church because I could not listen to the nonsense I heard spoken there any longer . . . The Japanese are a more valuable race than the Russians from Nature's point of view." He asserted that all professions ought to be open to women, and he gave a prescription for a good newspaper: "You must be democratic in politics but maintain an aristocracy in literature. All art is aristocratic in so far as it aims only at the very highest and must be content with nothing less. Popularity and democratic opinion have nothing to do with literature." Afterwards, when Morley Roberts asked him whether he was satisfied with the report, he answered with a prodigious sigh, "Oh, he got what I said, but none of my beautiful words, none of my beautiful words!"

In July he enjoyed a visit from Janet Ross, whom he had loved forty years ago. During her long residence in the Val d'Arno she had developed into a fabulous specimen of the expatriated Englishwoman, writing cookery books, selling expensive vermouth to her friends, and waging war on the peasants who shot songbirds. When she wrote a book of memoirs in 1890, Meredith arranged for its publication by Chapman & Hall, but forced her to omit all excerpts from his letters. Now she was delighted to find that "the old fire and brilliancy were there, and we talked for two or three hours about old times and old friends, most of them, alas, dead. 'You have something of Rose in you still, my dear,' he said, smiling rather sadly as I got up to go; 'those were pleasant days.' "

Age and pain had mellowed him. A platitudinous remark would still evoke a sarcastic or scornful onslaught, so that some self-conscious young writers who heard reports of these fearsome pounces refused to be introduced to him, in case they might be unable to hold their own. And there was no diminution in the ludicrous fantasies that he could invent at the expense of his friends. But listeners were no longer disturbed by a hard edge of cruelty in his jests. He cherished the few survivors of his old circle with a warmth bordering upon the sentimentality that he despised. A testimonial dinner was tendered to Greenwood in April, 1905; and E. V. Lucas, who visited Flint Cottage that morning, was entrusted with a bunch of violets from the garden, to be presented to the honored guest. A few weeks later Hardy paid a visit to Box Hill. "I am always glad to see him," Meredith told Gosse, "and have regrets at his going; for the double reason that I like him and am afflicted by his twilight view of life." In response to Hardy's request for advice, he encouraged him to continue writing *The Dynasts*, of which the first volume had been published; but he refrained from uttering his private opinion that it ought to have been written in prose.

Official recognition was eventually conferred. When he was sounded out regarding his willingness to be made a baronet he rejected the suggestion flatly—"a title would have sunk me," he declared. But he was more receptive toward an alternative. King Edward had recently founded the Order of Merit, with a strictly limited membership, selected for intellectual and artistic achievement. Suspecting that Morley, already a member, had something to do with the offer, Meredith let him know that "I could not be churlish in this case. Besides, I am to be ranked with and near you." After accepting it, he was notified, to his consternation, that he must attend an investiture, in levee dress, at Buckingham Palace—an impossibility to one in his crippled condition.

He spent August at Aldeburgh, Suffolk, where Clodd had for many years maintained a country home at which he gloried in entertaining his distinguished literary friends. The North Sea fishing village had been the birthplace of George Crabbe, and Meredith found it to be "a place without charm, like Crabbe's poetry; only grandeur of Sea. It lifted and steadied me to its own dead level." Shorter and other good talkers came down from London from time to time and enlivened him with the current literary gossip.

The procession of notable visitors continued when he was at home at Box Hill. Haldane brought David Lloyd George, a Welsh firebrand after his own heart. Another time, Haldane's companion was Sir John French, a military hero of the recent war, and Meredith launched into an argument with him about the disposition of troops at the Battle of Magenta. "No one with any military knowledge," the General declared, "could have imagined that at that stage a whole division could have been brought up to the point where you say they should have been." "General," Meredith retorted, "I have observed that cavalry leaders, however distinguished, are bad judges of the operations of mixed troops." Haldane decided that the moment was opportune for summoning the motorcar that was to take French back to Aldershot.

It was not only on military history that he paraded his knowledge. Nevinson observed that "his highest interest appears to lie far more in the great movements of the world than in what is called pure literature . . . I well remember his extreme disappointment when I could not tell him the exact origin of some disagreement between two little South American states, whose very existence was a matter of indifference to almost everyone else in England." His fascination with warfare and distant countries revealed a sense of unfulfillment in his own experience: he felt that he ought to have been a fighter or an explorer. He expressed his envy of the "rich, rough life" that Morley Roberts had lived in remote colonies.

With his growing infirmity, his faithful gardener Cole had taken on the duties of valet and bodyguard. In October, 1905, when tottering out on Cole's arm for a walk in the garden, he tripped over the scullery threshold and fell, breaking his right ankle. For a month he had to lie on his back with the leg in a "gallows," as he called it; "then permission to lie on the right side or the left—luxury immense, until the thought of people up and moving caused the bed to seem an implacable rack. However, I wore a smile through it, and chaffed Doctor, nurse, and myself. The thing to do in such a case is to rise humourously above one's body, which is the veritable rebel, not the mind." Edmund Gosse, never one of his admirers, commented acidly on the accident in a letter to Hardy: "He appears to be quite cheerful about that too. What a very curious thing temperament is—there seems no reason at all why G. M. should be so happy, and in some irrational way one almost resents it."

Morley meanwhile bestirred himself in the matter of the investiture, and the King graciously instructed an equerry to bring the insignia down to Box Hill and perform the ceremony in Meredith's bedroom. Three years later William Strang, A.R.A., was sent to make a portrait of him for the O.M. collection in the Windsor Castle Library.

The broken leg caused a change in his daily routines, for his power of walking was more restricted than ever. The dining-room at Flint Cottage was converted into a bedroom for him, and so he had to relinquish the pleasure of entertaining his visitors to any meal except an informal snack in the drawing-room. As life would be unendurable for him without a daily jaunt in the open air, a donkey chair was provided; and the neighbors became accustomed to the sight of the white-bearded author sitting in the little vehicle, wrapped in cape and rugs, while Cole guided "Picnic," the donkey, and Bessy Nicholls, Meredith's nurse, who had become another devoted retainer, brought up the rear. The long dynasty of dachshunds had been succeeded by a West Highland terrier, "Sandie," which also was invariably included in the entourage.

Meredith's political interest was keener than ever. Haldane being Secretary for War, and Morley Secretary for India, he was concerned over the destinies of the new Liberal Cabinet, and attracted comment in the newspapers by his remarks on Joseph Chamberlain, who was leading the Conservatives' election campaign in favor of imperial expansion and protective tariffs. Meredith called him a "motorman let loose" and denounced him as "a man of tremendous energy acting on one idea. You see it in the lean, long head and adventurer's nose." On election day, in spite of midwinter weather and his recent accident, he insisted upon being taken the whole six miles to Leatherhead and being carried into the polling-booth to cast his vote for the Liberal candidate. Afterwards he authorized a reporter to announce his gratification that the new Parliament contained for the first time a good quota of Labour members.

The sea air of Aldeburgh had been so good for him the previous year that he went there again for the summer of 1906. Every day he was wheeled out to the ancient quay, where he would sit sniffing the aroma of a handful of seaweed and watching an old ferryman slowly rowing his boat back and forth across the Alde. It was "my one intellectual amusement here," he reported, and he was annoyed when his nurse decreed that he must not sit in the breeze for more than five minutes, because he had caught a cough.

"I began with poetry," he told Clodd in 1905, "and I shall finish with it." Now that his writing was otherwise at an end, he was being treated as a literary classic who happened to have the idiosyncrasy of being still alive. G. Lowes Dickinson portrayed him in the character of Geoffrey Vivian in *A Modern Symposium*, a discursive novel much in Meredith's own vein. George Macaulay Trevelyan, a brilliant Cambridge historian, published an excellent book on *The Poetry and Philosophy of George Meredith*, and its subject was gratified to be anatomized by the grandnephew of Macaulay and the husband of a grandniece of Matthew Arnold. He told Trevelyan that the exposition of his meaning was clear and had his approval, and that he was even glad of the "trouncing" bestowed on him here and there in the book, "for it serves to counterbalance a degree of praise hardly digestible by reviewers." Soon afterwards, another capable book was written about him by Mrs Mary Sturge Henderson, entitled *George Meredith, Novelist, Poet, Reformer*; and one by Richard Curle followed a year later. An earnest Scot wrote a whole book to elucidate *The Shaving of Shagpat*. Arundell Esdaile compiled a full-dress bibliography of his writings. "They say this or that is Meredithian," he remarked to Clodd. "I have become an adjective."

And still the parade of literary pilgrims continued. His old armchair beside the fireplace had become, as Barrie said, "to many the throne of letters in this country." Bernard Shaw finally paid a visit, though it was not the Homeric battle of words that had been plotted a decade earlier. "He was shoved into a corner by his family, who wanted to hear *me* all the time," says Shaw. "I was forced, against my will, to talk all through the lunch, with Meredith, distant and deaf, trying to catch what I was saying and nobody paying the least attention to him . . . But I had half an hour of private talk with him in his study before lunch. He had supported the reactionary candidate in a recent election, imagining that he represented the principles of the French Revolution, and Meredith was apologetic when I explained to him that my Fabianism was the latest thing. He was a relic of the Cosmopolitan Republican Gentleman of the previous generation."

Gilbert K. Chesterton, as might be expected, gained a totally different impression of him:

*I came up quite close to him; he looked at me as he put out his frail hand, and I saw of a sudden that his eyes were startlingly young. He was deaf and he talked like a torrent—not about the books he had written—he was far too much alive for that. He talked about the books he had not written. He asked me to write one of the stories for him, as he would have asked the milkman, if he had been talking to the milkman. It was a splendid and frantic*

*story, a sort of astronomical farce, all about a man who was rushing up to*
*The Royal Society with the only possible way of avoiding an earth-destroying*
*comet; and it showed how even on this huge errand the man was tripped up*
*by his own weaknesses and vanities; how he lost a train by trifling or was put*
*in gaol for brawling. That is only one of them . . . I really had the feeling*
*that I had seen the creative quality; which is supernatural.*

This plot, of which Chesterton mentions only one episode, had been ripening in Meredith's brain for many years: as early as 1887 he mentioned a projected story about "a Knight of Perfectibility." It was to be a sort of fantastic exaggeration of *Beauchamp's Career*, recounting the life of a "Don Quixote of the Future," a wealthy young man who infuriates everybody with his importunate schemes for the improvement of the race. Meredith finally decided that H. G. Wells would be the ideal author to take over the scheme, and in May, 1904, he summoned Wells down to Box Hill to listen to a detailed recital of the story. Wells laughed uproariously at the comic scenes, but committed himself to no promise.

Meredith's opinions on political questions were never quite in conformity with other people's. His theories about national defense were partially put into practice when Haldane, as Secretary for War, established a Territorial Army; but he felt certain that only total conscription would be an adequate safeguard against the German aggression that he clearly foresaw. He was so excited over the prospect of liberal reforms in Russia that he sponsored a subscription in 1905 on behalf of the revolutionaries. Two years later, however, when Nevinson asked him to sign a manifesto condemning the Czarist regime, he refused because he regarded it as tantamount to "declaring war on the Russian government" and he had confidence in Grey's wisdom as Foreign Secretary. His concern over crises in Ireland, in India, in Egypt, was heightened when such incendiary friends as Hyndman and Blunt published pamphlets which in his opinion would cause more harm than good through their violence. For the same reason, even though he had been one of the earliest crusaders for equality for women, he wrote a long letter to *The Times* deploring the riotous demonstrations of the suffragettes.

His cautious avoidance of precipitate action had for a long time annoyed doctrinaire friends who knew that he shared their views and who therefore expected him to join in all their campaigns. Even though he had a high esteem for G. W. Foote, the belligerent editor of *The Freethinker*, he disappointed Foote's adherents by making no public gesture of sympathy when the editor was condemned to prison in 1883 for blasphemy. Meredith merely sent the prisoner an autographed copy of his new volume of poetry. A decade later, however, he contributed a cheque to a testimonial fund being raised for Foote, who hesitated to print his name in the list of subscribers in case it should bring Meredith into disrepute. Informed of these scruples, Meredith authorized Foote to include his name, since the subscription was "in recognition of high and constant courage."

In 1895 Frank Harris tried to get up a petition for the release of Oscar Wilde from prison. He says:

*I was informed on good authority that if Meredith headed the petition and I could get five or six other men of letters to support the request, the Government would grant it without further ado . . . To my astonishment he replied that he couldn't do as I wished, and when I pressed him to let me see him in the matter, he answered that he would rather not meet me for such a purpose as his mind was made up . . . A little later I made it my business to meet Meredith as if by chance and have it out with him. To my amazement he defended his want of sympathy. Abnormal sensuality in a leader of men, he said, was a crime, and should be punished with severity . . . He became emphatic, loud, rhetorical.*

If Harris had stopped to remember Meredith's writings he would have realized that the conquest of sensual impulses was the very basis of his whole ethical doctrine.

In his final years of fame, vegetarians, anti-vivisectonists, and other assorted cranks besieged him for support. He sent a subscription to Henry Salt, as secretary of the Humanitarian League, for its campaign against spring-traps for rabbits, but said that "on a point or two of your advocacy I am not in accord with you." The Hon Stephen Coleridge asked him to sign a petition opposing vivisection, and he replied:

*In my household animals are treated as one of ourselves, and I have not found friendship with a beast to be profitless . . . I know surgeons, upright, humane men, who insist on this method of research for the good of mankind, to which the members of it as well as animals are called on to be sacrificial victims. Do I make my position clear? To my regret it holds me from supporting you . . .*

When Coleridge drafted a compromise proposal to require that all experiments on animals must use anaesthetics, Meredith heartily supported it.

In response to an invitation to join the Rational Food Reform Association, when he was eighty, he wrote jauntily:

*I am unworthy to be among you, for I drink wine and I smoke. How preach to sinners when one is guilty of these vices and unrepentant? Eating of meat has never been to my taste. But an English cook who can make vegetables of good savour will not come to a country cottage even on liberal wages. So I have in some degree to conform to the national habit: excess in which accounts for numerous maladies, to say nothing of captious tempers. Therefore I wish well to your crusade, though unfit to join it.*

His consistent attitude in these matters revealed his personality. Contrasting himself with Hardy, he told Clodd that he "kept on the causeway between the bogs of optimism and pessimism." Sentimentality he always abhorred. His sympathies were well under the control of a cool and ironic rationalism. He suspected all crusades because he could see the merits and excesses of both sides. Though he passionately loved Nature, the evolutionary theory taught him that Nature was ruthless. It taught him, too, to believe in gradual processes and to respect the struggle for survival as the only route to betterment. Perfect happiness and universal welfare could not be suddenly created by legislative act. Indeed, he doubted the desirability of such a condition, even if it were attainable. His own life had exposed him to every sort of tribulation; and from his first book to his last conversations he proclaimed his creed that worthy character can be built and tested only through the endurance of buffets.

Some of his opinions, as uttered to reporters, were far from popular. The success of his books in the United States had instilled in him a strong admiration for American intelligence and a belief that the United States would predominate in the Anglo-Saxon world. In one interview he went so far as to assert that "we should merge ourselves with the American republic. But the English are so wedded to their old institutions that there is no hope of their opening their eyes to this until it is too late. What, for instance, should we do with our crown, or our monarch, in such an alliance? Nevertheless, it is the right thing to do."

His most sensational statement to an interviewer was that all marriages ought to be for a duration of ten years, after which the contract could be renewed only if both parties were satisfied. It was a suggestion guaranteed to stir the heart of the ha'penny press, and Meredith became known to a new segment of the public, in the guise of a dangerous social rebel.

Another subject on which he was always vocal was his disbelief in a future life. To Robertson Nicoll, who was a Presbyterian minister as well as an editor and critic, he declared, "You believe in it? But for my part I cannot conceive it. Which personality is it which endures? I was one man in youth and another man in middle age . . . I have never felt the unity of personality running through my life. I have been six different men, six at least."

Naturally, at his age, the subject of death was seldom far from his thoughts. "Fearlessness of death," he told Nevinson, "is essential for manliness. Doctors and parsons do a lot of harm by increasing the fear of death. Every night when I go to bed I know I may not wake up. That is nothing to me. I hope I shall die with a good laugh, like the old French woman. The curé came wailing to her about salvation, and she told him her best improper story and died."

Contrasting his helpless old age with the energetic man she had first known twenty years before, Mrs Comyns Carr says, "Life seemed to have crept up from his body and taken greater possession than ever of his head. Whenever he was speaking to any one of us he would fix his keen eyes on our faces, giving an impression of almost uncanny powers of concentration." His comic fantasies showed no signs of weakening: an article by Clodd in *The Quarterly Review*, applying the evolutionary theory to religion, suggested a tale of "The Hunting of Sir Reynard by the Fifteen Merry Prelates"; and a scholarly treatise on laughter by Professor Sully inspired him to compose mock-serious reviews by imaginary French pundits.

The development of the automobile was a boon to him. After about 1902 Mr Brandreth and his daughter Alice, now married to J. G. Butcher, a Tory M.P., took him for drives in their car, and he found a boyish delight in the speed of motion and the illusion of power. Later he sometimes hired a car for "a spin of 100 miles, a way of ensuring appetite and prolonged sleep." He even entertained an occasional thought of buying one for himself.

He was seriously ill again in the autumn of 1907, but recovered sufficiently to enjoy the tributes for his eightieth birthday. Clement Shorter took the lead in organizing a testimonial to overshadow the modest one of ten years before. Though some eminent writers were discontented that it should be in the hands of a second-rate journalist, who was suspected of eagerness to promote his own prestige, a total of two hundred and fifty famous names were attached to the document, which was mounted on vellum and bound in blue morocco. The only celebrities who withheld their signatures were Premier Asquith and

Lord Rosebery, political rivals who were united in their dislike of Meredith's style.

The birthday was made the occasion for a journalistic orgy. Reporters had interviewed him and photographers had waylaid the donkey chair for snapshots; every newspaper dedicated a leading article to "the Grand Old Man of Letters," "the last Great Victorian," "the Sage of Box Hill," or some other florid compliment. In addition to the large testimonial, which had included several American signatures, there was a special letter from fourteen American authors—Henry Adams, G. W. Cable, Julia Ward Howe, W. D. Howells, and so on. *The Daily News* printed a group of tributes from eminent fellow-authors. King Edward and President Roosevelt sent congratulations.

On the morning of the great day he had his usual outing in the donkey chair, with Lady Edward Cecil walking at his side. Then Shorter and Clodd arrived to present the testimonial. After lunch, surrounded with bouquets and congratulatory telegrams, he granted an audience to a few reporters, who sought to draw him out on public questions. At first he was coy: "When a man has climbed the stairs of eighty years," he said, "he should not use them as a pulpit." But gradually he launched into his opinions on the "bad taste and bad strategy" of the militant suffragettes, and on the need for universal military service—"the spirit of the soldier in every walk of life." In summary of his philosophy he announced, "Life is a long and continuous struggle. It is necessarily combative. Otherwise we cease. Let the struggle go on. Let us be combative; but let us also be kind." He dismissed the interviewers with a request that they should not write much about him. "Say that I am well, and that you found me sitting in my chair, delivering myself freely of very Radical sentiments."

Later in the afternoon the homage of the Society of Authors was presented by a delegation consisting of Anthony Hope Hawkins, Israel Zangwill, and Herbert Trench. "He read [the letter] aloud," says Hawkins, "with some pleasure, I think, yet *chaffed* it rather before us." While they had tea with him he regaled them with his opinions on poetry and the plots that he was offering gratis to younger novelists. Meanwhile a squad of reporters prowled behind the box hedges and wired every event of the day to the world's press. The whole amazing demonstration was more than a belated gesture of amends for neglect of a great artist. The participants were dimly aware that they were celebrating the obsequies of the Nineteenth Century.

He was still capable of a spurt of poetry. "Now and then I write some little verses," he told Morley, "and, the thing done, confess it to be only another form of idleness." In the summer of 1908 he published a vigorous patriotic piece, "The Call," to warn against the danger of invasion by Germany and to support Lord Roberts's plea for conscription. A little later, with Dr Plimmer's encouragement, he composed a noble blank-verse poem to be read at the Milton Tercentenary celebration of the British Academy, making his praise of Milton the occasion for a final utterance of his love of liberty and his British patriotism.

A French admirer, Constantin Photiadès, who was meditating a book about him, had a long interview in September. The visitor was impressed by Meredith's precise articulation, his impatient gestures, and his defiance of infirmity. He grumbled that he was not allowed to go for walks, as though this were a whim of his attendants; he boasted of his heavy smoking; in explaining why he no longer went to concerts, he minimized his deafness: "I hear all sounds in a wrong register, in a wrong key; this makes a series of false notes." The sensitive Frenchman was distressed to perceive that his literary idol was not a serene philosopher but an angry old man whose "supercilious and bitter modesty" betrayed that he had not forgiven the public for its one-time neglect. For hours Photiadès listened to the torrential monologue on journalists, on Tennyson and Swinburne, on Sandie the Scottish terrier, on Trevelyan's book, on plots for unwritten novels, on his Celtic lineage, on England's vulnerability, on French painters, French authors, French politics. Meredith read aloud part of his "Ode on Napoleon" with fiery intensity. Before it was all over, the young Frenchman was worn out with the strain of listening, the effort of shouting incoherent replies, the final humiliation of thinking that Meredith observed his fatigue. In the hall Miss Nicholls complained about her master's deafness: even his family could not always make themselves understood, but he would not succumb to an ear trumpet—"He is too proud."

His abnormal humility was inspired not merely by wounded pride, as Photiadès assumed, but also by an archaic conception of aristocratic reticence and a contempt for the modern journalistic violations of privacy. When over eighty he still forbade Hollyer to sell any copies of his photograph: "It might lead to the appearance of a singularly modest man in the shop windows between a bishop and a specimen of tarnished silver." For years he had been refusing permission for the reprinting of his poems in anthologies. In a conversation with Robertson Nicoll, "he laid great stress on the fact that he had never replied to a critic. Of this he seemed to be very proud. He owned that he had felt the temptation strongly on more occasions than one." These were simply other facets of what E. V. Lucas considered to be his vanity in dress: "His thick, strong hair, his pointed beard, his flowing pink tie, his rough tweed suit, all were trained with the greatest care up to the point where negligence and dandyism meet."

Alice Brandreth Butcher, now middle-aged, had undergone a year's crippling illness, and when she was able to come to see him in the summer of 1908 the sight of her crutches was so painful to him that on her later visits she had to hide them before entering his room. The last time she came, in November, he seemed very weary and slept through most of her visit. "I sat beside him in the failing autumn light, and the fire flickered in the grate. The silence was eloquent. When the hour came for departure he barely roused himself to give me his fare-well benediction." A less melancholy hour was spent by John Morley, now a viscount, when he visited him during the winter. "Found Mere-dith a trifle older in look," he noted in his diary, "but with a vigorous tongue and most gallant spirit. 'Going quickly down,' he said; but nothing morbid, introspective, pseudo-pathetic; plenty of hearty laugh-ter, as in days when we were both on a brimming stream: 'no belief in future existence; are our dogs and horses immortal? What's become of all our fathers?' "

A source of gratification in recent years had been the revival of friendly relations with Swinburne. Though eight years younger than Meredith, the volcanic poet was too deaf and feeble to go anywhere; but messages were transmitted through his housemate, Theodore Watts-Dunton, who was ubiquitous in literary activities. Indeed, Watts-Dunton began to take credit to himself as one of the first heralds of Meredith's genius, through his reviews in *The Athenaeum*, and he published a flattering sonnet on Meredith's seventy-sixth birthday. Nevertheless, he was jealous on behalf of his own special protégé, and in the midst of the eightieth-birthday furor he sent a letter to *The Daily Graphic* to point out that Swinburne had quite as good a claim to be called "the last great Victorian." When Swinburne died, in April, 1909, Meredith felt the blow almost more keenly than the deaths of much dearer friends, for this marked the last severance of ties with his early days. He issued a public tribute in the form of a letter to *The Times*. "I feel the loss of him as part of our life torn away," he wrote to Watts-Dunton, stating his intention of hiring a car and driving over to Putney to pay him a visit of condolence. In a letter to Foote, how-ever, enclosing a donation for the support of *The Freethinker*, he found fault with Watts-Dunton for permitting a religious service at Swin-burne's funeral; and he expressed the same opinion in a conversation with Clodd. On this visit Clodd found him still "full of fun and badinage," with a new chapter of Sir Reynard's conflict with the Prelates.

At the beginning of May he was occupied with plans for a holiday away from home at Whitsuntide; but his nurse was anxious about his fits of drowsiness, though these did not interfere with his daily outings. On Friday, May 14, in raw weather, he took his usual little drive, and caught a chill. The next day he insisted on going out again, and became worse. Though obviously in pain, he refused to be put to bed, and tried to prevent his nurse from calling the doctor. A serious heart condition was diagnosed, and his son and daughter were summoned. Unable to retain nourishment, he became steadily weaker. The local doctor called in the King's physician, Sir Thomas Barlow, for consultation. "I am afraid Sir Thomas thinks very badly of my case," the patient remarked calmly, after he left. During Monday night he was still conscious, though too weak to talk. His daughter could see in his eyes that he knew the end was near. He died early in the morning of May 18, 1909, facing the dawn that glowed above the green slope of Box Hill.

At once an unseemly argument burst out. Meredith had at various times expressed different wishes as to the disposal of his body: sometimes he favored cremation and the scattering of his ashes, again he preferred burial in the little churchyard at Mickleham, and at the time of his wife's death he obtained a family plot in the Dorking Cemetery. He always disapproved of ostentatious funerals. Nevertheless, officials of the Society of Authors demanded his burial in the Poets' Corner, whilst the militant freethinkers scoffed at the absurdity of holding even the simplest Christian ritual over his remains. Burial in the Abbey was refused by the Dean of Westminster, presumably on the grounds of Meredith's well-known agnosticism and perhaps particularly for his proposal about temporary marriages. Hardy remarked to Clodd that what the Abbey needed was "a heathen annexe." Amid uproar in the newspapers, a compromise was arranged. The body was cremated, the ashes were buried beside his wife at Dorking, and Westminster Abbey was the scene of a memorial service. On his tombstone the only inscription was his initials and the opening words of his favorite quotation from his own poetry:

> *Our life is but a little holding, lent*
> *To do a mighty labour. We are one*
> *With heaven and the stars when it is spent*
> *To serve God's aim. Else die we with the Sun.*

*Bibliography*

# Bibliography

ABLE, A. H., *George Meredith and Thomas Love Peacock: A Study in Literary Influence*. Philadelphia, 1933.

ANSTEY, F., *A Long Retrospect*. London, 1936.

AUSTIN, ALFRED, *Autobiography* (2 vols.). London, 1911.

AUSTIN, L. F., *Points of View*. London, 1906.

BAILEY, ELMER J., *The Novels of George Meredith*. New York, 1907.

BARRIE, JAMES M., *The Greenwood Hat*. New York, 1938.

BATTERSEA, CONSTANCE, *Reminiscences*. London, 1922.

BEACH, JOSEPH WARREN, *The Comic Spirit in George Meredith*. New York, 1911.

BENNETT, ARNOLD, *Journal*. New York, 1933.

BISPHAM, DAVID, *A Quaker Singer's Recollections*. New York, 1920.

BLUNT, WILFRID SCAWEN, *My Diaries* (2 vols.). London, 1921.

BRETT-SMITH, H. F. B. & C. E. JONES (eds.), *The Works of Thomas Love Peacock* (10 vols.). London, 1924–34.

BURNAND, FRANCIS C., *Records and Reminiscences* (2 vols.). London, 1904.

BUTCHER, LADY, *Memories of George Meredith*. London, 1919.

CARR, J. COMYNS, *Some Eminent Victorians*. London, 1908.

——— *Coasting Bohemia*. London, 1914.

CARR, MRS. J. COMYNS, *Reminiscences* (ed. by Eve Adam). London, [1925].

CARR, JOHN DICKSON, *The Life of Sir Arthur Conan Doyle*. New York, 1949.

CHARTERIS, HON. EVAN, *The Life and Letters of Sir Edmund Gosse*. London, 1931.

CLODD, EDWARD, *Grant Allen: A Memoir*. London, 1900.

——— *Memories*. London, 1916.

COLE, HENRY (ed.), *The Works of Thomas Love Peacock*, with a Biographical Note by his Grand-daughter, Edith Nicolls (3 vols.). London, 1875.

COLERIDGE, HON. STEPHEN, *Memories*. London, 1913.

COLLES, RAMSAY, *In Castle and Court House*. London, 1911.

COLLINS, J. P., "Conversations with George Meredith." *Pall Mall Magazine*, L (1912), 671–680.

COLVIN, SIR SIDNEY, *Memories and Notes of Persons and Places*. London, 1921.

COOLIDGE, BERTHA (ed.), *A Catalogue of the Altschul Collection of George Meredith in the Yale University Library*. New Haven, 1931.

[CORELLI, MARIE], *The Silver Domino: or, Side Whispers, Social and Literary*. London, 1892.

CRONWRIGHT-SCHREINER, S. C., *The Life of Olive Schreiner*. London, 1924.

—— (ed.), *The Letters of Olive Schreiner*. London, 1924.

CURLE, RICHARD H. P., *Aspects of George Meredith*. London, 1908.

DAUDET, LÉON, *Souvenirs des milieux littéraires*. Paris, 1920.

—— *Quand vivait mon père*. Paris, 1940.

DOBELL, BERTRAM, *The Laureate of Pessimism*. London, 1910.

DOLMAN, FREDERICK, "George Meredith as a Journalist." *New Review*, VIII (1893), 342–348.

DOUGHTY, OSWALD, *A Victorian Romantic: Dante Gabriel Rossetti*. London, 1949.

DOYLE, ARTHUR CONAN, *Memories and Adventures*. Boston, 1924.

DU MAURIER, DAPHNE (ed.), *The Young George Du Maurier*. London, 1951.

ELLIS, S. M., *William Harrison Ainsworth and His Friends* (2 vols.). London, 1912.

—— *George Meredith*. London, 1919.

—— (ed.), *A Mid-Victorian Pepys*. London, 1923.

—— *The Letters and Memoirs of Sir William Hardman*. London, 1928.

—— *The Hardman Papers*. London, 1930.

ELTON, OLIVER, *Frederick York Powell* (2 vols.). Oxford, 1906.

ESCOTT, T. H. SWEET, *Personal Forces of the Period*. London, 1898.

FIELD, MICHAEL, *Works and Days* (ed. by T. Sturge Moore). London, 1933.

FORMAN, M. BUXTON (ed.), *George Meredith, Some Early Appreciations*. London, 1909.

—— *A Bibliography of the Writings in Prose and Verse of George Meredith*. London, 1922.

—— *Meredithiana*. London, 1924.

GALLAND, RENÉ, *George Meredith and British Criticism*. Paris, 1923.

—— *George Meredith: Les cinquante premières années*. Paris, 1923.

GAUNT, WILLIAM, *The Pre-Raphaelite Tragedy*. London, 1942.

GEORGE, R. E. GORDON, "On Some Hitherto Unpublished Letters of George Meredith." *Bookman*, LXVI (1928), 615–620.

GETTMAN, ROYAL A., "Meredith as Publisher's Reader." *Journal of English and Germanic Philology*, XLVIII (1949), 45–56.

—— "Serialization and Evan Harrington." *Publications of the Modern Language Association*, LXIV (1949), 963–975.

GILCHRIST, H. H. (ed.), *Anne Gilchrist: Her Life and Writings*. London, 1887.

GISSING, ALGERNON & ELLEN (eds.), *Letters of George Gissing to Members of His Family*. London, 1927.

GOSSE, EDMUND & T. J. WISE (eds.), *The Letters of Algernon Charles Swinburne* (2 vols.). London, 1918.

GRETTON, MARY STURGE, *The Writings and Life of George Meredith*. London, 1926.

HAKE, THOMAS, & ARTHUR COMPTON RICKETT (eds.), *The Life and Letters of Theodore Watts-Dunton* (2 vols.). London, 1916.

HALDANE, ELIZABETH S., *From One Century to Another*. London, 1937.
HALDANE, RICHARD BURDON, *An Autobiography*. London, 1929.
HAMMERTON, J. A., *George Meredith: His Life and Art in Anecdote and Criticism*. London, 1909. Revised ed., Edinburgh, 1911.
HARDY, FLORENCE EMILY, *The Early Life of Thomas Hardy*. London, 1928.
———— *The Later Years of Thomas Hardy*. London, 1930.
HARDY, THOMAS, "G. M.: A Reminiscence." *Nineteenth Century and After*, CIII (1928), 146–148.
HARLAN, AURELIA BROOKS, *Owen Meredith*. New York, 1946.
HARPER, J. HENRY, *The House of Harper*. New York, 1912.
HARRIS, FRANK, *Contemporary Portraits, I*. New York, 1915.
———— *Life and Adventures*. London, 1947.
HARRISON, FREDERIC, *Autobiographic Memoirs* (2 vols.). London, 1911.
HAWTHORNE, JULIAN, *Shapes That Pass*. Boston, 1928.
HENDERSON, M. STURGE, *George Meredith, Novelist, Poet, Reformer*. London, 1907.
HILL, G. BIRKBECK (ed.), *Letters of Dante Gabriel Rossetti to William Allingham, 1854–1870*. London, 1897.
HIRST, F. W., *Early Life and Letters of John Morley* (2 vols.). London, 1927.
HORNBY, SIR EDMUND, *An Autobiography*. London, 1928.
HORNE, RICHARD HENRY, *Orion*. Melbourne, 1854.
HOUSMAN, LAURENCE, *The Unexpected Years*. Indianapolis, 1936.
HUEFFER, FORD MADOX, *Ancient Lights and Certain New Reflections*. London, 1911.
HUNT, VIOLET, *The Wife of Rossetti*. New York, 1932.
HUNT, W. HOLMAN, *Pre-Raphaelitism and the Pre-Raphaelite Brotherhood* (2 vols.). London, 1905.
HYNDMAN, HENRY MYERS, *The Record of an Adventurous Life*. New York, 1911.

JAMES, HENRY, *Partial Portraits*. New York, 1888.
———— *Notes of a Son and Brother*, New York, 1914.
———— *Letters* (ed. by Percy Lubbock) (2 vols.). New York, 1920.
JERROLD, WALTER C., *George Meredith: An Essay Towards Appreciation*. London, 1902.
JOPLING, LOUISE, *Twenty Years of My Life*. London, 1925.

KITCHEL, ANNA THERESA, *George Lewes and George Eliot*. New York, 1933.
KNIGHT, JOSEPH, *Life of Dante Gabriel Rossetti*. London, 1887.

LEFÈVRE, FREDERIC, *Entretiens avec Paul Valéry*. Paris, 1926.
LE GALLIENNE, RICHARD, *George Meredith: Some Characteristics*. London, 1890.
———— *The Romantic Nineties*. New York, 1925.
LEHMAN, R. C. (ed.), *Charles Dickens as Editor*. London, 1912.
LOWNDES, MRS BELLOC, *The Merry Wives of Westminster*. London, 1946.
LUCAS, E. V., *The Colvins and Their Friends*. London, 1928.
———— *Reading, Writing, Remembering*. London, 1932.
LYNCH, HANNAH, *George Meredith*. London, 1891.

McCABE, JOSEPH, *Edward Clodd*. London, 1932.
MacCARTHY, DESMOND, *Portraits*. London, 1932.
McCARTHY, JUSTIN, *Reminiscences* (2 vols.). New York, 1899.

McCLURE, S. S., *My Autobiography*. New York, 1914.
MACKAIL, DENNIS, *Barrie*. New York, 1941.
MACKAY, MONA E., *Meredith et la France*. Paris, 1937.
McKECHNIE, J., *Meredith's Allegory, The Shaving of Shagpat, Interpreted*. London, 1910.
MAITLAND, F. W., *Life and Letters of Leslie Stephen*. London, 1906.
MALLETT, SIR CHARLES, *Anthony Hope and His Books*. London, 1935.
MATZ, B. W., "George Meredith as Publisher's Reader." *Fortnightly Review*, XCII (1909), 282–298.
MEREDITH, GEORGE, *Letters to Alice Meynell*. London, 1923.
MEREDITH, W. M. (ed.), *Letters of George Meredith* (2 vols.). London, 1912.
MEYNELL, EVERARD, *Life of Francis Thompson*. London, 1913.
MEYNELL, VIOLA, *Life of Alice Meynell*. London, 1929.
MILNER, VISCOUNTESS, "Talks with George Meredith." *National Review*, CXXXI (1948), 449–458.
——— *My Picture Gallery*, 1886–1901. London, 1951.
MOFFATT, JAMES, *George Meredith: A Primer to the Novels*. London, 1909.
MORLEY, HENRY, *Early Papers and Some Memories*. London, 1891.
MORLEY, JOHN, VISCOUNT, *Recollections* (2 vols.). London, 1917.
MURRAY, HENRY, *A Stepson of Fortune*. London, 1909.

NEVINSON, HENRY W., *Books and Personalities*. London, 1905.
——— *Essays in Freedom*. London, 1909.
NICOLL, W. ROBERTSON, *A Bookman's Letters*. London, 1913.

O'CONNOR, MRS T. P., *I Myself*. London, 1910.
O'SHEA, KATHARINE, *Charles Stewart Parnell: His Love Story and Political Life* (2 vols.). London, 1914.
OXFORD and ASQUITH, EARL OF, *Memories and Reflections* (2 vols.). London, 1928.

PENNELL, ELIZABETH ROBBINS & JOSEPH, *The Life of James McNeill Whistler*. Philadelphia, 1908.
——— *The Whistler Journal*. Philadelphia, 1921.
PHOTIADÈS, CONSTANTIN, *George Meredith: sa vie, son imagination, son art, sa doctrine*. Paris, 1910. London, 1913.
POLLOCK, SIR JOHN, *Time's Chariot*. London, 1951.
PRIESTLEY, J. B., *George Meredith*. London, 1926.

ROBERTS, MORLEY, "Meetings with Some Men of Letters," *Queen's Quarterly*, XXXIX (1932), 62–80.
ROBINSON, E. A., "Meredith's Literary Theory and Science: Realism vs. the Comic Spirit." *Publications of the Modern Language Association*, LIII (1938), 857–868.
ROSS, JANET, *The Fourth Generation*. London, 1912.
ROSSETTI, WILLIAM MICHAEL (ed.), *Dante Gabriel Rossetti: His Family Letters* (2 vols.). London, 1895.
——— *Some Reminiscences* (2 vols.). London, 1906.
RHYS, ERNEST, *Everyman Remembers*. London, 1931.

SALT, HENRY S., *The Life of James Thomson*. London, 1889.
SASSOON, SIEGFRIED, *Meredith*. London, 1948.
SCHWOB, MARCEL, *Spicilège*. Paris, 1896.

SCOTT, WINIFRED, *Jefferson Hogg*. London, 1951.

SENCOURT, R. E., *The Life of George Meredith*. London, 1929.

SHARP, MRS WILLIAM, *William Sharp: A Memoir* (2 vols.). London, 1912.

SHORTER, CLEMENT K., "Chapters from my Reminiscences." *Bookman's Journal*, V (1921), 1–4.

———— "A Literary Letter." *Sphere*, LXXVI (1919), 204b, 224.

S[IDGWICK], A. & E. M., *Henry Sidgwick: A Memoir*. London, 1906.

SIME, GEORGINA J. & FRANK NICHOLSON, *Brave Spirits*. London, 1951.

SLADEN, DOUGLAS, *Twenty Years of My Life*. London, 1915.

SOLLY, HENRY S., *Life of Henry Morley, LL.D.* London, 1898.

STEVENSON, ROBERT LOUIS, "A Gossip on Romance" and "A Humble Remonstrance." *Memories and Portraits*. London, 1887.

———— "Books Which Have Influenced Me." *Essays in the Art of Writing*. London, 1905.

———— *Letters* (4 vols.). New York, 1911.

SULLY, JAMES, *My Life and Friends*. London, 1918.

SUTRO, ALFRED, *Celebrities and Simple Souls*. London, 1933.


TENNYSON, HALLAM, LORD, *Tennyson and His Friends*. London, 1911.

THORP, MARGARET FARRAND, *Charles Kingsley, 1819–1875*. Princeton, 1937.

TREVELYAN, GEORGE M., *The Poetry and Philosophy of George Meredith*. London, 1906.

———— *Grey of Fallodon*. London, 1937.

TYNAN, KATHARINE, *The Middle Years*. London, 1916.


VAN DOREN, CARL, *The Life of Thomas Love Peacock*. London, 1911.

VYVER, BERTHA, *Memoirs of Marie Corelli*. London, 1930.


WATTS, M. S., *George Frederic Watts* (3 vols.). London, 1912.

WAUGH, ARTHUR, *A Hundred Years of Publishing: Being the Story of Chapman & Hall*. London, 1930.

WILDE, OSCAR, "The Decay of Lying." *Intentions*. London, 1891.

———— *The Soul of Man*. London, 1895.

WINSTEN, STEPHEN, *Salt and His Circle*. London, 1951.

WOLFF, LUCIEN, *George Meredith, poète et romancier*. Paris, 1924.

WOODS, ALICE, *George Meredith as Champion of Women and of Progressive Education*. Oxford, 1937.


ZIPF, G. K., "New Facts in the Early Life of George Meredith." *Harvard Studies and Notes in Philology and Literature*, XX (1938), 131–145.

*Index*

# Index